GERMAN STUDIES

OXFORD UNIVERSITY PRESS
AMEN HOUSE, E.C. 4
London Edinburgh Glasgow New York
Toronto Melbourne Capetown Bombay
Calcutta Madras
HUMPHREY MILFORD
PUBLISHER TO THE UNIVERSITY

H G Fiedler.

GERMAN STUDIES

PRESENTED TO

PROFESSOR H. G. FIEDLER, M.V.O.

BY

PUPILS, COLLEAGUES, AND FRIENDS

ON HIS

SEVENTY-FIFTH BIRTHDAY

28 APRIL 1937

OXFORD
AT THE CLARENDON PRESS
1938

HERMANNO G. FIEDLER

DISCIPULI, COLLEGAE, AMICI

Accipe non uno conscriptum auctore libellum,
sit tibi multiplicis pignus amicitiae.
suaviloquo tu discipulos sermone beasti,
gaudia tu doctis das populoque libris;
te sequitur, Fidicen, Ludi symphonia nostri,
ipsa tuo auxilio stat magis ampla Domus.
nunc quintum decimum cum pergas claudere lustrum,
salve, quodque manet perfice laetus iter.

CONTENTS

THE FUNCTION OF CONVERSATIONS AND SPEECHES IN 'WITIKO'

By H. G. BARNES

ADALBERT STIFTER, born in 1805 at Oberplan in southern Bohemia, belongs to the generation of the Young Germans. He is in most things their antipode. His *Studien* (1844–50) and the more classical *Bunte Steine* (1853) are generally appreciated; his novels, *Der Nachsommer* (1857) and *Witiko* (1865–7), are much less widely read, despite Hebbel's jeering offer of the crown of Poland to any one who should finish the former. But even those who appreciate *Der Nachsommer* often fail to understand the peculiar qualities of *Witiko*, which seems to stand outside the tradition of the Goethean *Bildungsroman*, the consecrated type of the modern German novel. The subjective element in *Der Nachsommer* is considerable: Stifter's youth in Oberplan, his life as a private tutor in Vienna, his unhappy love for Fanny Greipl, and his keen interest in natural history, all are reflected either in Heinrich Drendorf or in Freiherr von Risach. In *Witiko* the subjective element is reduced to a minimum, unless the inclusion of Oberplan and the glorification of the forest peasants be considered in this light. It was perhaps for this reason that Stifter's contemporaries, with palates accustomed to highly subjective flavouring, found *Witiko* inordinately dull. Whatever the reason, Stifter's last novel came to be regarded as a regrettable experiment, in which an ageing author showed himself both mannered and verbose. To-day, to those who have read, and re-read, *Witiko*, there is little doubt that in this novel, rather than in the *Studien*, *Bunte Steine*, or *Der Nachsommer*, Stifter has made his most original contribution to German and European letters.

Witiko opens with the hero setting out from Passau in 1138 to seek his fortune in Bohemia. The main action of the novel comes to an end in 1158, when Wladislaw, Duke of Bohemia, accepts a royal crown from Frederick Barbarossa. Soběslaw, Duke of Bohemia, dies in 1140. His nephew Wladislaw is elected duke, despite the oath sworn by the nobles at Sadska that Soběslaw's son should succeed to the duchy. The new duke does not turn out to be the pliable instrument for which certain great men, in particular Načerat, had taken him, and in 1142 a rebellion breaks out in favour of Conrad of Znaim, to whom Soběslaw's son resigns his claim. Those who had opposed Wladislaw's election on grounds of justice now support him. At the battle of Wysoka, in which treachery prevents Wladislaw from obtaining a decision, Načerat is slain. Wladislaw fortifies Prague and hastens to Nuremberg to sue for aid from Conrad of Hohenstaufen. Returning with a German army he finds that the rebels have relinquished the siege of Prague and withdrawn to Moravia. They are defeated before Znaim in the following year and subsequently submit to Wladislaw. When Wladislaw accepts the crown from the Holy Roman Emperor, Bohemia, with order established within her boundaries, is incorporated into the political organization of Christendom and can play her part in restoring and maintaining order in the outside world, as in Italy and the Holy Land. The idea of *ordo*, which underlies the whole novel, here becomes manifest and gives *Witiko* a significance altogether transcending the nineteenth century: another reason why it was overlooked or misunderstood by Stifter's contemporaries. Closely interwoven with these political happenings is the rise to power of Witiko, the hero of the novel. His prudence, courage, and loyalty, and his exploits in the civil war, gain him not only possessions in the Bohemian Forest, but also the friendship of Duke Wladislaw and the hand of Berta, the only child of the powerful Heinrich von Jugelbach.

Such is the bald outline of events in *Witiko*. We can now attempt to analyse the form of the novel and examine the function of the conversations and speeches which occupy such a strikingly large place in its economy. From Stifter's correspondence we know that objectivity was the ideal he strove after in writing *Witiko*. His general attitude towards the historical novel comes out in the following passage:

Es erscheint mir . . . in historischen Romanen die Geschichte die Hauptsache und die einzelnen Menschen die Nebensache, sie werden von dem großen Strome getragen und helfen den Strom bilden. Darum steht mir das Epos viel höher als das Drama, und der sogenannte historische Roman erscheint mir als das Epos in ungebundener Rede.[1]

These remarks help to explain Stifter's reserve in the depiction of character. Throughout *Witiko* Stifter is on his guard lest he should do violence to historical reality by intervening with his own subjectivity to lend his characters thoughts and emotions which are not properly theirs. It would be difficult to cite an instance of Stifter's describing the inner life, the feelings and motives of his characters directly. These inward states are only shown indirectly as reflected in actions and spoken words. Stifter refers to historical subjects in another passage:

. . . so sind sie am schönsten, wenn sie einfältiglich herausgehoben und aus dem Munde des mitlebenden Volkes erzählt werden.[2]

In *Witiko* both description of event and characterization of person are conveyed 'aus dem Munde des mitlebenden

---

[1] *Stifters Werke*, Bong edition, Berlin, 1925, Erster Teil, p. lxvii.
[2] Ibid., p. lxvi.

Volkes', in other words by means of conversations and speeches. Stifter clearly considered this technique a safeguard against subjective falsification, for he adds:

Der Wille, vor der Wirklichkeit Ehrerbietung zu haben, wäre wohl da; aber uns Neuen mischt das Ich stets einen Teil von sich unter die Wirklichkeit mit und tauft ihn Wirklichkeit. . . .[1]

This objective technique becomes clearer when we compare it with the method of another historical novelist, Leo Tolstoy. He makes wide use of conversation but also employs direct description to convey the inward state of a character. One would search the nine hundred pages of *Witiko* in vain for a passage like the following from *War and Peace*:

'Yes, it is the same oak,' thought Prince Andrew, and all at once he was seized with an unreasoning spring-time feeling of joy and rejuvenation. All the best moments of his life suddenly rose to his memory. Austerlitz, with the lofty heavens; and his wife's dead reproachful face; and Pierre at the ferry; and that girl, excited by the beauty of the night; and the night itself, and the moon, and . . . all these suddenly rushed to his mind.[2]

Stifter's novel contains, however, many passages equally charged with emotional significance. One instance must suffice: Witiko's state of mind at Duke Soběslaw's funeral, which took place shortly after Wladislaw's accession, is conveyed indirectly, by purely objective means:

Witiko wohnte der Bestattung bei. Sein Fuß trat noch auf Reste von Tannenzweigen, die bei der Feier der Besteigung des Herzogstuhles verwendet worden waren, und sein Auge sah noch die Spuren im Schnee, wo sich das Volk getummelt hatte, da Münzen ausgeworfen worden waren.[3]

---

[1] *Stifters Werke*, Erster Teil, p. lxvi.
[2] *War and Peace*, The World's Classics, Book VI, Chapter III, p. 103.
[3] *Witiko*, p. 150. I am quoting from the Insel edition of *Witiko*, Leipzig.

Stifter's 'Ehrerbietung vor der Wirklichkeit' precluded
him from employing a technique of psychological representation which has now become so general that to-day
it is often overlooked that any other method is adequate
to the requirements of the novel.[1] He shuns all attempts
to read his characters' thoughts or analyse their emotions
and leaves the reader to draw his own conclusions. But
so carefully and justly are Stifter's characters drawn,
so successfully are appearance, speech, and action co-
ordinated, that no doubt as to the interpretation of a
character arises.

The use of conversation and speeches may be observed
from the way in which characters are introduced and
named. Until an occasion arises for a character to state
his name, or for another character to do so, he remains
anonymous. Witiko is thus simply 'der Reiter' for over
twenty pages, and not until he meets Berta and tells her
his name does the reader learn that 'der Reiter' is the
hero of the novel. In the same way Wladislaw is described
as 'der Scharlachreiter' throughout his long conversation

---

[1] The form of *Witiko* would seem to call for some modification of
Robert Petsch's strictures on Spielhagen in *Wesen und Formen der Erzähl-
kunst* (Max Niemeyer, 1934), p. 59. 'Aber es heißt das Kind mit dem
Bade ausschütten, wenn Fr. Spielhagen z. B. von dem dichterischen
Roman "zuerst und zuletzt verlangt, daß er nur handelnde Personen
kennt, hinter denen der Dichter völlig und ausnahmslos verschwindet,
so daß er auch nicht die geringste Meinung für sich selbst äußern darf:
weder über den Weltlauf, noch darüber, wie er sein Werk im ganzen
oder eine spezielle Situation aufgefaßt wünscht, am wenigsten über seine
Personen, die ihren Charakter, ihr Wollen, Wähnen, Wünschen ohne
seine Nach- und Beihilfe durch ihr Tun und Lassen, ihr Sagen und
Schweigen exponieren müssen."' (Petsch is quoting from the *Goethe-
Jahrbuch*, 1895, p. 5.) He continues: 'Damit wäre jede dichterische
Aus-, Vor- und Nachdeutung aus der Erzählung verbannt.' *Witiko* com-
plies with Spielhagen's requirements, as quoted by Petsch, almost completely, and yet the 'dichterische Aus-, Vor- und Nachdeutung' is one of
the salient features of Stifter's novel.

with Witiko in the second book. In the description of an
assembly only those already known by name to Witiko
are named and the enumeration concludes with the phrase:
'und noch viele, die Witiko nicht kannte'.[1] This technique
enables Stifter to withhold names with great dramatic
effect. When Witiko enters the assembly at the Wyšehrad
he notices an important figure:

Vorne in der Versammlung saß auch ein Mann in einem sammetnen
dunkelpurpurnen weiten Gewande, das ein Gürtel zusammenhielt,
in welchem aber kein Schwert hing. Auf dem Haupte hatte er
eine dunkelpurpurne Haube mit einer weißen Feder. Ein weißer
Bart floß auf das Gewand nieder.[2]

When Soběslaw's cross, which Witiko has produced as
proof of his mission, is passed round the assembly, we
read on p. 109:

Der Mann mit dem purpurnen weiten Gewande betrachtete es
genau und gab es dann weiter.

Not until p. 137 is this person named:

Da ... stand in der ersten Reihe der Mann mit dem weißen Barte
und dem weiten dunkelpurpurnen Sammetgewande auf, trat einige
Schritte gegen den freien Raum, kehrte sich gegen die Versammlung und sagte: 'Ich bin Načerat, der Sohn des Tas.'
    Ein allgemeiner Jubelruf folgte diesen Worten.

More dramatic still is the withholding of the identity of
a character who has already played a great part in the
action and now appears disguised. Witiko goes on a
journey to Passau with his servant Raimund and the
'Mann in dem braunen Gewande', whom Raimund treats
as an equal, ordering him to perform menial tasks. Only
when they come into the presence of the Bishop of Passau
is the identity of the 'Mann in dem braunen Gewande'
disclosed: it is Zdik, the fugitive Bishop of Olmütz.[3]

[1] *Witiko*, p. 738. An exception to this rule may be seen on pp. 260-1.
[2] Ibid., pp. 99-100.   [3] Ibid., p. 459.

With a different technique it would have been difficult
to achieve this dramatic effect by such simple means.
At the Imperial Diet in Nuremberg, where the number
of new characters to be introduced is large, Stifter
provides Witiko with a German companion, Wolfgang
von Ortau, who names for him—and the reader—all the
more important persons present.[1]

All political, social, and religious information essential
to the understanding of the novel is presented in conversations and more particularly in speeches and discourses. At the beginning of the novel Witiko and
Wladislaw discuss the internecine struggles which have
formed such terrible episodes in Bohemian history,[2] thus
supplying the reader with an historical background and
preparing him for the coming civil war. In the elective
assembly at the Wyšehrad an old man, the Župan Bolemil,
bases his argument on his experience of past civil wars,
repeating and amplifying the information supplied by
Wladislaw in the previous book.[3] When Witiko meets
Heinrich von Jugelbach for the second time their conversation contains comments on conditions in Bavaria
and Saxony.[4] Witiko, on his round of visits to his
neighbours Rowno, Osel, and Diet von Wettern, learns
—and with him the reader—the attitude of the small
nobility to the new Duke.[5] His conversation with the
Župan Lubomir is a further source of information for the
reader, as Lubomir explains to Witiko the two opposing
forces within the state.[6] The two bishops, Zdik of
Olmütz and Regimbert of Passau, take the reader further
afield in their discussion of religious and political affairs
in Christendom.[7] In what is perhaps the main speech of

[1] Ibid., p. 363.   [2] Ibid., pp. 70–85.   [3] Ibid., pp. 104–5.
[4] Ibid., pp. 431–2.   [5] Ibid., pp. 180–2, 206–7.
[6] Ibid., p. 193.   [7] Ibid., pp. 460–81.

the novel, Wladislaw explains and justifies his acceptance
of the royal crown with a wide survey of European
politics and the religious ideas underlying them.[1]

This technique of conveying historical information
through the characters has the advantage of allowing
repetition, a necessary device in an historical novel of
this length. Wladislaw and Witiko discuss civil wars in
the past with a certain detachment; the subject is resumed
in the Wyšehrad assembly but it is now discussed with
more insistence and personal interest, as it is no longer a
mere historical problem but a matter of some urgency.
Zdik in his colloquy with Regimbert of Passau[2] also
dwells upon the civil war, which has already broken out;
through Zdik the reader sees it mainly in a religious
perspective. When Witiko meets Berta after an interval
of some years she repeats to him all the personal details
she has heard about him from the time of his mission to
Prague down to the present.[3] Witiko's actions are set in
a new light, new motives are assigned and different
appraisals supplied and the reader's surmises are confirmed or corrected. When Witiko makes his request for
Berta's hand, he gives an outline of his career, which
Heinrich von Jugelbach then modifies where Witiko's
modesty has caused him to suppress certain facts.[4] From
these instances it will be seen that information is conveyed
in a natural way, as the characters only speak of what
properly concerns them. The reader's memory is continually refreshed and he insensibly acquires information,
which he might have resented had it come directly from
the author.

Another device employed by Stifter might be termed
dramatic retrospection. It often happens that the author

[1] *Witiko*, pp. 861–5.   [2] Ibid., pp. 462–4.
[3] Ibid., pp. 435–7.   [4] Ibid., pp. 712–16.

does not supply the motive of an action when it takes place
but leaves the reader to make conjectures. Only later,
when a particular deed has lost some of its immediate
interest and blended with the main action, when it can in
fact be seen in its wider bearings, does Stifter, by revealing
the motive, recall it to the reader's mind for further consideration. Stifter makes use of dramatic retrospection
most frequently with Witiko, many of whose earlier
actions remain at least partially obscure in their motivation. Berta's statements about Witiko's past activities and
his rejoinders are thus something more than mere recapi-
tulation; they supply the key to Witiko's inner life at a
moment when the reader is most keenly interested in it.
On Witiko's return to Oberplan after Soběslaw's death
in 1140, at a time when his career is apparently at an end,
one of his first actions is to ascend the Kreuzberg, from
which he gazes over into Bavaria.[1] Only two years later is
the motive of this action revealed, when Witiko confesses
to Berta that he was gazing in the direction of her father's
house but was ashamed to visit her as he was not yet a
'rechter Mann'.[2] The reader surmises at the time of
Witiko's visit to the Kreuzberg that he is thinking of
Berta, who has not been mentioned for over one hundred
pages. This surmise is not allowed to become certainty
until almost three hundred pages later,[2] lest Witiko's
activity in the forest and in the civil war should be thrown
out of perspective. But we know from his remark to
Wiulfhilt, Berta's mother, who is speaking of his first
visit three years before: 'Es ist so, als wäre seit jenen
Tagen keine Zeit vergangen',[3] that he has been constantly
thinking of Berta. Stifter's objectifying technique lends
itself to such reserve, and dramatic retrospection is its
natural corollary.

[1] Ibid., pp. 163–4.   [2] Ibid., p. 437.   [3] Ibid., p. 433.

Witiko's motives for allowing the Moravian rebel princes to escape near Pilsen are not fully disclosed until a year later, shortly before the battle of Znaim.[1] This makes the disclosure all the more striking, for had the princes not escaped, the battle of Znaim might not have taken place. Witiko's action thus gains new significance and the course of the battle is followed with an intensified feeling of suspense. In the battle Witiko retires and leads his men up a ravine to attack the enemy in the rear, thereby deciding the day. Only two years later, when Heinrich von Jugelbach is extolling Witiko's achievements, does the fact emerge that he had volunteered to carry out this dangerous operation.[2] Stifter's use of conversation allows him to exercise an economy in revealing motives which would seem unnatural were the direct method of psychological portrayal employed.

These are some of the advantages that may be claimed for Stifter's epic use of speeches and conversations. A more general advantage, in addition to that of vividness, remains to be noted: variety of style and point of view in the portrayal of character and event. By means of speeches and conversations Stifter is able to depict an action as it is reflected in different minds. In the more subjective novel only one style, one scale of values, and one point of view obtain, those of the author (or of the hero in the *Ich-roman*), and the action of the novel moves along one plane of sensibility. In *Witiko* it is otherwise, almost every notable action is not only described by the author but also shown reflected in at least one character's mind. We have already pointed out the different aspects from which the civil war is seen: it is first described objectively by the author, then related by Wladislaw in Nuremberg, who sees it on the military plane, and finally

[1] *Witiko*, p. 639.   [2] Ibid., p. 716.

by Zdik, who regards it as a divine punishment, not to
mention its countless reflections in the speeches of the
great noblemen, of the petty gentry and of the simple
peasants who take part in it. A good example of this
multiplicity of standpoint is the treatment of the battle
in which Witiko and his men defeat Wratislaw of Brünn.
The battle is tersely described by Stifter in a paragraph
that is justly famous for its impressive repetition: 'Sie
gingen vor'.[1] In the following book there occurs a further
more detailed description of the battle as experienced by
Sifrid von Milnet, who describes the encounter in the
light of the fame which it has brought the forest peasants
and their leader Witiko.[2]

The place of speech and conversation in the structure
of *Witiko* is nowhere more clearly exemplified than in the
second book of part one, which is wholly devoted to a
colloquy between Witiko and Wladislaw.[3] In this colloquy Stifter provides the exposition to the drama of the
civil war. Witiko is on his way to Prague to enter the
service of Duke Soběslaw. Near Chynow he falls in with
a troop of gaily dressed young horsemen, led by a youth
clad in scarlet. Witiko reins in his horse to allow them
to pass, but the scarlet rider calls out: 'Du einzelner Mann,
du reitest aus, das Herzogtum Böhmen zu erobern',[4]
showing thereby his own preoccupation with political
matters. This is Witiko's interpretation, as his retort
implies: '. . . deines Herzens Gelüsten wäre es, hier zu
schalten, weil du die Worte zu mir gesagt hast, die der
Schalk dir eingab'.[5] There follows a volley of pleasantries
from the scarlet rider, which contains a wealth of allusion
to Bohemian affairs and personalities. Apparently dissatisfied with the aimlessness of his existence, the scarlet

[1] Ibid., p. 606.   [2] Ibid., pp. 627–32.   [3] Ibid., pp. 59–90.
[4] Ibid., p. 59.   [5] Ibid., p. 60.

rider is both attracted and challenged by Witiko's poise and seriousness of purpose. To contrast the harmless nature of his present mode of life with the violence of earlier generations, he discourses to Witiko on the bloody feuds between the Slawnike and the Wrše and the sub-sequent struggles for the throne among the descendants of Přemysl. These horrors are related in a completely detached and dispassionate tone; only twice does emotion creep in. When the scarlet rider alludes to Wladislaw, the predecessor of the reigning Duke Soběslaw, his tone changes; enthusiasm and sympathy replace his previous detachment. But coolness marks his appraisal of Sobě-slaw and he concludes his survey with the promise which the nobles have sworn at Sadska, some two months back, that they will recognize Soběslaw's son as the successor to the throne. Sadska explains in part the scarlet rider's detached attitude, which is expressed in the following words:

Du siehst also . . . daß bei uns alle Sachen geordnet und befestigt sind, und daß es uns, die wir da reiten, nichts hälfe, wenn wir auch, wie du sagtest, das Gelüste hätten, in diesen Ländern zu schalten.[1]

Thus the reader is informed of the situation in Bohemia as Witiko finds it in 1138.

In addition, the character of the scarlet rider comes out clearly from his incidental remarks. Despite his apparent aloofness and frivolous bearing, his passionate interest in the welfare of Bohemia and his considerable political insight are only too evident. His winning manners, his graceful persiflage of Witiko's leather clothes, and his sovereign self-possession mark the true aristocrat, such as Stifter himself had often met in the great houses of Vienna. As they are about to part, Witiko asks the

[1] *Witiko,* p. 87.

scarlet rider, who has not yet disclosed his identity, who he is. The question and the answer sum up all the previous speeches and form a dramatic conclusion to this important book:

'Lebet wohl', antwortete Witiko.

Dann hielt er ein Weilchen stille und sagte zu dem Scharlach-reiter: 'Ich habe dir gesagt, wie ich heiße und woher ich komme, du hast mir manches erzählt und hast mir die genannt, welche dich begleiten, sage mir, wer bist denn du, daß du dich um dieses Land so kümmerst und was darin geschieht.'

'So höre, du Ledermann,' sagte der Scharlachreiter, 'ich bin der Sohn des edlen großmütigen hohen Herzoges Wladislaw, der in seiner Herrschaft keinen Tropfen Blut vergossen hat, ich bin der Enkel des ruhmreichen Königs Wratislaw, ich bin der Neffe jenes Herzogs Břetislaw, der im Walde von Bürglitz wie ein Stern zur Erde gesunken ist, ich bin der Neffe des unglücklichen Bořiwoy, der vor Swatopluk weichen mußte, und bin der Neffe des jetzigen Herzoges Soběslaw. Mein Name ist Wladislaw.'

'Wenn du das alles bist—', sagte Witiko.

'Nun, Witiko?' antwortete der Scharlachreiter.

'So solltest du ernster sein', sagte Witiko.

'Mein Sohn,' sagte der Scharlachreiter, 'hier führt mein Weg nach Morgen, dem Lande Mähren zu, der deine führt nach Mitternacht. Lebe wohl und finde dein Glück.'[1]

In the third book of *Witiko* speeches and discourses are employed by Stifter to represent action in progress and to complete the political exposition begun in the previous book. No fewer than thirty-five Bohemian noblemen are introduced in the assembly at the Wyšehrad and indivi-dually characterized by their speeches and the assembly's reaction to their words. In this way all the men and the political forces at work in Bohemia are depicted early in the novel. Stifter does not, however, present the reader with a static picture; the process of choosing a successor

[1] Ibid., p. 90.

to Soběslaw and the speeches for and against the different
candidates assume the character of a drama moving
swiftly to its climax. At the same time Stifter has con-
trived to keep the hero in the foreground, and in the first
part of this drama attention is focused on Witiko, who
has come to Prague on a mission from the dying Soběslaw.
He has been admitted to the assembly, but before he
speaks Bogdan, Domaslaw, Beneš, and Milhost demand
in more or less violent terms that he shall be punished as
a spy or traitor or simply for his effrontery in attempting
to enter the august assembly. The aged Bolemil in a
long speech recalling memories of civil wars is alone for
expelling Witiko without punishment. At this point
Zdik, the Bishop of Olmütz, intervenes and reminds the
nobles that they have promised to hear Witiko, who then
speaks and makes such an honest impression that he is
allowed to witness the deliberations.

The real discussion begins when Zdik, as president,
passes in review the various branches of Přemysl's descendants and formulates the question whether the premature
death of Soběslaw, before he has trained his son as
successor, will not invalidate the oath sworn at Sadska.
The assembly passes through various phases of opinion
and feeling and a definite rhythm is noticeable in the
sequence of speeches. Rowno and Diet von Wettern,
both small men, protest that they were intimidated at
Sadska and cannot therefore recognize Soběslaw's son as
the future successor to the throne. Milhost goes further
and declares that the nobility alone represents the nation;
he demands that the power of the dukes shall be restricted.
This feeling against the dukes is heightened by Domaslaw,
who denounces Soběslaw for promoting the interests of
'Bauern, Kaufherren, Münzer, Juden, Fiedelspieler' at
the expense of the nobility. Bohuš intensifies this animo-

sity by reviving memories of the many atrocities which the dukes have perpetrated. After this outburst, however, the feeling of the assembly turns from such anarchical tendencies, and Mireta, emphasizing the need of a leader, makes the first definite proposal: Conrad of Znaim. Osel, a small man, also declares that he would rather be governed by a duke than oppressed by one or several 'Lechen'. Znata, the brother of Načerat, utilizes this change in opinion to propose Wladislaw, the son of the former Duke Wladislaw. Another reaction then sets in, when Silvester, Bishop-elect of Prague, protests against the crime of breaking the oath of Sadska. Bolemil likewise protests, pointing out that the source of all their trouble is the lack of a law of succession. He prophesies that those who are now for Wladislaw will later turn against him. The fourth and last phase of the assembly now supervenes. Zdik declares the non-observance of the oath of Sadska to be no sin and proposes Wladislaw. Načerat then carries away the assembly with a brilliant speech of flattery and insinuation, and Wladislaw is elected amid acclamation. Silvester once more protests and, despairing of his influence over men's souls, he lays down his episcopal office.

With this summary of the Wyšehrad speeches in mind, it is possible to consider the different purposes they serve. We have said that they represent action, or rather movement towards an important decision by which all subsequent action is determined. It might be shown that not a single one of the thirty-odd speeches is without reference to later developments. From their words the reader already knows how the speakers will act in given circumstances. Znata, Bogdan, Milhost, Načerat, and other nobles are mainly concerned with increasing their own power; they either oppose all dukes or, more prudently,

secure the election of one whom they consider amenable
to their wishes. Rowno, Diet, and Osel are also for
Wladislaw; partly for selfish ends. But these ends do not
conflict with the well-being of the nation. They are not,
however, primarily concerned with questions of right and
wrong. Bolemil and Diwiš see in the election the seeds
of future civil war and oppose it on political as well as
moral grounds. Zdik acts from expediency, which he
considers must override the oath. Whilst Bolemil, knowing the weakness of human nature, is resigned to the
possibility of fresh strife and hopes that a law of succession
will avert the worst evil, Silvester stands for the moral
law without reference to political facts, and his absolute
standards come into conflict with what seems political
necessity. He is thus forced to withdraw from the world.
We shall see then that the speeches in the assembly fix
the pattern of the plot and foreshadow the final grouping
of the chief characters.

More important is their function of characterization.
A consideration of Bolemil, Silvester, Zdik, and Načerat
will make this clear. In the speeches at the Wyšehrad the
main traits of their characters are established, and what
follows in later books is but the amplification of these
traits and their application in the sphere of action. We
shall also notice Stifter's skill in differentiating apparently
similar characters. Each speaker in the assembly is
described as Witiko, or any other observer, would see
him, i.e. only from the outside. Bolemil is drawn with
extreme economy:

Er hatte ein dunkelbraunes Kleid, eine schwarze Haube ohne
Feder und einen langen weißen Bart. Er rief: 'Ich bin Bolemil!'
Ein sehr tiefes Schweigen entstand nach seinem Rufe. . . .[1]

He opens his speech by recalling his long experience of

[1] *Witiko*, p. 104.

different rulers and ends the impressive survey with the
simple words: 'So sind diese Dinge gewesen'.[1] He concludes with a reference to his freedom from human
passions and his detachment from earthly things:

So spricht Bolemil, ein alter Mann, der die Güter der Erde nicht
mehr liebt, keinen Menschen mehr haßt und sich nur zur Ver-
einigung mit Gott und seinen Heiligen vorbereitet.[2]

His second speech brings out his loftiness of mind and
his insight into human nature. He speaks without illu-
sions as to the effect of his words.

Meine Worte werden gewiß vergeblich sein, weil die Jugend und
viele Männer nach ihren Gelüsten vorwärts gehen; ich aber rede
sie, weil ich sie schuldig bin.[3]

He emphasizes the 'Heiligkeit der Ordnung', and is
sceptical of man's ability to choose his ruler:

Es scheint glaublich, daß man durch die Wahl immer sollte den
Besten erkiesen können; aber ich habe lange gelebt und viele
Menschen gesehen: wie wenige gibt es, die zu wählen verstehen,
und wie wenige, die wählen dürfen.[4]

Most men cannot even consider their own interests:

... so ist die große Zahl der Menschen so, daß sie zuerst ihrer
selbst gedenkt, und auch nicht recht ihrer selbst, sondern ihrer
Lust.[5]

Bolemil's age and wisdom command respect throughout.
His attitude to Witiko is in keeping with his whole
character; he is always scrupulously fair to him but
without that warm affection which another old man, the
Župan Lubomir, shows Witiko. Aloofness and detachment from human ties are Bolemil's outstanding qualities,
whereas Lubomir is significantly shown with his wife

[1] Ibid., p. 105.   [2] Ibid., p. 105.   [3] Ibid., p. 131.
[4] Ibid., p. 134.   [5] Ibid., p. 134.

Boleslawa and talks much of his children. Witiko's conversation with the old couple is one of the tenderest
passages in the novel,[1] and sheds light on Witiko's state
of mind when he has retired to the forest after Duke
Soběslaw's death. Bolemil is careful not to influence
Witiko's decision when he meets him on the way to the
civil war and thinks he is going to join the rebels. To
Witiko's question '. . . wer weiß, ob unsere Wege nicht
die gleichen sind', no reply is given: 'Bolemil antwortete
nicht, sondern nickte nur mit dem Haupte'.[2]

Bishop Silvester combines Bolemil's moral rigour with
Lubomir's warmth of feeling. He tries to dissuade Witiko
from entering the assembly, as it may cost him his life.[3]
In this solicitude for a stranger at a time of national crisis
we already see something of the character of this saintly
bishop. He cannot repeat too often that he is a weak
vessel. His opening words before the assembly are in
this strain:

Ihr seht, daß meine Haare weiß sind und mein Nacken gebeugt
ist. Ich rede nicht aus Lust oder Unlust oder für eine Person,
sondern als der, der zum obersten Seelenhirten dieses Landes
erwählt ist, wenn auch nicht würdig und noch nicht von seinem
erzbischöflichen Oberherrn von Mainz geweiht.[4]

These doubts about his person do not, however, affect
his conception of his holy office; he is the incarnation of
the moral law and throughout the novel he remains the
conscience of the nation. Since Duke Soběslaw is still
alive and his son duly recognized, the assembly is without
authority: '. . . die Versammlungen bestehen vor dem
Auged Gottes nicht'.[5] 'In christlicher Demut' he beseeches the nobles to keep their promise, and he declares
the election 'ungültig und sündhaft'. The bent figure of

[1] *Witiko*, pp. 199–200.   [2] Ibid., p. 242.
[3] Ibid., pp. 96–7.   [4] Ibid., p. 129.   [5] Ibid., p. 129.

the old priest, his humility and modesty, are forgotten,
the reader sees only the representative of the moral law.
Bishop Zdik tries to reason with him:

Silvester wischte sich mit seinem Kleide die Tränen ab und
sagte: 'Mein Sohn, es ist doch eine Sünde. Und wenn Gottes
Barmherzigkeit durch euren Erwählten das Land auf den Gipfel
des Heiles führt, so wird doch die Strafe auf die Häupter des
Meineides fallen.'[1]

After this prophecy Silvester disappears from the
public stage and returns to his monastery on the river
Sazawa, where he becomes the norm by which Witiko
and others measure their conduct. His prophecy is fulfilled, the country is visited with civil war, and in the
battle of Wysoka Načerat dies with Silvester's name on
his lips, whilst at Passau the fugitive Zdik acknowledges
the truth of his judgement. Witiko goes to him to hear
his verdict on his insubordination near Pilsen. Silvester
is in the monastery garden and replies to Witiko's greeting
deprecatingly:

Nenne mich nicht einen heiligen Vater, . . . es wäre wie Hohn und
Spott; ich bin in meinen Werken ein gebrechlicher Mensch, ich
konnte die Worte nicht finden, jene Versammlung zu bewegen,
und kann meine Klosterbrüder nicht leiten, sie lieben mich und
folgen mir nicht. Die Gemüse gedeihen leidlich, wenn ich sie
begieße und ihnen die gehörige Erde gebe. Ich bin nicht einmal ein
rechter Gärtner für den folgsamen Kohl und die gelben Blumen.[2]

Witiko however promises him obedience:

Wenn mir undeutlich ist, was ich tun soll . . . so erlaubet, daß
ich. . . . Euch um das Gute frage, an welchem das andere dann
hängt, . . . ich werde doch einer sein, der Euch folgt.[3]

Nadler has pointed out that Witiko withdraws to the
forest after each major political happening in order to
collect himself. On such occasions we read that he also

[1] Ibid., p. 142.   [2] Ibid., p. 418.   [3] Ibid., p. 418.

visits Silvester. When that is not possible Witiko always
refers to Silvester's example, thus indicating his state of
mind.[1] At the consecration of the site of his castle, which
marks the beginning of his overlordship in the forest,
Witiko bears public witness to Silvester by quoting his
words:

Ich werde bestrebt sein, das Gute zu tun, alles andere, sagt Silvester,
ist darin enthalten.[2]

Silvester leads a hidden life, appearing only five times
in all.[3] At the Wyšehrad he had declared Wladislaw's
election to be invalid, but in his last speech, in the council
convened to judge the rebel princes, he proclaims Wladislaw to be the rightful duke.[4] This speech is symbolical
of the new phase in Bohemian affairs: law has been
restored, the country is governed by a lawful ruler, and,
after this final judgement of Silvester, Wladislaw, as
lawful duke, can become king and incorporate his land
into the Holy Roman Empire, the organ of the reign of
law in Christendom.

Zdik, the Bishop of Olmütz, is carefully distinguished
from Silvester. He is a deeply pious man of generous
instincts, but a somewhat naive optimist without Bolemil's
grasp of reality and human nature and Silvester's fine
perception of moral right and wrong. In his desire to act
for the good of the land, he tends to overlook the principle
of justice. His speeches at the Wyšehrad leave the impression that he is trying to persuade not only his hearers
but also his own conscience. He appeals to reason rather
than to custom and justice,[5] and with a fine touch Stifter

---

[1] *Witiko*, pp. 511, 515, 690, 691, 694.   [2] Ibid., p. 710.
[3] Ibid., pp. 96–7, 129–42, 148–9, 417–23, 746–7.
[4] Ibid., pp. 746–7.
[5] Is it possible that Stifter has figured in this well-meaning bishop the
liberal tendencies of his own time?

makes him address the men of the assembly as 'Liebe, Getreue, *Einsichtige*'.[1] After his first speech some one exclaims with unconscious irony: 'Der Bischof ist ein gerechter Mann wie der heilige Adalbert'.[2] In his second speech Zdik's main argument is that civil war can only be avoided if a sufficiently large and powerful majority is behind the new duke; he entirely suppresses the question of a just claim to the throne, for which Silvester and Witiko sacrifice their careers. In his third speech Zdik asserts in opposition to Silvester:

Wenn wir das Versprechen, welches wir in Sadska gegeben haben, nicht halten, so begehen wir keine Sünde; weil die Vorbedingung, welche wir uns alle bei dem Versprechen gedacht haben, nicht erfüllt worden ist.[3]

He concludes with the artless proposal that should Soběslaw recover, the oath of Sadska should once more be recognized. His uncertain state of mind also speaks in his reply to Silvester's prophecy: 'Es geschehe, was muss . . . ein jeder kann nur nach dem gestraft werden, was er gesündiget hat'.[4] These words are likewise prophetic: Zdik's punishment is not slow in coming. He has to flee for his life from the Moravian rebels, and in his colloquy with Bishop Regimbert of Passau he admits his guilt: 'Ich bin ein Sünder und habe Strafe verdient, und was gekommen ist, das ist die Strafe'.[5] Despite this experience, Zdik clings to his old optimism. After the submission of the rebels he replies to Witiko's cautious remark: 'Die Fürsten werden jetzt wohl treu sein', with ill-founded confidence: 'Sie werden treu sein'.[6] Shortly after this assurance he is once more attacked by the Moravian princes and escapes with difficulty from a violent death. To the end Zdik remains convinced of the

[1] *Witiko*, p. 113.   [2] Ibid., p. 116.   [3] Ibid., p. 136.
[4] Ibid., p. 142.   [5] Ibid., p. 462.   [6] Ibid., p. 767.

reasonableness, if not of the justice, of Wladislaw's election. He explains to Witiko:

> Das Unglück, welches der hochehrwürdige Bischof Silvester geahnt hat ... ist eingetroffen und ist überwunden worden. Jetzt wird das Gute kommen, welches die vorausgesehen haben, die deshalb die Wahl Wladislaws gefördert haben.[1]

We have already noticed how Stifter draws the attention of the reader to Načerat in the Wyšehrad assembly. His very first words confirm the impression of vanity which the reader may have gained from his magnificent attire:

> 'Liebe, gewogene, ansehnliche Herren! Ich bin ein unbedeutender Mann in diesen großen und mächtigen Ländern.'
> 'Der bedeutendste', rief eine Stimme.
> 'Ein unbedeutender Mann', fuhr Načerat fort.
> 'Nein, nein, nein', rief eine Menge von Stimmen.
> 'Meine Worte sind nicht wichtig', sagte Načerat.[2]

In this exordium Stifter succeeds in conveying a good deal of information about Načerat: his power in the land, his popularity, his conceit, and his insincerity. He uses all the tricks of oratory, alternately flattering and threatening his audience. His feigned humility stands in striking contrast to Silvester's humbleness, and he emphasizes with a subtle threat that he has come to the assembly unarmed. He extols the might of the Bohemians, but points out that they are a peace-loving nation, whom the dukes have repeatedly dragged into wars and internal strife. He insinuates that the dukes can only rule through the nobility, and blandly reproves the dying Soběslaw for disregarding on occasion the counsel of his nobles. His motives in proposing Wladislaw are transparently selfish:

> Er ist gut und freundlich, er liebt unsere Kinder, teilt ihre Freuden und Leiden, hört ihre Meinungen, spielt ihre Spiele und scheut

---

[1] *Witiko*, p. 767.   [2] Ibid., p. 137.

ihre Rechte, er hat Ehrfurcht vor ihren Vätern und dem Rate derselben.[1]

After proposing Wladislaw, he continues with sneering irony:

Wenn ihr aber . . . den Sohn Soběslaws wählen werdet, so ist es gewiß, daß ihr überzeugt seid, daß derselbe noch mehr eure Rechte schützen, noch mehr euren Rat hören, noch mehr die Landeskinder beglücken wird.[2]

Načerat proves himself a master of innuendo, both here and in the brilliant speech which he delivers a year later at the Plakahof, where the discontented elements in the land have assembled. Whilst ostensibly thanking the host, Strich of Plaka, he arraigns Duke Wladislaw for ignoring his councillors, and fans up the flames of revolt merely by repeating his regret that Wladislaw has not seen fit to join the hunting party:

Ich rede immer von allerlei anderen Dingen und sage immer nicht unserem sehr guten Wirte unseren Dank für sein heutiges Fest, das er uns so gastherrlich gibt, und kann immer nicht davon wegkommen, zu bedauern, daß unser erlauchter Herzog nicht gegenwärtig ist.[3]

Načerat is the only deliberately evil character in *Witiko*; the others who appear as such are rather the creatures of passion and violence. He is the spiritual progenitor of the civil war, and the dying Soběslaw sees him in this light when he prophesies: 'Načerat wird gegen Wladislaw nicht siegen'.[4] That Načerat has done violence to his conscience appears from his dying words: 'Silvester, Silvester'.[5]

Stifter, true to his epic objectivity, refrains from any direct judgement on Načerat, but in one of the most dramatic scenes in this highly dramatic novel the futility of his scheming is seen as in a flash. Wladislaw is on the

[1] Ibid., p. 139.   [2] Ibid., p. 139.   [3] Ibid., p. 231.
[4] Ibid., p. 148.   [5] Ibid., p. 283.

road to Nuremberg and meets the followers of Načerat bringing home the bodies of their lord and his son for burial. An obscure man gives expression to what might be called the judgement of the people on Načerat. But this judgement is not free from human passion, and Stifter puts into Wladislaw's mouth words that depict Načerat *sub specie aeternitatis:*

Der Herzog Wladislaw und Zdik und Welislaw waren ganz nach vorne gekommen und sahen den Zug an.

Da rief Timeš, ein Begleiter Welislaws: 'Reißet das Aas aus seiner schönen Truhe und werfet es den Vögeln des Waldes hin. Da es noch in den prächtigen Kleidern ging, hat es Unheil gestiftet und ist schuld, daß tausend Menschen ihr Leben verloren, daß Städte und Dörfer rauchen, daß Felder dorren, daß Prag zerstört wird, daß Menschen nach Menschen umkommen und der Herzog Wladislaw als Bitter in die Fremde reiten muß.'

Der Herzog aber antwortete auf diese Rede: 'Načerat hat viel gewirkt und hat Böses getan; jetzt ist er ein Mann der Ruhe, und die Wandelbarkeit der menschlichen Dinge hat ihn getroffen. Einige verwünschen ihn nur noch; die hier um ihn sind, lieben ihn, wir haben nichts zu tun, stört sie nicht in ihrem Werke.'[1]

We have attempted to show from a few examples what use Stifter makes of speeches and conversations in *Witiko*, and to indicate the possibilities of the strictly objective method for the novel in general. It may be asserted that Stifter's recourse to speeches as the chief means of character-portrayal makes for verbosity. But to dismiss *Witiko* as intolerably prolix—and this was until recently the general verdict—betrays an almost complete misunderstanding of its peculiar form. This form, of which Stifter wrote: 'Gebe ich ... meinem Stoffe die Form, so ist sie doch von mir ganz unabhängig und hängt nur von dem Stoffe ab, ich muß sie finden, nicht erfinden',[2] was deliberately employed by a great master of economy,

---

[1] *Witiko*, p. 359.   [2] *Stifters Werke*, op. cit., p. lxvii.

for few novels contain as many pregnant laconisms as *Witiko*. A last example, the portrayal of Duke Soběslaw's death, an objective description and then characterization by a speech, is a brilliant vindication of Stifter's epic form. It should be sufficient proof, if proof be necessary, that *Witiko* is the work of a highly-disciplined artist:

Am vierzehnten Tage des Monates Hornung sprach der Herzog nicht mehr, er schaute durch das Fenster, welches nicht verhangen war, gegen Morgen, wohin noch viele Zweige seines Stammvolkes wohnten, und als die Nachmittagschatten in derselben Richtung zeigten, suchten seine Hände in der Wolle der Bärendecke und strebten sich zu falten. Der Bischof gab ihnen ein silbernes Kreuz, das sie festhielten. Das Zimmer füllte sich immer mehr mit Menschen. Der Arzt wachte über den Herzog, die Priester sagten leise Gebete, und ehe das Licht des Tages schied, tat er mehrere tiefe Atemzüge, dann sanken die Lider, und die Züge wurden starr.

Der Arzt gab mit der Hand ein Zeichen, daß alles vorüber sei.

Der Bischof sagte: 'Es ist vollbracht. Ihm wird das Viele belohnt werden, was er Gutes tat, und das Wenige verziehen, was er gesündigt hat. An ihm ist viel gesündigt worden.'[1]

The literature on *Witiko* is not extensive. The chief authorities are:

JOSEF NADLER, 'Witiko?' *Preußische Jahrbücher*, Band 188, 1922.

ADOLF VON GROLMAN, *Adalbert Stifters Romane*, Max Niemeyer Verlag, 1926.

FRANZ HÜLLER, *Adalbert Stifters 'Witiko'*, Eger, 1930.

WILHELM BIETAK, *Das Lebensgefühl des 'Biedermeier' in der österreichischen Dichtung*, Wien und Leipzig, 1931.

HERMANN BLUMENTHAL's valuable article: 'Stifters "Witiko" und die geschichtliche Welt', *Zeitschrift für deutsche Philologie*, Band 61, 1936, only reached me after the completion of this essay.

[1] *Witiko*, pp. 148–9.

THE FIRST FRENCH EDITION OF 'PETER SCHLEMIHL'

By L. A. BISSON

IN an article on German life and literature the French
critic and translator, Xavier Marmier, attributes the
first appearance in France of Chamisso's *Peter Schlemihl*
to the efforts of his friend and fellow translator Amédée
Pichot. Marmier is right, though there is no mention
of Pichot's name, or indeed of that of the original author,
in this first French edition,[1] whose inner history throws
an interesting light on publishers and authors and their
relations and activities in the early years of the nineteenth
century. The student of literature, primarily concerned
with the text and criticism of great masterpieces, tends
to forget or at any rate to lose sight of the purely commercial side of literary enterprise. It is a humbling and
possibly salutary thought that for the publisher it is the
market value of a work that counts, and the individual
author's personality becomes a minor consideration or is
converted into terms of hard cash. The rather equivocal
transactions in which the publication of *Pierre Schlémihl*
was involved offer an amusing if cynical illustration of the
way of a publisher with a manuscript and an author.

Perhaps it would be truer to say, of *one* publisher, for
Ladvocat's practice is an extreme example of the commercial exploitation of books and their writers. With his
meteoric rise to fame and prosperity, his magnificent
hotel on the Quai Voltaire, his evasions and subterfuges,
his numerous bankruptcies, his miserable end in hospital
in 1854, forgotten by his former associates, hated by his

---

[1] *Pierre Schlémihl*, Ladvocat, Paris, 1820.

former victims, his burial in the *fosse commune* because he
had lost the certificate of his *concession* in the cemetery of
Père-Lachaise—Ladvocat seems to have stepped straight
out of the pages of Balzac. But in the year 1820 he was
only on the threshold of this adventurous career. A
struggling young *libraire-éditeur* with a little wooden
boutique in the Palais-Royal,[1] he had, however, already
begun the complicated financial dealings which were to
become notorious among men of letters, and which, for
all his adroitness, seldom brought Ladvocat himself more
than the semblance of an uneasy prosperity. At this
early period, as throughout his whole career, he was
rarely, if ever, in a position to pay cash for a work, and
had recourse to an elaborate system of bills and promis-
sory notes, which were seldom honoured when they fell
due, but deferred or renewed or exchanged until the
hapless victim of these postponements almost gave up
hope of ever seeing Ladvocat's money. If he too was young
and struggling, he was often willing to be done with
it and accept payment in kind, that is to say, in books
which he needed then or might conceivably need in the
future. It was a mode of payment far more congenial to
the enterprising publisher; it got rid of surplus stock and
spared his scanty cash.

In 1820 Ladvocat had been for some time in touch with
Charles Nodier, in whom he recognized a potentially
valuable asset. Nodier was already well known, not to
say famous. He was a man of encyclopaedic knowledge,
and his knowledge was of an unusual kind; he could write
entertainingly, with charm and vivacity, on a variety of
themes; he could introduce, with conviction and authority,
just that exotic or macabre note which appealed to the
young generation of Romantics. Moreover, he was not

---

[1] Galerie de Bois, No. 195.

above doing odd jobs: translations, prefaces, compilations.
Here, clearly, was a person to be nursed; and Charles
was therefore paid more regularly than Ladvocat's other
authors, in cash rather than in kind, and at a distinctly
higher rate. What then could be more natural than that
Ladvocat, suddenly finding himself the possessor of a story
in manuscript, German in subject and origin, although
written in French, should turn to him to polish up the
style, especially when it was a story in a genre peculiarly
close to Nodier's own vein? No mention was made of
Chamisso's name or of the provenance of the manuscript;
indeed, on these points Ladvocat himself was in complete
ignorance. Such considerations would not have worried
him very much, for the actual authorship of a book had
little significance in his eyes. He was even known to get
some poor devil to execute a piece of work and then publish
it with Nodier's more profitable name on the title-page, as
he did with the translation of *The Vicar of Wakefield*.[1]
But in the case of *Peter Schlemihl* he was comparatively
innocent; a French version was sent or brought to him
bearing the name of neither author nor translator. From
all one knows of Ladvocat, one feels that for him it had
just dropped from heaven to minister to the wants of a
needy and deserving publisher. For him that was enough.
Why stir up trouble by inquiring further? And though
we can scarcely remain so easily satisfied as Ladvocat,
inquiry yields no very certain result. Between the publication of *Peter Schlemihl* in 1814 and the moment when
this French version came into Ladvocat's hands in 1820
there had been time to make many translations of the

---

[1] I have just received (January, 1937) a bookseller's catalogue containing this translation, 'par Charles Nodier'. Pichot, who knew the facts,
states categorically that Nodier had nothing to do with this or with several
other books on whose title-page his name appeared or with which Ladvocat
allowed it to be associated.

story; Chamisso, indeed, published what purported to be his own French version some months after Ladvocat's edition. Unless the earlier version which reached Ladvocat was by Chamisso himself—a possibility which the latter never admitted but which receives support rather than contradiction from his subsequent French translation—we can only assume that it was made by some unknown littérateur, presumably German, since it was found necessary to improve the French. But the motive which brought it to Ladvocat and the manner of its arrival remain a mystery, though we shall find some reason to suppose that the unknown translator was in fact, as already suggested, none other than the original author of the book.

Ladvocat, then, appealed to Nodier to tidy up the idiom and style of this heaven-sent manuscript, and Nodier liked the idea. His active imagination saw the possibility of little digressions, of adding bits of odd folk-lore, of clothing the German frame-work in his own whimsical and fantastic literary garb. In fact, he quickly lost sight of Ladvocat's humbler project altogether, and suggested writing another work on the same theme. But it was one thing to pay Nodier a couple of hundred francs for a bit of devilling and his name on the title-page; it was quite another to present the versatile Charles with a thousand francs down in advance, for these were the terms he proposed for an entirely new work. Things were not going well with the Maison Ladvocat; one wonders if they ever *were* when it was a question of payment. The publisher therefore turned down Nodier's suggestion unhesitatingly, but was still left with the necessity of having his manuscript prepared for the press, at a less ruinous figure and if need be by a less celebrated man of letters.

The man of letters was not far to seek; he was very much at hand in the person of young Amédée Pichot. In 1820 Pichot was twenty-five years old. He had come to Paris two years previously, after taking his M.D. at Montpellier, with a vague idea of practising as a gynaecologist. But in his heart of hearts he was already wedded to a literary career, and once arrived in Paris he devoted less and less time to his medical work, giving himself up to literary criticism and translation. Within a couple of years he had published his translation of Scott's poetical romances, of Moore's *Lalla Rookh*, and the early volumes of his *Byron*, as well as critical studies of Scott and Moore. In other words, he was completely in the clutches of Ladvocat, who paid him with bills and fair promises and —what was of equal importance even to the impecunious young Arlesian—kept him supplied with current English literature. No need this time to parley or drive a bargain. For over a year there had lain in Ladvocat's shop an edition of *Rousseau* in twenty-two volumes;[1] it was evidently not going to sell and was getting shop-soiled. Here was an obliging young man anxious for work; in exchange for this trifling service offer him the Rousseau and possibly a promise of something better in the future. Further, after glancing at the manuscript, Pichot declared that it required little alteration. The style would need to be simplified and the more obvious Germanisms removed. But the work, even as it stood, was sure to be a success.

[1] Rousseau, *Œuvres complètes*, Lefèvre, Paris, 1819. These volumes remained in Pichot's library, and vol. i bears the following note in his writing: 'Cette édition des œuvres de Jean-Jacques fut acceptée par moi pour ma révision d'un manuscrit de la traduction de *Pierre Schlémihl* dont j'ignorais l'auteur. J'ai raconté ailleurs comment j'ai appris que l'auteur de *Pierre Schlémihl* était le poète franco-allemand M. de Chamisso. Amédée Pichot.'

Ladvocat departed, well satisfied, and Pichot, not without a certain humorous appreciation of the publisher's little ways, set to work. As he had said, the manuscript needed relatively slight revision, and in the alterations he made he respected the thought of the unknown author as far as possible, but was naturally less scrupulous about the language of the equally unknown translator. When the work ultimately appeared in the same year, 1820, the only name it bore was that of its publisher; there was still no mention of the original author, and Pichot's share was unacknowledged. Ladvocat, however, was not going to lose an opportunity for propaganda. He let it be generally understood that Nodier was responsible for the mysterious work, and in the Prospectus was careful to point out the resemblance between it and *Jean Sbogar*.

Exactly a year later Pichot received a visit from the irate Chamisso in Paris. He had already called on Ladvocat and Nodier, who had clearly shifted as much of the responsibility as possible on to Pichot's shoulders. Indeed it was Nodier who had sent him, and Chamisso, it would seem, had been given the impression that Pichot had represented the story as his own. The angry author had brought the offending volume along with him, and extracted it from his pocket in dramatic fashion, ready to prove the literary theft. But he was disarmed by the obviously genuine surprise of the young man confronting him, and Pichot had no difficulty in showing him that the title-page claimed no authorship for any one, that the publication was entirely anonymous, and that his only offence was one of ignorance. Pichot's transparent honesty and simplicity completely convinced Chamisso of his innocence, and the two men parted on the best of terms. A little later in the same year there came signal proof of this. When Chamisso published his own French

version of *Peter Schlemihl* Pichot found that it was
practically identical with the version he had himself done
for Ladvocat, and was delighted to read this generous
admission in the Preface: 'Je crois en effet que c'est ainsi
qu'aurait écrit Schlémihl s'il avait voulu écrire en français.'[1]
Was there, however, more in this admission than Pichot
appears to have seen, more than an author's graceful
acknowledgement to an intelligent and sympathetic translator? Chamisso's behaviour is surely odd in thus re-
publishing as his own the version which Pichot had
re-written and Ladvocat had already published. Is it
possible that he was not only the original author, but also
the original translator whose Germanisms Pichot had
removed and whose clumsier phrases he had simplified
and polished into a clearer, more attractive French style?
There is an ambiguous note in the terms of his acknowledgement, which may even be construed as bearing out
this interpretation. Was it thus that Schlemihl-Chamisso
had indeed tried to write when *il avait voulu écrire en
français* the version which reached Ladvocat?

So the curtain falls on the little episode leaving each
of the three chief participants content with his share in it:
Ladvocat with an edition of a celebrated work which had
cost him nothing; Chamisso with all the credit of having
done a translation of his own book in a French style which
he certainly might not have achieved unaided; Pichot
richer by the complete works of Rousseau in twenty-two
volumes and more quiet amusement out of the whole
experience than often fell to the lot of those who had
dealings with Ladvocat.

[1] This Preface is dated: 'Au jardin botanique de Berlin, ce 10
septembre, 1821'.

FOUR PRAYERS IN GOETHE'S 'IPHIGENIE'

By J. BOYD

THE two crises in Goethe's *Iphigenie auf Tauris*, the
healing of Orest in Act III and Iphigenie's inner
conflict in Act IV, are among the problems presented in
Goethe's writings which have most constantly engaged
the attention of scholars; and the variety of the solutions
or interpretations which have been suggested illustrates
their difficulty. In the following pages an attempt is made
to throw further light on these problems by an investigation into four of Iphigenie's prayers. Even these have
been given varying interpretations and degrees of importance. Two of the Goethe biographers, J. G. Robertson
and A. Bielschowsky, present opposing views. Robertson
remarks:[1] 'We are not asked to believe that her [Iphi-
genie's] prayer in the third act has any part in her brother's
healing.' Bielschowsky,[2] on the other hand, emphasizes
Iphigenie's close contact with the gods, and adds that it
is only natural, 'daß die stärksten Affekte in einer An-
rufung der Götter sich entladen'. My object here is to
ascertain the place of two of the prayers in the two crises,
to estimate the importance of the four prayers for the
development of the plot, and to inquire to what extent
our conclusions affect the interpretation of the drama
as a whole.

The first prayer comes at the end of a monologue
(Act I, sc. i) in which Iphigenie describes her life as

[1] *The Life and Work of Goethe*, 1932, p. 118. His earlier article,
Goethe's 'Iphigenie auf Tauris' (Publications of the English Goethe
Society, 1924), sets forth similar views and need not be referred to.

[2] *Goethe, sein Leben und seine Werke*, 1922, i, p. 430.

D

priestess in Tauris and her longing for Greece. She
submits, she declares, to the high will of the goddess
Diana, and though not questioning her decrees, admits
with shame that she serves Diana, her saviour, with
reluctance. Yet she hopes for help from her. This brings
us to the point of the scene, namely, the prayer:

> So gieb auch mich den Meinen endlich wieder
> Und rette mich, die du vom Tod gerettet,
> Auch von dem Leben hier, dem zweiten Tode! (Act i, sc. i.)

This thought directs all Iphigenie's impulses, and the
main action of the play as a whole evolves slowly but
surely to the fulfilment of this prayer; when it is finally
answered in Thoas' 'Lebt wohl!', the play is finished.
Thus the 'Sehnsucht', which is the underlying *motif*, finds
its fullest expression in the form of a prayer; the outer
action is its fulfilment.

The second prayer, in Act I, sc. iv,

> O, enthalte vom Blut meine Hände!

is only a little less important and arises out of events which
have developed since scene i. We are told that two
strangers have been discovered on the shores of Tauris.
Thoas, hurt by Iphigenie's refusal to become his wife,
decrees that the rite of human sacrifice, which had been
abolished on her arrival, shall be re-established and that
the two strangers shall be the first victims. The abolition
of human sacrifice, we are told by Arkas, had brought
blessings; the goddess Diana had looked with favour on
the change:

> Hat nicht Diane, statt erzürnt zu sein,
> Daß sie der blut'gen alten Opfer mangelt,
> Dein sanft Gebet in reichem Maß erhört? (Act i, sc. ii.)

When the revelation that she is a descendant of Tantalus
fails to shake Thoas' resolve, Iphigenie suggests that the

goddess may have preserved her in Tauris in order that she should return home there to perform other duties. But Thoas hears in her remarks only evasion and refusal; and since she will not be his wife, he commands her to be wholly priestess:

> Sei Priesterin
> Der Göttin, wie sie dich erkoren hat;

and perform in future the ceremony of human sacrifice.

Iphigenie's reaction to this new situation is the natural one: she recoils from the thought, and appeals to the goddess to keep her hands free from blood. Human sacrifice is opposed to all her ideals; she conceives the gods as loving and kind, and far from taking pleasure in such sacrifice, they would, she believes, gladly extend man's brief span:

> Denn die Unsterblichen lieben der Menschen
> Weitverbreitete, gute Geschlechter,
> Und sie fristen das flüchtige Leben
> Gerne dem Sterblichen, wollen ihm gerne
> Ihres eignen, ewigen Himmels
> Mitgenießendes, fröhliches Anschaun
> Eine Weile gönnen und lassen. (Act I, sc. iv.)

Thus we find two of the chief *motifs*—the longing for home and the desire to remain unsullied by the guilt of performing human sacrifice—set forth by Goethe in the form of prayers to Diana. These prayers epitomize Iphigenie's character, they are the essence of the two monologues which reveal her personality, and they indicate her future conduct. As priestess to Diana, she could not have revealed her inmost soul in a more fitting or natural manner.

Iphigenie's next important prayer occurs just before Orest is healed (Act III, sc. iii). There are several factors which contribute to his healing. The first is the dialogue between brother and sister (Act III, sc. i) and consists of two parts: (*a*) his confession, and (*b*) the reaction of the *reine Schwester* to his confession. Robertson lays stress on the former. Iphigenie brings the hidden canker to light, and by compelling Orest to state his trouble in words, causes him to look upon it more objectively. But the next step, Iphigenie's reaction, is passed over by Robertson, and is only touched upon by Bielschowsky, who refers in general terms to 'der heilende Hauch der heiligen Schwester'.[1] It is of the utmost importance, in my opinion, that throughout the scene Orest is convinced of Iphigenie's nobility—he first regards her as the noble priestess and later as the noble sister. He addresses her as *du große Seele* whom he cannot deceive, as *du Himmlische* whose *holder Mund* extorts from him a confession of a deed which he would gladly bury in *das klanglos-dumpfe Höhlenreich der Nacht*. While they are yet ignorant of each other's identity, he tells the priestess of the fate of Agamemnon and the consequent murder of Klytämnestra:

> Klytämnestra fiel durch Sohnes Hand. (Act III, sc. i.)

It is significant that Iphigenie utters not a word of reproof; on the contrary, after questioning if the goddess had sheltered her in Tauris so that she should experience these horrors the more keenly, she inquires after the fate of Orest:

> Sage mir
> Vom Unglückseligen, sprich mir von Orest! (Act III, sc. i.)

When he relates that the spirit of Klytämnestra rose up to curse her son, and that in consequence there was no peace for him on earth, she repeats the word *Unseliger*:

> Unseliger, du bist in gleichem Fall
> Und fühlst, was er, der arme Flüchtling, leidet! (Act III, sc.i.)

[1] *Goethe*, 1928, i, p. 427.

Orest's statement *Ich bin Orest* follows immediately. Once again he expresses his desire to die, for he believes that his crime can only be expiated by his death. In her joy Iphigenie thanks the gods, who may be recognized by the abundance of their gifts, and she appeals that this long awaited happiness may not come to nought. When Orest confides his terror in face of the furies, she inquires:

Hast du Elektren, *eine* Schwester nur? (Act III, sc. i.)

whereupon he begs Iphigenie to desist, for she only seems to ally herself with the furies. Iphigenie's retort shows the faith she has in her power of healing:

O, wenn vergoßnen Mutterblutes Stimme
Zur Höll' hinab mit dumpfen Tönen ruft,
Soll nicht der reinen Schwester Segenswort
Hülfreiche Götter vom Olympus rufen? (Act III, sc. i.)

The lines not only illustrate the intimate connexion existing in Iphigenie's mind between the gods and herself, they also indicate the mission with which she believed she was entrusted—it is more definitely stated later—namely, the expiation of the curse of Tantalus; and so she is able to reply with conviction:

Du wirst nicht untergehn! (Act I, sc. i.)

The question now arises: Why should Iphigenie not condemn Orest's deed? In Euripides' *Iphigeneia at Aulis* Iphigeneia and her mother are lured to Aulis under the pretext of a marriage with Achilles; one cannot but have sympathy with Clytemnestra, for one feels there is motivation, if not reasonable justification, for her crime. Goethe robs her of this motivation and hence of our sympathy. Concerning Agamemnon, Goethe's Iphigenie utters not a word of blame—on the contrary, she speaks of him as *der göttergleiche.* Her attitude to Klytämnestra, however, is one of condemnation; death, in her opinion, is the fit punishment for her crime. To Orest's question:

> Und fürchtest du für Klytämnestren nichts?

she replies:

> Sie rettet weder Hoffnung, weder Furcht.

And when Orest tells of her death:

> Auch schied sie aus dem Land der Hoffnung ab,

her retort shows that she considers Klytämnestra ought to have expiated her crime by her own hand:

> Vergoß sie reuig wütend selbst ihr Blut? (Act III, sc. i.)

How different is Iphigenie's attitude to Orest's crime of matricide. What is the explanation? From the fact that neither the unknown priestess nor the loving sister utters one word of reproach, we may assume that she regards the murder as inevitable: since Klytämnestra had not taken her own life, the painful deed fell of necessity on Orest, Agamemnon's only son. And indeed she definitely speaks of Orest as the destined avenger of their father:

> Wie ist des großen Stammes letzter Sohn,
> Das holde Kind, bestimmt des Vaters Rächer
> Dereinst zu sein, wie ist Orest dem Tage
> Des Bluts entgangen? (Act III, sc. i.)

But Orest was placed in a dilemma; he was forced to commit one of two crimes: either to refuse to avenge his father or to become guilty of matricide. There could be no question regarding the proper course, and he chose what was for him the lesser crime, i.e. he performed his duty towards his father. But once vengeance is wrought, he is overcome by grief. Thus Iphigenie, recognizing in him a victim of circumstances or of the curse, brings, not condemnation, but sympathy and forgiveness to his troubled spirit:

> Ich bringe süßes Rauchwerk in die Flamme. (Act III, sc. i.)

Her sympathy and forgiveness, which have their full effect on Orest when he finally accepts her as his sister —for she, too, is a child of Klytämnestra—are, I believe, of vital importance for the next scene.

Orest's final recognition of Iphigenie presents a difficulty; almost up to the end of the scene Orest refuses to accept Iphigenie as his sister. The sudden recognition is brought about by her reference to an incident in her life of which a priestess in a remote land would not be aware, namely, that she had been offered as a sacrifice on the altar at Aulis, and that she had been saved by the goddess herself and brought to Tauris. Iphigenie then sums up the situation in which they are placed: Orest is a prisoner, doomed to die on the altar, while she, as priestess, is to perform the sacrifice:

> Vom Altar
> Riß mich die Göttin weg und rettete
> Hierher mich in ihr eigen Heiligtum.
> Gefangen bist du, dargestellt zum Opfer,
> Und findest in der Priesterin die Schwester. (Act III, sc. i.)

With his pessimistic belief in the inexorable cruelty of the curse, Orest sees the full implication: it is *die letzten Greuel unsres Hauses*; what more fitting end of the *alter Stamm* could the gods, in their insatiable thirst for vengeance, have thought out? Now, he believes, he will expiate his crime; it is not *Brudermord* incited by hatred or revenge; rather the gods have decreed that the loving sister shall slay her brother. Klytämnestra, he declares, can be satisfied; her spirit and all the furies she called down upon his head may behold the last, the most dreadful, deed of all. But for Iphigenie he feels only tenderness:

> Weine nicht! Du hast nicht Schuld. (Act I, sc. i.)

He has, he says, never loved anything so much as he could

have loved her ('wie ich dich lieben könnte, Schwester'). The fact that he is about to atone for his crime, as he believes, at the hands of a loving and beloved sister finally envelopes his mind in that visionary trance in which the emotions of the last dialogue are reflected: 'er sinkt in Ermattung'.[1]

Scene ii, in which Orest, in a state of semi-coma, describes his experiences in the underworld, is a natural outcome of scene i. Orest had realized through Iphigenie that there is forgiveness for his crime. That Elektra or any other of his friends might forgive him, was one thing; that Iphigenie, the perfect woman, the priestess and *reine Schwester*, should do so, was another. His experiences in the underworld are, in my opinion, nothing more than an intensified repetition of his experiences before the *Ermattung*: he now realizes that there is complete forgiveness for his crime *both here and hereafter*;

---

[1] In his article, 'Die Entsühnung des Orest in Goethes "Iphigenie auf Tauris" ' (*GJB.*, 1922 and 1924), in which some of the more important theories concerning the healing of Orest are summarized, P. Warncke gives a different interpretation. He sets special emphasis on Orest's *Schuldgefühl* and *Reue*, which distinguish him from his guilty forefathers and which impel him to long for death as an expiation for his crime. He admits the cure 'wird durch die Lichtgestalt der Iphigenie vermittelt—wenn jemand, so ist sie befähigt, durch ihr Vertrauen auf die Güte der Götter und ihre erbarmende Liebe, als Schwester und Priesterin, Orest den Frieden zu bringen'—but Orest, as he points out, 'hört von ihren Trostworten nichts ... und verkennt die Innigkeit der schwesterlichen Liebe'. Warncke is of the opinion that it is finally their *mutual love* which bears fruit: 'Der Strahl der Liebe Iphigeniens hat gezündet. Orest hat ihre Liebe durch alle Verdüsterung seines Innern hindurch gespürt und mit erwachender Bruderliebe erwiedert' (*GJB.*, 1924, pp. 133–6). K. Heinemann denies that Orest experiences any *Reue* at all: 'Wo steht in dem Drama auch nur ein Wort davon?' he asks (*GJB.*, 1899, pp. 212 ff.). M. Wohlrab, on the other hand, believes that Orest is healed, not by Iphigenie, but by himself through his *Reue* and his *Schuldbekenntnis* (*Neue Jahrb. f. d. klass. Alterthum*, 1899, ii. ii, pp. 86 ff.). See also Fritz Ernst, *Iphigeneia und andere Essays*, München-Berlin, 1933, pp. 13–30.

for he learns that his forefathers live in perfect harmony beyond the grave:

> Ist keine Feindschaft hier mehr unter euch?
> Verlosch die Rache wie das Licht der Sonne?
> So bin auch ich willkommen, und ich darf
> In euern feierlichen Zug mich mischen. (Act III, sc. ii.)

Even Agamemnon and Klytämnestra walk hand in hand, and so Orest feels he may approach her with the words: 'Sieh deinen Sohn! . . . heißt ihn willkommen!' Only one member of their family suffers eternal damnation, namely, Tantalus. But his sin was of a different kind. His was a sin against the gods, and as such—like in the Christian faith the sin against the Holy Ghost—can never be forgiven. With the full assurance that he can and will be forgiven, Orest awakes from his *Ermattung* as from a refreshing sleep.[1] Thus the scene symbolically expounds his full realization of a truth which had been implanted by Iphigenie in his conscious mind, namely, that there is for him complete and lasting forgiveness. The realization of this truth is the third factor contributing to his healing.

Scene iii deals with Orest's return to consciousness. He believes that he is still in the underworld and that Iphigenie and Pylades, too, have descended. It is now that Iphigenie offers her prayer to *die Geschwister*, Diana and Apollo:

> Geschwister, die ihr an dem weiten Himmel
> Das schöne Licht bei Tag und Nacht herauf
> Den Menschen bringet und den Abgeschiednen
> Nicht leuchten dürfet, rettet uns Geschwister! (Act III, sc. iii.)

That she should pray to both is natural: she herself was priestess to Diana, and Orest, who had appealed to Apollo at Delphi, found himself in his present unhappy

---

[1] Warncke stresses the importance of the refreshing sleep, *GJB.*, 1924, p. 137.

plight through his obedience to Apollo's command. Iphigenie could not believe that the gods would desert them now; and so in complete faith in their goodness, she makes her great appeal to Diana:

> O, laß den einz'gen, spätgefundnen mir
> Nicht in der Finsternis des Wahnsinns rasen!
> Und ist dein Wille, da du hier mich bargst,
> Nunmehr vollendet, willst du mir durch ihn
> Und ihm durch mich die sel'ge Hülfe geben,
> So lös ihn von den Banden jenes Fluchs,
> Daß nicht die teure Zeit der Rettung schwinde!
>
> (Act III, sc. iii.)[1]

The question to which we now come is: What part, if any, does Iphigenie's prayer play in Orest's cure? Professor Robertson says: 'We are not asked to believe that her prayer . . . has any part in her brother's healing.'[2] The remark is true, but the inference, to my mind, is misleading. In what way could we be 'asked' to believe it? It is equally true that we are not asked to believe that Orest's vision in the underworld plays any part—there is not a line in *Iphigenie* which says so—but we are nevertheless expected to *imagine* that it does. Yet such a vision is further removed from normal human experience. I cannot believe that the prayer is either a rhetorical outburst or a means of relief for Iphigenie's pent-up emo-

---

[1] Just as each of the former events leads logically and naturally into the next—the influence of Iphigenie on Orest compels his confession, the confession calls forth her sympathy and forgiveness, the realization of her forgiveness and the thought that he is about to die at her hands bring about the visionary trance with its assurance of a fuller forgiveness—so the prayer is a natural sequel to the preceding events. Orest's first lines in sc. iii show that he believes himself to be still in the underworld. Iphigenie's prayer to *die Geschwister* is calculated to convince him that he is in the land of the living, and her appeal to Diana is impelled by the fear that, with Orest in his present unhappy state (he only regains full consciousness in l. 1341), the time and opportunity for their escape may slip away.

[2] *Goethe*, p. 118.

tions; Goethe never stood farther from rhetoric than at this period, and Iphigenie's conception of the gods is too sublime for her to treat her prayers lightly or to doubt their efficacy. The fact that the prayer is followed by the complete healing of Orest is, in my opinion, a sufficient reason why it must be taken into account in the healing process. Immediately after her prayer Pylades addresses Orest, giving expression to exactly the same thoughts and sentiments as those contained in the prayer, only in a less divine way; at once Orest exclaims *zu Iphigenie*:

> Laß mich zum erstenmal mit freiem Herzen
> In deinen Armen reine Freude haben! (Act III, sc. iii.)

And addressing the gods, who, he declares, resolve man's *grausendes Erwarten in Segen*, he breaks out in a paean of joy and gratitude:

> Es löset sich der Fluch, mir sagt's das Herz.
> Die Eumeniden ziehn, ich höre sie,
> Zum Tartarus und schlagen hinter sich
> Die ehrnen Tore fernabdonnernd zu. (Act III, sc. iii.)

One reason Robertson gives for dismissing the prayer as one of the contributory factors in the healing process is: 'So unconscious is Iphigenie of her priestess-rôle that in the fourth act she is still ignorant that her brother has surmounted the crisis.'[1] Iphigenie's reactions are, to my mind, natural. Orest recovers from his trance to find himself suddenly cured. The minds of the three characters would scarcely attune themselves at once to the new state of affairs; there would be some doubt concerning the lasting nature of the cure. Moreover, they believed that the cure could only be effected when the conditions laid down by Apollo had been fulfilled, i.e. when the image

[1] Ibid., p. 118.

had been restored to Delphi. Pylades makes an attempt
to explain the premature cure:

> Die besten Zeichen sendet uns Apoll,
> Und eh' wir die Bedingung fromm erfüllen,
> Erfüllt er göttlich sein Versprechen schon.
> Orest ist frei, geheilt! (Act iv, sc. iii.)

Another objection by Robertson is that it was never
Goethe's way 'to untie a spiritual or emotional knot by
recourse to a religious miracle'.[1] Goethe's views on this
matter and the use he made of the supernatural in some
of his other works need not be discussed here.[2] Certainly
in *Iphigenie* he has presented Greeks—no matter whether
they are true to life or not—who still believe in their gods
and who accept them with all their attributes of power,
blessings, curses, revenge, oracles, &c. If we are to
understand *Iphigenie* aright, we must accept these characters as such; and of all the characters Iphigenie is certainly the last to doubt her gods or the power and effect
of her prayers to them.[3]

There are then, I suggest, not two, but four factors
which contribute to Orest's cure: (*a*) the relief obtained
by confession (sc. i); (*b*) the realization that in Iphigenie
he has found sympathy, pity, and forgiveness (sc. i);
(*c*) the extension of this realization to the conviction that
there is complete and lasting forgiveness for his crime
(sc. ii); and (*d*) Iphigenie's appeal to the gods.[4] These

---

[1] Ibid., pp. 118–19.

[2] See E. Franz, *Goethe als religiöser Denker*, Tübingen, 1932.

[3] With regard to the part played by the prayer, Warncke remarks:
'Iphigeniens rührendes Bittgebet . . . den Geschwistern gnädig zu sein,
des Freundes Zuspruch, der auf die sinnliche Wirklichkeit hinweist,
erwecken Orest aus seinem Traumzustand. Er empfindet seine Heilung
mit klarem Bewußtsein und wendet sich zum erstenmal in ergreifendem
Dankgebet an die Götter' (*GJB.*, 1924, p. 138).

[4] C. Lucerna ('Der morphologische Grundriß und die religiöse Ent-

four factors—two natural and two supernatural—are not of equal importance. Far from being of no importance, the prayer would for the three Greeks be of the greatest importance—and therefore we, too, must accept it as such. Besides, Goethe was artist enough to realize the dramatic effect of a *crescendo*, and for artistic reasons, if for no other, we must regard the factors not as diminishing, but as increasing in both intensity and importance.

The next question which arises is: Can we accept Orest's cure as *complete* and *lasting*? Let us first consider the question of completeness. Orest's words at the close of Act III show the change that has come over him. Nevertheless the three characters may be forgiven their initial caution. In Act IV, however, Pylades informs Iphigenie that their fears concerning the renewal of his malady outside the holy grove had proved to be unfounded. It is Orest, Pylades states, who is now the moving spirit in their plan for escape:

> Sein volles Auge glühte
> Von Mut und Hoffnung, und sein freies Herz
> Ergab sich ganz der Freude, ganz der Lust,
> Dich, seine Retterin, und mich zu retten.   (Act IV, sc. iv.)

wicklungsidee des Goetheschen Dramas Iphigenie auf Tauris', *GJB.* xxxiii, 1912, pp. 97 ff.) gives five factors; like Robertson he ignores (*b*) and (*d*), and subdivides (*a*) and (*c*). His process is as follows: '(1) Das Bekenntnis (Wiedererleben der Tat). Es entspricht einer Beichte; (2) Der Paroxismus der Seelenqualen entspricht der Reue; (3) Der im Wahn erlebte Tod vertritt eine Sühnung; (4) Die Vision eine Lossprechung; (5) Das Erwachen wird gefaßt als seelische Wiedergeburt, als Wieder-aufnahme in den Stand der Gnade.' A. S. Wilkins does not believe we can analyse the process at all: 'A sister's love and loyalty blot out the dark stains of the past, and restore a brother to peace and joy. It is impossible to analyse the manner in which this result is produced: *"Versöhnen ist immerdar der schöne Beruf der Frauen"*.' (Goethe's *'Iphigenie'*, *Transactions of the Manchester Goethe Society*, 1886–93, p. 73).

In Act V it is Orest who recognizes the true meaning of
the oracle of Apollo, which ran:

> 'Bringst du die Schwester, die an Tauris' Ufer
> Im Heiligtume wider Willen bleibt,
> Nach Griechenland, so löset sich der Fluch.' (Act v, sc. vi.)

The wise Pylades had believed:

> Der Götter Worte sind nicht doppelsinnig. (Act ii, sc. i.)

Even Iphigenie accepted the oracle literally (Act V, sc. iii).
But Orest, now in full possession of his faculties, declares:

> Wir legten's von Apollens Schwester aus,
> Und er gedachte dich! Die strengen Bande
> Sind nun gelöst; du bist den Deinen wieder,
> Du Heilige, geschenkt. (Act v, sc. vi.)

For his part Orest is convinced of the completeness of
his cure; he says:

> Von dir berührt,
> War ich geheilt; in deinen Armen faßte
> Das Übel mich mit allen seinen Klauen
> Zum letztenmal und schüttelte das Mark
> Entsetzlich mir zusammen; dann entfloh's
> Wie eine Schlange zu der Höhle. (Act v, sc. vi.)

Thus we see that Goethe is at pains to show the complete
nature of the healing. Not only is Orest himself convinced; he now possesses a clarity of vision and a perception of truth superior to that of any of the other
characters. Goethe could scarcely have done more to
show Orest's complete sanity.[1]

The lasting nature of his sanity is perhaps not so well
established—'Will they live happily ever afterwards?'
asks Professor Robertson.[2] It is more than probable that
in a play of a realistic type, we should be left with an
uneasy feeling that there would be moments when the

---

[1] Fritz Ernst, *Iphigeneia und andere Essays*, pp. 24–25.
[2] *Goethe*, p. 124.

'black past' would rise up again. But *Iphigenie* is not realistic.[1] It deals with the fable of the expiation of the Tantalus curse by Iphigenie.[2] Now the healing of Orest is only the first visible sign that the curse has run its course. Orest's unhappy plight was a consequence of the curse: his release from the pursuit of the furies is a direct result of its having been lifted. Thus, if we can believe that Iphigenie succeeds in expiating the curse—and if we cannot believe this, the whole play is pointless—then

[1] C. Schrempf is also not convinced of the lasting nature of the cure, nor even of the entire expiation of the curse. His views, which are the same as those of Robertson, who, as he states (pp. 125–6), follows Schrempf in this matter, may be explained by his attitude to the play. 'Die Geschichte der beiden Geschwister', he says, 'wird in Goethes Darstellung ein Symbol der allgemeinen Stellung des Menschen im und zum Leben. . . . Der Dichter bezeugt uns als objektive Wahrheit des Lebens, daß wir in der Obhut liebender Götter stehen, die besser für uns sorgen, als wir selbst es zu tun vermögen. Wir können also nichts besseres tun, als daß wir unser Heil ihnen anheimstellen' (*Goethes Lebensanschauung in ihrer geschichtlichen Entwicklung*, Stuttgart, 1907, ii, p. 232). Far from presenting 'ein Symbol der *allgemeinen* Stellung des Menschen im und zum Leben', *Iphigenie*, in my opinion, presents an *ideal* attitude to life. Nor is it true that the *objektive Wahrheit des Lebens* as set forth in the play amounts to an unquestioning acquiescence of an inactive, irresponsible humanity in a perfect, providential, divine guidance. The message of *Iphigenie* is rather that man must play his part; the gods have their laws, no less than *die Hölle selbst hat ihre Rechte*, and their law that man must fulfil his moral duty is no less inexorable than is the demand of actual life for his fulfilment of what Goethe termed *die Forderung des Tages*. It is true, as Schrempf observes (p. 233), in actual life the gods often enough disappoint man, when he puts his trust in them. But *Iphigenie* is not an *Abschnitt des Lebens*, and any insistence on its being symbolical of real life can only lead to a misunderstanding of its import. It presents not the real, but ideal, conception, as Goethe visualized it, of human conduct and of man's relationship to life and destiny.

[2] 'La maladie d'Oreste avait pour cause morale la conviction désespérée où il était que la fatalité condamnait toute sa famille à être criminelle; mais il découvre, ô délivrance! une sœur innocente et vertueuse: l'expiation est donc faite, et la malédiction antique a pris fin' (Paul Stapfer, *Études sur Goethe*, Paris, 1906, p. 123).

we must also accept Orest's cure as both complete and lasting.

We now come to Iphigenie's fourth prayer to the gods, that in Act IV, sc. v:

> Rettet mich
> Und rettet euer Bild in meiner Seele!

What is the meaning of this prayer? What emotions underlie it? What connexion has it with the *Parzenlied*, which follows? Let us review a few of the answers to these questions put forward by various scholars. Bielschowsky remarks concerning the prayer: 'Nun zwingen die Götter auch sie, sich zu beflecken. Sie fühlt ihren Glauben an die *Güte des Lebens* bedroht.'; and concerning the *Parzenlied* he says: 'Iphigenie singt das Lied von den unbarmherzig über die Schicksale der Menschen hinwegschreitenden Göttern, um sich von diesem trostlosen . . . Glauben durch Schauder *zu befreien.*'[1] W. Bittmann[2] asks the question: 'In dem reinen edlen Herzen dieser Himmlischen . . . sollte sich das Abbild "des größten Vaters" in dieses Zerrbild verwandeln?' G. Schlosser[3] remarks concerning the prayer: 'In dieser Gewissensnot wendet sich ihre Seele nach oben, woher allein Hilfe kommen kann, betend, rufend aus tiefster Not. . . . Mit diesem Gebet ist Gewißheit in ihr Herz zurückgekehrt.' He does not state what this *Gewißheit* is, or whether the *Parzenlied* is a product of it. Kuno Fischer[4] sees in the *Parzenlied* a memory of the curse

[1] *Goethe*, 1928, pp. 431–2. In the earlier editions further solutions were suggested, e.g., Sollte etwa so rasch ihr Glauben sich ins Gegenteil verkehrt haben? Sollte das Lied nur ein breiteres Ausklingen der Erinnerung an den Titanenhaß bedeuten? &c. (1922 edition, pp. 436–7.)

[2] *Eine Studie über Goethes 'Iphigenie auf Tauris'*, Hamburg, 1888, pp. 221–2.

[3] *Goethes 'Iphigenie' nach ihrem religiös-sittlichen Gehalt*, Frankfurt, 1875, p. 26.   [4] *Goethes 'Iphigenie'*, Heidelberg, pp. 22–4 and 51.

which threatens to destroy Iphigenie, and he contrasts
her present fear with the faith expressed in her prayer
in Act I, sc. iv:

> Und dein Blick ruht über den Deinen,
> Wie dein Licht, das Leben der Nächte,
> Über der Erde ruhet und waltet.

He then asks: 'Wer wird Recht behalten; der Glaube
und die Hoffnung Iphigeniens in ihrem Gebet an die
Göttin oder jenes alte, grausige Parzenlied?' Strangely
enough Fischer regards the prayer: 'Rettet mich', &c.,
as inspired by this memory—he reverses the order in
which they appear in the play: 'Die Erinnerung an das
Parzenlied erwacht, und sie fleht die Götter an, sie *vor
dem Fluch zu bewahren.*' His next statement: 'Sie ist
entschlossen, dem Könige die Wahrheit zu bekennen',
which indicates immediate relief from her fear, is belied
by her following verses and by the *Parzenlied*, which
closes the act. G. Witkowski[1] does not attempt an
explanation of the prayer, and with regard to the *Parzenlied* he merely remarks: 'Die Wahnsinnsszene des Orest
und das Parzenlied Iphigeniens sind die dramatischen
Höhepunkte der Handlung.' R. M. Meyer[2] is quite
non-committal: 'Die Priesterin Dianas ist keine über-
lebensgroße Heroine, und des furchtbaren Parzenliedes
entsinnt sie sich nur ungern.' H. Bulthaupt[3] believes
that Iphigenie cannot lie even if she would: 'sie verstrickt
sich selbst'; and he regards the prayer as a natural result
of her abhorrence of *das falsche Wort*: 'Ihre Sorge wird
zur Verzweiflung, die Notwendigkeit scheint sie zur
Lüge *zwingen* zu wollen, und qualvoll schreit sie auf:

[1] *Goethe*, Leipzig, 1923, p. 231.
[2] *Goethe*, Berlin, 1905, p. 312.
[3] *Dramaturgie des Schauspiels*, Oldenburg & Leipzig, 1893, vol. i,
p. 141.

"O, daß in meinem Busen . . .". The effect of her prayer
on a modern audience is explained, he believes, by its
Christian attributes: 'Wie nahe tritt uns diese Iphigenie,
die modern, die (man gestatte mir das Wort) *christlich*
empfindende! Die Griechin, die diese moralischen Scrupel
nicht kennt, vermöchte sie es uns so nachhaltig zu er-
greifen?' Unfortunately Bulthaupt does not explain how
the *Parzenlied* can be fitted into this Christian conception.
E. Franz[1] writes: 'Goethe ist der Schüler Herders, der
die Religion als höchsten Ausdruck der Humanität
feiert. . . . Iphigeniens hohe Kultur und Menschlichkeit
den Barbaren gegenüber findet ihren Ausdruck in ihrer
geläuterten Gottesauffassung.' But it sounds strange
when he adds: 'In der Stunde der Gefahr regen sich die
alten wilden Triebe des Titanengeschlechtes in ihr, und
sie fleht: Rettet mich . . .' F. Gundolf[2] remarks: 'In
diesem Gebet ist die Essenz alles dessen was ein Mensch
vom reinsten Willen fühlt, wenn ihm unter der Last
unverdienter Leiden oder verhängten Erbfluchs der
Glaube zu schwinden droht. . . . Das *Parzenlied* ist die
Erinnerung eines gläubig geläuterten Menschen an die
Möglichkeit, daß *Sühnung unmöglich sei*.' Carl Fries[3]
remarks: 'Das Ganze hat *die Bedeutung einer Warnung*
für sie selbst.' C. Schrempf[4] declares: 'Es ist für sie eine
Anfechtung, die das erworbene Vertrauen in die Götter
wieder gefährdet, daß sie . . . die Reinheit preisgeben soll,
auf der die bessere Zukunft der Tantaliden ruht. Es
regte sich wieder in ihr der furchtbare Argwohn, daß die
Götter vielleicht doch nur ihr rohes, höhnisches Spiel mit
den Sterblichen treiben. Aus tiefster Seelennot mußte sie

[1] *Goethe als religiöser Denker*, Tübingen, 1932, p. 222.
[2] *Goethe*, Berlin, 1922, p. 312.
[3] *Parzenlied und Völuspa*, GJB., 1912, pp. 86–87.
[4] *Goethes Lebensanschauung in ihrer geschichtlichen Entwicklung*, Stuttgart, 1907, I, pp. 230 ff.

die Götter anflehen: Rettet mich, und rettet euer Bild in meiner Seele!' He does not, however, show how *das grimme Lied*, as he calls it, follows on this appeal. Professor Barker Fairley[1] does not come to grips with either the prayer or the *Parzenlied*, but remarks concerning drama as a whole: 'There is scarcely a breath of revolt or self assertion in the poem'; and Professor E. M. Butler[2] believes: '. . . Even the Parcae's Song of Iphigenia [is] powerless to dispel our deep unanswerable conviction that all will yet be well.' J. G. Robertson has nothing to say about the *Parzenlied* beyond the remark that it is a 'grim song,'[3] but he does make an effort to get to the bottom of the prayer, and to his interpretation we shall return.

Let us consider briefly the events which lead up to the prayer. Between Acts III and IV there is a scene which is not portrayed—the council at which the plan is evolved, and of which Orest speaks at the end of Act III, sc. iii:

> Es bedarf hier schnellen Rat und Schluß.

In the course of Act IV we are given details concerning the plan. Iphigenie's part is to deceive the king, so that the image can be safely conveyed from the temple. Though she recoils from deception, she resolves to play her part (Act IV, sc. i).

In scene ii she is reminded by Arkas of the kindness she had experienced 'since her arrival to this day' at the hands of Thoas, a noble man, we are told elsewhere, who had become to her a second father. In her next monologue (sc. iii) Iphigenie reveals the conflict which Arkas' untimely reminder had evoked in her soul: she now hates the lie doubly, for it means the deception of her best

---

[1] *Goethe as revealed in his Poetry*, London, 1932, p. 28.
[2] *The Tyranny of Greece over Germany*, Cambridge, 1925, p. 102.
[3] *Goethe*, p. 124.

friend. She excuses her temporary lapse by her overwhelming joy in finding a long-lost brother and by the
prospect of an early return home.   But she realizes now
that she is leaving 'Menschen' behind:

> Nun hat die Stimme
> Des treuen Manns mich wieder aufgeweckt,
> Daß ich auch Menschen hier verlasse, mich
> Erinnert. Doppelt wird mir der Betrug
> Verhaßt. O, bleibe ruhig, meine Seele! (Act IV, sc. iii.)

In this state of mental turmoil she is found by Pylades
(sc. iv). On learning that Arkas is about to inform the
king of the intended purification of the image, he proposes
carrying it off forthwith, but Iphigenie seeks to restrain
him. Realizing her qualms, Pylades now speaks a number
of lines which, to my mind, are of vital importance:

> So hast du dich im Tempel wohl bewahrt;
> Das Leben lehrt uns, weniger mit uns
> Und andern strenge sein; du lernst es auch.
> So wunderbar ist dies Geschlecht gebildet,
> So vielfach ist's verschlungen und verknüpft,
> Daß keiner in sich selbst, noch mit den andern
> Sich rein und unverworren halten kann. (Act IV, sc. iv.)

For Iphigenie, Pylades insists, there can be only *one*
course, namely, to save her brother; and when she still
hesitates, he reiterates the thought:

> Man sieht, du bist nicht an Verlust gewohnt,
> Da du, dem großen Übel zu entgehen,
> Ein falsches Wort nicht einmal opfern willst. (Act IV, sc. iv.)

How little her noble purpose had been understood by
Pylades, becomes clear in Iphigenie's next monologue
(sc. v). He had regarded her reluctance to deceive the
king as a mere scruple; she was unwilling, he believed, to
sacrifice any of those virtues which exalted her above
other mortals and thus to degrade herself in her own self-

esteem. How different were the real facts. Iphigenie
here confesses that she had hoped, through a pure heart
and a blameless life spent in seclusion and dedicated to
the service of the goddess, to counterbalance the sin of
Tantalus and to expiate the curse:

> O, soll ich nicht die stille Hoffnung retten,
> Die in der Einsamkeit ich schön genährt? (Act iv, sc. v.)

But now it would seem as if this hope is to prove vain:

> So hofft' ich denn vergebens, hier verwahrt,
> Von meines Hauses Schicksal abgeschieden,
> Dereinst mit reiner Hand und reinem Herzen
> Die schwer befleckte Wohnung zu entsühnen! (Act iv, sc. v.)

What were the exact circumstances which were
threatening to frustrate her hopes? Like Orest, she was
placed in a dilemma; she, too, had an option: either to
sacrifice her brother, or to deceive the king. As Pylades
had said, there could be only one course. But in saving
her brother, she would sully her soul. Thus the gods
were not threatening to refuse to raise the curse; they
seemed to be taking the subtler course of depriving her
of that virtue by which she had hoped to expiate it. If
these things should come to pass, she fears that her
reverence may turn to contempt and her love to hate:

> O, daß in meinem Busen nicht zuletzt
> Ein Widerwille keime! der Titanen,
> Der alten Götter tiefer Haß auf euch,
> Olympier, nicht auch die zarte Brust
> Mit Geierklauen fasse! (Act iv, sc. v.)

On these thoughts her prayer follows naturally:

> Rettet mich
> Und rettet euer Bild in meiner Seele!

What do these words really mean? Professor Robertson
gives the following interpretation: 'If ye gods do not

stand by me now in my hour of need, my faith in you will be destroyed, and with it my whole confidence in a providential guidance of human affairs from on high. Take your choice: accede to my prayer, and I will continue to believe in you; disappoint me, and I repudiate you.'[1] And he asks: 'Is this not arrogance in its most desperate form?'[2] Nothing, in my opinion, could be further from a true estimate of Iphigenie's mentality at this moment. She is not defiant, she does not arrogantly or presumptuously place the gods before a choice; on the contrary, she believes that they are placing her before one—the choice of two sins, either of which will be her undoing. In anguish she implores them to save her, to keep her free from guilt, so that she may yet perform her life's task. With no other thought than this, she beseeches them: 'Rettet mich'.

But it is no less important that she should preserve her high ideal of them. She had conceived them as loving gods. Diana herself had saved her from the altar in Aulis; thus she is able to say:

> Denn die Unsterblichen lieben der Menschen
> Weitverbreitete, gute Geschlechter,

[1] *Goethe*, p. 123.

[2] Professor Robertson admits that such arrogance towards the gods of Greece ought to have ended in tragedy—'the gods must inevitably leave the mortal in the lurch . . . who arrogantly challenges them as Iphigenie does; who dares presumptuously what she dares'—and as a reason for their unexpectedly lenient behaviour, he suggests that 'we must deem his heroine lucky in for once finding the gods of Greece in good humour and willing to close an eye' (pp. 123-4). In a review Professor L. A. Willoughby expresses complete agreement with Robertson's views; 'his criticism', he says, 'is thoroughly objective, inspired by sanity. . . .' And referring to Professor Fairley's discussion of a 'harmonious fusion of the ancient and modern spirit in *Iphigenie*', he remarks: 'Nowhere is the revolt against the old order so tragically brought out as in her *defiant* speech to the gods: "Rettet euer Bild in meiner Seele!"' (*Modern Languages Review*, 1933, pp. 123 ff.)

Und sie fristen das flüchtige Leben
Gerne dem Sterblichen, wollen ihm gerne
Ihres eigenen, ewigen Himmels
Mitgenießendes, fröhliches Anschaun
Eine Weile gönnen und lassen. (Act i, sc. iv.)

She refuses to regard them as blood-thirsty:

Der mißversteht die Himmlischen, der sie
Blutgierig wähnt; er dichtet ihnen nur
Die eignen grausamen Begierden an. (Act i, sc. iii.)

And, she believes, Diana is not only *gnädig* and watches over mortals (Act I, sc. iv), she is wise as well:

Weise bist du und siehest das Künftige. (Act i, sc. iv.)

But now it would seem as if the gods were about to destroy the exalted conception, which during her years as priestess in Tauris she had built up; and in anguish lest she should lose her ideals, she beseeches them: 'Rettet euer Bild in meiner Seele!'

Here a climax is reached; there is a pause. A thought strikes her: 'Is my conception of the gods as noble and loving, is this "Bild in meiner Seele", the true one? Are they not perhaps jealous, spiteful, cruel, and unforgiving? Is not the conception which was instilled into me in my youth—so different from this present "Bild in meiner Seele"—possibly the just one?' And now a song—one which she had gladly forgotten—comes back to her mind. It is the song which the Parcae sang when Tantalus was banished from the table of the gods and which she had learnt from her nurse.

This song, as Bielschowsky remarks, *ist ihrem ganzen Glauben zuwider*.[1] It would perhaps be more correct to say that it is opposed to that faith which she had acquired since the days when she first learnt the song: in other words,

[1] *Goethe*, 1922, i, p. 436. In the edition of 1928 the paragraph has been altered considerably, p. 431.

it expresses a conception of the gods directly opposed to the present *Bild* in her soul, which she now implores the gods to preserve; for it represents the conception held by the descendants of Tantalus under the spell of the curse.

We thus leave Iphigenie at the end of Act IV, not in *Gewißheit*, as Schlosser suggests,[1] but in a state of doubt; she struggles and prays to retain her high ideals of the gods, while as a result of her present circumstances she is pursued by the memory of that conception which she had learnt in her youth and which she fears may perhaps prove to be the true one after all.

Between Acts IV and V—as was the case between Acts III and IV—we must suppose a development of the plot which is not portrayed, but which is nevertheless of vital importance: Iphigenie frees herself from the doubts which had assailed her in the end of Act IV, she regains her old faith in the gods as loving, magnanimous beings, who are able and willing to help. In consequence, she rejects Pylades' plan of subterfuge and deceit, and puts her trust once more in truth and goodness.

Does her conduct in Act V bear out this hypothesis? Let us trace the events briefly. In scene i Arkas speaks of the proposed ceremony of purifying the defiled image as *der heilige Vorwand*. In scene ii Thoas expresses his conviction that he is being deceived by Iphigenie, ascribing her deceit to his own excessive indulgence. In scene iii we have the great dialogue between Thoas and Iphigenie. Iphigenie is as yet ignorant of the fact that counter-measures have been taken, but, as Bielschowsky puts it, 'sie hat innerlich den Plan des Pylades schon abgetan'.[2] This is evident when, to Thoas' remark:

Die Vorsicht stellt der List sich klug entgegen,

---

[1] *Goethes 'Iphigenie' nach ihrem religiös-sittlichen Gehalt*, p. 26.
[2] *Goethe*, i, p. 433.

she replies:

> Und eine reine Seele braucht sie nicht. (Act v, sc. iii.)

She determines to take the step which she knows will end either in the full attainment of her wishes or in disaster. She addresses Thoas:

> Ich werde großem Vorwurf nicht entgehn,
> Noch schwerem Übel, wenn es mir mißlingt;
> Allein euch leg' ich's auf die Kniee! Wenn
> Ihr wahrhaft seid, wie ihr gepriesen werdet,
> So zeigt's durch euern Beistand und verherrlicht
> Durch mich die Wahrheit! (Act v, sc. iii.)

She tells how Apollo had sent Orest and Pylades from Delphi to carry off the goddess:

> Apoll schickt sie von Delphi diesem Ufer
> Mit göttlichen Befehlen zu, das Bild
> Dianens wegzurauben und zu ihm
> Die Schwester hinzubringen, und dafür
> Verspricht er dem von Furien Verfolgten,
> Des Mutterblutes Schuldigen Befreiung. (Act v, sc. iii.)

Convinced that they are fulfilling the will of the gods, Iphigenie refuses to believe that Thoas, as a believer in the Greek gods, will oppose them; he dare not destroy them:

> Verdirb uns wenn du darfst! (Act v, sc. iii.)

Thoas hesitates, a natural reaction to a sudden request to forego his claim to both image and priestess; but Iphigenie pleads:

> Laß mich mit reinem Herzen, reiner Hand
> Hinübergehn und unser Haus entsühnen! (Act v, sc. iii.)

In scene iv Orest enters and Iphigenie informs him that she has confessed all; she now pronounces what are, in my opinion, among the most momentous lines in the whole play:

> Verzeih mir, Bruder! doch mein kindlich Herz
> Hat unser ganz Geschick in seine Hand
> Gelegt. Gestanden hab' ich euern Anschlag
> Und meine Seele vom Verrat gerettet. (Act v, sc. iv.)

She is well aware that all is lost, if Thoas should prove unworthy of her trust, i.e. if he should be deaf to *die Stimme der Wahrheit und der Menschlichkeit*. But whatever may be the outcome, she has at least the comfort of knowing that she has saved her soul from deceit; the gods have heard her prayer: *rettet mich.*

Is there a corresponding answer to the second part of the prayer? Does she retain her high ideals? Iphigenie had hoped for two things above all else: to return to Greece, and there to expiate the curse. But the fulfilment of these hopes was dependent on the gods being good and kind; if they were truly the gods of her fathers, she could only expect hatred and revenge. In Act V, sc. vi, she experiences the full truth of her statement that the gods are to be recognized in the abundance of their gifts. In this scene she realizes that her brother is healed, that the curse is lifted—of this her brother's cure is proof— and, when the solution of the oracle is found, the three Greeks are allowed to depart with Thoas' blessing. All this is made possible by her timely confession to Thoas; had she persisted in trusting to Pylades' plan, instead of putting her faith in the gods, all would have been lost. It was her renewed faith in their goodness in the beginning of Act V which was the means of bringing about this happy issue. Her faith has been vindicated; the gods have proved abundantly that her ideal conception was the true one, they have heard her prayer: 'Rettet euer Bild in meiner Seele!'

Finally, how do the above remarks affect the interpretation of the play as a whole? We have seen that these,
the most important of Iphigenie's prayers, are followed
by their ultimate fulfilment; the gods seem willing to grant
her every wish. Is there any explanation? Does she contribute anything towards their fulfilment? Writing in
1827, Goethe gave the full credit to Iphigenie:

> Alle menschliche Gebrechen
> Sühnet reine Menschlichkeit.

Professor Robertson believes that 'too much weight
has been ascribed to this afterthought of Goethe's';[1] and
he continues: 'He was here imposing on his drama a
conception of the redeeming power of *reine Menschlichkeit*
similar to that which effects the salvation of Faust. But
the idea is foreign to *Iphigenie auf Tauris*.'[2] The question
of Faust's salvation by *reine Menschlichkeit* may be passed
over here; but the fact that Goethe's dictum was an 'afterthought' lends it all the more weight. Pronounced after
a lapse of some forty years, we can be sure that the *critic*
in Goethe was speaking; it is of more value as a verdict
and as an interpretation. Had it been pronounced in the
'eighties, we might be tempted to regard it as an *Idee*
worked consciously into the drama. As we have seen,

---

[1] *Goethe*, p. 121.

[2] Hume Brown expresses the opposite view. 'The theme he chose in
the particular case of *Iphigenie*,' he states, 'was one which involved the
presentation of a definite philosophy of life and of human conduct. This
philosophy was summed up for him in the phrase *reine Menschlichkeit*,
pure humanity, which Goethe had set before himself as the ideal after
which he must strive, if he were to live his full life. . . . As it was under
the daemonic element in nature that he wrote *Egmont*, so it was under this
new inspiration that he wrote *Iphigenie*, which is at once a paean of "pure
humanity" and an illustration of its victorious power' (*Life of Goethe*,
1920, i, pp. 357–8). P. Warncke calls *Iphigenie* 'das Hohelied reiner
Menschlichkeit, die Verherrlichung der menschen- und völkerverbin-
denden Idee edler Humanität' (*GJB.*, 1922, p. 113).

Iphigenie regarded her virtue and her faith as of para-
mount importance—she was prepared to risk all in order
to save them. Her conception of the gods as good and
kind was the basic element of her faith; and this conception, which finally proves to be the true one, is the main-
spring of the action leading to the expiation of the
curse. Apart from his obedience to the oracle, Orest contributes nothing to his cure; as far as he is concerned, it
is a gift of the gods. Iphigenie has something to offer,
but even before her life of service as priestess began,
Diana saved her from certain death on the altar. Life
itself, with its opportunity of expiating the curse, was
therefore a gift. The reason for the granting of the gift
was that Iphigenie had offered herself as a willing sacrifice, she had acquiesced in the will of the gods, she was
the first of the descendants of Tantalus who had not been
found wanting in the virtues of *Rat, Mäßigung, Weisheit
und Geduld*.[1] Thus it is only when we reach Iphigenie in
the long line, that we find circumstances propitious for
the gods to lift the curse. According to Iphigenie's conception, the gods are only too willing to bestow their
blessings; had they wished they could, she well realized,
have withheld them. Their blessings are neither obtained
by barter nor bought by service: they are conferred by
grace. But man must prove himself worthy; he must merit
them by his virtue. In our play it is Iphigenie's virtue
which fulfils this condition. It is her reliance on truth,[2]

---

[1] 'Die Lösung des so aufgefaßten Fluches erfolgt, wenn aus diesem
Geschlecht ein Mensch entspringt, der von der wilden Art seines Hauses
nichts geerbt hat. Es ist Iphigenie' (G. Witkowski, *Goethe*, pp. 228–9).
'Against this mass of accumulated horrors there stands out the pure saint-
like figure of Iphigenie. She is the only one of her race whom the breath .
of perdition has not touched' (K. Francke, *A History of German Literature*,
p. 351).

[2] 'Nicht eine Verherrlichung der "Wahrheit", durch die sie Thoas

her blameless life, her ideal of the gods, her faith in man, her nobility of character, her perfect sympathy, in a word, her *reine Menschlichkeit* which calls forth the blessings of the gods, which facilitates the good work they would do, which, as Goethe put it, in our play expiates *alle menschliche Gebrechen.*

bezwingt, soll man als Hauptton heraushören—sie ist nur ein einzelner Zug in der reinen Menschlichkeit dieser Priesterin' (R. M. Meyer, *Die deutsche Literatur bis zum Beginn des XIX. Jahrhunderts,* Berlin, 1920, p. 488).

ACTOR AND PUBLIC IN GOTTSCHED'S TIME

By W. H. BRUFORD

IN studying the condition of the theatre and drama in Gottsched's time, it is useful to keep in mind the distinction now commonly made by German scholars[1] (since Hermann Reich's *Mimus*, 1903) between two types of dramatic performance, 'Mimus' and 'Drama'. The one is a theatrical entertainment pure and simple, in which the maximum use is made of every device that will hold the attention of an audience—realistic acting and slapstick comedy, with a crudely emotional or humorous appeal; exhibitions of the actors' agility, strength, or other physical attractions, a powerful voice, for example; and striking scenic effects. The other is drama in the full sense of the word, in which many of these primitive elements are still indispensable, but only as instruments employed by the dramatist to body forth what he has created in his imagination, a unified whole, 'some possibility of life seized on by the poet's mind, and imagined as a single movement of events . . . an idea shaping itself forth in the action of life' (Lascelles Abercrombie). It is also helpful to remember what sort of people the actors were whom Gottsched was trying to win over for his new ideals, and what sort of audiences they usually had to play to. A study of the social factors shows what formidable difficulties had to be faced by any reformer who aimed at converting the 'Mimus', which was the usual fare in the popular theatre of the day, into a real 'drama'.

[1] Cf. particularly R. Petsch, 'Zwei Pole des Dramas', in *Deutsche Vierteljahrsschrift für Literaturwissenschaft und Geistesgeschichte*, ii, 1924 (and in his *Gehalt und Form*, Dortmund, 1925).

W. Flemming[1] has classified the drama of the baroque period according to the social status of its patrons. Opera was maintained by absolute princes and their courts, literary tragedy and comedy appealed to the educated middle classes, officials for the most part, and was acted by students and Gymnasiasten, and the Latin drama of the Jesuits in the south, though it offered most to scholars and courtiers, was not without attractions for the common man. The town populace were the principal support of the strolling players, the English Comedians and their successors, though courts would often engage them, especially in the early days, and all classes might be represented to some extent in their audiences. This was the professional German theatre of that age. It was only through the English Comedians that the German public came to know what professional actors could do, and it is only from that time that one can properly speak of 'actors' and a 'public' in Germany at all. Much the same classification will serve for Gottsched's age. It was this professional theatre that he wished to reform.

That an ambitious young scholar, as eager as any one in that age to win favour with the great, should condescend so far as to seek the personal acquaintance of strolling players, and should even entertain the hope of exercising a good moral influence through them, must have greatly surprised his friends, for the social standing and moral reputation of actors and actresses were very low. They were regarded by most respectable citizens, as their predecessors, the *fahrende Leute*, had been since the days of the *Sachsenspiegel*, as *unehrlich*, beyond the pale. J. C. Brandes, the actor and playwright, could not even in 1764 marry the lady of his choice in Königsberg, her home, but had to go to Breslau for the ceremony, to satisfy her family, because

---

[1] Introduction to *Barockdrama*, *I* (Deutsche Literatur), Leipzig, 1930.

of the prejudice that still existed against his calling, and Iffland, when he ran away to the stage in 1777, had to plead with his father for years before he was forgiven. In 1787 a comparatively broad-minded writer in the Hamburg *Journal aller Journale* has to admit that although the theatre is so popular, there is still much prejudice against actors. As to actresses, he feels it is often justified, for they are in general *eigennützig, kokett, leichtsinnig und wankelmütig*. He does not advise any one, unless very talented, to take to the stage, if any more reputable career is open to him. Good old-fashioned citizens, to whom any strangers were a little suspect, naturally could not feel that homeless wanderers were of their own kind. 'Bring the washing in, the players are coming!' was still their attitude quite late in the century. The first professional actors had been foreigners, and a large proportion of the Germans who took to the stage were at their wit's end before they resolved on so desperate a step. G. H. Koch was in such financial straits in 1728 as a law student in Leipzig[1] that he had thought of enlisting, the last resource of so many young men, before he joined the Neubers' troupe. Many of the university men who were to be found among the actors had been moved by similar motives. There must have been a certain glamour about the stage, too, for young impressionable people, even before the sentimental age. The famous Velthen, a young man of good family and already a Magister, after some successes in an amateur student company in Leipzig, married the daughter of the Prinzipal Paul, who often visited the town, and joined his troupe. In many other cases too a love affair brought a troupe a new recruit, or a girl ran away, as Karoline Weissenborn did with the student

[1] C. H. Schmid, *Chronologie des deutschen Theaters*, ed. P. Legband, Berlin, 1902.

ACTOR AND PUBLIC IN GOTTSCHED'S TIME   65

Johann Neuber, and joined a company with her lover, because any one with a good presence, especially if backed by a little education, was sure at least of being given a trial on the stage. But when once engaged in this precarious and despised profession, they found it very difficult to leave it for anything better. They might find themselves associated with acrobats and dancers, clowns and marionette players and conjurors. 'Der große Haufe vermischte zu leicht den Künstler, dessen Fach Talente und Anstrengung erforderte, mit dem Marktschreier, dem Seiltänzer, oder gar—dem Tanzbären', as the Hamburg writer quoted above says, for it was only gradually, in the course of the eighteenth century, that legitimate drama came to be distinguished from something very like what we now call 'variety', the whole aim of all but a few idealists among the Principals being to amuse an audience by any means in their power, to content themselves, in a word, with 'Mimus'.

The attitude of society to these wanderings troupes is clearly reflected in the regulations made for their benefit by the town councils. They were not allowed to perform in any town without first obtaining the permission of the town council and paying a fee. Their programme had to be submitted for approval, the prices they might charge for admission, the length of their stay (seldom more than a fortnight), and the times of their performances were determined by the council, and they were warned on pain of a fine not to cause disorder or to offend against public morals. These were quite normal precautions, that might be compared with many other regulations of the paternal governments of that day, but the council often went further. In one Swiss town even in 1757 Ackermann's company was forbidden to seek quarters in private houses, in another to accept any invitations from citizens.

4343   F

In earlier days such injunctions had been very common, and, as the records show, not unnecessary, especially after women had begun to appear on the stage, in the second half of the seventeenth century, 'Denn ein wanderndes Mädchen ist immer von schwankendem Rufe', as Dorothea said to Hermann. Their dress and morals gave particular offence to the Pietists, and the Puritan attack on the stage in England was followed by a corresponding movement in Germany. Anton Reiser's *Theatromania* (1681) started a long controversy; respected actors like Velthen were refused communion and even in 1760 Karoline Neuber's coffin had to be lifted over the churchyard wall because the minister would not hand over the keys of the gate for the burial of an actress.

The state governments seem on the whole to have been better disposed towards the players than those of the towns, but everything depended on the personal tastes of the ruler of the state. The greatest desire of every Principal was to be in the good books of some prince and his court, and although from the Thirty Years War on the courts reserved their chief favours for Italians and Frenchmen, a prince might occasionally help a German troupe through the winter and quite readily gave the better troupes *Privilegien*, which, though they did not confer a monopoly on the troupe, gave it official recognition as the court troupe of the state concerned and recommended it to the town authorities in that state. In Berlin it was the ruling house, in Velthen's time, which defended the actors against the narrow-minded clergy. The aristocracy in general were pleasure-loving and far from strait-laced in the matter of morals. It is evident from actors' memoirs (Christ, Brandes) that 'Protection' from people of rank, not always won by purely artistic merits, might mean much for a troupe and was eagerly courted. Young

officers especially sought the favours of actresses and
often admitted actors to their company, as they came to
be men of some cultivation. Even in Gottsched's time
actors were not content with their low social standing,
particularly if they came, as some did, of a good middle-
class family and had enjoyed, as a surprisingly large
number of actors in the better troupes had, some sort of
university education.[1]

Frau Neuber received a succession of recruits, some of
them her best actors later, from the universities, particularly Leipzig, where even in the period of her decline
she still received support from the students, Lessing being
foremost among them. By the strict control which she
attempted to exercise over the behaviour of her young
actresses she did something to raise their social position
too, and her example was followed in the better troupes
later, notably by the Ackermanns. The presence of
Studierte among the actors would not in itself account for
the willingness of so many troupes to attempt to raise the
literary level of their repertoire even at the risk of financial
loss, but it may well have contributed something towards
the movement. Above all, these contacts with court,
university, and literary circles, together with the growing
interest of the public in the drama as a serious form of

[1] In the seventeenth century several of the earliest German troupes
had consisted wholly or mainly of students—cf. R. Proelss, *Kurzgefaßte
Geschichte der deutschen Schauspielkunst*, Leipzig, 1900, p. 103. Velthen
was a Magister of Leipzig, and Schmid (*Chronologie*) mentions the following as having been either the sons of professional men, or students themselves: (in Velthen's and his widow's troupe) Salzsieder, Dorseus, Müller;
(in the Haack troupe) Kohlhardt (son of a minister), Hofmann; Principal
Förster; Karoline Neuber was the daughter of a notary, married a student,
and took into her troupe at various times, amongst other ex-students,
G. H. Koch, Fabrizius, Uhlich, Heyderich, Schuberth, Wolfram,
Döbbelin; while in Schönemann's troupe we find J. C. Krüger, G. F.
Kirchhoff, and some already mentioned.

art, tended inevitably to raise the general level of taste and education among actors, and at the same time to give them a higher standing in society, so that the great actors of the permanent theatres which grew up in the classical age, men like Schröder and Iffland, were lionized in their prime like the leading authors of the day. But the social position of actors in general was still precarious for all that, as we gather for instance from the words of the Hamburg critic quoted above, or from Goethe's faithful picture of the relations between actors and other classes in *Wilhelm Meister*. Schönemann, appealing to Gottsched for more student actors in 1742, had claimed that 'reason had now made his profession an honourable one', but he was anticipating developments more than a little in saying so.

The social origins and status of the professional actors are an important factor to consider in connexion with Gottsched's reform of the theatre, for they go far to explain the low level of taste reflected in their performances. But in their acting they were of course only free in a limited measure to express themselves, being professionals dependent on their takings. The bad taste they exhibited was due at least as much to their audiences as to themselves. What were these audiences like? Except on the rare occasions when a prince was their patron, the actors played to any whom they could attract in as large a town as possible, preferably at fair time, when strangers were plentiful and a festive spirit prevailed. The Mecca of all such wanderers in the eighteenth century, as already in the seventeenth, was Leipzig with its fairs. Next in popularity came Hamburg, then Frankfurt am Main. These were of course the most important commercial centres of the day. The capitals of some of the larger states were also profitable places of call, especially in carnival time, Dresden, Braunschweig, Hannover and, from the forties, Berlin. Nürnberg and the other leading Reichsstädte of the south were worth an occasional visit, as were the Baltic ports Kiel, Lübeck, and Rostock. From mid-century on Danzig and Königsberg in the north-east and Breslau in the south-east were regularly visited by good troupes, and the German Swiss towns were toured by Ackermann during the Seven Years War. Strassburg, though French, had attracted good German troupes since the time of the Neuberin, and she was also the first manager of note to produce German plays in St. Petersburg, though her stay there was very brief. She provided the Viennese theatres with their first good actors in regular German plays and acted there herself in her later years. Many Viennese actors were to be found in different parts of Germany, but in spite of these exchanges Austria, which meant in the main Vienna, remained an area apart, developing under special conditions.

The usual audience of a travelling troupe would be made up of craftsmen and apprentices, shopkeepers and clerks, and a few merchants, officials, and professional men, with a handful of officers and noblemen perhaps in court towns. It is the taste of the lower middle class that is reflected in the surviving plays, a class with very little education and very few cultural traditions in Gottsched's day. The average craftsman, if he could read at all—in the absence of good 'German' schools a large proportion must have been illiterate—would read little but his bible and catechism and an odd *Kalender* or moral weekly. He would perhaps have seen something of other towns in his youth, but when newspapers were still a rarity and travel so slow and difficult, he was usually only interested in the affairs of his own little town, and passively at that. Most audiences were rowdy and inconsiderate. Johann Neuber writes admiringly to Gottsched of the good police arrangements made by the French in Strassburg: 'Das sieht hier anders aus, als bei uns, und bei so guten Anstalten ist's nicht zu verwundern, daß die französischen Komödianten in gutem Zustande sind.' In front of his usual audience the strolling player did not need to be reminded that he had *weiches Holz zu spalten.* Taught by the English Comedians, he gave the kind of entertainment that his audience could appreciate, and it might be quite a good entertainment, adapted with considerable art (as Anna Baeseke, for instance, has recently proved for the English Comedians[1]) to the conditions of the theatre and to this particular type of audience, but necessarily on a low cultural level.

Carl Heine's analysis of the themes treated in the surviving serious plays of the itinerant stage before Karoline Neuber shows us clearly what the audience liked. They were fond of pictures of 'high life', in the first place. All serious plays have their scene at court, and their heroes are princes, noblemen, or illustrious persons. 'The splendour of which the masses caught glimpses in real life and which they painted in still brighter colours in their envious day-dreams' had to surround the heroes of the stage, though it was usually a gilt and tinsel affair. There were scenes of martial splendour and pastoral episodes for contrast, in which the idea of a return to nature and even a certain 'naturalistic' coarseness were anticipated. The springs of action were ambition and love. The qualities admired in the hero were steadfastness, faithfulness, devotion, and magnanimity, and those detested in the villain were treachery, disloyalty, and cruelty. Full use was made

---

[1] *Das Schauspiel der englischen Komödianten in Deutschland, seine dramatische Form und seine Entwicklung,* Halle, 1935.

of stock theatrical devices, eavesdropping, misunder-
standings, disguises, assumed names and characters,
and a *coup de théâtre* was usually provided at the close.
True tragedy was avoided; streams of blood might flow
in the course of a play, but the hero was seldom allowed
to die at the end. And comic relief was always amply
provided by Hanswurst in his many disguises, in scenes
where he might play the Sancho Panza to his Don
Quixote of a master, or which might have no connexion
with the plot at all. These scenes, in which the clown's
powers of improvisation were given full scope, and into
which local allusions, spiced with the broadest of jests,
could be freely introduced, were together with the farcical
almost wholly improvised *Nachspiele*, the delight of the
crowd and the chief source of offence to the reformers.[1]

It was clearly a naïve, uncultivated audience that could
find pleasure in these performances, the kind of audience
that barn-stormers could depend on both in Germany and
England for a century or so to come. One would have to
go to the cinema for the nearest modern equivalent, as
Flemming suggests. It is at any rate some such audience
that Hollywood only too often seems to have in view, and
it counts on pleasing it still with much the same kind of
fare as was provided by the Wanderbühne, high life,
thrills, cheap heroics, physical strength and beauty, and
farcical comedy. The films are more sentimental, no
doubt, and less obscene than the old plays, because of a
more efficient censorship, the strength of the Puritan
tradition in Anglo-Saxon countries, and the predominance
of women in the modern audience. There are still greater

[1] Carl Heine, *Das Schauspiel der deutschen Wanderbühne vor Gottschea*,
Halle, 1889. For a full analysis of the comic element, see B. Aikin-
Sneath, *Comedy in Germany in the first half of the eighteenth century*,
Oxford, 1936.

differences due to the totally different technical and
economic conditions in the two cases, the presence in the
one and absence in the other kind of performance of
living actors in the closest touch with the audience, giving
to it and receiving from it every moment, and directly
dependent on its favour, with no assistance worth mentioning from press or other advertisements or from interested financial backers. In the one, improvisation and
comparatively simple staging were accordingly inevitable,
in the other, everything is planned and everything is
expensive. But there is a fundamental similarity between
the two for all that, which must result from the fact that
both satisfy the elementary human needs of a comparatively unsophisticated audience.

The type of regular play which Gottsched admired had
been created for a very different kind of audience; it
reflected in its content the very different society of Paris,
and the conventions it employed were in an entirely
different tradition from those current in Germany at this
time. The difficulty was not that these plays were of
foreign origin—nearly all the plays of the Wanderbühne
had been based on foreign models—but that they had
not been adapted, as Shakespeare and Calderon had been
earlier, to suit a popular German audience. What could
a good tradesman of Hamburg make of the refinements
of love and honour, the restrained passion, the elegance,
of plays written in an age of great national achievements
and in a language chastened by the Hôtel de Rambouillet,
for a few thousand noblemen and upper middle-class
officials and lawyers in Paris? Molière of course was a
different matter. He had after all run a troupe in the
provinces himself, and in Paris sought to please the bour-
geois of good sense rather than the courtier, with his
pictures drawn from ordinary life, so that Velthen had

already been able to play some of his lighter comedies with success. But how could audiences accustomed to loosely constructed plays, in which every happening in the plot was presented in action on the stage, and thrilling horrors alternated with buffoonery, appreciate the dignity, the logical structure, and the antithetical eloquence of tragedies whose characters talked endlessly about what had been or was about to be done, but never did anything exciting before one's eyes, and never allowed themselves a joke?

Plays of this nature did not easily make an immediate appeal even to the cultivated middle-class German, but the prestige of the French stage, as of French culture in general, at least disposed him to admire them. He could not help being repelled by the crudeness of the popular plays, the absurdity of their plots, the bad taste and indecency of their humorous passages, the total lack of style in their language, and he was attracted by the corresponding merits of the French classics. Scholars like Gottsched were greatly impressed too by French dramatic theory in Dacier and the rest, and since for them art was the handmaid of morality, they could not but approve of a theatre founded, as they considered, on the principles dictated by reason and good morals. Drama of this type, Gottsched thought, could continue the good work begun by moral weeklies like his *Vernünftige Tadlerinnen*.

In addition to its intellectual and ethical appeal, the social prestige of French drama must have raised it considerably in the eyes of Gottsched and many of his contemporaries. Like everything French, French tragedy and comedy were accepted as models of their kind by almost every one in court circles in Germany. It was the ambition of every prince to possess a French theatre and an Italian opera. Even in Weimar at the height of

German classicism, Karl August and many, perhaps the majority, of his court preferred French drama to anything German authors had produced. Goethe and Schiller themselves translated a French play or two, and those plays of Goethe which are most obviously the product of a court atmosphere (*Tasso* and *Iphigenie*) closely resemble French classical tragedy. Court circles had encouraged the performance of French tragedy in German translations from the end of the seventeenth century, first in Braunschweig and then in Dresden, where the court poet, König, was the chief influence behind those performances of *Regulus* in German by Hofmann's company by which, as Gottsched tells us in the preface to his *Sterbender Cato*, the reformer's attention was first drawn to the merits of French tragedy and its possibilities on the German stage. König too supported the application of the Neubers for the Saxon Privilegium, revised the translation for their first experiment with a regular play, and supplied them with rich costumes from court stores in Dresden, thus giving the new enterprise the benefit of a blessing from the highest social circles.[1] It was from Braunschweig that the Neubers were supplied with the manuscripts of Bressand's translations made a generation earlier for that court. Other translations were furnished by patricians like Lange, Bürgermeister of Leipzig, and Herr von Führer, Ratsherr and Castellan of Nürnberg; and Georg Behrmann, who along with Gottsched supplied the first original plays on the new lines (*Die Horazier*, *Timoleon*) was a rich Hamburger in a high official post. The original backing of this enterprise came, it will be seen, from court,

---

[1] 'Die neue Garderobe überredete die damaligen Zuschauer, als ob das Stück, wozu sie gebraucht wurde, den Beifall des Hofes hätte, und nun wagte es niemand dem Geschmacke des Hofes zu widersprechen.' Schmid, *Chronologie* (Reprint, p. 43).

official, and learned circles, or from the patricians of the towns, who at this time for the most part shared the court philosophy of life and art, and it was only where the support of these 'better' circles was continued that the Neubers had any success with their verse plays, as can be seen from Johann Neuber's letters to Gottsched. He writes from Hannover, for instance, in 1730 that he has had more success there than he had anticipated, especially in view of the fact that troupes like that of 'the famous Harlequin Müller' (their great rival later in Leipzig) had disgusted the better class and made shopkeepers so distrustful that the Neubers had to pay cash for everything.

'Da wir aber unsere so genanten Verse Comoedien anfingen, und die neuen Kleider anzogen, kam es bald anders. Die zur hiesigen Landes Regierung bestelten geheimen Räthe machten den Anfang, und weil es denen gefiel, folgten die übrigen von Adel und alle vornehme bald nach, und nun gesteht Jedermann: sie haben dergl. noch nie gesehen. Hingegen der Pöbel welcher vorigen Comödianten die Nahrung gegeben, kan sich noch nicht darein finden, weil man nicht genug Gelegenheit hat, grobe Possen zu machen.'

The Neubers were faced with peculiar difficulties everywhere, for they fell between two stools. They had not a sufficient number of good plays to satisfy the cultivated, and they lost the support of the masses in performing even the few they had, in spite of all their efforts to meet the popular taste too with lighter fare. We find them most often performing in court towns like Dresden, Braunschweig, Wolfenbüttel, Blankenburg, or in Leipzig, which was dominated by the taste of Dresden. Even in Gottsched's town, in 'Klein-Paris', they had all sorts of difficulties to contend with, were often absent for years at a time, and finally had to give way to their rivals. In Hamburg, a stronghold of the rising middle class, they never had a real success despite all their efforts. They played there in 1735 for nearly eight months, with a most varied repertoire of 75 plays and 93 Nachspiele.[1]

'Wen Gottsched und Cato nicht in die Bude lockten, den zog *Harlekin, die lebendige Uhr*, oder *der Mann mit zwei Köpfen*, oder *der listige Herr Schnapphahn.* . . . Bei einem Stücke: *die verwünschte Prinzessin*, oder *das lebendige Todtengerippe*, wurde unter andern auf dem Anschlagzettel Aufzüge und Kleidungen beschrieben, auch angezeigt: "daß die Ritter ganz geharnischt vom Kopf bis auf die Füße, auch mit Helm, Schild und Federn geziert seyn würden." '[2]

But it was all in vain. They left the town in debt and their last performance was banned, because Karoline Neuber had revealed her intention of telling the Hamburg public what she thought of it.

It is clear that literary drama of the new type was too strange and difficult for the ordinary middle-class audience, and that those *bessere Stände* who could appreciate it were not numerous or enthusiastic enough to justify by practical results the idealism of the Neubers in what Devrient calls their *Opposition gegen die Majorität.* It is an exaggeration therefore when the same writer asserts: 'Gottsched und die Neuber haben die Kluft geschlossen, welche so lange zwischen der Dicht- und Schauspielkunst, zwischen der höheren Bildung und dem volkstümlichen Theater lag.' They were able to lay a few planks across the gap, no more. Gottsched's alliance with the Neuberin and the banishment of the Harlequin are important because they mark a turning-point; they are rightly seized upon as symbolic happenings in the history of the German stage and drama. But before the gulf between literature and the theatre

---

[1] For titles, see Reden-Esbeck, *Caroline Neuber*, Leipzig, 1881, pp. 107 ff.

[2] J. F. Schütze, *Hamburgische Theatergeschichte*, Hamburg, 1794, p. 224.

could be stoutly bridged—it has never yet been filled in—
a new type of literary play had to be evolved and a number
of changes had to take place in German society, changes
so slow that at the time they were scarcely perceptible, as
is the way with many far-reaching social developments.
It was not enough to produce a sufficient number of
classicist plays to fill the repertoire; what was needed
was a type of play better adapted to the views and tastes
of the rising middle class, and this was found in the
domestic drama. This genre was popular from the beginning in Germany. It was received with an enthusiasm
such as *Der sterbende Cato* and its like had never evoked.
Lessing was the first modern German author whose plays
were both literature and 'good theatre'; he rightly criticized Gottsched for his advocacy of a type of drama which
could not possibly make a deep appeal to the German
public generally.

Among the social changes which favoured, after Gottsched's time, the popularity of a more literary drama
there was, first, the gradual rise in the general level of
taste and education, as German literature of every kind
developed and the reading public expanded. It was this
slow change, rather than the banishment of the Harlequin
—Frau Neuber herself could not get rid of him except
in name, as Lessing pointed out—which gave the death-
blow to Hanswurst and his type of humour. Along with
this went the weakening of traditional religious beliefs
under the influence of rationalism, and the corresponding
growth of an interest in art and letters, in *die Welt des
schönen Scheins*, as an alternative means of escaping from
the ugly reality of life in the Germany of that day. There
followed the period, reflected in *Wilhelm Meister* and
some of Schiller's essays, when the theatre became for
enthusiasts, and they were many, a kind of temple, at

least in theory, for in practice it constantly disappointed them. But the efforts of the more practical idealists like Lessing had meantime resulted in the establishment here and there of standing theatres, subsidized by a court or later by a city, which were able to follow with much greater hope of success the Neubers' principle of opposing the majority, though even the best of them had still to make very great concessions to popular taste.

These were far-reaching changes, but it is curious to note how through them all many of the features that we have observed in Gottsched's day still persist. Like Gottsched, authors were still prone, when writing plays, to start from theoretical considerations and to lose sight of theatre and public, and this continued to be so all through the following century. As Paul Ernst and others have pointed out, the 'higher' German drama since the classical period has been in the main book-drama; few dramatists have produced works of art which are also real plays, as Lessing did.[1] The history of the German theatre remained, as Julius Bab says, the story of an attempt to build a house from the roof downwards, 'die vergebliche Suche nach der verlorenen Einheit',[2] and the study of the reform of the theatre attempted by Gottsched and the Neubers shows more clearly perhaps than any later episode the difficulties inherent in any attempt to build up a flourishing theatre without a public.

---

[1] A classification of German dramatists in this respect is sketched by Anna Baeseke in the introduction to *Das Schauspiel der englischen Komödianten*, pp. 17 ff.

[2] *Das Theater im Lichte der Soziologie*, Leipzig, 1931, p. 173.

FORMAL VALUES OF THE GERMAN LYRIC ON THE THRESHOLD OF THE 'BAROQUE'

By AUGUST CLOSS

I. *The Meaning of 'Baroque'*

WE purposely reject an *a priori* use of the term 'baroque'. In discussing Hofmannswaldau, for instance, who is often described as characteristically 'high baroque' the title will in some ways be found to be apposite, though his style cannot be designated as pure 'baroque', and reveals itself rather as a synthesis of renaissance and 'modern' ideals. Hofmannswaldau lacks both the ecstatic vein of Quirinus Kuhlmann and the religious fervour of Gryphius. But the term 'baroque' has attained great significance not only in German but European literary criticism. We shall here not be concerned with it in its timeless aspect as a recurrent aesthetic ideal, but as an historical phenomenon limited to a definite period.

The term 'baroque' first found popular use principally in the domain of art criticism. Regarded from the renaissance point of view, 'baroque' was rejected as a positive stylistic phenomenon by Burckhardt and Nietzsche, as also by B. Croce. Riegl won deeper insight into the problem in explaining its appearance as the development of an 'optic' concept of art compared to the 'haptic' ideals of the renaissance. Dagobert Frey traced the gradual conquest of a 'simultaneous' by a 'successive' type of vision. To Pinder, the beauty of baroque is the expression of a young, virile race. Spengler, on the other hand, sees in baroque the Faustian death-struggle of doomed Europe. Worringer regards baroque as the 'gothic' principle of

style, their reconcilable enemy of all classic aspiration, and
a characteristically Germanic or Northern concept. Dehio
also applies timeless, racial values to the term. To Hau-
senstein, baroque is synonymous with restless excited
movement and high-strung nerves. In spite of this tempting variety of interpretations, not one of them can find
a strict analogy in literary criticism.

The subject-matter, style and type of a German seventeenth-century poem are subject to their own special laws.
Wölfflin's categories (open—closed, &c.) do not cover any
baroque phenomenon in literature. Nor is baroque, as
Strich wrongly tries to prove, akin to old Germanic form.
German baroque was born under different conditions to
those that produced the baroque architecture of Bernini
or Borromini, or even the paintings of Rubens, Rembrandt,
van Dyck, Hals, &c. In Germany human lives and
fashions alike reflect the horror and upheaval of the Thirty
Years' War, the uncertainty due to an economic and
aesthetic subservience to foreign influence, until gradually
racial individuality emerged triumphant over its ruins.

In the field of the German lyric, the conflict, as our
inquiry will prove, was largely fought out between *Pagan-
ism* and *Christianity*. The true synthesis with which Hofmannswaldau's playful harmonies but toyed, was not
achieved before Goethe. Viewed from this angle the German lyric of the baroque period appears as a vain attempt
on the part of the German genius to revive the spirit of
antiquity. The point of extreme tension—the 'high-
baroque'—would in this case possess a negative value.
Hofmannswaldau is not entirely 'high-baroque'. Moreover, mystics like Spee, Gryphius (quite apart from Jakob
Böhme) remain a class apart. Ermatinger believes the
essential quality of the baroque to lie in the culmination
of man's struggle between the joys of the flesh and the

dream of an after-life, but such a concept remains equally one-sided ignoring as it does many undeniable historic phenomena of the baroque.

Nevertheless, it is useless to seek like Strich a unified lyric style of the seventeenth century. That characteristic alluring quality of movement which Strich finds lacking in the sixteenth century fails to appear even in many seventeenth-century poems, as do those insistent variations on a theme which will appear to us important features of German seventeenth-century verse. It is still more danger-ous indeed to try and gather the entire phenomena of the period under an *a priori* denominator entitled 'high-baroque'. A study of *single* aspects of the question such as the consciousness of the ego, the antithesis between art and nature, the concept of man's mortality or symbols of man's attitude towards life as reflected in the rich metaphor of seventeenth-century poetry is more likely to bring enlightenment on the significance of baroque as an historic style.

Contrasted with the profound serenity of Goethe's classic *Weltanschauung*, that of the seventeenth century appears dictated by accident as though history were but the whim of 'Fortuna'. The seventeenth-century poet is little interested in the description of character but revels in heroics and fame, in courtly manners and pleasures of the flesh, in short adventures in the name of the sword or 'amour'. His hero aspires to no harmony of body and soul, but struts and swaggers with *bravura* gestures. He lives but in the present. Dafnis's 'Carpe Diem' remained till Arno Holz's time an assuaging sop to our dread of mortality, though itself restrained through consciousness of death. Just as the baroque painter registers the fleet-ing impression through the flash and gleam of colour, so the seventeenth-century poet catches the whim of the moment. His temperament is too restless to render nature eternal. *Emotion* is chained by the fetters of *reason*.

A *plethora of words* provides poetry with abundance of material, often rendering images more intense, but producing simultaneously a general impression of turgid redundancy or violent tension—a state of affairs accentuated by a mania for 'synaesthesia'. The writers of the renaissance period also sometimes rendered light by sound, optic by acoustic effects (thus Kepler in *Harmonice mundi* (1619) and before him Leonardo da Vinci, Giordano Bruno, &c.). In the philosophy and poetry of the seventeenth century (Athan. Kircher's *Ars magna lucis et umbrae*, 1645, or Harsdörffer, &c.), pictura-poesis is attempted by a blending of the senses of sound, sight, touch, taste, and scent, whilst the rational and irrational elements stand side by side in unbearable tension.

The *rhetorical* element is a characteristic trait of seventeenth-century dependence on the court and on publicity. The drama mirrors the fate of dynasties. Class feeling guides personal sentiment. Learned men fawn at the feet of their rulers and patrons. On the other hand, the voice of revolt is heard not only in the lower but also in the upper strata of society. Thus, on the threshold of the sixteenth century, we have Julius von Braunschweig's drama *Vincentius Ladislaus*, to be followed by Jakob Böhme's unrhetorical mysticism and Czepko's works, folk-songs, religious songs, Grimmelshausen, Moscherosch, &c.

The seventeenth-century *metaphor* is surcharged with synaesthesia added to an ornate verbosity that springs alike from the intellect and from a pathos of sentiment, suffocating all sense of form. The emotional value of the theme thereby becomes disseminated as a chaos of sensual intellectual atoms. Where, however, true aesthetic feeling exists, as in Paul Fleming's later poems or Gryphius's verse, the emotional element also remains; with weaker talents, rhetoric turned to mere formula. Personal expression yields to type.

At the same time, the etiquette of the Habsburg court in Vienna spread its influence particularly over South-German culture. It is certainly right to question the universal importance of Versailles in the development of German baroque literature. For the palace was only completed three years after Hofmannswaldau's death, Louis XIV entering into residence there as late as 1682. Racine's theatre was not inaugurated until 1667. On this account Günther Müller calls the seventeenth century the 'Habsburgerzeit' though this universal title is scarcely justified to the same extent as the designation 'Stauferzeit' for the twelfth to the thirteenth century, the Austrian court hardly exerting a powerful influence on Lutheran districts. The humanists' proud scorn of the *profanum vulgus* prepared the way for courtly literature. The Jesuits then amalgamated the absolutist aristocratic with the ecclesiastic ideal in their spectacular festivals and dramas, depicting heavenly and profane love. Even the baroque novel became the stage for history, statecraft, and intrigue. Barclay's *Argenis* provided a model for the court manners of the subsequent period. Form and wit become the fashion of the day. The anecdote tended to become epigrammatic.

A mania for quotations reflects the overpowering influence of culture on literature. The isolation of the object from its cosmic relationship to the universe was but the natural outcome of an artificial attitude towards life. The mask, however, is dropped in the face of death. A study of the problem of death provides F. W. Wentzlaff-Eggebert with a new interpretation of seventeenth-century poetry in which he differentiates the writers of the period according to whether they tend to exalt this life or the next. Stoic resistance (Gryphius) and mystic yearning (Spee, Scheffler, Kuhlmann . . .), each find their own way of rising triumphant over the transitoriness of existence. At the close of the century, a precursor of our modern age —Christian Günther—stands staring death in the face undaunted and steeled by faith in himself and in the dawn of a new world.

II. *The Development of Content and Formal Values*

A. *'Gesellschaftslied'*. At the time when the post-Lutheran evangelical hymn was rapidly developing, the so-called Italian 'Gesellschaftslied' enjoyed a short-lived period of glory which reached its zenith on the threshold of the seventeenth century. It was immediately preceded by a lyric style which as a legacy of courtly medieval poetry forms a bridge between the Minne- or Meisterlied and the German renaissance. The 'cultured' lyric or *Renaissancelyrik deutscher Musiker*, in vogue about the year 1500, is not without its merits, though it was all too soon cast in the shade by the contemporary folk-song. To-day such song books as those printed by Öglin (editor of the first German *Liederbuch*, Augsburg, 1512), P. Schöffer (Mainz, 1513), Arnt von Aachen (Köln, 1515), Egenolf (1535) are treasured because they not only reflect the spirit of the age but present an example of the linguistic influence of humanism on the German lyric of the early renaissance. Relatively speaking more formal in tone than the folk-song and certainly more elegant in expression than the Meisterlied, they point in retrospect to the Minne lyric and simultaneously herald the future as fore-runners of Opitz.

The poems in Georg Forster's (d. 1568) *Frische Teutsche Liedlein* (1539—) are culled largely from various collec-

tions of the period, in particular from Öglin, P. Schöffer,
Ott, &c. Forster tampers with his sources in a true
dilettante manner. Words are sacrificed for the sake of
the melody. (See Forster's references to his own methods.)
The collection is rich in both themes and forms. The
folk-song element alternates with verbal virtuosity, didactic phrases, and purely foreign or mongrel expressions:

> Es ritt ein Jeger hetzen auß . . .
> Bene venertis . . .

or: 'Wir zogen in das Feldt . . . Strombetta mi-a-la-mi,
presenti alla mostra Signori.' According to Böhme (*Alt-
deutsches Liederbuch*) this song was composed during the
first two decades of the sixteenth century. The refrain
really means:

> *Trompetet mi-a-la-mi, erscheint zur Musterung, ihr Herren.*

In spite of its untrustworthy philological renderings
Forster's book is of the utmost importance in providing
examples of songs popular shortly before and after Luther's
death. In addition to the Italian elements mentioned above,
we may discover signs of influence from the Netherlands:
'Ich weet ein Vrauken . . .'

Towards the end of the sixteenth century the Italianate
form of the German Gesellschaftslied suddenly burst into
full blossom. Its origin may be traced back to a definite
occasion, i.e. to the appearance in 1574 (1576) of the
Netherlandish poet Regnart's collection of *Villanelles*, the
first in the German tongue. Hence Regnart was one of
the first to stimulate the growth of the German 'Kunstlied',
which thus originally seems to have been inspired by
musical *tendances*. This, however, does not imply that
Italian influence only reached German lyric poetry through
the agency of music. We shall later also meet with the
Petrarcian lyric which played no less significant a part

in the formation of German style. At first the text was considered of second-rate importance. Italian music ruled the market. Since Petrucci had inaugurated the printing of music in 1502, Italy had gained a monopoly over the music of Europe. The introduction of the chromatic scale and the development of a new type of song resulted in the gradual disappearance of the *Cantus firmus* which had enjoyed such popularity in Germany and particularly in the Netherlands. The fact that the individual voices now began to gain independence gave the Italian song a character peculiarly its own. As mentioned above, Germany first made its acquaintance through Regnart's Villanelles. These are three-part folk-songs which the Italian peasants and labourers sang at work. The German folk-song is indeed usually regarded as a three-part song (two *Stollen* and one *Abgesang*) though it is in reality but two-part, for its two *Stollen* are not so sharply divided according to verses as in the case of the Villanelle. On the other hand, the German folk-song often uses the popular octo-syllabic verse whilst Italian virtuosity is inclined to favour the more melodious form of seven or eleven syllables.

Regnart adopted the metre of the Villanelle and at first also adhered to its content. Afterwards he composed German words to fit the new verse-form; that the text retained an Italianate flavour is not surprising. Velten, for instance, points out that the typical Villanelle beginning with ♩ ♩♩ caused Regnart to accentuate the beginning of his German verses. Thus form and content of the German lyric were much enriched, e.g. the song 'Venus, du und dein Kind . . .', derived from an Italianate verse pattern, became the prototype for many a German song. It is found, for instance, in Paul von der Aelst's famous compilation of songs (1602, Deventer: *Blum und Ausbund allerhand auserlesener weltlicher, züchtiger Lieder*

und Reime). The latter incidentally represents a treasure-
trove of Italian, French, High- and Nether-German songs
of the period, many being taken from Forster's collection.
An example of adherence to Italian themes is afforded by
Regnart's *Brunnenlied*.

In the course of time, however, Regnart emancipated
himself ever more from Romance influence and instead
took up the tradition of the German folk-song, as may
be proved by a comparison between various Villanelles
collections. By 1580 the sudden influx of Italian renaissance forms had ebbed. Regnart's followers: Lechner,
Harnisch, Gregorius, Lange, Brechtl, &c., poured old
wine into new bottles whose labels bore the would-be name
of Villanelle. Among that company Pinello, alone attempting no more than translation, escaped the styleless vulgari-
ties of the plagiarists.

In the last decade of the sixteenth century the German
song burgeoned with new and lovelier blossom. Again
Italian music and visits to Venice provided a source of
inspiration for the Northern poets, chief amongst whom
was Christoph von Schallenberg. Interest was primarily
concentrated on the Italianate text, but it was now not so
much the Villanelle as the Canzonetta with its four- or
five-lined verses that fascinated the German composers.
Whilst Cesare Zacharia's *Canzonette suave et dillettevole*
(1590), with its German and Italian text, failed to exert
any great influence on German collections (excepting of
course V. Haußmann's additions to Zacharia's songs),
Christoph von Schallenberg's works must rightly rank
as the glory of the Italian-German 'Gesellschaftslied'.
Through his ability to transfuse Italian texts with truly
German feeling, new Southern themes were often fitted
harmoniously into songs.

The form of the Madrigal seems to have made its

first appearance under H. L. Haßler (1596: *Newe teutsche Gesänge*). His contemporary, Valentin Haußmann, whom we had occasion to mention above, was not blessed with the good fortune that enabled Haßler or Schallenberg to experience Italian music on Southern soil. Thus Haußmann, especially in the early stages of his career, whilst in no way claiming to originate new melodies, is more inclined to affect the folk-song tone, in which indeed he was far more successful than in his later attempts to achieve that reconciliation of German and Italian elements in which Haßler so often excelled. Haußmann's strength lies rather in the comparatively individual quality of his texts which he shapes to the alien musical form. But true aesthetic harmony can scarcely be achieved where the pattern is but fitted on the theme like a fashionable dress on a rustic body. The discrepancies between Southern and Northern elements in the Italianate German song of the early seventeenth century, whether in the form of Villanelle, Canzonetta, or Madrigal, could of necessity lead only to a speedy decay.

The 'Quodlibets' that provided an amusing pastime for idle hours were more to the public's taste. The Italian 'Gesellschaftslied' was moreover doomed to oblivion on the appearance of Opitz, who rejected the Villanelle, Canzonetta, and eleven-syllable verse in favour of the alexandrine. Generally speaking, he proved more prone to French influence, though by this roundabout path Italian elements naturally found a new means of entry into the German lyric.

Shortly before this transitory, though intensive cultivation of the Italian song ceased, a more patriotically inclined genius arose in the shape of J. H. Schein in Leipzig. In spite of reminiscences of Haßler, his *Venuskräntzlein* (Wittenberg, 1609) already intimates a rebirth of the native tradition. The folk-song had, in the meantime, suffered complete eclipse. Schein's *Musica boscareccia oder Waldliederlein* (1621–) is of great interest from the point of view of musical history, offering one of the earliest examples of the introduction of the Italian 'concert style'. Its sub-title reads as follows: 'In drei Stimmen mit Beglei-tung des Generalbasses'. The *basso continuo* is here used according to the Italian manner, though retaining cer-tain peculiarities of style. The accusations made against Schein's use of foreign words are scarcely merited, for the full-blooded *Landsknechtlied* itself contains similar transgressions. Nor do they suffer from the preciosity and *raffinement* of Stefan George's 'tonal verses' which are based on no existing language. Of Schein's 'Woodland Songs', one at least, 'Frau Nachtigall', was happily rescued from oblivion by Hoffmann von Fallersleben. It offers an important instance of Schein's folk-song propensity. The poet's individuality appears most marked in his short collection *Studentenschmaus* (1626). One song, 'Frisch auf ihr Klosterbrüder mein', with its alternative solo and chorus, contains the refrain 'Sa sa! sa sa!', still popular in student songs of the present day (cf. Erck I, no. 176, *Deutsches Liederbuch*). Another, 'So da, mein liebes Brü-derlein', creates 'the moist and merry *Stimmung*', with its metrical use of diminutives: 'Brüderlein—Trünkelein—Gläslein'. . . . Inspired by Claudio Monteverdi's madri-gals, Schein also tried his hand at *Diletti Pastorali* (1624) and composed instrumental suites in *Banchetto musicale* (1617), in which appear the 'pavane' and its afterdance the 'galliarde', the vivacious 'corrente', the 'allemande' herewith making its first appearance in German song-books.

J. H. Schein thus belongs to the tail-end of the move-ment though he reached heights which the majority of

other poets of convivial songs scarcely rivalled. Not only
was P. Fleming a great admirer of Schein, but the vast
quantity of imitations which his works inspired bear witness to the influence Schein exerted on the following
period. The baroque elaboration to which the convivial
songs succumbed under the influence of the Petrarcian
manner will be discussed later. In the meantime we must
cast a glance at those absurd *pastoral conceits* which were
already intimated in the works of P. von der Aelst. Though
Italian songs may have introduced such themes into the
German song, the pastoral only attained real popularity
after Tasso's *Aminta* had been translated into Latin and
Guarini's *Pastor fido* into German.

B. *Opitz (1597–1639).* From the previous chapter we
shall have gathered how far we may accept the statement that modern German poetry begins with the
year 1624, even though Opitz does not derive from
the Italian convivial lyric. The above year witnessed the
publication of J. W. Zinkgref's selection of German poets
containing also Opitz's *Aristarchus* and Zinkgref's own
poems. The edition proudly boasted a new era of German
poetry. However, it was not Zinkgref but Opitz who
became its critic and formal arbiter.

His *Buch von der deutschen Poeterey* (1624, Breslau)
may be considered a land-mark in the history of German
literature. It offers no aesthetic philosophy but is a handbook of prosody, providing a criterion by which to judge
both the past and the future. The work breathes the
influence of Ronsard and Scaliger, but originality in the
sense demanded later on by the 'Sturm und Drang' was
here not intended. It sought rather to draw up a compre-
hensible rhythmic system of poetic form. Opitz's fame,
and title as model creator of forms—'Princeps poetarum
Germaniae'—put all the German intelligentsia in the

shade, and continued throughout the seventeenth century well into Gottsched's era. The latter's fanatic classicism which Opitz on the whole carefully avoided with regard to both form and content, finally led to the pitfalls of reason and formalism. World-wide vision and cosmic emotion only found true expression through the classic poets whose poems appear at once so supremely individual and yet of universal significance. On the other hand, Opitz's relation to nature and mankind and to his friends remains hide-bound by humanistic social forms and pedantic accuracy. One must here, however, not conceive of a special intellectual class existing as a sort of parallel to the chivalry of the 'Minnesingers'.

German literature was thus forced to pass through Opitz's school of discipline in order to recover from the plethora of subject-matter that had flooded the sixteenth century. Thus it subjected itself to a rigorous training in both German and foreign verse construction. In his capacity as remoulder of language and form Opitz appears as a high-light in German literature. The fact, however, that he turned to alien models whose spirit was in many cases remote from native ideals, certainly proved a means of making Germany (which could not boast a Paris!) acquainted with foreign culture, but it retarded the process of unification and simultaneously laid bare the gulf between Opitz's learned, quotation-ridden works and the genius of the German people, which his fervent patriotism failed to reconcile. It must not be thought that Opitz was ever aware of his lack of mystic and folk-bound powers. He remained isolated in his intellectual world in which, however, as a Protestant Silesian, he discovered many an aristocratic patron (including indeed not a few of the anti-Protestant party!). He thus became a European celebrity. The Netherlandish poets Daniel Heinsius,

in Holland, and Hugo Grotius, in Paris, he counted
amongst his illustrious friends. In 1628 he was knighted
by Kaiser Ferdinand. Political embassies and the pane-
gyrics he wrote in honour of his patrons endowed his
learning with an enticing sparkle. It was Opitz's aim
to rival the foreign humanists.

Already in his Latin article 'Aristarchus sive de con-
temptu linguae Teutonicae', Opitz at the age of twenty-
one appears fully aware of his own worth as champion
of German poetry. But, as the very title proves, he steps
into the ranks as a humanistically minded patriot, or
better as a patriotic German humanist. Certainly Opitz's
finest German verses in the well-known *Trostgedicht in
Widerwärtigkeit des Krieges*, written during the early years
of the disastrous Thirty Years' War, though bearing a
later dedication, were inspired by profound love of the
fatherland. The words in *Geistliche Poemata*, p. 397:
'Wir sind ja deutsch geboren' are full of warm-hearted
faith. Yet how little of the spirit of Gryphius and
Grimmelshausen seems to move in this long poem in
four books and rhymed six-foot verses with its formal
pedantry:

> Ich wil die Pierinnen
> Die nie nach teutscher Art noch haben reden können,
> Sampt ihrem Helicon mit dieser meiner Hand
> Versetzen bis hierher in unser Vaterland .... (loc. cit., p. 337.)

In the hour of approaching death, words of deeper
emotion seem to spring from the poet's heart, but even
here they fade beneath the veneer of cold rhetoric. The
poet knows that evil threatens to be the conqueror. Death
ends all pain and at the same time glorifies the patient
endurer who suffers God's will to be done and whom our
Lord will recompense in the life to come. Edified by
reason, man's courage should be steeled to stoic serenity

(*firmitas animi, constantia*). Emotion gives way to didactics: p. 399, 'Was ist doch nur der Tod?'.

Opitz was also the author of *Lob des Krieges Gottes* (with a Latin dedication dating from the year 1628) containing the characteristically humanistic introductory *Hymne*: 'O Mars, ich singe dich, du starker Gott der Kriege, . . .' A divine genealogy is divulged, Juno and Jupiter are presented as the parents of Mars and his descent from Sparta explained, whilst the variability of his name according to different races and localities, as also his divine attributes and heroic deeds, his amours and offspring, his favourites amongst the nations, are duly accounted for. The patriotic note is not missing in that Mars appears as the deity of Germany. Mars is the virile fighter. Women exist but to bear children—an intimation of Schiller's theoretic ideals!

War in its tumultuous passion is affirmed by Opitz. Mars incites and seeks the enemy. He kindles the spirit of man. Fame hastens before him. The two steeds—Terror and Fear—accompany him. The poem reaches its zenith in the horrible vision of Bellona, the wife of Mars, with her blood-coloured hair, bearing the fire-brand. Rape, poverty, hunger, thirst, envy, pestilence, and solitariness at last yield to palm-crowned victory. Burdened by mythological allegorical reference and excessive in length, the verses enter on a catalogue of man's discoveries and inventions, to end with a survey of the German fatherland which is threatened by the Turks and must at last withdraw its blood-stained hands from the war-god. There follow yet further expositions on the praise of Mars with certain quotations and allusions.

This poem gives sure proof of the fact that the pedantic German poetry of the seventeenth century is not so remote from life as is often supposed. Topical events are, however, most sharply reflected by the dramas of the period, as we see in Gryphius's views on the divine right of kings as displayed in *Carolus Stuardus*.

Opitz's patriotic sentiments are again passionately expressed in the 'Vorrede' of the *Weltliche Poemata*. In his dedication (1628) to Fürst Ludwig zu Anhalt he sings the praise of Augustinian Rome when the art of poetry flourished under the protection of noble patrons. The court of Charlemagne and of the Staufen, the renaissance of Italy and France, should likewise proffer an example to the wise and virtuous regent whom German poetry will render immortal. Just as Alexander ever bore a dagger and a 'Homer' at his side, the German prince should ever keep his poet at hand. The latter, however, must uphold the purity of language as once the patriotic Roman had craved forgiveness for using a foreign word when lacking the necessary expression in the mother tongue.

The *autonomy* of the poet with regard to worldly possessions is strongly marked at the beginning of the *Poeterey*. As Opitz well knew, genius cannot be born of method and laws and he was therefore chary in the matter of influence. The importance he laid on the intellect nevertheless betrays his affinity with the *Aufklärung* which would have set reason itself on the throne of poetry at the time when German verse had lost all dignity through formal confusion. *Style now became a symbol of conscience*. Hence the refined scholar Opitz in the sixth chapter of his *Poeterey* demands primarily elegance and grace of words, which must be pure (i.e. good High German) and lucid. Mixed languages, padding and impurity of rhyme, lack of clarity in the syntax (such as ambiguity regarding nominative and accusative in the neuter) are tabooed. The seventh chapter is full of schoolmasterly rules against the hiatus, and acclaims the iambic alexandrine with a pedantic *cae-sura masculinae terminationis* following the sixth syllable as the model of heroic verse. The characteristically *German* accentuation as basis of syllable enumeration in contrast to the quantitative reckoning of the classics provides a rare and refreshingly homely note in this handbook of rules for German poets.

For the *sonnet*, which a hundred years later was banned by Gottsched, Opitz likewise recommends the alexandrine or alternatively the French *vers commun*. The sonnet, which reached Germany from Italy by way of France, was now restricted to an exact scheme: fourteen lines, of which the first, fourth, fifth, and eighth are rhymed, as also the second, third, sixth, and seventh, whereby feminine or, as the case may be, masculine endings in each group are interchanged with masculine or feminine ones in the second. The last six lines (two terzine) can be treated at will, though the rhyming of lines 9 : 10, 11 : 14, 12 : 13 is advised as favourable.

How deeply not only Opitz the theoretician but Opitz the verse-maker is rooted in renaissance tradition (though foreshadowing a new style) may be proved by the following analytical contrasts:

The sonnet: 'Dies wunderliche Werk, das Gott hat aufgericht . . .' is a product of reason, built up with a virtuosity of crescendo, deduction, and concluding point that defies the harmonious canon of classical verse. The first verse introduces the theme: Nature is nothing without its suns (the two suns represent the eyes of the beloved). The second verse brings the crescendo: I, wretched wight, bear the light of two suns. Day and night are thereby treated as antithesis and as such related to the ego. Third verse: The author suffers death by day more than ten thousandfold and ever new pain. Fourth verse:

Near—far, day—night; concluding point = Rather, I chose death near the sun which inflames me.

How serene (in contrast to Opitz's poems) appear Gottfried Keller's lines: 'Augen meine lieben Fensterlein!' Sensuous joy and contemplation balance each other when the poet turns to the thought of life's light extinguished. On the other hand, what erotic frivolity is reflected by Philipp von Zesen's musical lines: 'Das achte Lied auf die der überirdischen Rosemund liebes-reizenden Augen!' The latter indulges in exquisite variations on the word *lieb* which appears in every single line, three times in fact in the last but one, though only once in the last, but here it achieves an effective crisis in the midst of three verbs which all end with the two syllables *loben*.

We are likewise tempted to draw a comparison between Opitz's poem and Weckherlin's 'Ihr Augen, die ihr mich mit einem Blick und Blitz'. This sonnet is also a piece of virtuosity, but of a type more reminiscent of Opitz. It begins with rhetoric and works with antitheses. First verse: Eyes can punish and reward, chastise and spare...; further the antithesis: sharp—sweet. The second verse brings the crescendo: the tool of love, triumphal arch, crowns . . .; the antithesis: illumined—shine. The third and fourth verses abound with alliteration, assonances, enumerations, which are concluded by the final verse with its parenthetically pointed antithesis 'nature—art', but the poem lacks the force of Opitz's sonnet. Yet the inner tension between supposition and deduction, expectant confusion and final conclusion appears both with Opitz and Weckherlin happily wedded to the sonnet form.

The influence exerted by Opitz is shown by many imitations of the form of his poem: 'Ihr schwarzen Augen ihr und du, auch schwarzes Haar'; cf. Stieler's 'Die Nacht,

die sonst den Buhlern fügt und süße Hoffnung macht';
Chr. Weise's 'So geht das liebste Kind von euren Augen
aus'; Angelus Silesius's 'Ihr keuschen Augen ihr, mein
allerliebstes Kind'; Schirmer's 'Ihr Augen voller Brunst
und du, du Purpur-Mund'; Fleming's 'Aurora schlummre
noch . . .', &c.

The formalistic tendency of such poetry colours and
simultaneously veils the poet's attitude towards *nature*.
She is not sufficient in herself (cf. August Closs: 'Georges
Goethebild' *Germanisch-Romanische Monatsschrift*, XXIII,
1935. The poet does not submerge his identity in hers.
She is but a decorative background, the painted scene in
which the author himself plays an actor's part or gives this
role to his hero. We would here mention in particular
Opitz's sonnet 'Vom Wolffesbrunnen bei Heidelberg', as
it treats of a definite object in a neighbourhood well
known to us. The comparison appearing in the first verse,
'Fountain—Prince', is an external invention, the 'land's
crown and head' and 'life' (nymph) a pale abstraction,
whilst the concluding line finally brings a cumbrous *pointe*.
The intellectual conceit, not emotion aroused by nature,
produces the *Stimmung*.

Contrasted with Opitz's poem, Sigmund von Birken's
fountain-song 'Hellglänzendes Silber . . .' betrays unexpectedly rhythmic, sensuous power. The awakened senses
are here in the first verse almost attuned to impressionist
concepts, though not indulging in vague synaesthesia, e.g.
silvery light and the broad shadows of the many-branched
lime tree. The second verse with its rhetorical question
is yet closely bound to the impression, though tending
towards abstraction. The third verse betrays the poet of
the seventeenth century with its *pointe* fixed on winter,
decay, and death. The metric formula is clearly maintained throughout.

J. W. Zinkgref's 'Sauerbronnen-Liedlein' and other fountain-songs (by G. Finckelthaus or H. Aßmann Frh. von Abschatz) also fall within the tradition of the period when the romantic nature worship of the stifled city masses had not as yet usurped the fashionable sojourn at the spa. Nature is but a foil to the actors. How must society have revelled in the description of the fount in 'Amadis' which the author intended as a parallel to the fate of Argenis and Poliarchus! C. F. Meyer's sensuous architectonic vision 'Aufsteigt der Strahl . . .' and Rilke's magic objectivity in the 'Römische Fontäne' are yet unknown to seventeenth-century poets.

Of great importance is Opitz's song in the tone of Ronsard's 'Ma belle je vous prie': 'Ach, Liebste, laß uns eilen . . .'. The 'carpe diem' motif here takes on a peculiar form that may be described as 'haptic', a dance-like tripping over the surface lacking all sense of depth, whilst emotion flees before intellectual virtuosity that plays with the transitoriness of life (a favourite theme of the seventeenth century). Any individual note is obscured by traditional abstraction: the gift of beauty, the cheek's embellishment, &c. Homburg, a poet of Upper Saxony, in his rendering of the Ronsard-Opitz song, accentuates rather the landscape element: Flora, flower, clover, heath, &c., than characteristic human allusions. Simon Dach's May-song: 'Komm, Dorinde, laß uns eilen . . .' appears when compared to Opitz and Homberg almost coarse in its simplicity. Nature and the human heart are in harmony. Tree speaks to tree, bough entwines with bough. Nature reflects itself in the springtide of love, though expression sometimes takes on the form of 'reflection'. Where Dach, however, gives free vent to poetic intuition, his freshness, the directness of his vision, raise him above the level of Opitz and Homburg.

Opitz's store of themes and forms was by no means limited to those mentioned above. Amongst his poems 'Vielguet'—an occasional song in rhymed couplets and alexandrines—describes the royal farm of his lord Heinrich Wentzel von Münsterberg in Silesia. The contents (that which is reputed good often engenders evil) are learned and witty and have a religious undertone. Apparent dignity is but illusion:

> Die Ähre beugt sich, worinnen Körner sind.
> Die aufrecht steht, ist Sprew und fleuget in den Wind.

Amidst the ocean of man's unrest, the prince's 'Vielguet' is a harbour of peace where one may dwell in merriment though with temperance—a wish-fantasy. Beneath the pastoral mask fashionable at that time lives a yearning for joy, serenity, for Horace's '*Beatus ille*'.

Opitz's festive play *Dafne* (put to music and performed by H. Schütz in 1627) brought the very heavens to the feet of an amazed audience. Ovid, the connoisseur in the art of love, speaks the prologue. Naked little Cupido breaks the proud will of the python-slayer Apollo who is now inflamed with passion for Dafne and pines and smarts for love. Everything in life must yield to *Amor's* power (which is here not presented as an affair of state) until at last Fortuna requites the indefatigable hero with her favours as in John Barclay's *Argenis*, which thanks to Opitz's translation became a model for German seventeenth-century novels. The significance given to Eros in the Petrarcian mannerisms of the European love-poems will, I trust, become clear in the course of the following chapter.

C. *Round about Opitz*. The term 'Petrarcism' was coined by Ronsard and was often used by Opitz himself, having been distorted to the verbal form *petrarquiser*. One of his earliest sonnets (a translation from the Netherlandish),

'Was will uber Puesch / wz wil ich uber Sand . . .', already
betrays Petrarcian conventions: 'Die Lippen sind Corall,
die Wangen sind Rubin . . .'

Paul Fleming (1609–40), who hails Schein and Opitz
as his models, having learned the Petrarcian manner from
the latter, excels his master in preciosity of style:

> Die Wangen sind Berill, die Lippen ein Rubin, . . .
> . . . das Kinn der Perlen Art, der Hals von Alabaster . . .
>
> (*Poetische Wälder*, iv, p. 153.)

H. Pyritz, in his systematic study of Fleming, boldly
traces the source of the entire German stock of metaphors
and mythological references to Petrarca (1304–74) himself. The gold of Petrarca's love-lyrics degenerated into
the rusty coinage of hackneyed similes: cheeks like roses
or rubies, lips like coral gates, hair like gold, a countenance
like diamond, breasts like marble balls, hands like jewels,
eyes like crystal, or the stars, &c. Name and *motif* were
thus derived from Petrarca, the cliché itself, however,
must fall to the account of his followers and satellites.
These were represented in Italy by Pietro Bembo, in
France by the Pléiade, in England by Surrey, Wyatt, &c.,
in Spain by Montemayor, in Holland by Daniel Heinsius,
whose Petrarcism cast its influence on Opitz even before
the latter became acquainted with Montemayor. Especial
attention must be paid to the new Latin poetry of Europe
as a mediator of Petrarcian forms, for from this inter-
national platform the 'allure' of such preciosities penetrated
even to the seventeenth-century German song.

In the mouth of the Petrarcians their master's passionate antithetical utterances were petrified to a system
of formulas, a virtuoso's *cadenzas* on love's joy and love's
defeat, embellished with a surfeit of hyperbole. Petrarca
himself had already praised the beloved's golden hair,
her rose-red mouth, had scolded Amor, sighed and pined

under his mistress's wayward tricks. Tears gush from his death-entreating eyes. He therein unconsciously approaches the mannered idealism of the Troubadours and the *Dolce Stil Nuovo* which raised *Amor* to the rank of a virtue. Guido Cavalcanti (13th cent.), Guido Guinizelli (13th cent.), and Dante, in his *Vita nuova*, are the greatest exponents of the tender style which afterwards degenerated into the virtuosity of Cino da Pistoia.

It would exceed the scope of this chapter to enter more deeply into the question of Petrarcian sources, such, for instance, as the *Anacreontic-Sapphic* prototype. The Platonic concept (cf. Timaios) of man's relation to the Universe and the treatises on Eros whom the Renaissance regarded as a cosmic, life-giving power (cf. Pico della Mirandola, Ficino, &c.) fertilized the anthropomorphic attitude of the period. Such inter-relationships have as yet scarcely been dealt with in any detail, least of all the references to *microcosmos* and *macrocosmos* or Paracelsian concepts which frequently crop up in the German lyric.

At present we would examine the range of formulas (flame of love, praise of love, love-sickness) which, already discernible in Opitz's poetry, now flood the German lyric, although Paul Fleming refrains from endowing them with that steely cynicism in which the second Silesian school rejoiced. The anacreontic flavour is scarcely noticeable. Fleming delights in genuinely Petrarcian eroticism. Thus his starting-point is the late Renaissance and Opitz, whose formalized type of song appears to have for him an especial appeal. Later on he adopts an inflamed Petrarcian manner and without borrowing directly from Petrarca himself, raises it to a place of first importance in the seventeenth-century German lyric. Nevertheless, it hardly deserves the name of baroque. Such a designation would hardly fit here, for Fleming's later development clearly betrays a consciously anti-baroque attitude. His poetic intuition was far profounder than Opitz's and eventually far surpassed the latter's love-lyrics, in particular the odes, though not his religious songs. Yet Fleming's epitaph on Opitz contains the following eulogy: 'Du Pindar, du Homer, du Maro unsrer Zeiten.' But the Reval period and a journey to Persia had the effect of freeing Fleming from the influence of Opitz and his verbal conventions.

A work of truly poignant expression never came from his pen, nevertheless we may thank him for many a song of tender charm, both simple and frolicsome: 'Wie er wolle geküsset seyn . . .', 'Aurora schlummre noch . . .' (*Odes*, book V). This fifth book of *Odes* is a treasury of melodious rhymes abounding in assonance and alliteration. A playful tone runs through the *Brautlied*, his bridal song with its sweet alternating refrain: Amaryllis—Mirtyllus. The crown of Fleming's love-lyrics is considered to be 'Anemone' (*Odes*, V. 42).

Fleming's *religious verse* is less compelling, though not without a certain individuality. Certainly the ode 'In allen meinen Taten' still has power to admonish our conscience. But the Christian sentiments expressed in 'Laß dich nur nichts nicht tauren' may easily be unmasked as the stoic creed of self-discipline: 'Sei dennoch unverzagt.' By its side Storm's 'Oktoberlied', which was born of actual experience, only shows how dependent on purely typical values is Fleming's poem whose concluding line reminds us of Augustine's maxim: 'In te ipsum redi, noli foras ire.' Yet in comparison to other poetic reflections of the seventeenth century (with the exception of Gryphius's verse) Fleming's appears pleasingly simple. Th. Hoeck's 'Der Autor beweint das Leben', for instance, is burdened by humanist pedantry. The opening lines, which remind us of Hans Sachs, match the clumsily learned style of the remaining verses. Hofmannswaldau's 'Gedanken bei Antretung des fünfzigsten Jahres', on the other hand, betray the wit of the verbal juggler.

Opitz's fame cast Fleming, Weckherlin, and others into the shade. We can hardly recall any anthology of seventeenth-century German verse whose preface or dedication does not boast the name of Opitz. He was also the hero of the Königsberg school of poets.

During the heyday of literary activity in Königsberg, the East Frankish regions of Germany produced their own school of poets, the Nürnberg circle whose speciality was the pastoral. Their aesthetic doctrine bears close resemblance to Opitz's linguistic reforms and those of the German *Sprachgesellschaften* whose cause was championed by Justus Georgius Schottelius. His *Opus de lingua Germanica* is the most important seventeenth-century contribution to the study of the German language. In his dedication to the Duke of Braunschweig and Lübeck he cites the Celtic language as the principal source of the German tongue—one of many outlived theories found in his lengthy, rambling work. And yet its patriotic enthusiasm cannot but galvanize even the present-day reader. Schottelius traces the origin of words, thereby paying special attention to the relationship between object and expression. The mystic doctrine of the 'natural language' (possibly attributable to J. Böhme) seems to have had some influence here. Schottelius is evidently acquainted with the φύσει- and θέσει-theory. He regards the stem words as the foundation of a language. They derive from nature and symbolize objects. He proudly commends the descriptive tonal colour of the German tongue which in comparison to Greek, Latin, Hebrew, &c., is so rich in imitations of animal and natural sounds. Schottelius

also examines image-rhymes, i.e. rhymes which offer typo-
graphic representations of the object in question: an egg,
a pyramid, a goblet, a cross, &c., and thus theoretically
justify their right to live. This affords a departure from
Opitz's ideas. In the *Haubtsprache* considerable space is
devoted to the discussion of the pictorial lyric, although
Scaliger had already approached the subject in his prosody.
An anticipation of the modern lyric! This decorative
arrangement of lines in seventeenth-century verse bears a
superficial resemblance to the form of Holz's 'Phantasus',
but the rhymed anapaests and dactyls were severely rejected by Holz. On the other hand, certain logical unities
reminiscent of those in 'Phantasus' may sometimes be
detected in Schottelius's quotations (cf. August Closs:
'Zur Phantasus-Zeile' in *Dichtung und Volkstum* (*Euphorion*) vol. 37, 1936). In the seventeenth century this man-
nerism was put an end to by the classic ideologies of
Boileau.

In traversing the pages of the *Teutsche Haubtsprache* we
often meet with the name of G. Ph. Harsdörffer (1607–58),
whose works and opinions are those cited with profound
esteem. He not only founded the Nürnberg 'Pegnesi-
scher Blumenorden' but furthered its activities in many
directions. His *Frauenzimmergesprächspiele* (1641–) and
Nürnberger Trichter (1647–) advocate a union of painting
and poetry, picture and word. The Nürnberg School
thereby not only became an influence in German literature of the period but foreshadowed the tonal imagery
and symbolism of Brentano's musical lyric of the soul.
Harsdörffer attempts exact acoustic reproduction of the
impression aroused, of an idea or some experience,
e.g. war, tempest. A surfeit of merely jingling sound
and poverty of imaginative vision, however, prevent him
from attaining anything like the verbal richness of the

modern naturalistic school. The tyranny of pure rhyme, formal rhythm, assonance, and repetition outweigh all expressive values. Harsdörffer's style of tonal paintings probably achieved the fame it did, because he was one of the first German poets to work in this direction. Nevertheless, the assertion made by W. Kaiser and others, that German literature could reap but little benefit from such innovations, is unjust. Moreover, such critics are evidently too tied to the purely rational significance of word and content as exemplified by the work of Fischart, Hans Sachs, &c.

In his tonal paintings Harsdörffer was primarily influenced by the pastorals and Marinistic foibles of Italian fashion. The poetry of Spain (Montemayor), of France (Pléiade), and the Netherlands doubtless also left their impression on his work. In the course of his struggles against the bombast and exaggerated imitations of his own style, Harsdörffer was eventually forced to retreat into the background, his aims forgotten until with the rise of Romanticism, German poetry set out once more on paths somewhat similar to those he had trod.

The virtuosity of the seventeenth-century German lyric leads in a direct line to the *galanteries* of Hofmannswaldau. At the same time, however, a wave of religious fervour awakened expressions of profounder sentiment above all in Gryphius, in protest against the frivolities of current literature. The Silesian poet Czepko represents as it were a bridge between the early baroque humanism of Opitz and the mystic death-yearning of Gryphius.

SOME GERMAN PARTICLES AND THEIR ENGLISH EQUIVALENTS

A STUDY IN THE TECHNIQUE OF CONVERSATION

By w. e. COLLINSON

A SUITABLE motto for a brief survey of problems concerning the German particles and their rendering in English would be the following words taken from the autobiography of the veteran Egyptologist Professor Erman:

> Wie oft habe ich mir mit den beiden Zauberworten geholfen 'ach was' und 'nu gerade'; mit diesen beiden Worten kann man über manches hinwegkommen und manches erreichen.

Ach was and *Nu gerade* obviously represent attitudes taken up by a human being to his experiences. In actual conversation we are rarely content with making a bare objective statement. Sometimes we show hesitancy, using words like *vielleicht*, 'perhaps', and pick our way cautiously; sometimes we clearly manifest our confidence or the strength of our convictions, using words like *sicher*, *bestimmt*, 'certainly', 'definitely', and plunge straight ahead. In every case we are seeking to influence our partner in some way. This is done (*a*) more indirectly or implicitly, e.g. by what Dr. Alan Gardiner calls the 'elocutional' factors, which would include stress, intonation, grouping, pauses, relative speed of utterance, or (*b*) directly and explicitly, e.g. by using what Dr. Gardiner calls the 'locutional' factors, such as specific words and word-groups or a certain order of words. These nuancing expressions or 'attitude-words' may on the face of it merely indicate the speaker's reaction to what he is communicating—but it is to be noted that he desires his

partner to share that reaction! Such words are, for instance, *vielleicht*, *wahrscheinlich*, *sicher*, but they may, like
the English 'surely', address themselves particularly to
one's partner and ask for an assurance or reassurance.
In practice it is not always possible to make such a division.
The essential point is that there are definite means not
created by the individual speaker, but acquired by him
while learning his mother-tongue, to enable him to express
his varying attitudes to the content of his communication
and to his partner. By his tone or choice of words he
may show not only familiarity, respect, intimacy, or indifference, but also try to influence his partner in specific
directions. Whole groups of words may become detached
from their original setting and crystallized or stereotyped
(*grammatikalisiert*) to render explicit a definite attitude,
e.g. *sag mal* (to obtain information), *hör mal* (to give
information), 'look here', *allons*, *tiens*, 'in all conscience',
'to all intents and purposes'. They do not convey any
additional information in regard to the matter communicated, but are what Marty calls *interesseheischend*—they
serve to fix the listener's attention to what is considered
essential and to guide his feelings in the way desired. As
the term 'particle' is often widely used to include all
flexionless parts of speech it is safer to adopt for our purpose the term 'modal particle' for any single word, or
'modal particle-group' for any combination of words used
with the purpose of indicating an 'attitude' whether to
subject matter or to partner. Some particles in German,
like *erst*, *mal*, *noch*, *schon*, are primarily temporal; here we
are concerned purely with their modal functions. At the
same time it would be a valuable piece of historical research to follow the almost imperceptible stages by which
a purely temporal group like the OHG. *thana noh* ('Christus
und die Samariterin': *thanna noh so saz er*) passes through

the transitional MHG. *dannoch* ('Der arme Heinrich', 163 f.: *Ein wēnec fröuwet er sich doch von einme trōste dannoch*) to the purely modal *dennoch* of Modern German.

In view of their importance for a thorough understanding of idiomatic spoken German it is surprising how little attention has been devoted to them. Apart from the bilingual dictionaries, which treat them very cavalierly, far and away the best sources of information for comparative studies is O. G. Curme's *Grammar of the German Language*. In Dr. Eggeling's *Advanced German Composition* there are some valuable notes on certain particles, and in the school edition of Goebel's *Rübezahl* (London, 1903) there is a useful section by the editor of the series, Dr. Otto Siepmann. An instructive article by Miss Hildegard Gauger of Tübingen, 'Das Adverb als Gefühlsträger in Englisch und Deutsch', *Neuere Sprachen*, xlii. 404, draws attention to an unpublished dissertation presented by her at Tübingen under the guidance of Professor Franz in 1922. She gives a bibliography which enables us to dispense with further details. Apart from that the most interesting side-lights on the German particles come from Romanic scholars, especially A. Tobler with his article on the French *par exemple* in the fourth volume of his *Vermischte Beiträge zur französischen Grammatik* (Leipzig, 1901), in Leo Spitzer (*Italienische Umgangssprache*, Bonn, 1922), and the same author's *Stilstudien* (vol. i, *Sprachstile*, Munich, 1928). Finally there is much material in the German dialect dictionaries, e.g. Mensing's *Schleswig-Holsteinisches Wörterbuch* and the *Rheinisches Wörterbuch* now in course of publication.

In the course of a brief article the treatment must be selective and summary to a degree. Typical cases must be chosen from the great mass of material drawn from such sources as novels, dramas, and notes made in actual

conversation. German exchange-students (especially Fräulein Ilse Sueßmann from Silesia) have given much valuable help. With them the usual procedure has been either
for me to submit to their scrutiny passages containing
particles embedded in a definite context and to ask them
for a full description of the psychological functions of the
particles as they appear to them, or on the other hand for
me to construct specific speech-situations, e.g. peremptory request, ironical question and the like and ask them
to deal with the situation in their own way in German.
It was interesting to find on an extensive background of
agreement certain divergences in the use of colloquial
particles according to region, e.g. between a Hamburg
lady and one from Silesia, an Oldenburger and a Heidel-
berger, &c. The dialectal and regional divergence in the
use of modal particles would form a good theme for a
German dissertation. My chief concern is with those used
in the standard language, particularly in the educated
colloquial of northern and western Germany, leaving aside
such regional features as *man*, *halt*, and *gelt*, still more so
dialectisms such as the Schleswig *riktinog*.

To bring out the agreement and contrast between
German and English in fulfilling similar speech-functions
the following organization suggested itself. Taking Büh-
ler's classification of speech-functions as *Kundgabe* or outward manifestation of inner states issuing normally in
exclamatory sentences or unrealized wishes, *Auslösung*
or 'actuation' of one's partner to do something asked for
or to answer a question put and *Darstellung* or 'statement',
i.e. the conveyance of information, we take as our major
categories the following: (1) exclamatory utterances, (2)
wistful utterances, (3) requests and commands, (4) questions, (5) statements. The first four will be more copiously
illustrated than the last, in connexion with which only a

few specific points will be raised. After the presentation
of the material it will be possible to draw attention to
certain typical procedures in English where they differ
from the German.

In order to study the technique of conversation in
German and English respectively it is advisable to build
up contexts and adduce some of the more typical means
of indicating the speaker's attitude.

It is noteworthy that there is at times a discordance
between the locutional and the elocutional factors. Thus
a request or command need not necessarily be expressed
in an imperative sentence. A peremptory command may
be put in the form of a statement in the present indicative
but with commanding intonation, e.g. *marsch, sofort gehst
du dahin*, cf. 'now then, off you go there at once'; or as
an impatient question with rather menacing tone, e.g.
*wirst du [nun endlich] deine Schularbeiten machen oder
nicht?* 'are you going to do your homework or not?'; or as
an admonition assuming in advance 'compliance on the
part of the person addressed' (Eggeling), e.g. *willst du
wohl machen, daß du fortkommst?* in contrast with 'you
jolly well get off and be quick about it'. Sometimes,
indeed, there is a discordance between both the locutional
and the elocutional factors on the one hand and the
speaker's attitude on the other. Thus a polite request is
often put in the form of an interrogative sentence with
question-tone, e.g. *wollen Sie nicht bitte Platz nehmen?*
'won't you please sit down?', 'won't you sit down, please?',
or in the form of a statement, but with the past subjunctive
to indicate the tentative approach, e.g. (giving a direction
to an assistant) *vielleicht würden (könnten) Sie die Arbeit
mitnehmen und zu Hause durchsehen*, 'perhaps you wouldn't
mind taking (would be so good as to take) the work home
with you and looking it through', often with slight rising

rather than low falling intonation. There is no need to deal here with such camouflaged requests or orders as underlie the statements (supplying merely the premise and leaving the conclusion to be drawn): *es klingelt*, 'there's a ring at the bell', or 'the kettle's boiling'; but a word may be added in regard to an ironical request or challenge, when the tension between the actual utterance and the effect to be produced is greatest of all, e.g. *bitte schön, dann klettere doch mal auf den Baum*, 'all right, go (right ahead) and climb the tree [I would if I were you]', with an intonation somewhat like the low-rising tone of encouragement used to children: 'come on, there's a good boy', but with a different voice-quality and facial expression.

Beginning with exclamation, we find that exclamatory sentences evoked by admiration do not afford much material, for they are usually brief and 'attitude' is sufficiently shown by the speaker's intonation, e.g. *was für eine schöne Buche*, 'what a fine beech'; *wie schön die Buche ist*, 'how fine the beech is'; or with an introductory asseveration, e.g. *beim Himmel* (*bei Zeus, alle Achtung, Donnerwetter*), *das war eine Leistung*, 'by Jove (by Jiminy, my hat), that took some doing' ('that was *some* achievement'—with the American emphatic use of 'some'). Some speakers use the particle (*ein*)*mal*, e.g. *das ist mal ein hübsches Bild*, 'that's a pretty picture for you (I must say)'; *das heißt* (*ein*)*mal eine nette Situation*, 'well, that's a nice kettle of fish, by Jove (by George, I must say)'.

In 'wistful' utterances the typical particles are 'doch' and 'nur (bloss)' and their combinations, e.g. *wenn der Zug doch bloss* (*endlich*) *kommen würde*, 'if only the train would come', sometimes prefaced by the interjections 'oh' or 'ach' just like 'oh' in English. Sometimes *erst* is used, e.g. *wenn der Sonnabend erst mal da wäre*, 'if only Saturday were here'; *wäre ich doch erst zu Hause*, 'oh, if only I were at home'. Apprehension is sometimes expressed by a particle group, e.g. *wenn er aber doch nicht zur rechten Zeit kommt*, 'but supposing he doesn't come in good time after all'. Impatience is shown in *wenn das Konzert doch nun mal endlich (doch mal erst) anfangen würde'*, 'if only that wretched concert would start!'

In imperative sentences the typical particles are *mal*, *doch*, *nur (bloss)*, *auch*, and *ja*. The following rough classification of the chief speech-situations will help us to discriminate them:

1. In a comparatively unemotional utterance made by a speaker to some one with whom he is on familiar terms a slight amount of liveliness is added to a request by *mal*, e.g. *kommen Sie mal her*, 'just come over (along) here'. A greater briskness is conveyed by adding *ja*: *komm mal 'nen Augenblick her, ja?*, cf. will you (won't you).

2. If the person addressed does not comply promptly a more insistent request is put forward by *doch*: *kommen Sie doch*, 'do come along [won't you?]. A greater urgency is indicated by *doch schon*: *komm doch schon*, 'come at once, I say (I tell you)'. By itself *schon* may indicate a speaker's impatience at the unnecessary fuss his partner is making, e.g. *hören Sie schon auf mit dem Geld (jetzt könntest du aber endlich mal mit der Geldfrage aufhören)*, 'do stop talking about the money'.

3. Sometimes a speaker anticipates reluctance on the part of the person addressed and reinforces his request with *doch mal*, e.g. to encourage him to undertake some seemingly difficult task, as in: *na, versuch's doch mal (bloß mal), es ist ja gar nicht so schwer*, 'do just have a try, you'll find it's not so hard'. However, *doch mal* may be used also to excite interest, as when an adult turning the pages of a book sees an interesting picture and calls to a child:

komm doch mal her, 'I say, come and look here'. A mother
might ask a governess politely, as it were casually, to see
what the children are up to, e.g. *sehen Sie denn doch mal
zum Rechten bei den Kindern*, 'you might just go and have
a look at the children, will you?' Another particle of
encouragement is *nur*, e.g. *treten Sie nur ein*, 'come right
in', or: *fang nur an*, 'you just start'.

4. If the speaker divests himself of all responsibility
for a proposed action on the part of the person addressed
he may use the request forms with *bloß*, *schon*, or a fuller
word, e.g. *geh bloß (schon), wenn du durchaus mußt*, 'go
by all means if you must', or in statement-form: *meinet-
wegen kannst du ihn besuchen gehen*, '(you can) visit him as
far as I'm concerned'.

5. On the other hand he may set his partner's mind at
rest in regard to any consequences likely to be produced by
the expected action, e.g. *erzähl's ihm ruhig (getrost)*, or: *das
kannst du ihm ruhig (getrost) erzählen*, 'don't mind telling
him', 'don't hesitate to tell him', 'tell him by all means
if you like'.

6. The speaker wishes to impress upon his partner the
necessity of remembering to fulfil a request. The mildest
form of admonitory particle is *auch*, e.g. *vergiß es [aber]
auch nicht*, 'be sure not to forget', 'now don't go and forget'.
The following are more explicit: *sei bestimmt pünktlich*,
'make quite sure you're punctual'; *sieh bloß zu, daß du
pünktlich bist*, 'take good care to be punctual', 'just see to
it that you are punctual'; and in a negative request or
prohibition: *um Himmels* (or *Gottes*) *willen, komm nicht
zu spät*, 'for goodness' (heaven's, the lord's) sake, don't be
late'; *erzähl's ihm auf keinen Fall*, 'don't tell him on any
account'; *was auch geschieht (mach was du willst, tu was
du willst, aber . . .) erzähl keiner Menschenseele davon*,
'whatever you do, don't tell a soul'. The most characteristic

admonitory particle is, however, the strongly stressed *ja* (combinable with *doch*). Thus a mother may say to a child: *iß ja deine Suppe auf*, 'mind you eat up all your soup', sometimes using an indirect command with *daß* and relegated verb in isolation from a main clause, e.g. *daß du mir ja nicht an die Glaskästen gehst*, 'now mind you don't go near the glass cases'. Occasionally a kind of interrogative locution is employed, e.g. *wollen Sie's bitte ja nicht vergessen*, 'you'll be sure to remember, won't you, please'. Examples of prohibitions reinforced by *doch ja* are: *glauben Sie doch ja nicht alles, was Ihnen dieser Mensch erzählt*, 'for goodness' sake, don't believe all this man tells you', or: *doch bitte* in *halten Sie mich doch bitte nicht für den Herrn, der diese Bemerkung gemacht hat*, 'for goodness' sake (I beg of you), don't take me for the man who made that remark'.

In many of the above instances of requests *doch* retains its original adversative function, a note of protest somewhat analogous to that of 'surely' in English, but it is often rendered by an emphatic 'do' which may in addition be strengthened by a tag-question like: won't you. Used with both it makes a mere polite request almost officious or at least effusive, e.g. *lassen Sie mich doch Ihnen bitte die Sachen abnehmen*, 'oh! do let me take your things', *aber bitte, nehmen Sie doch Platz*, 'do please sit down'.

In regard to questions a simple one like: *kommt er?* may be posed as an alternative: *kommt er oder nicht?* 'is he coming or not?', which may be made more insistent and even threatening by repeating the verb: [*hör mal*] *kommt er oder kommt er nicht?* 'look here, is he coming or is he not coming?' *Nonne*-questions and *num*-questions are in both languages expressed by a positive and negative statement respectively, each ending with a tag-question undifferentiated in German *nicht wahr?* but in English with a negative or positive tag in contrast with the form of the statement (*er wird kommen, nicht wahr?* 'he will be coming, won't he?'; *er wird nicht kommen, nicht wahr?* 'he won't be coming, will he?'). The tags occur more frequently in English than *nicht wahr?* in German and extend to all the auxiliary verbs (can, must, may, need, dare), and are like direction-indicators pointing to yes or no. The questions in which they figure may be called 'directed questions'.

The particles used in German questions include certain ones like: *mal, doch, auch, nur,* which, as we have seen, are prevalent with imperatives. *Ja* occurs in statements uttered with question-tone. A particle less used in requests than in the question is *wohl*; another typical question-particle is *etwa*. To distinguish the various functions of these and other particles we may, as in the case of commands and requests, set forth certain interrogative situations classified singly as follows:

1. A speaker wishing to introduce a new topic or change the subject feels his way with a question which, to avoid brusqueness, is provided with an introductory formula and padded with a particle like *eigentlich*, e.g. [*Sag mal, Laura,*] *wieviel Leute hast du eigentlich eingeladen?* 'tell me, Laura, how many people did you actually ask?' (more familiar: 'I say, Laura, . . .')

2. If he wishes to ask politely, but somewhat casually, whether his partner has at any time had a certain experience, he uses *mal* or *schon mal*, e.g. *sind Sie schon mal in Paris gewesen?* ['have you, 've you] ever been to Paris?' He also uses *mal* in inviting his partner to share some activity with him in the near future, e.g. *wollen Sie mal rudern?* 'what do you say to a row?', 'how about going for a row?', the *mal* indicating the smallness of the effort required (*einmal* like 'just for once in a while'). To indicate lively interest in his partner's communication he may

use *denn,* e.g. *wer denn?* 'why, who?'; *was ist denn passiert?* 'why, whatever has happened?' Sometimes *denn* indicates impatience, *warum tust du's denn nicht?* 'well, why don't you do it then?'; *warum denn nur?* 'why on earth?'

3. The speaker indicates his curiosity as to how a certain matter will turn out. This he can do by an explicit statement beginning with *ich bin gespannt, ob . . .,* 'I wonder whether . . .'. The indirect question itself may be used independently as a sort of 'musing' or pensive question reinforced by *wohl* appropriate in a soliloquy, e.g. *ob er wohl kommen wird, wann er wohl kommen wird,* 'I wonder if (when) he will come'. *Doch* is used if the speaker in his musings is conscious of an obstacle, *ob sich die Baronesse nicht doch verlobt?* 'I wonder whether the baroness will not get engaged after all.'

4. The speaker puts forward a presumption and expects it will be confirmed, e.g. *Sie haben wohl jetzt Ferien?* 'I expect (no doubt) you are now having your holidays?' The *wohl* of expectancy is a useful device in a polite request put in the form of a question, e.g. *könnten Sie wohl den Brief mit in den Kasten stecken?* 'I wonder if you'd mind posting this letter with yours' (*mit* indicating the modesty of the request), or: *würden Sie wohl so liebenswürdig (freundlich, nett) sein und den Brief mitnehmen?* 'I wonder if you'd be so good as to take this letter.'

5. The speaker is feeling his way towards making a request, say for a loan, does not venture to express by *wohl* used alone his confidence that his request will be granted, but often prefers to use a particle of mere possibility as though he had not given the matter much thought, e.g. *hast du wohl zufällig (vielleicht, vielleicht zufällig) etwas Geld bei dir?* '[I say] do you happen [by any chance] to have any money on you?'

6. Instead of appearing confident or assuming a casual

attitude the speaker fears that the person addressed may
not be taking the matter as seriously as he himself. He
then uses *auch* in a manner analogous to that of the
admonitory request, e.g. *paßt du auch auf?* 'are you sure
you're paying attention', 'are you really attending?' This
particle is used with the responsive particle *denn* if a
previous utterance has produced a feeling of expectation
which is, however, questioned, e.g. A: *Er verdient gut.*
B: *Ist er denn auch glücklich?* A: 'he is earning good money.'
B: 'Well, is he any the happier for it?' 'Are you sure he
is . . .?' This *denn auch* is totally different from *doch auch*
in a context when the speaker protests that not only
others but he too must be treated fairly, e.g. *man will
doch auch essen und trinken, nicht wahr?* 'after all, people
want to eat and drink, don't they?'

7. The adversative or protesting quality of *doch* makes
it peculiarly appropriate when an anxious speaker asks
his partner to reassure him in a situation in which things
look bad, but may yet turn out more favourably. The
speaker may seek to reassure himself by deliberately using
a strong particle of conviction, e.g. *aber natürlich wird er
kommen, nicht wahr? Er kommt doch selbstverständlich, nicht
wahr?* 'Surely we can take it for granted that he will
come, can't we?' Sometimes the same type of combination
occurs in a 'follow-up' question, e.g. *du kennst doch das
Bild? natürlich doch?* 'do you know the picture? why, of
course you do, don't you?' On the other hand the speaker
may ask his partner to reassure him by asking explicitly:
du bist doch ganz sicher, daß er kommt, nicht wahr? 'you
are quite sure he's coming, aren't you?' *Doch auch* expresses a greater measure of confidence, e.g. *du bist doch
auch ganz sicher, daß . . .*, 'I take it you are quite sure that
. . .'. The appeal to his partner may, however, be implicit
in the particle, e.g. *er wird aber doch [bestimmt] kommen,*

nicht wahr? 'but he will quite definitely be coming, won't he?' In addressing this type of question in the second person as directly concerning the partner the speaker may indicate a more anxious state of mind with: *du wirst doch aber kommen?* 'but you will be coming, won't you?', a more hopeful feeling with: *du wirst aber doch kommen?* 'you will certainly be coming, won't you?' and a hope tinged with anxiety with: *du wirst aber doch hoffentlich kommen, nicht wahr?* 'you will be coming, I hope, won't you?' The speaker's well-founded anxiety lest his partner should not be able to comply with a request is indicated by *ja wohl doch* with a negative or virtual negative, e.g. *Sie haben ja doch wohl kaum Zeit?* 'I'm afraid you won't have time, will you?' If in addition to feeling anxious the speaker feels moved to protest at the apparent reluctance of the subject, he says: *er wird doch wohl kommen?* 'I suppose he will be coming, surely, won't he?'

8. The speaker is taken aback by the communication he has just received and can hardly believe his ears. He is reluctant to take his partner's words at their face value and expresses his hesitancy by the particle of possibility *etwa* (cf. can it in any way be possible?), often reinforcing it by the protesting *doch* placed before or after. His attitude is made explicit in: *wollen Sie etwa behaupten . . .?* 'do you mean to tell me . . .?' or: *du willst mir doch nicht etwa sagen, daß . . .*, 'you surely don't mean to (are not going to) tell me that . . .', *hör mal, du meinst doch nicht etwa im Ernst, daß . . .*, 'I say (look here) you don't mean to tell me seriously that . . .'. The attitude of unwillingness to accept uncongenial evidence is implicit when the particles are used without the verb of assertion, e.g. *hat er es etwa doch verplaudert?* 'he surely hasn't told any one, has he?', or more emphatically: *hat er es doch etwa verplaudert?* 'he surely hasn't gone and told any one, has

he?' Sometimes the doubt in the speaker's mind is due to his awareness of the time-factors involved, whence the time-particle *noch* in: [*es ist schon spät*] *möchten Sie etwa doch noch zur Kirche gehen?* 'you surely are not thinking of going to church now, are you?' With the first person *etwa* is used familiarly in apologizing—the speaker makes himself out to be reluctant to believe that he himself could have been so guilty as he appears. Thus if practically sure he is late for an appointment he may try to pass it off with: *komme ich etwa zu spät?* 'don't tell me I'm late', or: *hab' ich es etwa an der nötigen Delikatesse fehlen lassen?* 'surely people can't say I've been lacking in delicacy'—when he fears he has been guilty of tactlessness. A jocular incredulity is also expressed by *etwa*, e.g. in reply to a speaker talking of settling in a certain neighbourhood in which the person addressed has a business the latter may say: *wie (was), willst du mir etwa Konkurrenz machen?* 'what (why), were you [by any chance] thinking of competing with me?'

9. The speaker, while not rejecting or disbelieving what his partner has told him, leaves open the possibility that his partner may be wrong and therefore asks what conclusions should in that event be drawn. Here *doch* as the affirmative response in rebuttal of a negative question is clearly appropriate, e.g. A: *er wird nicht kommen.* B: *wenn er aber doch kommen sollte?* 'but what if he did', 'but supposing he did come after all?'

10. The speaker is trying to recollect some name or fact which eludes him. The milder musing particles are *noch* and *denn*, e.g. *wie heißt er noch (denn, denn noch)?* 'what was his name, whatever was his name, now?' To show some impatience at his own forgetfulness ('memory like a sieve') he often says: *wie heißt er auch schon?* or: *wie im Himmel heißt er denn nur?* 'oh lor, what was his name?'

11. The counterpart of a recollecting question is one

indicating the unexpected emergence of something the speaker finds it difficult to understand. Here the typical particle is *nur*, e.g. *was hast du nur?* 'why, what's the matter?' or: 'whatever is the matter?'

The above may be regarded as typical instances of particles used in questions. They all occur together with various other nuancing words and in various combinations in the statement. The cases are so numerous that here only a small selection can be given to illustrate certain characteristic English renderings.

In regard to the use of the particles in the statement only a few salient features can be touched upon here. The subject is vast and complex, and the admirable work done by Curme and Eggeling invites further investigation in the use of the simple as well as of combined particles. In passing we may note the expostulatory use of *auch*, not very much unlike its use in questions (are you sure) and requests (be sure to), e.g. in Eggeling's [A: *Sie wissen hier gut Bescheid*] B: *Ich wohne auch schon lange hier*, which might be rendered: 'Well of course (to be sure, after all) I've lived here some time.' Eggeling, too, draws attention to the use of *auch* in a tentative suggestion showing readiness to fall in with a person's wishes, e.g. [*wenn du nicht mitkommen willst,*] *kann ich auch allein gehen*, which might be rendered: 'I suppose I can go alone all right.' Then there is the indication of irony in Eggeling's *das hilft mir auch was*, 'a [fat] lot of good that will do me', cf. the more emphatic use of *gerade* in: *na, das wird gerade viel nützen (helfen)* or: *das hat gerade noch gefehlt*, 'that's just about done it'. Further, there are the uses of *ja* in pointing to a fact already known or assumed to be known to one's partner, e.g. *ich gebe mir ja Mühe*, 'I do take pains, you know', and in indicating that in view of the certainty of an occurrence, further anxiety is superfluous, e.g. *sei*

mir nur nichte böse, ich will es ja nicht wieder tun, 'please
don't be cross, you see I'll never do it again. These and
other uses of *ja* are admirably treated in Paul's *Deutsches
Wörterbuch*. Next there is the reassuring use of *schon*,
e.g. *ich werde schon darüber hinwegkommen*, 'I'll get over
it all right (never fear, don't worry)'. Sometimes the reassurance is, to say the least, ironical, e.g. in W. Busch:

> Zuerst hast du es gut, mein Sohn,
> Doch paß mal auf, man kommt dir schon!

'but look out, they'll be after you all right!' One particular point I have not so far seen mentioned. Whereas
Eggeling discusses: *das ist schon wahr, aber . . .*, 'that
may well be true, but . . .', he does not mention the
propitiatory use of *schon* as a brief reply, e.g. *hast du mich
denn nicht lieb?* to which the reply was: [*das*] *schon, Puck,
aber davon gibt es so verschiedene Sorten*, 'why, yes, of
course, but . . .'. From an example like: *ich hab's schon
ausgerichtet*, 'I've seen to it already, and so it's all right',
it is not difficult to see how this particle could acquire
the nuance of encouraging, consoling, or setting at ease.
Finally there is a curious use of *wohl* in a sharp rejoinder
to a question which is resented, e.g. [A: *denken Sie, daß
mir das Eindruck macht?*] B: *Ich werde wohl denken, was
mir beliebt*, 'I suppose I can think what I please'.

These are merely a few gleanings from a vast store of
material. It would be an alluring task to pick out in
German a certain number of simple particles, combine
them in pairs or triplets or even larger groups, and try to
discover which groups are the most commonly used,
which have the most characteristic functions, and which
cannot be combined with which, or at least not in a particular order. It will be found that the following order in
the specific particle-groups mentioned appears to be
impossible in German: *noch auch, schon auch; auch denn,*

noch denn, ja denn; wohl ja, schon ja; noch nur, in contrast with the regular: *auch noch, auch schon; denn auch, denn doch; ja wohl, ja schon; nur noch.* There must be some reason for this state of things if it could be discovered. Occasionally a slight change in the order makes a considerable difference to the feeling-tone. Thus a person asking politely for leave to absent himself for a moment could say: *ich möchte mir eben doch noch die Hände waschen,* 'I should like to go and wash my hands, please'. On the other hand, a child excusing itself a little impatiently from coming at once in obedience to its mother's call might rather say: *ich möchte mir doch eben noch die Hände waschen,* rendered 'can't I just get my hands washed first?'

In regard to the more characteristic combinations the following cases might be noted in which the English equivalent diverges considerably from the German: The use of the consequential particle-group *denn auch* in such phrases as: *dieses Versprechen hat er denn auch gehalten,* 'and this promise he duly kept'; the protesting group *denn doch* in: *das geht denn doch zu weit,* 'that's going too far, I must say', *das trieb denn dann doch die Sache auf die Spitze,* 'that just about brought matters to a head'; the defiant *erst recht* [*nun gerade*] in Paul's example: *nun wollen wir erst recht vergnügt sein,* 'now we will make merry with a vengeance'; the presumptive group *ja wohl* in: [*wenn Vater Moral donnert*] *weißt du ja wohl,* [*so halt ich mir bloß die Ohren zu*], 'you ought to know by now', 'I think you might know'; the resigned *nun einmal* in: *na, so ist er nun einmal,* 'well, that's just his little way' (Eggel.) or: *so ist's nun mal* or *es is nun doch mal so,* 'well, there it is [it can't be helped, there's nothing for it, it's no use worrying]'. Sometimes *mal* alone suffices, e.g. in Wilhelm Busch:

> Es ist mal so, daß ich so bin,
> Weiß selber nicht warum.

Whereas *nun mal* expresses an attitude of submission to fate or the world in general we find that a half protesting, half resigned attitude to the unreasonableness of human beings may be expressed by *ja doch*, e.g. *bei Junggesellen ist ja doch immer was entzwei*, 'oh well, things are always getting broken in bachelors' establishments'; *lossagen mußt du dich ja doch von mir*, 'well, you see, you'll have to give me up anyhow'.

The last example quoted opens up a further interesting line of inquiry, viz. the correlation between certain particles and particle-groups and certain gestures. *Nun mal* is very much like a shrugging of the shoulders, *erst recht* or *nun gerade* perhaps a clenched fist of defiance. The particles used in trying in vain to recollect (*noch, bloß*, &c.) are like scratching one's head or the downward jerk of the clenched hand (gesture of annoyance) or clicking the finger and thumb (gesture of impatience or fidgetiness). Being the expression of attitudes these particles are all more or less in the nature of phonetic gestures or *Lautgebärden*.

It is evident from a consideration of the various equivalents of German particles that English adopts a number of totally different procedures in indicating 'attitude'. Fräulein Gauger in *Neuere Sprachen* noted a few of these, and all that is necessary here is to summarize and supplement her findings. The chief procedures in English are as follows: (1) use of intonation with or without specific word or phrase, the tone being often sufficient to suggest a mood of playfulness, irony, anxiety, reproach, or the like; e.g. 'a lot of good that will do!' (2) use of strong stress especially of the auxiliary, e.g. 'will he come?' expressing doubt, 'I do hope he'll come'; (3) addition of a tag-question, e.g. 'isn't he', 'won't he', 'won't you', &c.; (4) inserting at the beginning of the sentence an interjection like 'oh', 'oh, I do hope not', or a quasi-interjectional word like 'why',

'well', or an expletive like 'by Jove'; (5) reinforcement of
the main verb by the use of 'been and', 'gone and', e.g.
'he's gone and betrayed us', cf. the well-known joke in
Punch in which the maid says to the mistress: 'Please
mum, the butcher's been and gone and never come'; (6)
the use of quasi-particles or particle-like phrases, e.g. 'you
know', 'you see', 'mark you' (cf. Ger. *wohlgemerkt*, *notabene*;
Fr. *par exemple*), 'I suppose'. The examples given have
shown occasional blends of these procedures which on the
whole bring English conversation more into line with
French than with the other Germanic languages.

A thorough survey of this field could not in any case
stop short with English and German. It would explore
the agreements and differences between High German
and the other Germanic languages, which have often
adopted forms through Low German. Thus the Dutch
nu eenmaal and Danish *nu engang* would be studied in
relation to the German *nun einmal*. Particles not existing
in German, e.g. Dutch *stellig*, *heusch*, *trouwens*, would be
examined in their peculiar functions and, in particular,
attention could be drawn to the Dutch discrimination of
doch and *toch* in contrast with German *doch*, and of Danish
ja and *jo* in contrast with German *ja*. Even that would not
be sufficient, for in due course the English procedures
would have to be compared with the French and the chan-
nels of influence investigated. These are all lines of
investigation which cannot be pursued here. Enough
has, however, been brought forward to illustrate the truth
of the statement that the acquisition of a living language
is an unending task. Wherever one turns there are riches
innumerable waiting to be collected, sifted, and put in
their right setting. It is a task in which the close collaboration of native speakers of all the languages compared is
eminently advisable.

PAUL ERNST'S THEORY OF THE NOVELLE

By Dr. Kathleen Cunningham

BEFORE proceeding to outline Paul Ernst's theory of the Novelle it is necessary to emphasize the fact that his pronouncements on the subject are made from the standpoint of the creative artist and that they are therefore not free from a certain dogmatism. In theorizing about the Novelle Paul Ernst does not proceed primarily from a number of concrete examples and endeavour to derive a theory of the genre from them; he proceeds rather from his own bias as a creative artist. Moreover, his aesthetical speculation is and must be, in the very nature of the case, unsystematic. Some of his theoretical pronouncements on the Novelle as a genre have, it is true, arisen from his preoccupation with the works of other artists, but very many of them are the result of his own experiences as a writer of Novellen. In other words, his theory of the Novelle is written from a prejudiced standpoint and the very farthest thing from his mind was the erection of his speculations into a system. He himself gives us the clue to his attitude in this matter in a passage in *Der Weg zur Form*, in which he says that when a poet theorizes there can be no question of his producing definitive investigations, for he is not 'scientifically interested': 'his preoccupations are with reality in so far as it forms the material for his work, and with his craft; everything else is a matter of indifference to him'.[1]

Having cleared the ground thus far, the next thing we must do is to ascertain the bias, the vantage-point in the

[1] *Der Weg zur Form*, 3rd ed., Munich, 1928, p. 273 (quoted as *W.z.F.*).

aesthetical field from which Paul Ernst is writing. This
is easily done. When he first began to write at the close
of the last century he was associated for a very brief
period with the writers of the naturalistic school, and his
first dramatic and narrative works were naturalistic in
subject-matter, style, and technique. But a very few years
sufficed to show him the faulty foundation on which the
whole structure of naturalism was reared. Paul Ernst
severed his connexion with naturalism because he could
not accept the principal tenet in the naturalist creed, the
so-called milieu theory which regarded man as the product
of his environment. He tells us himself in his own account
of his artistic development that when he had completed
his first plays he was immediately conscious of the fact
that he had been working along wrong lines; it became
clear to him that by adhering too closely to nature he
could not represent 'the important things', namely 'moral
struggles'.[1] He felt the same dissatisfaction with a volume
of poetry and with his first Novellen; their chief blemish
seemed to him to be a lack of form, and although they
were to a certain extent poetical they were in every respect
inartistic. These disappointing experiences with his own
work forced Paul Ernst to take stock of his position. He
refers to the years between 1898, the date of publication
of his naturalistic plays, and 1900 as years of struggle
in which he was ceaselessly preoccupied with problems
of form. At last in the year 1900, during a journey to
Italy, he found an answer to many of the problems that
had beset him ever since he first began to doubt the efficacy
of naturalism. He tells us that now for the first time he
recognized the extraordinary difficulties that confront the
dramatist and that for the moment he contented himself
with the easier form of the Novelle. In many respects

[1] *W.z.F.*, p. 20.

Paul Ernst's Italian experience reminds us of Goethe's; in his case also Italy seems to have meant for him a kind of crystallization of tendencies that had already been latent in him. In Italy, and above all in the classical Novelle of Boccaccio, Paul Ernst found a positive answer to those questions of form which up till then he had answered only negatively himself.

The immediate result of this preoccupation with Boccaccio was the collection of *Altitaliänische Novellen* which he edited with a foreword in 1902. Here for the first time we find a comprehensive and fundamental exposition of his views on poetry and art, and as he himself has more than once insisted in his critical writings that he has not altered his position radically since then, we are justified in regarding this foreword as his artistic credo. Quite briefly, it is a classical credo. The poet, one of the group of people in the foreword who are discussing the circumstances under which the great Italian literature arose, tells the company of the joy that he experienced when he first came into contact with the Italian Novelle:

> Und dann rühmte er, welche Freude er gehabt, als er durch Zufall auf die große Menge der alten italienischen Novellen gestoßen; wie hier die alte Weltanschauung herrschte, welche den Menschen zum Mittelpunkt machte und zu einem freien Herrn über sich und die Welt . . .[1]

A few years later Paul Ernst had occasion to restate and to define more precisely the classical standpoint expressed in this foreword. Protesting against the label 'neo-classicist' which had been applied to him and some other poets with kindred aims, including W. von Scholz and S. Lublinski, he declared that never for a moment had there been question among them of a 'resuscitation of the

[1] *Altitaliänische Novellen*, Ausgewählt und übertragen von Paul Ernst, 2nd ed., Leipzig, 1907, vol. i, p. 33.

past'; 'on the contrary', he wrote, 'we are thoroughly conscious of belonging to the twentieth century, and some of us have taken much trouble and have sacrificed years in trying to understand our own age in its ultimate causes. Our aim is not classicism but a classical quality, that is to say, we are not concerned with questions of matter but of form.' The rest of this statement of aims is a definition of the term 'classical quality' and is of vital importance for the understanding of Paul Ernst's aesthetical theory, including his theory of the Novelle:

Wir verlangen von uns, wenn wir ein Kunstwerk schaffen, daß wir die für dieses Werk erforderlichen Mittel in dem für unsere Begabung höchstmöglichen Grade beherrschen; daß wir nicht die Kunstformen vermengen; daß unsere Subjektivität zurücktritt vor dem objektiven Anspruch des Werks; daß wir keine Surrogate verwenden.[1]

These are severe demands, and the artist who set himself such a high standard was equally uncompromising in his judgements on the works of others. There must be no mingling of the art forms; drama is one thing, narrative is another; and the nineteenth century, which tried to mingle them, represents nothing more or less than an artistic chaos: this is the aesthetical prejudice with which we must start if we would find logical satisfaction in Paul Ernst's theory of the Novelle.

Paul Ernst's most significant contribution to the theory of the Novelle is found in the essay *Zum Handwerk der Novelle*, written in 1903, and incorporated in *Der Weg zur Form*. He begins by emphasizing the relation between the drama and the Novelle and the essential differences between these two art forms and the novel. Like Schiller and Grillparzer, he regards the novel as not being an art form in the strict sense of the word, *Halbkunst* being the

---

[1] *Ein Credo*, 1st ed., Munich, 1912, vol. 1, p. 175 (quoted as *Credo*, i).

rather derogatory term which all three theorists apply to
this Cinderella among the literary kinds. According to
Paul Ernst the drama and the Novelle, by their very
nature, are of all the poetical kinds the most strongly
bound and limited by rules; elaborating this relationship,
he arrives at the following formula:

> Wie das Drama eine abgezogene Kunstform ist, welche wichtige
> Inhalte des Lebens, das heißt Punkte, um welche sich bei den
> Menschen Kräfte lagern, in einem sinnlichen Gewand gibt, durch
> dessen Anblick diese Kräfte gelöst werden . . . so ist es auch die
> Novelle.[1]

He then goes on to stress the part that structure plays in
both the drama and the Novelle, reminding us, as he does
so, of an important difference between the German and
the Latin peoples in their attitude towards form. The
Germans, he insists, just because they have a stronger
sense of reality in art and are more moved by it than the
Latins, are correspondingly less sensitive to artistic form
as such. The mere fact that the Novelle is subject to the
same external conditions as the novel, being perused in
private by individuals and not enjoyed in common with
others like the drama, has, he believes, brought about a
deplorable confusion in style between these two literary forms. When we read a Novelle, he says, we take
pleasure in the characterization, the language, atmosphere, thoughts, and perhaps even the didactic purpose
of the author, and forget that, as with the drama, the
most important thing for the Novelle is the structure,
everything else being of secondary consideration.[2]

To illustrate his theory of the Novelle as an abstract
art form, Paul Ernst summarizes a Novelle by Giovanni
Sercambi, an Italian who wrote in the year 1375.[3] 'Here',
he declares, 'a whole human destiny, in so far as it is

[1] *W.z.F.*, p. 69.　　　[2] Ibid.　　　[3] Ibid., pp. 70 ff.

bound up with character and circumstances, is decided in a single point, which is an unusual happening.' If the poet had worked according to naturalist theories he would have shown the accumulation of miseries that the hero experienced in exile; in the Novelle, however, all that is gathered together and concentrated in a single symbolic incident, which sheds an illuminating light backwards and forwards over the hero's life. Moreover the incident in question is of a strange and peculiar kind that impresses itself on the imagination of the reader. Ernst reflects that in reality actions spring from a thousand impulses and motives, and that here, instead of leading us through a labyrinth of psychological subtleties, the poet concentrates this multitude of motives in one single 'foreground thought'. The author is not concerned with reality but with a significant problem in the life of an individual, and the manner in which this is represented reminds Paul Ernst of the kind of 'shorthand' with which in a Greek relief a door is used to indicate a whole house.[1]

After this general characteristic Ernst proceeds to differentiate between three types of Novelle. The most significant of these is that which reveals the relation between character and fate, and their mutual interdependence; Sercambi's Novelle is of this type, but a still finer example in modern literature is C. F. Meyer's Novelle, *Die Versuchung des Pescara*. After summarizing the problem that lies at the root of this Novelle Ernst goes on to observe that 'in this truly novellistic content' we see immediately the difference between this genre and tragedy. Here, he maintains, we have the same problem as in *Wallenstein*, with the important difference that, whereas in Schiller's play the hero actually yields to temptation, betrays his emperor and meets his downfall

[1] *W.z.F.*, p. 71.

in consequence of his action, in Meyer's Novelle the hero
who is assailed by temptation is already a dying man and
the temptation remains a temptation; the problem in the
one case is tragic, in the other novellistic, a warning, says
Ernst, to the fools who are still tempted by the apparently dramatic but in reality novellistic structure of
Meyer's Novellen to dramatize them.[1]

Meyer's material, he continues, is not only more profound and wider in scope that Sercambi's childish tale,
the actual narrative has also become richer. Nevertheless,
in spite of these circumstances, or, more accurately, just
because of them, we can see in Meyer's Novelle the distinctive features of the genre as an abstract art form:
thus Meyer avoids wherever possible all detailed direct
descriptions, charging the actual conversations with more
momentum, so that these are far from being a copy of
reality but give, as it were, an extract of reality; what
cannot be communicated by means of conversations is
concentrated in quite brief remarks, all such direct narration being reduced to the barest minimum; moreover a
vivid sense of the actual situation is produced in the mind
of the reader by a clever choice of images, such only being
used as impress themselves strongly on the imagination.[2]

The second type of Novelle is not concerned with the
workings of fate, and the events it describes are of less
far-reaching significance. Nevertheless, here too the central incident or event must be one that is characteristic
for the individual concerned and peculiar in its own way.
Ernst emphasizes the quality of strangeness as the most
essential feature of this type of Novelle, which he finds
most often represented in the early beginnings of the
genre and the most striking examples of which are found in
the *Cento novelle antiche* and in the Old Castilian collection,

[1] Ibid., pp. 74 ff.   [2] Ibid., p. 73.

Conde Lucanor; its effect, he observes, is similar to that of comedy, in which, in contrast to tragedy, in the end nothing is changed but everything remains as it was; another point of contact is the tendency that both have to portray types rather than individuals; finally, both appear to Paul Ernst to be strongly influenced by social conditions and are in consequence much more inclined to date than other forms of literature.[1]

Paul Ernst calls a third type of Novelle 'the witty retort', a variation of the genre which he says we hardly understand rightly to-day. Our failure to understand this type to-day demonstrates how certain art forms become extinct in consequence of changes in our general cultural outlook; its *raison d'être* was the formulation of a witty answer, the art of playing with words, which was less common then than it is to-day.[2]

Paul Ernst is inclined to be pessimistic about the prospects of the revival of the art of the Novelle at the present day. He sees the chief reason for the dissolution of the genre in the relativist outlook of the modern age; the modern tendency towards formlessness must of necessity have a disintegrating effect on a genre in which, to use Ernst's own words, there must be 'a beginning and end, cause and effect'. In view of these circumstances he can think of only one possibility, namely the 'Arabesque', a form which he says was first created by Arnim and Brentano, and the best example of which is Arnim's *Isabella von Aegypten.*

In the *Schlußwort zur Judenbuche*, which was originally published in 1904 in Paul Ernst's edition of Annette von Droste-Hülshoff's Novelle and which now forms part of *Der Weg zur Form*, we also find a number of significant statements concerning the Novelle as an art form.

[1] *W.z.F.*, p. 74.   [2] Ibid., p. 75.

In this essay, as in the one just discussed, Paul Ernst starts his investigation by stressing the differences between the dramatic and the narrative forms. The critic of the drama, he maintains, can disregard the personality of the dramatist almost completely, 'for the forms of the drama are so compelling that not much more than the choice of material is in the hands of the dramatist', everything else proceeding according to 'immutable laws'; the reason for this is that the drama must produce an immediate effect on many people at once, and the number of means whereby such an effect can be achieved is so small and their employment is possible only under such binding conditions that the individuality and aim of the poet necessarily appear under the guise of talent; for this reason Paul Ernst thinks that the critical attitude that judges the dramatist as a 'craftsman' is altogether just.[1]

'The Novelle and, to a still greater extent, the novel are subject to other external conditions', and here Paul Ernst repeats a contention made in the previous essay: the mere fact that they are read in private by individuals means that they do not depend for their success or failure on the immediate effect that they produce; if, out of every hundred readers, there are eighty who detest a Novelle, the influence of the other twenty, if they esteem it, is sufficient to spread its fame; but if twenty out of a hundred spectators at a play remain indifferent, their influence is sufficient to kill the enthusiasm of the others. The book which is read has, therefore, at its disposal a much greater number of means of producing an effect than the drama which is heard and seen. For this reason the critic who judges a Novelle and, still more, a novel, need not restrict himself to the purely technical aspect, or, as Paul Ernst puts it, to actual 'craftsmanship' in the same degree as the

[1] Ibid., p. 85.

critic who judges a drama; in other words, the personality of the author counts for much more in the narrative forms than in the drama.[1]

Paul Ernst then proceeds to say something of the personality of Annette von Droste-Hülshoff and its effect on her art. He sees her as an aristocratic nature, the descendant of an ancient family, who grew up amongst people with fixed and ordered views, and knowing little of 'what we to-day call freedom'; as one who had a respect for tradition and a reverence for authority and who, because of the many links that bound the noble families with the ordinary people in those 'patriarchal' days, was able to obtain a knowledge and an understanding of other people. This type of education was, he considers, in many respects beneficial to her art, for an aristocratic nature will always, other things being equal, produce something more valuable than others, but it may also produce a certain disregard for the purely technical aspect, as compared with the actual ethos of the work of art. In support of this view Paul Ernst quotes a remark of Annette's from which it is obvious that she was more concerned with the philosophical and ethical content of her poetry than with the actual mode of expression;[2] and, having cast his net thus widely, he proceeds to show the effect of this attitude of mind on the composition of the *Judenbuche*.

In the course of his analysis he points out that the main content of the Novelle, that is the murder of a Jew and the discovery of the murder through the awakening of the murderer's conscience in a peculiar way, was based on actuality; such an event had actually taken place, and the poetess often heard her grandfather relate it. Now, according to Paul Ernst, Annette was one of those individuals

---

[1] *W.z.F.*, p. 86.   [2] Ibid., p. 87.

in whom the creative process was almost entirely unconscious; in the minds of such individuals 'a material develops
to a certain extent by itself' and finds its own 'adequate
form' without any conscious effort on the part of the
artist.[1] Ernst goes on to say that when Annette had
completed her Novelle in the form in which we know it
to-day she became acquainted with a written version of
the incident as it actually happened; during the course of
her own composition she had remembered only the principal circumstances of the story as originally told to her by
her grandfather; and now, when confronted with the
written version of the actual story, expressed her regret
at not having known it before composing her Novelle,
for, she said, the simple truth is always better than the
best invention.[2] We have therefore, according to Paul
Ernst, in Annette's Novelle 'the result of an unconscious
activity of the artist's imagination which allows the actual
happening to grow dim in the memory' and invents a
new version in its place.[3]

Ernst has nothing but praise for the manner in which
the author has managed to avoid depicting the actual
psychological processes in the mind of the hero and has
yet succeeded in arousing in the reader a vivid sense of
the mental agony that he endured. He points out that
for this purpose the matter-of-fact milieu of the actual
happening and the stupidity of the real murderer could
not be used; the suicide of the real murderer appears to
the reader as fortuitous; what actually took place in his
mind is incapable of being represented poetically, and a
true poet will realize that such depths of the subconscious
cannot be expressed in words; 'one can only arouse in
the reader, by the use of certain means, the impression

[1] Ibid., p. 88.   [2] Ibid., pp. 93 ff.
[3] Ibid., p. 94.

that they exist'.[1] Ernst then shows how, through the description of the hero's environment and the rather circumstantial account of his early history, Annette has managed to produce in the reader a mood that makes it easy for him to realize, on looking back, what mental torture the hero has endured. The manner in which this is done is, in Ernst's opinion, beyond praise. We can, he says, only recognize the 'great artistic wisdom' of the author, who does not describe for description's sake but merely narrates and then only such things as prepare us for the overwhelming part that conscience plays in the story.[2]

The *Judenbuche* satisfies Paul Ernst both in regard to content and form. 'A Novelle', he declares, 'must contain in its main part something irrational, something whereby that which is narrated reveals itself as unusual and surprising; preferably this should be connected with some clearly marked object, as in Boccaccio's classical Novelle, with the falcon that the impoverished knight sets before his lady as a meal.' The irrational connexion between the beech tree and the murder, which is heightened by 'the complete silence in regard to the psychological state of the murderer', gives Annette's Novelle its special 'novellistic significance'; without it it would merely be a 'tale'.[3]

In conclusion, Paul Ernst again stresses the fact that Annette was one of those artists in whose production conscious artistic effort plays very little part; to a certain extent she must be described as a 'dilettante'. We have, therefore, he believes, in the *Judenbuche* a quite remarkable example of the autonomy of artistic form; although the artist was unaware of the fact and would actually have liked to write a true story, 'the necessities of form',

---

[1] *W.z.F.*, p. 95.   [2] Ibid., pp. 95 ff.
[3] Ibid., p. 96.

without any conscious effort on her part, so altered the original version in her mind that a classical Novelle has arisen.[1] In view of the fact that the author's other prose works have 'no very outstanding value' and that the *Juden-buche* is the only Novelle she wrote, Paul Ernst is inclined to the view that in this case we have an example of a material that has developed and found shape of its own accord. He uses the expression *Eigenbewegung des Stoffes* to describe this unconscious process: the material itself contains all those 'forces' which 'allow it to develop into a Novelle'; 'these', says Paul Ernst, 'develop in a poetic-ally gifted individual like a grain of seed in the earth'.[2]

In an introduction to a collection of Goethe's Novellen and fairy tales which he edited for the Insel-Verlag in 1913 and which has since been republished in the *Tagebuch eines Dichters*, 1934, Paul Ernst repeats his contention regarding the strictness of the laws that bind the writer of Novellen.

'The Novelle', he says, 'is a close art form and offers the poet who knows how to use it the extraordinary advantages of every close art form.' By its very nature it has a limited compass beyond which it cannot go and should, therefore, have afforded Goethe the support that he needed. Ernst implies here that Goethe was an artist with a decidedly epic tendency who should have benefited very much by having to confine himself within the restricted range of the Novelle. Like Spielhagen and other theorists, he expresses the view that Goethe shattered the Novelle form in the *Wahlverwandtschaften*, and suggests that he did so because of his failure to find 'the fruitful moment in which the destiny of the characters must decide itself', for, he continues, the Novelle compresses the 'growth and development of processes in a single point in which every-thing from forwards and backwards and from the sides

[1] *W.z.F.*, p. 97.   [2] Ibid.

meets together'.[1] The test of the structure of a Novelle
is its oral narration: the good Novelle should still be
entertaining when narrated quite simply and without
elaboration. Ernst points out that Goethe is supposed to
have narrated the Novellen that he included in the *Wan-
derjahre*, before he wrote them down, and that for the
most part he did not invent the stories himself but took
them over from other sources and gave them a higher form,
in some cases the highest possible form.[2]

In the same essay Ernst makes an interesting comparison between Goethe and Kleist as writers of Novellen.
In Goethe's Novellen he finds a remarkable antithesis to
Kleist's, for, although both are examples of 'the complete
mastery of the novellistic form', they are entirely unlike
each other in descriptive method. The difference, as
Ernst sees it, is mainly that between youth and age:
Kleist, the young man, does his utmost to reproduce
reality and to hold fast the momentary, while Goethe, the
old man, tries to represent what is lasting and what lies
behind reality. One might say that Goethe's style is
'abstract' as compared with Kleist's; we should be careful,
however, about using this expression if we mean it as a
reproach. We must distinguish, he thinks, between 'various degrees of reality'; the older we grow the more purely
intellectual and the less superficially sensuous our perceptions become; this must not be understood to mean that
the sensuous element is entirely lacking in the perceptions
of a great poet like Goethe, but rather that the perceptions
have more form, for the older man, says Ernst, 'recognizes
behind the flowering exterior that he sees the skeleton
that he does not see'. We should, he thinks, bear this
in mind if we would fully appreciate Goethe's Novellen.[3]

---

[1] *Tagebuch eines Dichters*, Munich, 1934, p. 80 (quoted as *T.e.D.*).
[2] *T.e.D.*, p. 81.   [3] *T.e.D.*, pp. 81 ff.

Paul Ernst mentions another interesting difference between Kleist and Goethe: Kleist's chief preoccupation in
his Novellen is the representation of passions, while
Goethe's is the painting of pictures; very often the climax
of Goethe's Novellen is such a picture as, for example, in
Novelle. Ernst ascribes this circumstance also to the
difference in age between the two poets: Kleist's experience of the passions is still immediate and unbroken; for
him they are the centre of everything; they and the movement of his own soul are the only things he knows, while
'the whole external world seems to exist only for him and
his passion'; the mature man, on the other hand, 'who has
himself experienced many things, with their beginnings
and climaxes, the resistance of the outside world, the
decline and extinction of passion, and who has observed
similar processes in the case of others', cannot possibly
regard himself as the centre of the universe; 'he realizes
that the destinies of all human beings are interlocked', the
sufferings of the ones being necessary for the happiness
of the others, and that such sufferings do not possess 'the
exclusive importance' that he himself formerly ascribed
to them. In other words, the attitude of Kleist to the
world is subjective and tragic, while Goethe's is objective
in that it seeks to comprehend the world as a whole, thus
triumphing over the purely tragic standpoint and arriving
at 'harmony and beauty'.[1]

After these general remarks Ernst goes on to discuss
individually some of the stories that he has included in his
collection. The first of these is the *Bekenntnisse einer schönen
Seele*, which, he says, cannot be regarded as a 'Novelle in the
strict sense of the word'; but inasmuch as a whole life is
here envisaged and represented from one particular aspect,
the *Bekenntnisse* have much in common with the Novelle.[2]

[1] Ibid., p. 82.   [2] Ibid., p. 83.

Another point of interest in this essay is the comparison between the framework of the *Unterhaltungen der deutschen Ausgewanderten* and the framework of the *Decamerone*. Ernst finds Goethe's framework 'less felicitous' than Boccaccio's; 'it contains too much conversation, and the Novellen appear as concrete illustrations of abstract ideas'. Boccaccio's framework on the other hand is 'merely a framework'; at the same time it surpasses Goethe's in sheer artistry, for the stories that are set within it are divided into ten groups, and not only has each of these its own introduction but each of the individual stories has one also. Goethe's framework seems to Paul Ernst to be less convincing than Boccaccio's: we have, he says, the same feeling regarding it as we have about the employment of a similar device by the romanticists; it seems as though the stories would gain by being detached from the framework.[1]

It has already been indicated at the beginning of this essay that the point of departure for all Paul Ernst's aesthetical theory is his insistence on the absolute separation of the literary kinds. It is not, therefore, surprising to find that one of his favourite critical pastimes consists in pointing to Novellen that are not really Novellen but rather the first chapter or chapters of novels, and dramas that are not really dramatic but novellistic.

Probably the most convincing of such analyses is that devoted to a tale by Selma Lagerlöf, the material of which seemed to Paul Ernst at first sight a good subject for a Novelle. But on closer examination it was clear to him that the incident with which Selma Lagerlöf closes her story is not the end but the beginning of a development. He points out that the material in itself is 'a charming anecdote'. Now according to Paul Ernst, the anecdote

[1] *T.e.D.*, pp. 83 ff.

tends even more than the Novelle to give an abstract of
life, so much so that it can hardly be considered as belonging to the poetical domain at all. Selma Lagerlöf, a true
poetess, has not the necessary 'coldbloodedness' to write
an anecdote; 'if she were less than she is she would have
written an excellent anecdote'; but, as it is, she has written
a tale, 'die den inneren Drang hat, eine Novelle zu werden
und das nicht werden kann'.[1] At the end of the story there
is opened up the prospect of a conflict which, in Paul
Ernst's view, constitutes the subject for a novel. If the
poetess had more of that constructive, organizing ability
of which Paul Ernst speaks elsewhere, more *bauende
Vorstellungskraft*, she would have realized that this was not
a good subject for a Novelle, for, he declares:

> Die Novelle ist eine dichterische Form; das heißt, sie gibt ein
> geschlossenes Bild. Aber bei der Erzählung der Lagerlöf führt
> eine Tür aus dem Geschlossenen ins Freie.[2]

We find an interesting pendant to the view expressed
here in a criticism of *A Doll's House* in the first edition of
the *Credo*.[3] Paul Ernst asserts that the plot of this play is
not dramatic but novellistic, and compares it unfavourably
with the plot of *Ghosts*, which, he says, is essentially tragic.
He points out in a rather humorous analysis of Ibsen's
material that the hero is very much the average man who
behaves rudely to his wife in a crucial situation, namely
when he learns that she has committed a forgery for his
sake; after a few days he will probably see the matter in
its right perspective, will make it up with her, thank her
for what she has done, and at the same time admonish her
gently, pointing out that nice little wives should not do
things like that. But in Ibsen's play the nice little wife

---

[1] *W.z.F.*, p. 430.
[2] Ibid., Cf. also M. Florin, *Paul Ernst als Novellist*, Diss. Münster,
1926, pp. 32 ff.   [3] *Credo*, i, pp. 35 ff.

of the first act has developed into a magnificent and awe-inspiring creature with 'claims to freedom and self-determination'. This development, Paul Ernst maintains, is novellistic: the Novelle says that she leaves her husband and children and goes out into the wide world, whereas in reality the point at issue between them would have solved itself rather prosaically in the ordinary give and take of married life; thus the end of the play, as originally written by Ibsen, presents us with the 'surprise', the 'irrational element', the 'pointe' which is characteristic of the Novelle.

This point of view regarding Ibsen's play is, of course, not peculiar to Paul Ernst: it is to be found in most criticisms of the play. Spielhagen formulated it differently, but he meant much the same thing when he said that it was not a drama but a few chapters of a novel in dialogue form, the beginning of which lies far before the beginning of the play and the end of which falls long after the fall of the curtain.[1]

I have indicated in the beginning that we must not expect a systematic aesthetic of the Novelle from Paul Ernst; his theoretical pronouncements on the subject are indeed very far from constituting a system. Nevertheless we cannot deny to them a certain unity and cohesion that have their origins in a well-defined, not to say one-sided, aesthetical outlook. The key to Paul Ernst's theory of the Novelle is, as already remarked, his own classical standpoint; the point of departure is the rigorous distinction that he draws between the literary kinds. Compared with his views on this question, the attitude of Schiller in the letter to Goethe of 29 December 1797 is revolutionary; and yet Schiller was only facing facts; because the conditions under which the epic and dramatic kinds originally arose have disappeared for ever, he insisted that the

[1] *Beiträge zur Theorie und Technik des Romans*, Leipzig, 1883, p. 310.

modern poet was obliged to mingle them. In this letter
he was merely anticipating the process of breaking down
the barriers between the kinds that began with romanticism and went on right through the century. Soon the
theorists were to be confounded by the appearance of
lyrical and epic drama and of dramatic epic. Now the
originality of Paul Ernst's theory of the Novelle is that,
though faced with the novellistic practice of the great
nineteenth-century exponents of the genre,[1] and with the
bulk of the theory on the subject, he nevertheless affirms
with great decision the essential differences between the
Novelle and the drama as art forms. For him there are
specifically novellistic and specifically dramatic materials.
The material treated in *Die Versuchung des Pescara* may
strike us superficially as being very similar to that treated
in *Wallenstein*, but, in Paul Ernst's view, the essentially
passive role of Meyer's hero marks this material as being
distinctively novellistic. This matter forms such a conviction with him that he insists in his analysis of the *Judenbuche* that the forms have their own life, that there are
materials which are so essentially novellistic that they are
capable of developing their own adequate form with little
or no conscious effort on the part of the artist. This is
the conviction that also lies at the root of his analysis of
the tale by Selma Lagerlöf, in which he shows that the
author has not written a Novelle but the first chapter of
a novel; she has not written a Novelle because the subject
was incapable of novellistic treatment. Similarly, *A Doll's
House* is not dramatic but novellistic.

In conclusion, it may perhaps again be emphasized
that Paul Ernst's classical standpoint is not the outcome
of pedantic investigations into the meaning of form: it

[1] Cf. H. Pongs, *Möglichkeiten des Tragischen in der Novelle*, Berlin,
1932; E. K. Bennett, *A History of the German Novelle*, Cambridge, 1934.

goes much deeper than that; it is much more an attitude
to life than an attitude to art, or perhaps it would be more
correct to say that the attitude to art is determined by the
attitude to life. In this sense it is true to say that *Der Weg
zur Form* is more than a collection of essays dealing with
the epic and dramatic forms; it is primarily a vigorous
Kampfschrift directed against the relativist outlook and
the levelling tendencies of the nineteenth century. In
other words, the type of aesthetical speculation that we
find here is the same as we find in Lessing's *Hamburgische
Dramaturgie* and in Otto Ludwig's *Shakespearestudien.* In
all three cases the writers are conducting aesthetical cam-
paigns for causes that they themselves believe to be right;
in all three cases there is an arch-enemy who must be
subdued, and whether he bears the double head of Cor-
neille/Voltaire or the single head of Schiller or Gerhart
Hauptmann, the attitude is the same and the motto is
'No quarter!'

SOME OBSERVATIONS ON JEAN PAUL

By H. C. DENEKE

THERE are times and seasons when it is of special interest to revive first-hand impressions of authors rarely read. Jean Paul has never been forgotten, but the widespread popularity once accorded to his work has gone. There is little likelihood that he will ever be reinstated as the beloved novelist of the German upper middle classes. The leisurely fashion of his day has long departed, the world into which he would lead us has suffered disenchantment and is remote. Much can be said and much has been said to break his spell. Nevertheless the spell has not faded altogether and, in view of the striking reversals accorded to his work in the nineteenth and twentieth centuries, it may seem worth while to linger over the timeless quality upon which his power rests. Creative writers amongst his compatriots have been well aware of this quality. Men of genius have responded to it and have drawn from him in one way or another, using his ideas, answering to his stimulus, finding illumination in his insight, his delicate perception, his humour, his mastery of language. And these have been very different people, from E. Th. A. Hoffmann, whom he fathered, to Heine, who owes him ideas, and notably to Keller, Raabe, and Stifter, or again to Hölderlin, the Tieck of *Franz Stern-bald*, and Novalis. In this century Stefan George—prominent among creative writers and a most fastidious critic —has associated himself with those to whom Jean Paul is timeless and taken his share in promoting a Jean Paul revival. And this by rediscovering in him the sheer poet. It is strange, perhaps, that this side should have been

neglected so long. But an explanation is not far to seek,
for Jean Paul's sentimentality remains an outstanding
fact and in the Germany of post-romantic days the danger
of baseless dreaming was a bugbear. The very intensity
of Jean Paul's appeal to his public while it lasted may well
have bred some carping criticism and heavy judgements
from certain professional teachers and literary historians,
particularly in the latter half of the nineteenth century.
His oddities and his bad habits became fair game for those
who teach style by demonstration, and for pastors and
masters intent upon tempering idealism with virility,[1] and
so current judgements upon him have not infrequently
been perfunctory. The idyllic stories and his humour
were settled into a perspective of temperate praise and
his romantic writing was passed over.

'I will tell you of a poet, one of the greatest and most
neglected, and will detach from the rich resources of his
lifework . . . some pages . . . startling in their kinship
with you of the present day', writes Stefan George[2] before
quoting a passage that he has selected to show Jean Paul's
power to express visionary things. It is a prose poem
embodying the impulses of minds that mix and mingle
in the exaltation of silent love and of great thought. A
deep mutual look, tears dropping, an eloquent eyelid
downcast, a long embrace may have prompted it some-

---

[1] Gervinus, *Geschichte der deutschen Dichtung* may be regarded as
barometric for 1844 ff., Paul Nerrlich, *Jean Paul*, for solid work towards
the rehabilitation of Jean Paul, 1876, 1889 ff. Wilhelm Dilthey, *Jean
Paul*, provides an excellent historical critical survey from notes approximately of 1906 now made accessible in *Von deutscher Dichtung und
Musik*, edited by Herman Nohl and Georg Misch, 1933.

Eduard Berend has become the chief authority on Jean Paul, especially
through his edition *Jean Pauls Sämtliche Werke, historisch-kritische
Ausgabe*, 1925 ff., and *Die Briefe Jean Pauls*, 1922 ff.

[2] Stefan George, *Gesamtausgabe der Werke*, publ. Bondi, Berlin,
vol. xvii, *Tage und Taten*, p. 60, Lobreden Jean Paul.

where in actual experience, for we are aware of these gestures remotely. But an ethereal impersonality pervades the atmosphere and in delicately graduated words there are conveyed to us impressions of sounds that swell and sigh and of radiance in sparkling light and white and blue with the associations of a temple, of tree tops, and a wonderful flower (the pledge retained from a visionary dream), birds of paradise and then the stillness of night to encircle a union of two souls. Stefan George claims Jean Paul as the true ancestor of contemporary impressionist art and it is here that his rediscovery has some revolutionary significance and that he and Wolfskehl would urge a larger circle of people to become acquainted with the 'undiscovered Jean Paul of word music and of dreams' and invite them to draw upon an impulse for poetry evinced in him more powerfully than in any other German. It is recognized that Jean Paul's novels as such have paid their toll to time, but those long left aside are here summoned to yield purple patches which are prose poems, while *Titan* is once more taken seriously. It must be admitted that impressionist art is not every one's fare, and that Stefan George's poetry itself sometimes calls for special pleading. Nevertheless, the fine lyrical quality that he has perceived in the prose-poetry of Jean Paul is not therefore a mere figment of his brain. The specimens that he and Wolfskehl have selected can stand and plead for themselves.[1]

Taking Jean Paul's writings as they stand one is con-

---

[1] See Stefan George und Karl Wolfskehl, *Deutsche Dichtung*, vol. i, Jean Paul (1900), Vorrede zur zweiten Ausgabe (1910): 'Denn um all dieses handelt es sich nicht, sondern darum, daß der noch ungesehene Jean Paul der Töne und Träume, durch diese Seiten offenbart, zum erstenmal von einer Gemeinschaft gesehen wurde, und die größte dichterische Kraft der Deutschen (nicht der größte Dichter, denn der ist Goethe) nun nicht mehr gänzlich ungenutzt daliegen muss.'

fronted with very individual work which defies pigeon-
holing. One finds oneself in the company of a personality
in the making, very complex in its impulses, and the
strangest mixture of *naïveté* and self-consciousness; a dis-
orderly mind, in its wealth, its eccentricity, its imaginative
flights, its depth, its fondness for detail, its fullness. One
thing emerges: Jean Paul is concerned with the human
soul as poets are, that is not as an abstraction but as a
living thing. His works record an impressive endeavour
to hold fast his vision and then to interpret actual life in
the light of it. And his chief novel, *Titan*, read as a whole,
is the document both of this endeavour and of its ultimate
failure, for the facts of life defy him; sustained inspiration
is denied.

The rare quality in his creative gift induces speculation
as to why it stops short as it does. This question has
frequently engaged the attention of his critics and inter-
preters and it is of high interest since it brings us face to
face with his mind. Jean Paul's mental attitude results
from his particular response to the intellectual influences
of his age, and leads him to hold a balance[1] between an
ideal world of the imagination that is revealed in dreams
and visions and a material world of sense that can be
coloured by, and so can support, the ideal world, but that
also proves a check. Full fusion of the two is, on the whole,
treason to the visionary world which links us to eternity
and must ultimately prevail. Jean Paul's intuition of the
grandeur and the high destiny of the human spirit is his
profoundest inspiration, and he has expressed it fully.
With it, too, his perception of how men fall short. For
human existence is paradoxical: 'in action how like an
angel! in apprehension how like a god!' and yet a 'quint-
essence of dust'. Perhaps the general reflection that the

---

[1] See preface to *Quintus Fixlein*.

gods often convey their rarest gifts in strange disproportion should provide us with sufficient answer to the puzzle why none of his books attains to artistic perfection as a whole. On the other hand the very profundity of his inspiration challenges the comparison with his greater contemporaries Goethe and Schiller and then of how they met the outstanding intellectual and moral problem of their time. Emotion, rediscovered and over-emphasized in the days of *Sturm und Drang*, called for reconciliation with the demands of full reason. The synthesis that was required, and that nowadays unfolds itself impressively before our eyes in the classicism of Goethe and Schiller and in the philosophy of Kant, was then in the making. Jean Paul did not attain to it, and it is arguable that, in failing to attain to it as a thinker or as a man, he also failed as an artist. Perhaps in this failure he was merely fulfilling the law of his nature. The problem of the age did not come to him as one of passion that is directed towards a great objective. It came as the need to save the belief and the high instincts which had revealed to the imaginative child Friedrich Richter his central intuition of the majesty of the human spirit. Without this, faith must die and Jean Paul's best faculty perish. He could not sacrifice the predominance of imagination. He was too intellectual and too profound to escape the influence of rationalism, which touched him first on its destructive side, and too sensitive not to respond to the age of Werther. The clash of class distinctions had entered into his soul as it did into young Schiller's. In coming to terms with the intellectual and moral problem of his time he does not fully face the difficulties but he gleans his humour. Measured by Goethe and Schiller he is seen to evade the problem by a retreat upon his own best intuition. At the hand of Kant, and upon the basis of Jacobi's philosophy, he found a foundation

for his faith in God and in immortality. The way of
this isolates him intellectually from Goethe, the naturalist
and thinker, and from Schiller, the moralist and thinker,
and from both in their artistic aim of objectivity. It
associates him intimately with Herder, the thinker and
theologian, and leaves him free to express universal human
values on his own terms. His vision of the grandeur of
man's spirit becomes in his hands the romance of poor
men in the Germany that he knew best. By immortalizing
its narrowness and its potential spirituality he expressed
experience that both Goethe and Schiller had left aside.
In this there rests his historical significance and his touch
with future generations.

Whatever may be thought of Jean Paul's novels as a
whole on artistic grounds, he finds adequate forms of his
own for things that he has to say. Among these his power
of wielding emotional tension is interesting. His imagination is strong in conceiving fruitful situations, in com-
plicating these by packing them with associations of
thought and feeling from what has gone before or pre-
monitions of what is to come. Then he unravels and
recomplicates by charging his sentences with allusions
that reach out far, or by following some change of mood
temperamentally through a set theme, while he writes
from visual impressions that are animated by what they
signify. Perhaps no writer can be more expressive. The
flutist Vult's return to his native village, unrecognized
and after long years of absence, is an instance. He left it
in disgrace, running away from paternal rule, and comes
back at dusk with the complex feelings of one who loved
the place and has hated the life there. Recollections rush
in upon him:

Draußen fand er das Dorf so voll Dämmerung, daß ihm war,
als steck' er selber wieder in der helldunkeln Kinderzeit und die

ältesten Gefühle flatterten unter den Nachtschmetterlingen. Hart
am Stege watete er durch den alten lieben Bach, worin er sonst
breite Steine aufgezogen, um eine Grundel zu greifen. Er machte
einen Bogenumweg durch ferne Bauernhöfe, um hinter den Gärten
dem Hause in den Rücken zu kommen. Endlich kam er ans Back-
ofenfenster und blickte in die breite zweiherrige Grenzstube —
keine Seele war darin, die einer schreienden Grille ausgenommen;
Türen und Fenster standen offen; aber alles war in den Stein der
Ewigkeit gehauen; der rote Tisch, die roten Wandbänke, die
runden Löffel in der hölzernen Wandleiste, um den Ofen das
Trockengerüste, der tiefe Stubenbalken mit herunterhängenden
Kalendern und Heringsköpfen, alles war über das Meer der
langen Zeit, gut eingepackt, ganz und wie neu herübergeführt,
auch die alte Dürftigkeit.

Soon he is perched in an apple-tree and peering in the
gathering darkness through the window into the brightly
lighted room where, as the description develops, he sees
how his imaginative brother Walt, the stranger on this
earth, is questioned by a local lawyer with a view to his
vocation for a notary's profession. The figures are grouped
round a table, the old father listening with the interest
of an amateur expert, the mother trying to sum up the
examiner, while Goldine, the handsome hunchbacked little
Jewess, an adopted orphan, sits knitting a red sock, all
ears. When Walt comes in, the contrast between his
idealistic enthusiasm and what is expected of him brings
the climax for the scene.

Jean Paul very frequently lifts out some central event
or some central theme and uses it so as to focus the reactions of different temperaments or characters. It is a
favourite method. In interesting instances he subtilizes
the situation by playing off emotional tension in some
person or persons against unconcern in others. At the
beginning of *Titan* the enthusiastic hero Albano is
travelling by boat across Lago Maggiore to Isola Bella.

The landscape is atmospherically pictorial and Albano's
emotions are tense. He is consciously luxuriating in his
sensations and concentrating on his intense longing to
see his lovely birthplace and meet a mysterious and unknown father. These two *motifs* of desire are drawn out
and wrought into the description of a chapter that rises
to the crest of a wave. Albano's mood is focused by his
companions. He is seated between the gentle Greek artist
Dian, who responds to his mood, and the caustic German
humorist Schoppe, who sees beyond it and furnishes perspective. Dian ties a black scarf over Albano's eyes so as
to give him the joy of one grand impression on reaching
the island, Schoppe the educationist had informed recent
inquirers after this striking youth

mit einer närrischen Quadratur seines Runzel-Zirkels um die
Lippen weitläufig . . . mein Telemach ist's und ich mache den
Mentor dabei—ich bin die Rändelmaschine und der Prägstock,
der ihn münzt—der Glättzahn und die Plattmühle, die ihn bohnt
—der Mann der ihn regelt.

Another time in *Titan*, Jean Paul has a scene which
grows to its climax as those concerned in it listen to music.
It is at the court of a petty prince where all high instincts of
the soul are quelled and we know that it is against a background of scheming elders that the young people there
dream their visionary dreams of romance. We are made
aware of a setting such as Wieland uses when he presents
nymphs and cupids and garlands in the stylized scenery
of rococo days with temples, groves, and fountains.
What is decorative setting in clear outline to Wieland
gives to Jean Paul nodal points for a musical description
in which setting is surcharged with feeling. In the ducal
pleasure gardens at Lilar, with their chestnut avenue,
the stone figures, the grotto fitted with bewildering mirrors, the marvellous moving staircase and the waterworks

that can be turned on to play sprays as a surprise, a group
of young people are taking a walk. We know the complex
cross-currents of feelings and loyalties between them,
particularly for the idealistic hero Albano and his delicate
lover Liane, shadowy as she is, yet articulate in music.
And there are Princess Julienne, bringing well-bred ease,
and Rabette, Albano's foster-sister, a raw country girl,
and baby Helena, Dian's little girl, with childlike impulses and gestures, and Roquairol the cynic, Liane's
brother, Albano's friend, the smirk of whose bows and
the swish of whose coat-tails strike a false note when he
first walks past the Princess. A visit to a little room by
the waterworks is suggested. It holds a musical instrument made of glass, where the player can sit concealed,
and there Liane takes her seat. Above, on the bridge, a
fine red sunset gilds the listeners as she plays and makes
the spraying water sparkle in gold. With the description
of the sound, the light and the colours there are subtly
conveyed the sentiments of all and of each present, Albano's
love *motif*, moody and half in longing and in passionate
discontent, Roquairol in cool detachment as he turns on
the waterworks, Princess Julienne, anxious that all should
feel comfortable with one another, little Helena quite
unperturbed, as she drops her auriculas into the rushing
water for the pleasure of seeing them washed away. Rabette is surprised into distress by the sudden revelation of
beauty and of feeling hitherto unknown. Rushing below
to embrace Liane, the madonna-like, impersonal player,
she is soon joined by Albano whose mood has been broken
and the music in its suggestion of superhuman things
becomes the focus for a union of souls. The effect of such
a description must be found in Jean Paul's text, no mere
account of the situation can render it. A setting like
Wieland's has been used for purposes beyond Wieland's

range of clear outline, witty contrast, and good sense, for
Jean Paul's description has learnt from the Werther tradition, where figures and landscape blend with mood, and
it has been influenced by the luminous radiance of Wilhelm Meister. But his touch is not Goethe's nor his
effects. He lacks Goethe's objectivity, the creator's gift
to withdraw while his creatures pursue or seem to pursue
a life of their own.

Something more akin to objectivity enters into a scene
from low-life in which Jean Paul uses his gift for contrasting types of people not in their sensitiveness to exalted
emotional tension but in their reaction to a central event
of a humorous kind. It is an exploit of Count Albano,
at the age of eleven or twelve on the estate of his guardian,
Wehrfritz, at Blumenbühl. The little boy is suspended
in mid-air on a bird-pole, hanging, slung by a rope round
his middle, in the upper branches of a tall tree. The
farm-hands, who will do anything for him, have been
persuaded to raise him up there by the pulley-arrange-
ment of the pole. A company of anxious, responsible
grown-ups collects below. The proud, defiant little boy,
every inch a miniature prince, threatens to cut himself
down if they interfere with him. The farm-hands enjoy
the joke. Meanwhile the impotent tutor, Wehmaier,
passes from stage to stage of nervous terror moving in
Jean-Paulean phraseology from the 'Plongierbad des Eis-
schauers über die Kühnheit' to the 'Tropfbad des Angst-
schweißes über die Gefahr'; he fears his pupil will be
dashed into twenty-six atoms like Osiris, or the thirty
that were once Venus of Medici, and all this when the
young devil was getting on so well in languages and likely
to bring credit upon his teaching! So the caricature of a
tutor is torn between fear and vexation when a carriage
appears containing Wehrfritz. This man, a counterpart

of our country squire of old, is an unstylized humorous character and well drawn in the scenes where he appears; non-self-conscious, downright, blustering, true to life, an honourable *Hausvater*, decent in his dealings and averse to the sophistications of courtiers, fond of his charge and afraid to show it too much. He is simply outraged at the indignity of the situation. It was the boy's birthday, he himself has arrived with the gift of a piano and has brought a teacher with him; there was to have been a pleasant ceremony. And he thumps at the window of the closed carriage and breaks it. But the driver has his eye on the little boy. He explains that the key of the carriage-door is lost (actually it is in his pocket), jumps on the box and drives off to the nearest locksmith. Then Albano, getting tired, allows himself to be lowered at his tutor's orders and is told to report to his guardian. Once more the full flavour of the scene depends on what comes before and after and on Jean Paul's words.

The famous scene at the beginning of the *Flegeljahre*, where co-legatees are assembled to hear the will of van der Kabel read, is similarly constructed in principle. The sheer invention of so fruitfully absurd a situation as arises from the clause that demands from the legatee spontaneous tears shed within exactly half an hour by the clock, would stamp Jean Paul as great among the world's humorists. As an artist in episodic characterization and in expressive grouping Jean Paul cannot easily be matched for the rare combination of wit, delicate perception, and poetic radiance.

The nearest approach to constructive character development is his presentation of Roquairol the villain in *Titan*, on whom he has bestowed care, since he intended him to typify a man who became a victim to the special temptations of that age. The novel was to be an argument against the exaggerated passions which the age of *Sturm und*

Drang discovered and the young romantics cultivated, and, inasmuch as Jean Paul's experience led him to such condemnation, he was approximating to Goethe's view and was consciously marking disagreement with the romantics. Roquairol, 'mixed ethereal and mud', was possessed of qualities that in juxtaposition always intrigued Jean Paul. His imagination was seized by what is sinister in such a figure—its suavity, its unexpected violence—and by the contrast with the radiance that is showered upon Albano and the women. He can go as far as the threshold to view such a soul, can place it in relation to its opposite and point to its destructiveness. Taken as a whole this character leaves the impression of a fine sketch that degenerates into caricature. Perhaps a realist method alone could have made Roquairol convincing. Jean Paul fails to give him flesh and blood, the archangel ruined whom we hoped to know ends as a melodramatic cad. The whole of Jean Paul's plot and of his thesis carries no conviction and is, in some ways, curiously outrageous. Tragedy remains outside his range and for moral issues he is capable of using a light-hearted and perfunctory pen.

The phenomenon of Jean Paul's hold over his readers cuts into the social history of his day. He was no revolutionary, but he exploits to the full the impulses of defiance for privilege that rests on descent or cash, or office, or acres. The actual world disgusts him and seems sound only with those in humble station whom he sees as one who has suffered their wrongs and lived among them. His own escape from the checks imposed by a stark matter-of-fact world had been through the world of mind. The ethereal world of enchantment that he had created had exercised a magical attraction upon passive discontents, aristocratic ladies who lived in bondage, mostly with unloved husbands and in complete economic dependence,

thwarted in their finer feelings and intellectual aspirations. These failed to distinguish between Jean Paul and
Johann Paul Friedrich Richter just as he failed to distinguish between dreams of souls in love and the women
who helped to prompt these dreams. On analogous lines
in the nineteenth century we might perhaps account for
his popularity among middle-class readers of the Biedermeier age, who, being shut out from the opportunities
that a wider public and social life offers, withdrew into
themselves and home life. Much of this popularity was
due to his direct appeal to German sentiment in its combination of idealistic flights and the search for poetry in
trivial things. His choice of hero attaches to the Parzival
tradition surviving in the figure of a youth unspotted by
the world and slow to learn its ways. Here, too, he is
writing from impulses ingrained in the nation.

Humour and pathos blend in him in a way that is
wholly his own. Perhaps it is hardly true to say that Jean
Paul develops progressively when he has once found himself. But he learns as a writer and improves in the skill
with which he summons old impulses. In his last novel,
Die Flegeljahre, the perspective is widened on the idyllic
and narrowed on the romantic side by the creation of the
immortal twins: Walt, the dreamer, and Vult, the man of
the world, the very opposites of one another but united
by close ties of affection. Again these figures must not
be measured by a realist standard, again the development
that he had in mind for them fails in that it was never
carried out, but in their imaginative setting they are alive,
for each is a side of Jean Paul himself. Their disagree-
ments and reconciliations call forth some of his best and
most characteristic moments, so once more the delightful
little scene in which pent-up anger and penitence dissolve
into the tenderness and humour of Vult plaiting an absurd

and humiliated Walt's pigtail. It implies knowledge of
the complex psychology and situations which led Vult
to persuade his transparent brother to assume a disguise
and act on false pretences. The whole has misfired. The
disguise has been gently removed by Vult. A few lines
may give a flavour of the situation which is developed in
Jean Paul's best manner.

Als Vult im Mondlicht dem betrübten Schelm das dünne Nan-
kingröckchen wie einen Gehenkten am Aufhängbändchen hinlangt'
und er es überhaupt überlegte, wie lächerlich der Bruder mit dem
Korkwams der Verkleidung auf dem Trocknen sitzen geblieben,
so dauerte ihn der getäuschte Mensch in seinen weiten Steifstiefeln
unsäglich, und ihm brach mitten im Lächeln das Herz in zwei
Stücke von—Tränen entzwei. 'Ich will dir'—sagt' er, sich hinter
ihn wie hinter ein Schießpferd stellend—'das Zöpflein machen.—
Nimm aber das Zopfband zwischen die Zähne, das eine Ende!'

It is because of his inveterate idealism that idyllic
moments, one way or another, are his best, for in these
he can best wield the facts of life to suit his outlook.
A Wuz or a Lenette are true to life and are idealists
because of a besetting notion that disregards all obstacles,
Wuz in his temperamental optimism, Lenette in her
relentless energy for keeping her house spick and span;
in them and many others humour is quite unconscious;
the conscious humorists, Leibgeber and Schoppe, bring
Jean Paul's own perspective and are restlessly torn between a haunting idealism that they wish almost forcibly
to impose upon life, and a baffling impotence. Vult, the
last of the conscious humorists and the simplest, has
abandoned such a struggle and turned a laughing rogue
except perhaps in his music and certainly in his love and
protection of his brother Walt, the dreamer, which makes
him human. Before the fact of Walt who can believe no
ill of any one and take no evidence about the ways of

men in life, Vult's cynicism ceases. The story remains a fragment, but no end could be finer than the fragmentary one by which Vult, since his attempt to shield and mould his brother has brought him face to face with a hopeless tangle, gets up from their bed and leaves him. Walt, lost to the world, is meanwhile recounting to him, in fine prose poetry, his marvellous dream of last night, while Vult goes off into the world as it is, piping, piping in receding sounds as he goes. We are left with Walt, the dreamer.

Jean Paul made the most of his gifts and his greatness stands. What there is of weakness has remarkable psychological and historical interest and it is incident to his strength.

LUTWIN'S LATIN SOURCE

By A. C. DUNSTAN

FOR some years Professor Eis has occupied himself with the study of Middle High German religious verse, and has been able to show that the Sudetenland has been active in this branch of literature. In his *Beiträge zur mittelhochdeutschen Legende und Mystik*[1] he examines Lutwin's *Adam und Eva*, and reaches the conclusion that the language of the poem points to Sudetenland. He finds documentary evidence that the name Lutwin is known in this district, and sees Lutwin's source in the Latin *Vita Adam et Evae*, which is contained in two of the manuscripts of the *Magnum Legendarium Austriacum* (referred to as MLA.). Eis edits this Latin text for the first time.[2] Thus Eis sees in the source further evidence pointing to Sudetenland as the home of Lutwin's poem.

The evidence that Lutwin's poem is based on the MLA., or on a version of the *Vita* very close to MLA., rather than on any other version of the *Vita* is not conclusive, as the present paper tries to show.

We now have the following printed Latin texts of the *Vita Adam et Evae*: W. Meyer edited a text based on a number of manuscripts in Munich and one in Paris.[3] He divided his manuscripts into three classes (referred to as Meyer I, &c.). J. H. Mozley edited a text based on twelve manuscripts found in various English libraries.[4] Eis edited a text based on the two manuscripts of the

---

[1] *Germanische Studien*, Heft 161, Berlin, 1935.
[2] Ibid., pp. 241–55.
[3] *Abhandlungen d. Bayer. Akad. d. Wiss.* xiv Bd., 1878.
[4] *The Journal of Theological Studies*, vol. xxx, no. 118, 1929.

MLA. already mentioned. L. Katona published a text based on two incunabula.[1]

There are various Middle English versions of the story, which serve to check the Latin texts.[2]

In attempting to discover the source of a work we must accept as the best evidence common errors. The next evidence, not so reliable, is afforded by peculiar readings. Common omissions come last.

When we examine Lutwin's poem and the various groups of Latin texts we find that Lutwin and MLA. have one error only in common. This is found in the passage in which Satan upbraids Eve. Some of Meyer's MSS., § 38, read: 'nunc autem non potes portare si tibi incepero exprobrare', some of Mozley's have a similar reading, whilst the MLA. reads: 'nunc autem non potes portare Seth', which fully accounts for Lutwin:

> Mahtu nit uff dinem kragen
> Dinen sun von hynnen tragen. (ll. 2557–8.)

To balance this there is one error common to Mozley and Lutwin. Where Satan, in the form of a serpent, attacks Seth, Meyer, § 37, reads: 'ecce subito venit serpens bestia et impetum faciens morsit Seth', MLA. has a similar reading, but some of Mozley's MSS. read: 'subito uenit serpens bestia impietatis et faciem Seth momorsit',[3] which accounts for Lutwin:

> Die selbe tufeliche slange
> Beis Sed durch ein wange. (ll. 2535–6.)

[1] *Magyar Tudomanos Akad.*, köt. 18, sz. 10, 1904.

[2] *Canticum de Creatione*, edit. K. Horstmann, *Anglia*, i. Bd., 1878; *Altenglische Legenden*, ed. K. Horstmann, Heilbronn, 1878; *Archiv f. d. Stud. d. n. Spr.*, lxxiv. Bd., *The Wheatley Manuscript* (E.E.T.S., No. 155), edited Mabel Day, 1921.

[3] The Middle English versions agree, e.g.: 'sodenly ther come an eddre, a foule best with-oute pite, as it were a fende, and boote Seeth wykkedly in the face' (*Archiv f. d. Stud. d. n. Spr.*, lxxiv. Bd., p. 351).

The evidence given by peculiar readings is limited also to one clear case as far as MLA. is concerned. The Latin texts of Meyer and of Mozley, § 51, tell us that Eve was buried 'cum magno fletu', but the MLA. reading 'cum magno festo' is followed by Lutwin:

> Die kint noment zu hant
> Ire muter und begyngent ir
> Begrebede mit grosser zier
> Und mit grossen hochziten. (ll. 3626–9.)

To balance this again there are two peculiar readings in Mozley's MSS. which are found in Lutwin. In MLA. and Meyer, Seth embraces the dead body of his father, § 46: 'et cum esset Seth amplexans corpus patris sui lugens desuper', but some of Mozley's MSS. read: 'Cum autem Seth et mater eius Eua amplexati essent corpus Ade et luxissent super illud', which is followed by Lutwin:

> Mit grossem jomer umbefingen
> Seth und das arme wip
> Adam den doten lip. (ll. 2988–90.)

According to MLA. and Meyer God gives Adam into Michael's custody, § 47: 'Tunc vidit Seth manum Domini extensam tenentem Adam. Et tradidit Michaheli dicens: Sit in custodia tua . . .', whilst in Mozley God gives Adam's soul:[1] 'Tunc . . . animam patris sui tenentem . . ., Sit hec anima in c. t. . . .', which Lutwin follows:

> Er leit sine götliche hant
> Uff das houbet Adams sele
> Er entpfalch sü sant Mychahele. (ll. 3127–9.)

There are two omissions which MLA. shares with Lutwin. Satan is ordered to adore Adam, who is described

---

[1] This is found in the English translations also: 'God tok Adam soule, þat Seth it seiʒe,/& bitok it seyn Miʒhel . . .' (Horstmann, *Altenglische Legenden*, l. 546 f.).

in Meyer, § 14, as 'imaginem dei Jehova', in MLA. as 'imaginem Dei', which is followed by Lutwin:

> Der gebildet ist nach got. (l. 1399.)

But Mozley's reading 'ymaginem Domini Dei' is fairly close to that of MLA., and the English *Canticum de Creatione* reading: 'To gon and worschipen godis ymage' (l. 268) considerably weakens any claim on the part of MLA.[1]

Another omission is found in the passage in which Eve addresses the serpent. Meyer, § 37, reads: 'Et dixit Eva ad serpentem voce magna', MLA. omits *voce magna*, as does Lutwin:

> Eva zu der slangen sprach:
> 'Ach verfluchtete slange . . .' (ll. 2540–1.)

But though Mozley reads *uoce magna*, and some of the English translations follow this reading, the words are omitted in the *Cant. de Cr.*: 'To þe addre seide she þo:/ 'sey, þow cursede beste' (11.647–8.).

Here again to balance MLA. there are omissions common to Mozley and Lutwin. In Meyer, § 21, and MLA. twelve angels and two virtues help Eve at the birth of Cain, but one of Mozley's MSS., viz. Winchester MS., and Katona's text omit the two virtues,[2] which accounts for Lutwin:

> E das er die wort gesprach,
> Zwölff engel er by yme sach,
> Die hette got dar gesant. (ll. 1770–2.)

We find, therefore, that the evidence in favour of MLA. is balanced by the evidence in favour of Mozley's

---

[1] *Ein deutsches Adambuch*, ed. H. Vollmer, Hamburg, 1908, reads (verse): 'pit Gotes pild an' (p. 12).

[2] L. Horstmann, *Altenglische Legenden*, has 'twelve angelus', omitting the virtues (p. 224). So also *Ein deutsches Adambuch*: 'darnach vnlang kamen zu ir zwelff engl' (p. 15).

text as far as common errors, peculiar readings, and
striking omissions are concerned.

Eis makes out a list of parallels between MLA. and
Lutwin which are not to be found in Meyer. But an
examination of Mozley's text shows that these parallels
are not peculiar to MLA. and Lutwin. Thus, whereas
in Meyer, § 5, Adam is to do penance, the MLA. expresses
Eve's resolve to do penance: 'Domine mi, quantum
cogitasti peniteo, quod ego induxi tibi laborem et tribu-
lationem.' This appears in Lutwin:

> Davon, Adam, sage mir,
> Was wiltu nemen zu büsse dir,
> Durch das ich gesundet han?
> Du hast daran nit missetan:
> Dye büsse sol ich alleine han. (ll. 986–90.)

But Mozley's Balliol Coll. 228. reads: 'Sed tu Domini
mi quod cogitastis me penitere penitebo . . .', and Queen's
Coll. 213: 'D. mi iudica mihi debeam penitere . . .'.

When Adam was borne to Paradise angels stood by
the chariot according to Meyer, § 25: 'et multa milia
angelorum erant a dextris et sinistris currus illius.' In the
MLA. *currus* is omitted, as in Lutwin:

> Ouch sach ich by den ziten
> Zu der rehten und lincken siten
> Engel manig tusent schar. (ll. 2180–2.)

But MLA. is not alone in omitting *currus*. Most of
Mozley's MSS.[1] omit the word, and the Balliol MS.
shows still more clearly that the angels are on the right
and left of God, not of the chariot: 'a dextris et sinistris
maiestatis sue.'

In Meyer's text the angels who sided with Lucifer

---

[1] *The Wheatley Manuscript* also omits *currus* (p. 89). Also *Archiv*:
'another companye of aungeles beyng on the right syde & on his lefte
syde (p. 349).

were lower in rank, § 15: 'hoc audientes ceteri qui sub
me erant angeli', whereas in MLA. *sub me* is omitted.
Thus Lutwin:

> Das hörten etliche engel do,
> Die volgeten mir ie so. (ll. 1423–4.)

But Mozley has 'qui sunt mecum' in some manuscripts.[1]
Eis finds that *ire* disturbs the metre in line 3617:

> Hiemitte sü von bette gie,
> Sü viel an ire baren knie
> Und reichet ire hende hin ze got. (ll. 3615–7.)

and attributes it to MLA.: 'Tunc Eva expandit manus
suas orans et inclinans genua in terram.' Here Meyer,
§ 50, has *manus* for *manus suas*. But *suas* is not peculiar
to MLA., Mozley has: 'expandit manus *suas* et respiciens
in celum inclinans genua *sua* in terra.'[2]

Another slight parallel between MLA. and Lutwin is
to be found in the passage in which God reproves Adam
for obeying his wife instead of God. Meyer, § 26, reads:
'quia plus audisti vocem uxoris tuae', whilst MLA. has
prius for *plus*, which can account for Lutwin:

> Der hastu vor mich
> Gefolget, das weis ich. (ll. 2209–10.)

This slight parallel in favour of MLA. may be balanced
by three in favour of Mozley's text. Lutwin tells us that
the devil, disguised as an angel, led Eve:

> Der tüfel in engels cleit
> Furte Evam by der hant. (ll. 1266–7.)

---

[1] Inferiority is absent also in *The Wheatley Manuscript* (p. 84) and the
Cant. de Cr. reads: 'þo alle þe angel herden þis / þat fellen with me out of
blis' (ll. 283–4). Also *Ein deutsches Adambuch* (verse): 'daz sprachen auch
die gesellen mein / die mit mir von himel geschaiden sein' (p. 12).

[2] *The Wheatley Manuscript* agrees: 'hir hondis' (p. 97), also *Cant. de
Cr.*: 'and op here hondis hild' (l. 915), also *Ein deutsches Adambuch*: 'auff
ire knie vnd rechte ire hent' (p. 27).

MLA. and Meyer, § 10, read only: 'erexit eam diabolus
et perduxit eam ad Adam', whilst Mozley's Winchester
MS. has *angelus i. diabolus* and the Balliol MS. *angelus
s. diabolus.*

Another minor parallel between Mozley and Lutwin
occurs in the passage:

> Do Eva reht hat vernomen,
> Das sü also betrogen was
> Von dem leiden Satanas (ll. 1298–1300.)

Here MLA. and Meyer, § 11, read: 'cognovit, quod
diabolus suasit exire de flumine', but Mozley: 'cognovit
q. d. *seduxit* eam et de flumine exire persuasit.' That
Lutwin's *betrogen* translates *seduxit* is suggested by the
line:

> Wie bistu ander stunt betrogen (l. 1290.)

which translates Meyer, § 10, 'quomodo iterum seducta
es'.

A further parallel between Mozley and Lutwin is to
be found in the passage:

> Adam usz dem Jordan
> Mit zorn rieff den tüfel an
> Owe, du böser geist . . .' (ll. 1310–2.)

Here MLA. and most of Meyer's MSS. ascribe the
speech to Eve, § 11: 'Eva cecidit . . . et exclamavit dicens:
Ve tibi . . . ', whilst Mozley's MSS., with two of Meyer's,
give the speech, as in Lutwin, to Adam: 'Adam excla-
mauit dicens, Ve tibi . . .'

Eis shows that twelve passages in Lutwin must be
based on a text common to Meyer I and MLA. Of these
twelve passages seven are to be found in Mozley.[1] The
passages not found in Mozley are 1048–50, 2238–40,

---

[1] These passages are: 2124–8, 2146–8, 2231–5, 2241–5, 2375–81,
2579–82, 2623–4.

2265, 2618–19, 3158–63; but even here Mozley's MSS. contain elements found in Lutwin, which do not occur in Meyer I and MLA. Thus Lutwin tells us that the fishes remained still during Adam's repentance:

> Do er die wort volsprach,
> Zu hant er die vische umb sich sach
> Stille ston unt nit fliessen. (ll. 1048–50.)

This agrees with MLA. and Meyer I, § 8: 'Statim omnia animantia venerunt et circumdederunt eum ex aqua Iordanis et steterunt ab illa hora non agentes cursum suum.' In Mozley the river stops: 'et aqua fluminis stetit in illa hora.'

But Lutwin tells us:

> In leide kerte er sinen synn;
> Er rüff mit klegelicher stymme
> Und mit jomers gryme . . . (ll. 1035–8.)

This is to be found in Mozley: 'et rauce facte sunt fauces (*v.l.* uoces) eius', but is absent in MLA. and Meyer.

Further Lutwin tells us that Adam summoned the fishes to mourn with him, and they came and mourned:

> Ach, Iordan, ich sage dir,
> Du solt helffen klagen mir.
> Samene, was in dir swebe
> Und naturlichen lebe,
> Vysch und was swymendes sy,
> Das sü mir stont klagende by. (ll. 1038–43.)

and the fishes came:

> Und gebarten dem gliche,
> Sam in leit umb in were;
> Und klageten sin swere,
> Der do stunt gnaden lere. (ll. 1053–6.)

MLA. and Meyer I, § 8, contain ll. 1038–43: 'Et dixit Adam: Tibi dico, aqua Iordanis, condole mihi et congrega

mihi omnia natantia, quae in te sunt et circumdent me ac
lugeant pariter mecum', but do not contain ll. 1053–56.
Mozley's text contains both passages: 'Tunc dixit Adam,
Tibi dico Iordanis . . . et lugite mecum . . . lugentes (*v.l.*
lugencia) erant omnia animancia cum Adam.'

Eis[1] remarks that Lutwin's ll. 1053–56 (viz. how the
fishes obeyed Adam's summons) can be derived from
Adam's summons to the fishes. It is, however, not
necessary so to derive them, since Mozley supplies both
passages. Lutwin seems to have followed in this section
a text containing two elements from MLA. and Meyer I,
and two elements from Mozley.[2]

In one case the difference between MLA. and Meyer
on the one hand and Mozley on the other is slight, but
nevertheless striking. Lutwin says:

> Ein kunig gar so mynneclich,
> Gottes sun Jesu Christ. (ll. 2618–19.)

for which MLA. and Meyer, § 42, offer 'amantissimus
rex Christus filius dei', whilst Mozley omits *rex*.

Another parallel between MLA., Meyer, and Lutwin
concerns the healing of Seth:

> Der tüfel sprach: 'ich vare von dir,
> Als du hast geboten mir'.
> Hiemitte er von yme verswant.
> Seth wart gesunt zu hant. (ll. 2579–82.)

MLA. and Meyer I, § 39, read: 'et dixit bestia ad Seth:

---

[1] Op. cit., p. 79.

[2] *Cant. de Cr.* contains the summons (ll. 148–53), the hoarse voice
and obedience to the summons (ll. 172–4): 'þanne seyde Adam to Jordan:
Water . . . Gadere alle þe fisches . . . To helpen me make mone . . . his
voys wax hors, his cheke sor. / and alle þe bestis þat weren þor / ffor him
sorweden alle.' *Ein deutsches Adambuch* also contains the summons, and
how the fishes obeyed it: 'das sich in dir gesamen dy visch vnd klaine tier,
dy helffen all klagen vmb mich . . . auch sah er her swimmen dy creaturen
vnd vmb in kläglich geparen' (p. 8).

ecce recedo, sicut dixisti, a facie imaginis dei. Statim
recessit plaga de dentibus a Seth.' Mozley has 'Ecce
recedo . . . et statim recessit et Seth plagatum dentibus
dimisit', which is against line 2582,[1] but, on the other
hand, has *ut iussisti*, which covers line 2280 better than
sicut dixisti, and *et statim recessit*, referring to Satan, which
explains line 2581,[2] left unexplained in MLA. and Meyer.

Lutwin has a long passage (ll. 3207–3307) on Adam's
burial. In the manuscripts of Meyer and of Mozley
Paradise (Meyer III: Calvary) is given as Adam's burial
place. Lutwin does not name the burial place. MLA.
reads: 'Et sepelierunt Adam et Abel Michahel et Urihel
angeli portis paradysi videntibus Seth et matre eius.' Eis
sees MLA. influence here, but Lutwin names the angels
Mychahel and Gabriel. Further Lutwin tells us that the
angels brought '*Zwey* snewise rehte cleit' (l. 3217),
whilst MLA. reads: '*tres* sindones bissinos.' That Lutwin's source differed from MLA. is proved by the
English translation 'God comaundet tweyn angelus to
bringe *twey* cloþes . . . þat on to do vppon Adam and þat
oþer to don vppon Abel, his sone'.[3]

Eis sees in:

> Das grüne oleyboumes riss
> Das uss dem paradis
> By dem engel was gesant,
> Das trug ein engel in der hant,
> Bis das grab was bereit;
> Daryn wart Adam geleit
> Und sin lieber sun Abel. (ll. 3235–42.)

evidence that Adam was buried outside Paradise. This

---

[1] Mozley's Balliol MS. reads: 'et recessit placata sensibus', which looks
like a bad attempt at *plaga de dentibus*.

[2] *Cant. de Cr.* is similar: 'I wil don as þow me bed, / ffro þe now gynne
y te' / and vanschede out of here siȝt.' (ll. 683–5.)

[3] Horstmann, *Altengl. Leg.*, p. 226.

evidence is not conclusive since Katona's text reads:
'dixit Adam filio suo Seth, Numquid misit mihi angelus
Domini aliquid? Respondit Seth, Misit tibi angelus
ramusculum trium foliorum . . .', and this branch which
was sent out of Paradise some time before Adam's death,
was planted at Adam's head, as Katona's text shows:
'Seth uero filius eius plantauit ramum ad caput patris sui.'

Eis sees in MLA. the main, but not the only source of
Lutwin's poem, 'Lutwin hat ausserdem bestimmt auch
einen Text der Gruppe Meyer III gekannt, wie drei
Stellen beweisen'. The Latin manuscripts hitherto printed,
however, do not cover the whole of Lutwin's poem, and
there is no need to assume that Lutwin had more than
one version of the *Vita* before him. There is one striking
passage, dealing with Satan's fall (ll. 1407–15 and
1442–7), which is very similar to a portion of the *Vita*
which has been incorporated in the *Gospel of Bartho-
lomew*,[1] and Lutwin's source must have contained this.

Another passage in Lutwin which no known Latin
version of the *Vita* has supplied concerns Abel's body,
which remained above the ground without rotting:

> Und der rehtikeit hort
> Abel, der uff dem velde dort
> Manig jare was dot gelegen,
> Dem sunne, wint nach der regen
> Nie geschadet umb ein har. (ll. 3221–5.)

Since this occurs in Armenian translations of the *Vita*[2] we
can assume that Lutwin found it in his source. This is

---

[1] Latin text edited by Moricca in *Revue biblique*, Paris and Rome,
Oct. 1921. See pp. 512–13 for the passage referred to.

[2] See E. Preuschen, *Die apokryphen gnostischen Adamschriften aus dem
Armenischen übersetzt* (Festschrift B. Stade, Gießen, 1900). We are told
that the earth would not receive Abel after Cain had murdered him
(p. 184), and 'Sein Leib bleibt unverweslich und ohne von den Würmern
zerfressen zu werden' (p. 198).

made the more certain by its inclusion in a Middle English translation.[1]

The omissions in the various versions of the *Vita* are often striking. Jagic tells us that the Slavonic version, of which he examined nine manuscripts, omits Satan's own story of his fall, but he shows that it is known in Slavonic.[2] Although this important part is omitted, the making of Adam from eight parts, and the naming of Adam from the stars visited by the angels are included, as in Mozley's Balliol MS. Mozley's Winchester MS. omits everything between §§ 25 and 33.

Eis assumes that Lutwin went directly to the Bible for some of his material, e.g. the crime and punishment of Cain (ll. 1908–52 and 1995–2100), 'dass er nicht etwa die biblischen Berichte in einer Schrift schon verarbeitet vorfand, sondern sie selbstständig nachschlug, geht aus seinen wiederholten Hinweisen auf die Genesis hervor, wie 212 f. und 1908'.[3] But Biblical passages are found in some of the Middle English translations, and Meyer remarks that one of his Latin manuscripts, viz. 3, contains three chapters from the Vulgate, at the beginning and a passage (on Cain) between §§ 23 and 24.[4] Mozley's Balliol MS. also expands the story of Cain. This suggests that Lutwin found his material in the *Vita* used by him. His reference to Genesis may not prove more than that he knew that the matter was to be found there, too.[5] In some

---

[1] *Cant. de Cr.*: 'ȝete lay Abel aboue erþe' (l. 573).

[2] *Slavische Beiträge zu den biblischen Apocryphen. Denkschriften d. kais. Akad. d. Wiss.*, philo-hist. Kl. Wien. 1893, pp. 45–9.

[3] Op. cit., p. 87.

[4] *Abh. d. bayr. Akad. d. Wiss.* Bd. 16, Abth. 2, München, 1882, p. 210.

[5] Some translators were more ignorant. Thus *Cant. de Cr.* (Ed. MS.) reads: 'And as we finden in lecture / Y wot not wheþer it be in holy scripture' (ll. 49–50).

cases one may suspect metrical and rime requirements,[1]
e.g.:

> Das dirte wasser Tygris
> Also uns Genesis
> Das buch kundet sunder wan. (ll. 211–13.)

Mozley's Balliol MS. begins with the creation of Adam
from eight parts, proceeds to the naming of Adam
(Anatalim, Disis, Archtos, Mensembrios), contains a long
passage on the rivers springing from Paradise (Gyon,
Physon, Tygris, Eufrates), has a long passage on Cain,
and works the legend of the Holy Rood into the *Vita* to
make a unity. Lutwin's poem is certainly not based
directly on the text of the Balliol MS., but since the
Balliol MS. contains these elements in common with
Lutwin one may assume that Lutwin worked on a *Vita*
which also contained these elements.

To give in detail a comparison between Lutwin's poem
and all the Middle English translations would occupy too
much space. A short comparison of Lutwin and one of
these versions (MS. Vernon 393)[2] shows some interesting
parallels. The English version begins before the Creation:
'þer nas no þing þat was quik' (Lutwin: 'Do niht was und
nieman lebete', l. 98), and the 'holigost . . . wiþouten
beginning, & schal be wiþouten endyng' (Lutwin: 'Die
lebetent in der eynikeit / Vor der welte one angenge',
ll. 85–6; 'Aber er one tougen swebete / Unsegelich in
der gotheit / Mit der ewen ewikeit', ll. 99–101). God
made heaven and earth (Lutwin, ll. 128–38). In Paradise
'þe murþe þat þer-inne is, non eorþlich may hit telle no
seo' (Lutwin: 'Das paradis so wunnesam / Das heisset
wol der wunne gart, / Wanne so schönes nie nit wart, /

---

[1] Cp. also line 148: 'des mahtent uns die buch gewis', where a rime for
the (missing) *Dysis* is required.

[2] Horstmann, *Altengl. Legenden*, pp. 220–6.

Das sich yme glichen müge, / Nach zu sprechen dar zu
tüge / Von menschlichem synne', ll. 133–8); the rivers
Fyson, &c. (Lutwin, ll. 154–222); creation of Adam and
naming of Adam from the stars (Lutwin, ll. 139–53);
God created Eve 'of Adam's ribbe' (Lutwin, ll. 226–76);
in the absence of the guardian angels Satan tempts Eve,
who tempts Adam (Lutwin, ll. 392–533); Adam and
Eve banished from Paradise (Lutwin, ll. 534–838). Then
follows the *Vita* proper.

Some further points of likeness may be mentioned.
Adam made a house, 'swinke he most & trauaylen, & Eve
moste spynne' (Lutwin, 'Wie Adam hacken und Eva
spynnen mustent', heading to p. 25); the story of Cain
at length; the burial of Adam and Abel, 'God comaundet
tweyn angelus to bringe twey[1] cloþes . . . þat on to do
vppon Adam, and þat oþer to do vppon Abel his sone'
(Lutwin: 'Mit zwein engeln . . . Das sü balde brahten
dar / Zwey[1] snewise rehte cleit / . . . Der here Adam
gedecket mitte / . . . Und . . . Abel', ll. 3212–22).

It may be noted that the *Canticum de Creatione* (Edin.
MS.) ends, like Lutwin's poem, with Noah, and for the
same reason, viz. the story of Adam is carried down to
the common parents of us all, which makes a good conclusion. It suggests that the Latin sources used by Lutwin
and the English translator also ended here.

The above analysis shows that no case can be made out
for regarding the Latin text of the MLA. as the special
type of the *Vita* used by Lutwin. Lutwin's poem contains
much that is common to the texts of Meyer, Mozley, and
MLA., and contains a little found only in each one of these
three groups. The evidence of other translations, e.g. the
Middle English versions, suggests that Lutwin found in his
source matter contained in none of the printed Latin texts.

[1] All the printed Latin texts read *three*.

LUTHER: EXEGESIS AND PROSE STYLE

By WALTER ETTINGHAUSEN

THERE have been isolated attempts[1] to belittle the
virtues of Luther's prose style, though critics in the
main have at all times recognized its unique quality.[2]
This recognition, extended to Luther even by some who
oppose him in point of doctrine,[3] has often been accompanied by puzzlement and by a feeling that facts essential
to a final judgement of his style are still wanting.[4] And
to the corollary—a natural demand for further research—
there has been unstinting if varied response.

We have, on the one hand, well-stocked ossuaries,[5]
which seem, for all their worth and pioneering spirit, to
have carried us not very far in the right direction. It may
be our own fault that we have not achieved more where

[1] e.g. V. Hasak, *Der christliche Glaube des deutschen Volkes*, Regensburg, 1868; F. Pfeiffer's collection of pre-Lutheran 'Predigtmärlein' in
Germania, iii (1858), p. 409; J. M. Lenhart, 'Luther's Indebtedness to
the Catholic Bible', *The Fortnightly Review*, St. Louis, Missouri, xxxvii
(1930), p. 103.

[2] Esp. A. E. Berger, *Martin Luther*, Berlin, 1895–1921, II. ii. pp. 624–
711; J. Koestlin and G. Kawerau, *Martin Luther*, Berlin, 1903, i. pp. 459–
62, ii. pp. 434–5 and *passim*; K. Burdach, *Vorspiel*, i. ii. pp. 37–8; H.
Boehmer, *Luther*, London, 1930, cap. vi; F. Funck-Brentano, *Luther*,
Paris, 1934, pp. 273–90; and many others.

[3] Esp. H. Grisar, S.J., in *Luther*, Freiburg i. Br., 1924–5; cf. id.,
Martin Luther: his life and work, St. Louis, Mo. and London, 1930,
pp. 421–2.

[4] Boehmer, op. cit., pp. 332–42; A. Risch, in *Neue Kirchliche Zeitschrift*, xxii (1911), p. 132; J. M. Reu, *Thirty-five Years of Luther
Research*, Chicago, 1917, pp. 78–87.

[5] 'It is not possible to gather all the materials out of which a work of
literature has grown; and if we could have them all in our hand, they would
only be *dry bones*; the spirit that breathed upon them is everything.'
L. Cazamian, *Criticism in the Making*, New York, 1929, p. 14.

Pietsch[1] and Franke[2] led. On the other hand, we have seen in recent years more than one attempt[3] to pin down the spirit which, in Cazamian's sense, 'breathed' on Luther's prose works. It is this second line of inquiry, more in tune with the 'psychological' trends of our age, that appears to promise the most hopeful results. *Le style est l'homme même* is an old adage; a man's style can tell us all about his personality. What we are trying to do is to make Luther's personality tell us something about his style.

Our task is complicated by the fact that Luther was a man of genius; a genius, certainly, in the sense that he was the plaything of a *daimon* no less imperious than that of Socrates or Goethe. Genius transcends categories, the *daimon* is an elusive faery spirit; so we can perhaps never familiarize ourselves with Luther as with men not victims of a higher than themselves. But we may at least try to grasp the nature of this *daimon* imperative,[4] and to watch it at work.

To Luther, as has been suggestively remarked,[5] 'truth was far more important than beauty'; it need not concern us here to define his particular view of that truth whose manysidedness a contemporary politician has been at pains to stress. It is sufficient that Luther felt and

[1] P. Pietsch, *Martin Luther und die hochdeutsche Schriftsprache*, Breslau, 1883.

[2] C. Franke, *Grundzüge der Schriftsprache Luthers*, Halle a. d. S., 1913–22, 3 vols. Cf., too, such highly specialized piece-work as C. Sang's *Die appellative Verwendung von Eigennamen bei Luther*, Gießen, 1921.

[3] H. Preuss, *Martin Luther. Der Künstler*, Gütersloh, 1931; W. G. Moore, 'The literary quality of Luther's style', *MLR.*, xxviii (1933), pp. 338–51. To Dr. Moore personally I am indebted for much ready help and advice.

[4] On the workings of the *daimon* cf. J. P. Eckermann, *Conversations with Goethe*, 11 March 1828.

[5] E. M. Butler, *The Tyranny of Greece over Germany*, Cambridge, 1935, p. 4.

believed himself a mouthpiece of divine revelation.[1] He
strikes the true prophetic note in 'his treatise *An die
Ratsherren* (1524), in a passage beginning: 'Weyl myr
Gott den mund auff gethan hatt und mich heyssen
reden . . .'[2] In *Gebet wider den Türken* he is even more
confident on the subject of his mission and guidance:

> Wir sind gleichwol eben der selben Leute, den Gott sein wort
> befolhen, und durch seinen Geist uns predigen lesst, Ja eben so
> wol sind wir solche Leute, als Mose, Josua, Elias und alle ander
> Heiligen, Denn wir desselben Gottes wort und Geist haben, den
> sie gehabt.[3]

Luther can have been in no doubt that what he preached
was divinely inspired and therefore true.

It is—to give but one illustration—to this passionate
inner conviction of the truth, rather than to frayed nerves
or quick temper, that we should attribute Luther's frequent, and frequently deprecated, resort to merciless
sarcasm and unrestrained abuse. The prophet in him
thus characteristically reacted to opposition. Within the
compass of a single work, *Wider Hans Worst* (1541), we
find Luther raging against an eclectic, chimerical host of
'Beuttel dresscher oder Beutelschneider', 'lester Heintzen,
schand Meintzen', 'Rottengeister', 'weibische Memmen',
'Doctor Saw', 'Filtz und Trunckenbolt', 'Teufel Heintz
und Heintz Teufel', 'tolpel, knebel und rültze', 'Teufels
dreck', 'Esels Dialectica'—to select only a few instances;
in other works he is scarcely less violent. And it is no
everyday spasm of spiritual or intellectual arrogance that
makes a man exclaim:

---

[1] H. Preuss, *Martin Luther. Der Prophet*, Gütersloh, 1933, esp. cap.
iv; Boehmer, op. cit., cap. v. Preuss (p. 119) sums up his findings thus:
'Luther hat sich als besonderer beauftragter Bote Gottes, d. h. aber als
Prophet, gefühlt, gewußt, und hat dies auch in aller Öffentlichkeit
erklärt und für sich in Anspruch genommen.'

[2] Preuss, op. cit., p. 115 *ad fin.*   [3] Ibid., p. 117.

Was fur leute sind, die also reden, weis yderman wol, nemlich, tolle unsynnige narren odder lotterbuben, die uber tissche von eisern vogeln sagen so uber den see fliegen, odder von schwartzem schnee der ym somer fellt, damit sie ein gelechter den gesten anrichten (iii. 431).[1]

Ein ander bracht fragen aus Sanct Thomas und Scholastern, ein ander predigt von den Heiligen, ein ander von seinem heiligen Orden, ein ander von blaw enten, ein ander von hüner milch; wer kan es alles erzelen das unzifer? (iv. 271).

Habt jrs gesehen jr scharffsichtigen fleddermeuse (iv. 338).

Er ist ein trefflicher man, in der heiligen Schrifft fertig, behende und leufftig, wie eine Kue auff dem Nusbawm oder eine Saw auff der harffen (iv. 349).

God, perhaps for the first time, was speaking German, or so, at least, Luther must have felt. It would be surprising indeed if so elemental a force had not left a profound and permanent impression on the language. It must not be supposed, however, that Luther was content to let his *daimon*, or the Word of God, speak through him haphazard. He was determined to find worthy expression for his message, and beauty, though overshadowed by truth, found in him an earnest cultivator. The *Sendbrief von Dolmetschen* (1530) is too familiar to require paraphrase here; every student knows that Luther was anxious to write a German not only clear and simple (*rein und klar teutsch*) but beautiful (*ein fein, schön, loblich deutsch*), while renouncing the *filtzicht zötticht deudsch* of the kind of man who *meulet ein wort odder zwey die helfft*. Repeatedly in his letters and table-talk[2] Luther stressed the importance

---

[1] Luther's works (except where the contrary is expressly stated) are quoted from O. Clemen's handy 'Bonn' students' edition in 8 volumes. For the sake of clarity I have in some cases slightly modified the punctuation.

[2] e.g. *Tischreden*, nos. 3573, 3612, 5335, 5465, in vol. viii of the 'Bonn' edition; Luther's letter to Link, in Enders' edition of the *Letters*, x. 134.

of clear, straightforward German; he never tired in his
efforts to enrich his native tongue.

Yet we must not exaggerate the significance of this
preoccupation of Luther's with language; it should not
be thought that Luther modelled his prose style as a
potter models clay.[1] The implication is no more than
that Luther had a 'feel' for language as such and that in
this 'feel' an important prerequisite for a good prose style
existed. To uncover the hidden founts of that style we
must delve deeper.

Luther's obsession with revealed truth found a natural
outlet in exegesis. While still quite a young man, he was
interpreting the Scriptures at Wittenberg, and from the
time he assumed the mantle of his teacher Staupitz until
his death in 1546 he was engaged in constant study and exposition of the Word. The very idea underlying his translation of the Bible was, in the widest sense of the term,
exegetic; it was his aim to 'popularize' the Message which
alone promised salvation. And if, in teaching, explaining,
and expounding, he achieved superlative prose, are we to
deny the probability that the credit for this achievement
rests largely with the mysterious force that moved him?

In his *Kleiner Katechismus* Luther discusses, for
instance, the prayer 'Unser teglich brod gib uns heute'
and asks explicitly: 'Was heisst denn teglich brod?'
Echo, the *daimon*, answers:

Alles was zur leibs narung und notturft gehört, als essen, trincken,
kleider, schuch, haus, hoff, acker, vihe, gelt, gut, frum gemahl,
frume kinder, frum gesynde, frume und trewe öber herren, gut
regiment, gut wetter, friede, getrewe nachbarn und des gleichen
(H. Lietzmann's *Kleine Texte*, no. 109, p. 18).

[1] Except in works of great importance, e.g. the translation of the Bible,
where he confesses that he sometimes searched for weeks on end for the
mot juste (iv. 183); cf. 'im Hiob erbeiten wir also ... das wir yn vier tagen
zu weilen kaum drey zeilen kundten fertigen' (ib.).

It is hard to admire sufficiently the vitality and elasticity
of a mind that can interpret *teglich brod* exegetically by
gut wetter. Or have we here more than a lively, flexible
mind? Is it not perhaps a case of that genius to which
two and two produce five more naturally than four? At
the very least, it is exegesis that has given birth to good
prose. We find in this short passage the assonances, the
word-arrangement and the rhythm that are the characteristic marks of Luther's style. We see, moreover, a
mind that expresses itself freely in 'concrete', pictorial
terms, for all its depth eschewing the abstract. In a
German dissertation[1] the writer comments on a passage
in Luther's translation of Aesop's fables which, for all
the difference in subject-matter and mood, presents remarkably similar features. Where Steinhöwel, a previous
translator, faithfully describes a larder, 'darinn allerhand
spys behalten was', Luther expands to 'da war voll auff
von Brot, Fleisch, Spek, Würste, Kese, und alles'. It is
the same process at work; exegesis again (albeit secular),
and in 'concrete' language.

The extent of Luther's prose achievement is sometimes
not fully appreciated, because it is hard to picture to oneself the difficulties he had to overcome. The abyss that
yawns between Luther and his forerunners may perhaps
best be illustrated by one passage (out of the many that
might be cited) in his version and in an earlier translation.
(The term 'version' is used advisedly, as will be shown
below.) Nahum iii. 1–4.[2]

Wee dir statt der sünden gancz	Wehe der mörderischen statt,
der lüge. vol zerreyssung. Es wirt	die vol lugen und rauberey ist, und
nitt weychen von dir der raube.	von jrem rauben nicht lassen will.

[1] W. von Both, *Luther und die Fabel*, diss., Breslau, 1926, p. 32.

[2] For these and other early German versions of the Bible, cf. W.
Walther, *Luthers Bibelübersetzung kein Plagiat*, Erlangen and Leipzig,
1891. These verses from Nahum may be found at p. 36.

Die stymm der geysel unnd die stymm der gähe des rads und des gryssgramenden pferdes und des hyczenden vierredrigen wagens. Und des aufsiczenden reytters. und des scheynenden schwercz. und des blicenden spyess. und der erschlagen menig. und des schweren fallss. Es ist nit end der ass. Und sy werden fallen in jren leychnamen, umb der menig willen der unkeüschunge der unkeüscherin der schönen. und der genämen. und der habenden die übelthat. die do hat verkaufft die völcker in jrem unkeüschen. und die gesinde in jren zaubernussen.

Denn da wirdt man hören die gaysseln klappen, und die reder rasseln, die rosse schreyen, und die wägen rollen. Er bringt reütter herauff, mit glentzenden schwerdten, und mit blytzenden spiessen, Da ligen vil erschlagen unnd grosse hauffen leichnam, das der selbigen kain zal ist, unnd man uber jre leychnam fallen muss. Das alles umb der grossen hurerey willen der schönen lieben huren die mit zauberey umbgeet, die mit jrer hurerey die haiden, und mit jrer zauberey lande und leütte erworben hat.[1]

Comment is almost superfluous, but it may be well to stress the main points. The earlier translation is clearly the more faithful rendering; the second verse, literally translated from the Hebrew, reads: 'the sound [or *voice*] of the whip and the sound of the noise of the wheel and the galloping horse and the bounding chariot.' Luther has sacrificed not a tittle of the essential meaning of the original, but has rendered the sense of the passage in characteristic German. By the use of finite verbs, *hören*, *klappen*, *rasseln*, *schreyen*, *rollen*, which it is in the nature of Hebrew to omit, he presents a lively, 'concrete' picture. The interplay of onomatopoeia and alliteration, *die gaysseln klappen*, *und die reder rasseln*, completely vanquishes the literal 'die stymm der geysel unnd die stymm der gähe des rads', both for clarity of expression and for aesthetic effect. Though there are indications (e.g. *der habenden die übelthat*) that the earlier translator used an original other than the Hebrew, yet, even if we make

---

[1] Luther's text is from the Augsburg edition of 1532; hence *gaysseln*, *kain*, *haiden*.

allowances for this, we cannot hide from ourselves the superiority of Luther's version.

Luther, in fact, has done more than translate, as a comparison of his text with the original or with the Revised Version will show. Once again we have before us what is essentially a piece of exegesis; Luther is *explaining* and interpreting the Word of God. Had he been content simply to translate, he could not have produced a version materially different from that of his predecessor. His German would necessarily have been as limp and obscure, and of prose style there could have been no question. He might have offered us a German Septuagint, grotesquely literal; instead, he has re-created the sacred text and published something not unlike an original composition. In short, it is primarily the triumph of Luther, the master of exegesis, on whom Luther the stylist depends for his very existence.

It is impossible in a short article to multiply instances; for further comparisons of Biblical passages the reader is referred to Walther, op. cit.[1] But it must not be supposed that the evidence for the debt of Luther's style to his exegetic mind is to be found solely, or even mainly, in his translation of the Bible. His entire literary output testifies to the power of this striking psychological trait.

If we accept the thesis that Luther was primarily an interpreter, it follows from this that he must have interpreted his every idea in terms of some other idea or series of ideas; explanation presupposes a *tertium quid*. The more we read of Luther, the more conscious we become of the frequency with which this *tertium quid* takes the

---

[1] A close examination of Luther's Old Testament in the light of the Hebrew original would throw much light on Luther's prose style. A beginning was made some years ago in Gundolf's Heidelberg seminar, but these first attempts (on the Psalms) were not continued.

form of a pictorial (*anschaulich*) simile or metaphor. Once again, by a more devious path, we find ourselves face to face with Luther's leaning towards the 'concrete' in language. His mind is powerfully associative, but its feelers are all put out in the same direction. Time and again we are startled at Luther's association of ideas, which to us, who have no share in his *daimon*, often seems incongruous. Who can read the simile of the cow on the walnut-tree without a start? And there is no dearth of parallels:

The Roman Curia is pictured as the 'Romisch treudelmarckt, da man schlussell, brieff, siegel, sund, gnad, got, hell, alle ding keufft und tausschet' (ii. 87).

Of unscrupulous men of business: 'sie haben alle wahr unter yhren henden ... und drucken und verderben alle geringe kauffleute, gleich wie der hecht die kleyne fisch ym wasser, gerade alls weren sie Herrn uber Gottes Creaturen' (iii. 19).

Of the same: 'wie ettliche geytzigen blasen ... frisch widderumb dasselb auch auff zynse treyben, das ymmer eyn zyns den andern treybe, wie das wasser die möl rad' (iii. 37).

Of naive theologians: 'kindisch und alber reden sie vom hymel, auff das sie Christo einen ort droben ym hymel machen, wie der stork ein nest auff eym baum' (iii. 446).

A false syllogism derided: 'Christus ist etlicher gestalt nicht bey uns, drumb ist er allerdinge nicht bey uns, frisch a particulari ad universale, Der Schultheis ist nicht mit roten hosen ym bade, drumb ist er nicht ym bade' (iii. 380).

Of the grace of God: 'Lieben deutschen, keufft weyl der marck fur der thür ist, samlet eyn, weyl es scheynet und gutt wetter ist, braucht Gottis gnaden und wort, weyl es da ist. Denn das sollt yhr wissen, Gottis wort und gnade ist ein farender platz regen, der nicht wider kompt, wo er eyn mal gewesen ist' (ii. 446).

Any reader of Luther may convince himself that these extracts are typical; in each case an idea is made clear and *interpreted*.

It is no far cry from the association of ideas to the

association of sounds, and we are not surprised to find
in Luther (notoriously a musical man)[1] a rich crop of every
kind of vocalic and consonantal assonance. To turn from
pre-Lutheran German prose to Luther is, in this respect as
well, to pass from medieval night to Renaissance day, as even
cursory comparison of Luther with his forerunners will
show.[2] Assonant words and phrases indeed, ranging from
the simplest to the most complex constructions, occur in his
works with such frequency that one might justifiably refer
the reader to 'Luther, *passim*'. A few examples, however,
will not be out of place. To take the simplest forms first:

im tunckeln munckelt, schleicher und streicher, schinden und
schelen, reutter und reuber, keyn ander fuge noch farbe, brassen
und brangen, die grossen Rolande und Risen, löcher und lücken,
blenden und schenden, klagens und fragens, mit platten und kappen,
zu flicken und zu lappen, der Romanisten runtzen und gruntzen,
fladdert und fleucht, webt und schwebt, webt lebt und tobet, es
klapt noch klinget nicht, flüchtige fladder geister, lauter tillens
tellens, flugs und frölich, guten groben grumpen.

These are typical of the countless instances of rhyme,
assonance and alliteration found in Luther's works. It
may be objected that some of these phrases (e.g. *runtzen
und gruntzen*) were quite probably in common use, and
indeed Luther's celebrated recipe for the composition of
good German tends to confirm this view.[3] But this is not

[1] Cf. H. Preuss, *Martin Luther. Der Künstler*, pp. 95, 97, 103, 119,
&c.; Boehmer, op. cit., cap. iv; H. Kretzschmar, *Luther und die Musik*
(Peters-Jahrbuch, 1917); K. Anton, *Luther und die Musik*, 1918.

[2] A useful anthology of pre-Lutheran prose carefully selected for its
merits may be found in Hasak, op. cit.

[3] *Sendbrief von Dolmetschen*, iv. 184: 'man mus nicht die buchstaben
inn der lateinischen sprachen fragen, wie man sol Deutsch reden . . .
sondern, man mus die mutter jhm hause, die kinder auff der gassen, den
gemeinen man auff dem marckt drumb fragen, und den selbigen auff das
maul sehen, wie sie reden . . . so verstehen sie es denn, und mercken, das
man Deutsch mit jn redet.'

the point: it is not claimed that Luther invented these phrases—all that matters is that he used them so naturally and with such freedom.

The following sentences are more elaborate in structure, but they speak for themselves; lack of space unfortunately forbids detailed comment. The reader is invited to examine them in the light of the foregoing remarks and to ask himself whether they do not reveal a felicity and a naturalness unknown in pre-Lutheran prose and by no means a common feature at any period in the history of German writing:

was hilffts aber viel flicken und pletzen am peltz, da haut und har nicht gut ist?

wurtz, wein, saltz, speck, fladen, palmen, und der gleichen.

allein seinen gehorsam jnn leiblichen, losen, leichten sachen, als fleisch essen, feyren, fasten, kleiden.

Gott . . . muss zu hulff haben brieff, bullen, pergamen, bley, blech, schnür, kleyn und gros, wachs, grün, gelb und weys.

wie er des frids, nutzs, schutzs, gutts, freyheyt, und gemach der gemeyne geneust.

man darff dem Pöfel nicht viel pfeiffen.

das wir noch eine weile gute zeerlinge bleiben, und lassen neerlinge und wehrlinge sein.

es seyen heisselwort, odder lasselwort, thettelwort odder leselwort.

wer die brod mit zenen odder zungen zu drückt, der zu drückt mit zenen odder zungen den leib Christi.

dazu kleider und schuch, essen und trincken, haus und hoffe, weib und kind, acker, vihe und alle güter, mit aller notturft und narung dysses leibs und lebens reichlich und teglich versorget.

Finally we may cite a familiar passage from *Vom ehelichen Leben* that is perhaps the supreme example of this type of almost musical prose:

ach solt ich das kind wiegen, die windell wasschen, bette machen,

stanck riechen, die nacht wachen, seyns schreiens wartten, seyn
grindt und blattern heylen, darnach des weybs pflegen, sie erneeren,
erbeytten, hie sorgen, da sorgen, hie thun, da thun, das leyden und
diss leyden? (ii. 352).

The perfection of this piece of early German prose is such
that one does not immediately realize how it *might* have
sounded. Something is undoubtedly due to the occasional
omission of the definite article; compare for sound 'das
kind wiegen, den stanck riechen, die windell wasschen,
das bett machen, die nacht wachen' with Luther's arrangement. Or read the last dozen words with *diss* and *das*
transposed. It is not, of course, suggested that Luther
deliberately selected or shaped his phrases; the assumption is merely that here a naturally associative mind has
dictated words and clauses linked to one another by their
sound. Can it be doubted that, in a previous example, it
was sound rather than logic that dictated *blech* after *bley*?

If all these examples *prove* nothing, at least they confirm what we know of Luther. And they allow us to put
forward the suggestion that Luther's prose style deserves
to be examined on new lines, to which the modern science
of psychology points the way. The study of Luther's
style has usually been divorced from the study of his life
and teaching. The rhythm of his prose has been more
often related to the rhythm of this or that *Kanzleistil*[1]
than to the rhythm of his own mind; for that mind has a
movement of its own, and that it communicates that
movement, has been little heeded or forgotten. And yet,
if we think of English writers, who would interpret the
style of individualists like Doughty or T. E. Lawrence in
the light of the prose of gone centuries?

T. E. Lawrence, a tragic, sensitive, scholarly sufferer
—and in this respect not altogether unlike Luther—

[1] Cf. Franke, op. cit.

infused all the conflicting qualities of his mind into his prose[1] and created a style inimitable and unique. We interpret his prose by what we know of his mind. Why should we not do as much for Luther? We have tried long enough to interpret his mind by what we know of his prose.

We have seen that, primarily, Luther illustrates his works and, if we may extend the metaphor, blends his words. If, now, we bear in mind that Luther was essentially a preacher and interpreter of the Word, that his thoughts turned naturally to exegesis and explanation, and that he felt and believed that a higher Force was speaking through him, then a great deal becomes clear, or at any rate clearer. We have, after all, outlived the epoch of materialistic criticism, which shied at genius and the intangible.

To sum up in a word. The fundamental characteristic of the exegetic mind, of the mind that teaches and preaches, is *association*, fluent, even facile. When we find abundant evidence of this association, both of sound and of sense, in Luther's prose style, are we not, then, to understand that style as the wholly natural expression of his personality or, if you will, of his *daimon*?

[1] Cf. particularly the opening pages of *The Seven Pillars of Wisdom*.

WACKENRODER'S APPRENTICESHIP TO LITERATURE: HIS TEACHERS AND THEIR INFLUENCE

By A. GILLIES

'DU hast alle meine Gefühle verfeinert und veredelt,' wrote Tieck to Wackenroder in May 1792, 'Du bis jetzt fast der einzige Mensch der mich wirklich kennt und der mich versteht. . . . Ich habe es nie so lebhaft gefühlt als jetzt, wie sehr ich Deiner bedarf, um zu leben, im eigentlichen Sinn . . . alle meine Kraft versiegt, die reizende Natur verliert ohne einen Freund, der mit uns empfindet, alles Schöne, statt des Belebenden des Frühlings sieht man in jedem Wesen nur, wie ein jeder Atemzug ihn näher zum Grabe rückt, alles verdorrt und verlischt in meiner Seele.'[1] This is a striking confession, the more so, as Tieck's attitude to his friend was frequently, indeed usually, one rather of masterful superiority than of effusive sentimentality. Yet, even allowing in this instance for some exaggeration on the part of the overwrought young student, it is clear that Wackenroder, at the age of nineteen, possessed qualities of feeling and outlook that exercised an unusual fascination over Tieck. It has been recognized that it was through him that Tieck became a medievalist, that what was at first little more than a fascinated attachment to the flashing externalities of the Middle Ages—largely prepared by his juvenile absorption in *Götz von Berlichingen* and nourished by the influence of Bernhardi and Rambach—was transformed into a real and sincere desire to penetrate into the spirit

[1] W. H. Wackenroder, *Werke und Briefe*, hg. F. von der Leyen, Jena, 1910 (henceforth referred to as *WW.*), ii. 34 f.

of medieval poetry.[1] But it is nevertheless surprising that the creator of the '*kunstliebender Klosterbruder*'—more particularly as regards his initiation into literature and art—has hitherto scarcely received the attention proportionate to this position.[2] For Wackenroder had the advantage of a literary training that might well have been the envy, not only of Tieck but of many another contemporary, a training that could well withstand and ultimately overcome the scornful scepticism of the friend who found nothing more to say of the *Minnesänger* than that they were monotonous.[3]

Wackenroder owed his interest in German literature to one of the most enthusiastic and strangely neglected German scholars of the time—Erduin Julius Koch. Scherer dismisses Koch, to be sure, as a well-meaning dilettante,[4] as he is when compared with Scherer's hero, but his ranking must be considerably higher when he is judged in his place at the end of the eighteenth century. Of his importance for Wackenroder, who took a course in German literature under him in autumn 1792, there is clear evidence. Wackenroder's own sincere report is worth quoting:

Da hab ich [he wrote to Tieck in December 1792] denn manche

[1] J. Brüggemann, *Ludwig Tieck als Übersetzer mittelhochdeutscher Dichtung*, Diss. Tübingen, 1908, p. 4, and G. Klee, *Zu Ludwig Tiecks germanistischen Studien*, Progr. Bautzen, 1895.

[2] Cf. especially, in addition to R. Haym, *Die romantische Schule*, Berlin, 1928[5], *passim*; P. Koldewey, *Wackenroder und sein Einfluß auf Tieck*, Leipzig, 1904; A. E. Lussky, *Tieck's Approach to Romanticism*, Borna-Leipzig, 1925; O. Walzel's introduction to his edition of the *Herzensergießungen eines kunstliebenden Klosterbruders*, Leipzig, 1921; works on more special points are noted below.   [3] *WW*. ii. 148.

[4] W. Scherer, *Jakob Grimm*, Neudruck der 2. Aufl., Berlin, 1921, p. 51. For a treatment of the whole question of the growth of Germanic studies the reader is referred to R. von Raumer's indispensable work, *Geschichte der germanischen Philologie*, Munich, 1870.

sehr interessante Bekanntschaft mit altdeutschen Dichtern gemacht und gesehn, daß dies Studium, mit einigem Geist betrieben, sehr viel Anziehendes hat. Ich habe mir auch einige Stücke abgeschrieben, und schmeichle mir jetzt öfters mit der (wenn auch kindischen, doch ergötzenden) Hoffnung, einmal in dem Winkel mancher Bibliothek, Entdeckungen in diesem Fach zu machen, oder wenigstens es durch kleine Aufklärungen zu erweitern. Schon Sprache, Etymologie und Wortverwandtschaften (besonders auch das Wohlklingende der alten Ostfränkischen Sprache) machen das Lesen jener alten Überbleibsel interessant. Aber auch davon abstrahirt, findet man viel Genie und poetischen Geist darin.[1]

He follows up this slightly apologetic passage with the remark that such studies are important 'für Geschichte der Nation und des Geistes',[2] having, in the meantime, read the *Heldenbuch*.[3] At every point, in fact, we see him completely in Koch's power—the perfect echo of his master; the desire to ransack libraries, and the emphasis on etymology and on *die alte ostfränkische Sprache* were among the principal planks in Koch's programme.

Koch's career (1764–1834) reads like a Temperance pamphlet. Beginning as a teacher at the *Pädagogium der Realschule* in Berlin in 1786 and entering the Church in 1790, he was suspended from his office in 1808, and finally removed in 1815 for unworthy conduct and, though an attempt was made by those who knew his ability to employ him in the University library at Breslau, he sank into oblivion a drink-sodden half-wit pauper. Yet in his youth this incorrigible old dipsomaniac had been without doubt one of the most learned authorities of his time in the field of German literature, had sketched out a programme which the brothers Grimm, some twenty years afterwards, began to realize in practice, and had written a work which was the predecessor of Goedeke's *Grundriß*. But like Goedeke, weighed down by his encyclopaedic

[1] *WW.* ii. 130.   [2] *WW.* ii. 168.   [3] *WW.* ii. 177.

erudition, he seems to have had little success as a teacher, and but for his influence on Wackenroder and the poets of the *Wunderhorn* would have passed into complete oblivion.[1]

The time of his association with Wackenroder was clearly his sanest and most fruitful. In 1792 he wrote a *Hodegetik für das Universitätsstudium in allen Fakultäten*, and in the next year published a whole series of works: an address *Über deutsche Sprache und Literatur. Ein Aufruf an sein Vaterland. Nebst einer ausführlichern Nachricht von dem öffentlichen Auftritte der Gesellschaft Deutscher Sprach- und Literatur-Forscher zu Berlin;*[2] a revised edition of J. G. Sulzer's *Kurzer Inbegriff aller Wissenschaften*, with the ambitious title *Encyclopædie aller philosophischen Wissenschaften*; a *Literarisches Magazin für Buchhändler und Schriftsteller* (2 vols. Berlin, 1792–3); editions of the *Reise einer Französischen Emigrantin durch die Rhein-Gegenden in Briefen an einen Deutschen Domherrn, als Nebenstück von Försters Ansichten*, and of the *Odeum Friedrichs des Großen*, an anthology, with an introductory account of the poets centred around that monarch. Participation in the work *Für Deutsche Sprache, Litteratur und Cultur-Geschichte. Eine Schrift der deutschen Gesellschaft zu Berlin. Herausgegeben von J. F. A. Kinderling, J. P. Willenbücher, E. J. Koch* (Berlin, 1794) was followed by the completion of his most famous production, his *Compendium der deutschen Literaturgeschichte* (vol. i, 1790; vol. i, ed. 2,

---

[1] *Weimarisches Jahrbuch*, i, Hannover, 1854, pp. 58–72 (by Hoffmann von Fallersleben). Cf. also H. Lohre, *Von Percy zum Wunderhorn* (Palaestra, 22), Berlin, 1902, pp. 111 f. and 128, and R. Steig, *A. von Arnim und C. Brentano*, Stuttgart, 1894, pp. 121, 139, 142, 163, and *Arnim und Bettina*, Stuttgart, 1913, p. 20.

[2] Koch had founded this society in 1788 on the cessation of Adelung's *Magazin für Deutsche Sprache*, in order to continue the work of that periodical.

1795; vol. ii, 1798—the latter volume bearing the supplementary title *Grundriß einer Geschichte der Sprache und
Literatur der Deutschen von den ältesten Zeiten bis auf
Lessings Tod*). These titles would incline us to believe that
Koch was nothing more than a belated *Popularphilosoph*—
which is indeed the case; but there is in addition a valuable
statement of policy in his work, which by reason of its
date, its penetration and completeness entitles him to a
place of some merit in the history of German studies, as
the predecessor of the Romantic philologists.

His *Hodegetik* is not the least interesting from our point
of view. After a dedication to Wackenroder's father
(among others), Koch, turning to his *Abiturienten*, lays
particular stress on the Classics, Ancient History, and
Archaeology which—as we should expect from a keen
pupil of F. A. Wolf—he looks upon as the foundations
of all study, and goes on to urge his students to report to
him periodically on their application of his recommendations. We know that Wackenroder kept in constant touch
with his master during his university years. The *Compendium* was the first attempt to list and classify extant
material on the history of German literature. Though not
easy to use, it is extraordinarily complete—for the study of
the sixteenth and seventeenth centuries it was the standard
work of reference until the appearance of Goedeke—is
built up on scientific lines and gives biographical and
critical notes in addition to its bibliographical data. There
was little of the amateur about Koch.

But his aspirations are more clearly set out in the
Literarisches Magazin. His line of approach represents a
fusion of the strictly philological procedure of his teacher
Wolf (to whom the first volume of this work is dedicated)
with the critical demands of Herder, who is frequently
alluded to with approval. Among his suggestions are:

a learned periodical, an 'East Frankish' (!) dictionary, a history of the German language, an account of German proverbs and of Germanic legends and mythology. Of the literary historian he has very definite requirements to make: a biography of a poet must not be limited to bare externals but should give a regular *Culturgeschichte* of the times—'er (the critic) habe die Dichtwerke dieser Männer, als den wahrsten Abdruck des vollendeten oder unreifen Geistes, der sie schuf, und als unbestechbare Zeugen der Empfindungen, des Geschmacks, kurz des ganzen Geistes-Charakters, so lange und gründlich studiert, bis er deren Individuelles in Form und Materie völlig kennen gelernt hat'.[1]

Koch's address *Über Deutsche Sprache und Literatur* is undoubtedly, considering its date, a very remarkable performance; his ringing challenges and general vigour of presentation make it a document of unusual interest to modern times. Jakob Grimm himself, indeed, could not have been more explicit or enthusiastic. It is a rare and little-known document that would fully merit, if space permitted, being quoted *in toto*, for its sentiments were those with which Wackenroder was armed when he entered upon his student life. From Wackenroder they passed to Tieck, ultimately bearing fruit in his *Minnelieder*, which supplied A. W. Schlegel with material for his Berlin lectures and first aroused Jakob Grimm's interest in medieval literature.[2] There is therefore a direct line of succession from Koch to the Grimms, with a second one in support passing through the editors of the *Wunderhorn*, who were personally acquainted with him.[3]

[1] i. 77 f.

[2] Ludwig Tieck, *Kritische Schriften*, i, Leipzig, 1848, p. ix, and J. Grimm, *Kleinere Schriften*, i, Berlin, 1864, p. 6.

[3] R. Steig, *A. von Arnim und C. Brentano*, Stuttgart, 1894, pp. 121, 139, 142, 162, 163.

Ich verlange [wrote Koch in a significant passage] . . . daß der werdende *Deutsche Philolog* zuvor ein *Griechischer und Römischer* Philolog geworden sey. Dann erst darf man hoffen, daß unsere biedere Sprache und Literatur aus ihrer unverdienten Verborgenheit hervorgerissen werden könne, wenn geübte und talentvolle Erklärer und kritische Bearbeiter des *Homer* und *Horaz*, des *Thucydides* und *Tacitus*, des *Aristoteles* und *Cicero* sich unsern *Oberdeutschen* und *Niederdeutschen*, *Fränkischen* und *Schwäbischen* Sprachschätzen jedes Zeitpuncts und jeder Gattung *herablassen*, oder vielmehr es als ein patriotisches Verdienst ansehen, jene von Griechen und Römern hergeholten Fertigkeiten und Kenntnisse auf die Erklärung und kritische Bearbeitung unserer weniger schönen, aber für uns nicht minder reichhaltigen Sprachdenkmale, willig und ausdauernd anzuwenden. Dann erst darf man hoffen, daß besonders die Geschichte unserer Literatur nicht fernerhin aus Biographien Deutscher Dichter, aus Inhaltsanzeigen Deutschgeschriebener Werke, und aus archivarischdiplomatischen Beschreibungen alter und seltener Drucke bestehen werde. Sondern auch hier wird man alsdann den seelenerhebenden Ideen folgen, welche wir von Griechen und Römern allein erhalten konnten. Aber wann wird diese Sonne am literarischen Horizonte unseres Deutschen Vaterlandes aufgehen? Wann werden Deutschgeborene Philologen, wie F. A. *Wolf*, C. G. *Heyne*, David *Ruhnken* aufhören zu glauben, kritisches Studium der vaterländischen Sprache und Literatur sey Entwürdigung des neueren Philologen? [1]

It is clear that Wackenroder's apprenticeship to German literature under such a teacher was nothing superficial or amateurish; it was a deadly serious occupation. During his university years he constantly turned to his master,[2] who was no doubt only too ready with hints and advice as to what should be read; it is indeed hardly too much to say that he stood completely in Koch's power as far as German was concerned. In Göttingen and Cassel he took notes for the *Compendium*,[3] and in the latter city made the

---

[1] *Über Deutsche Sprache und Literatur*, Berlin, 1793, pp. 13 ff.

[2] R. Köpke, *Ludwig Tieck*, Leipzig, 1855, i. 174.

[3] *Compendium*, ii. 1798, Vorrede, iii and *Weimarisches Jahrbuch*, i. 66

acquaintance, at his teacher's instance, of Wilhelm Johann Christian Gustav von Casparson, the editor of *Willehalm*,[1] and of the Hessian minister Ernst Martin von Schlieffen (to whom the second volume of Koch's *Magazin* and the work *Für Deutsche Sprache* were dedicated), the patron of Johannes von Müller and author of unsigned essays in the *Deutsches Museum* on Heinrich von Veldeke, Hartmann von Aue, and others.[2]

But before he left Berlin for the University, Wackenroder had already developed other interests—in music and art. Of the latter he wrote to Tieck in terms full of envy at the opportunities the Göttingen library presented and of anticipation of the prospects Erlangen would offer.[3] His teacher in this subject was none other than Karl Philipp Moritz,[4] who after his return from Italy had been appointed, through the influence of Karl August of Weimar, professor at the *Akademie der bildenden Künste*, where he delivered extremely popular lectures. At that time Moritz was bringing out his *Reisen eines Deutschen in Italien aus den Jahren 1786 bis 1788* (3 vols., Berlin, 1792–3) and his periodical *Italien und Deutschland in Rücksicht auf Sitten, Gebräuche, Litteratur und Kunst* (6 vols., Berlin, 1789–93). It is known how great an impression he made on the youthful Wilhelm von Humboldt, and Wackenroder, too, must have found his lectures an extremely profitable preparation for his visit to Nürnberg (with which Moritz was well acquainted) and for Fiorillo's classes at Göttingen. As regards music, Wackenroder had already declared his desire to make progress in practical composition, as a step towards better appreciation,[5]

---

[1] Cf. W. Scherer, *Jakob Grimm*, ed. cit., p. 34.
[2] Ibid., p. 51.   [3] *WW*. ii. 131.
[4] R. Köpke, *Ludwig Tieck*, i. 90.
[5] *WW*. ii. 2.

and inquired earnestly of Tieck about the reputation and taste of Forkel, the Göttingen professor of music.[1]

Much of the ardour Wackenroder showed in the Erlangen term of 1793 was clearly the direct result of Koch's assiduous instruction, seconded by the influence of Moritz; for we know that the former's vision of a 'Geschichte der Deutschen Menschheit' included attention to art and culture of all kinds. There is no doubt that this rapturous summer, one long enchanted succession of castles and monasteries and medieval relics, together with the memorable meetings in Nürnberg with Panzer and Murr, to whom he had recommendations,[2] and his discussions with Meusel and Harleß at the University,[3] caused Wackenroder—and with him Tieck—completely to surrender himself to the new and entrancing field of German and other medieval art and literature. His diary overflows with enthusiasm for the paintings he came upon during his Franconian wanderings.[4] The teachings of Koch and Moritz were driven home by the rich experiences of reality. By his rediscovery of Nürnberg, Wackenroder achieved at a blow what the indefatigable antiquarian Murr had long been striving for.[5] From the

[1] Ibid., p. 112.   [2] Köpke, op. cit. i. 160 f.
[3] Ibid., p. 155.
[4] R. Wolkan, 'Ein unbekanntes Tagebuch Wilhelm Wackenroders', Süddeutsche Monatshefte, ix. 2 (1912), pp. 265, 267 seq.
[5] Christoph Gottlieb von Murr (1733–1811) was the leading authority on Nürnberg antiquities and author of a vast number of works on art, literature, and local history and institutions. Wackenroder could not possibly have consulted any one better qualified or more desirous of spreading interest in this work. Murr's Bibliothèque de Peinture, de Sculpture et de Gravure, 2 vols., Frankfurt and Leipzig, 1770, was a standard work of reference. (Fiorillo notes his indebtedness to it in his Geschichte der zeichnenden Künste von ihrer Wiederauflebung bis auf die neuesten Zeiten, 5 vols., Göttingen, 1798–1808, I. vi.) Shortly before Wackenroder's visit he had published his Beschreibung der sämtlichen Reichskleinodien und Heiligthümer, welche in der des H. R. Reichsfreyen Stadt Nürnberg

infectious *naïveté* of the *Herzensergießungen* there is a direct line, through *Franz Sternbald* and Hoffmann's *Meister Martin der Küfner*, to Richard Wagner's *Meistersinger von Nürnberg*.

It was with such preparation as this that Wackenroder proceeded to Göttingen, where he matriculated as a student of law on 18 October 1793.[1] He was very conscientious in his attendance at lectures and took copious notes.[2] Of his teachers he stood nearest to the lecturer in art, Fiorillo.[3] Johann Dominicus Fiorillo (1748–1821),

aufbewahrt werden, Nürnberg, 1790, and was also in an excellent position to give advice regarding Bamberg—his *Merkwürdigkeiten der Fürstbischöflichen Residenzstadt Bamberg* appeared at Nürnberg in 1799. In Göttingen Wackenroder studied assiduously his *Journal zur Kunstgeschichte und zur allgemeinen Litteratur*, 17 vols., Nürnberg, 1775–89 (*v. infra*). Nearly 6,000 items are listed in the auction catalogue of Murr's library (*Catalogus Librorum quos V. C. Christophorus Theophilus de Murr . . . collegerat*. Noribergae, 1811). (J. B. C. Grundy (*Tieck and Runge. A Study in the Relationship of Literature and Art in the Romantic Period, with especial reference to 'Franz Sternbald'*, Strassburg, 1930, p. 43) has reminded us that Wackenroder and Tieck probably saw the de Praun collection in Nürnberg (of which Murr published a catalogue in 1797), with its very strong Italian and Dürer sections, and also draws attention to the visit to Cassel, with its large Dutch collection. Köpke's words on the Nürnberg days are well worth quoting in this connexion: 'In voller Kunsttrunkenheit durchsuchten die Freunde Kirchen und Kirchhöfe. Mit Rührung standen sie an den Gräbern Albrecht Dürers und Hans Sachs', sie sahen die Burg, Bürgerhäuser und Sammlungen, was nur irgend einen Namen hatte. Eine versunkene Welt stieg vor ihren Augen wieder empor, und unwillkürlich bevölkerten sie diese Straßen und Plätze mit den Gestalten ihrer Phantasie. Von selbst ward das Leben des alten Nürnberg zu einem Kunstroman' (i. 160).)

[1] I am indebted to the University authorities for this information. Wackenroder lodged in the Stumpfebiel during his two terms at Göttingen. It is probable that the friends arrived at the University much earlier, for Tieck was already a borrower from the library on 1 October. (On Tieck's use of the Göttingen library see my article 'Ludwig Tieck's English Studies at the University of Göttingen, 1792–1794' (*Journal of English and Germanic Philology*, April 1937).) [2] Köpke, op. cit. i. 177.

[3] Grellmann, who usually signed Wackenroder's library slips, does not

who had studied at Bayreuth, Rome, and Bologna, had
come to Göttingen in 1781, where he was made curator
of the engravings in the University library.[1] He taught
drawing and the history of art, becoming *extraordinarius*
in 1799 and *ordinarius* in 1813. His classes, we are told,[2]
were especially designed for students intending to visit
Italy and France, and it was no doubt his teaching that
was responsible for the plan to go to Italy, which the
three friends, Wackenroder, Tieck, and Burgsdorff
formed.[3] In the preface to the *Phantasien über die Kunst*
(1814 edition), Tieck tells us how much his friend
enjoyed the society and instruction of Fiorillo.[4]

That Wackenroder knew his teacher's work *Über
die Groteske. Einladungsblätter zu Vorlesungen über die*

appear to have any special significance in view of Wackenroder's later work.
He was the author of a work on the gypsies, and his lecture subject was
'Statistik von Deutschland' (*Göttingische Anzeigen von Gelehrten Sachen*,
1793, p. 1478; 1794, p. 501).
  [1] Pütter, *Versuch einer academischen Gelehrten-Geschichte von der
Georg-Augustus-Universität zu Göttingen*, ii, Göttingen, 1788, p. 198.
  [2] Pütter, op. cit., fortgesetzt von Saalfeld, iii, Hannover, 1820, p. 370
Fiorillo's lecture subjects during Wackenroder's two terms were 'Anfangs-
gründe der Zeichenkunst und Mahlerey', and 'Geschichte, Theorie und
das Mechanische der Mahlerey' (*Göttingische Anzeigen von Gelehrten
Sachen*, 1793, p. 1478; 1794, p. 501).   [3] Köpke, op. cit. i. 184.
  [4] *WW*. i. 200. But the latter himself is a more explicit informant
he wrote (*Geschichte der zeichnenden Künste in Deutschland*, iv, Hannover,
1820, p. 83 and note): 'Der Herr Baron v. B[urgsdorff?], ein liebens-
würdiger und geistvoller junger Mann, bezog mit seinen Freunden
Ludwig Tieck, und Wackenröder [!] aus Berlin, die hiesige Universität,
und ich hatte das mir unvergeßliche Vergnügen, diesen drey jungen
Männern ein Privatissimum über Kunstgeschichte, Theorie der Mahlerey
u.s.w. vorzutragen. Tieck hatte einen scharfen, durchdringenden Blick,
der auf der Stelle alles faßte, er zeichnete sich nur wenig auf. Wackenröder hingegen konnte nicht genug zu Papier bringen und kam auch
außer den Stunden in mein Haus, um die Kupferstiche, Bücher und andere
kostbare Werke zu besehen und sich noch manches zu notieren.' In a
note Fiorillo adds: 'Ich erinnere mich, daß er unter anderen sehr viel aus
Matthes Quad von Kinkelbachs Schriften excerpierte.' On Quad *v. infra*.

Geschichte und Theorie der bildenden Künste (Göttingen, 1791) goes without saying. Indeed it was no doubt his first introduction to Fiorillo's ideas, and it is possible that this essay can provide a hint as to the origin of the figure of the Klosterbruder. For in a note[1] Fiorillo quotes the well-known attack of St. Bernard on the artistic leanings of the Cluniac monasteries, and it is not inconceivable that the art-loving monk may have been originally thought of in direct opposition to this passage of St. Bernard's; for Wackenroder must have been greatly pained to see art looked down upon as ungodly and incompatible with true devotion—the whole of the *Herzensergießungen* is one long statement of the contrary. It is well known, of course, that the actual title of the work was suggested by the musician Reichardt,[2] who was reminded of the 'Klosterbruder' in Lessing's *Nathan*, and that Tieck supplied the preface with the fiction that the author was a member of

---

[1] 10 n. The reference is to *S. Bernardi Opera Omnia*, Parisii, 1719, i. 545, and in Fiorillo's translation the passage runs: 'Was soll in Klöstern vor den Augen der mit Lesen beschäftigten Brüder diese lächerliche Abentheuerlichkeit, diese wunderbare, ungestalte Schönheit und schöne Ungestalt? Was sollen da die garstigen Affen, die wilden Löwen, die ungeheueren Centauren, die Halbmenschen, die gefleckten Tiger, die fechtenden Soldaten, die Jäger mit ihren Hifthörnern? Hier sieht man unter Einem Kopfe viele Körper, dort wieder viele Köpfe auf einem Rumpfe; hier an einem vierfüßigen Thiere einen Schlangenschwanz, dort an einem Fische den Kopf eines vierfüßigen Thiers. Das eine Thier hat vorn die Bildung eines Pferdes und schleppt das Hintertheil einer Ziege nach sich; ein andres trägt Hörner und endigt sich hinten in einem Pferdeleib. Kurz, es zeigt sich überall eine große und bewunderungswürdige Mannigfaltigkeit der Bildungen, daß man mehr Behagen findet in dem Marmor als in Handschriften zu lesen; daß man lieber den ganzen Tag hinbringt mit Betrachtung aller dieser Dinge, als mit Nachdenken über das göttliche Gesetz.' The last sentence must have struck Wackenroder particularly unfavourably. The passage is taken from the *Apologia ad Guillelmum Abbatem*, is directed 'contra Cluniacensium superfluitates', the chapter heading being: 'Luxum et abusum in templis et oratoriis exstruendis, ornandis, pingendis arguit.'   [2] Köpke, op. cit. i. 221 f.

a religious community. But the actual figure of the monk was Wackenroder's own idea, as Tieck himself states in the 'Nachschrift' to *Sternbald*.[1] We may imagine how Wackenroder, no doubt with considerable diffidence, imparted to Tieck as a secret the fact that he had composed the work, and how the latter, with the aid of Reichardt, took it under his wing and prepared it for the press, evolving on the strength of Wackenroder's fiction a title of novel attractiveness.

Fiorillo's lectures, if we may judge from his published work, which no doubt reproduced their substance, must have meant a very great deal, as regards both matter and method, to so eager a pupil as Wackenroder. The *Geschichte der zeichnenden Künste in Deutschland* (4 vols., Hanover, 1815–20) emphasized, it is hardly necessary to say, the close connexion between art and religion in the Middle Ages: Wackenroder must have heard of more than one art-loving monk and have been quickly convinced, if he was ever doubtful, of the significance of the Church's efforts on behalf of art. In addition, of course, Fiorillo gave prominence to the life and work of Dürer, with bibliographical notes. It was no doubt he, moreover, who impressed upon Wackenroder the importance of Vasari—one of the principal sources for the *Herzensergießungen*.[2] Some of the essays in his *Kleine Schriften*

---

[1] 1798, i. 374—'Mein Freund . . . wählte absichtlich diese Maske eines religiösen Geistlichen, um sein frommes Gemüt, seine andächtige Liebe zur Kunst freier ausdrücken zu können.' Tieck's note in the Vorrede to the 1814 edition of the *Phantasien über die Kunst* would also imply that the conception of the 'Klosterbruder' was Wackenroder's own, though Tieck also denies that it had any special intention (*WW.* i. 199 f.). O. Walzel, however, in his edition of the *Herzensergießungen* (Leipzig, 1921, pp. 27–32) ascribes the idea solely to Tieck (and Reichardt).

[2] Cf. E. Dessauer, *Wackenroders Herzensergießungen in ihrem Verhältnis zu Vasari* (Studien zur vergleichenden Literaturgeschichte, vi), Berlin, 1906, p. 248 f. and P. Koldewey, op. cit., *passim*.

(2 vols., Göttingen, 1803–6) deal with very significant
topics.[1] But Fiorillo's method, as set out for us in the
introduction to his principal work, the *Geschichte der
zeichnenden Künste von ihrer Wiederauflebung bis auf die
neuesten Zeiten* (5 vols., Göttingen, 1798–1808),[2] was no
doubt equally attractive to Wackenroder, and probably
of even greater influence on his work. It is the historical
approach of Winckelmann applied to European art—the
study of the artist's life and personality within the immediate background to which he belonged and within the
general course of development of his art.[3] In Fiorillo's
own words:

> Ich habe daher immer mein Augenmerk darauf gerichtet, in
> dem Mahler nicht den Bürger, den Gatten, den Hausvater, den
> Freund u.s.w., sondern den Künstler zu zeigen; sein Talent und
> seinen Styl zu charakterisieren; vorzüglich die künstlerische Ge-
> schlechtsfolge, Ableitung und Verkettung der Manieren übersehen
> zu lassen, wie ein Stamm sich in verschiedne Zweige getheilt und
> ausgebreitet hat, wie hinwieder aus Vermischungen des Charak-
> ters einer Schule und eines Landes mit dem eines andern, neue
> Erscheinungen hervorgegangen sind; endlich die beständige Ebbe

[1] Cf. especially *Fragmente zur Geschichte der Mahlerey und Bildhauerey in Deutschland, von den Zeiten Carls des Großen bis zum Anfang des fünfzehnten Jahrhunderts*; *Über die Quellen, welche Vasari zu seinen Lebensbeschreibungen der Mahler, Bildhauer und Architecten benutzt hat*; *Literarisch-kritische Untersuchungen über die verschiedenen Ausgaben des Vasari*; *Über die Nothwendigkeit des Studiums der Naturkunde für den Mahler, Bildhauer und Architecten*; *Über den Dominicaner Francesco Colonna und sein berühmtes Buch Hypnerotomachia*; *Beyträge zur Geschichte der Mahlerey in Deutschland*; *Einige Nachrichten von dem Cardinal Bembo und von Raphael.* In the first essay Fiorillo had noted that few monasteries followed out St. Bernard's prohibition of artistic work strictly.

[2] A section of the important series to which Bouterwek's history of literature belonged—*Geschichte der Künste und Wissenschaften seit der Wiederherstellung derselben bis an das Ende des achtzehnten Jahrhunderts. Von einer Gesellschaft gelehrter Männer ausgearbeitet.*

[3] It is noteworthy that A. W. Schlegel worked carefully through this history of Fiorillo's and corrected the style (1. xx).

und Flut des herrschenden Zeitgeschmacks und der Mode zu schildern;[1]

or again:

Endlich habe ich nach Vermögen der Kritik die Kunst mit ihrer Geschichte zu vereinigen gesucht, weil keine ohne die andere bestehen kann: wenn jene unentbehrlich ist, um die Thatsachen in ihr wahres Licht zu stellen, so giebt diese hinwiederum den Überblick der Gegenstände, aus deren Vergleichung erst ein richtiges Urtheil hervorgehen kann.[2]

Thus, Fiorillo's approach admirably supported the point of view of Koch. It must not be forgotten, moreover, that in Göttingen the historical method was also represented by Gustav Hugo (1764–1844), the founder of the historical law school in Germany before Savigny. Hugo signed some of Wackenroder's library forms and Wackenroder no doubt attended his lectures; at least he must have been personally known to him.

To these influences must be added that of the University musical director, Johann Nikolaus Forkel (1749–1818), who was originally one of Göttingen's main attractions for Wackenroder.[3] A man of tremendous learning in his own field, he lectured on the theory of music[4] and was the author of a number of works on musical history. Koldewey[5] has already drawn attention to Wackenroder's absorption in the first volume of his *Allgemeine Geschichte der Musik* (Leipzig, i, 1788, ii, 1801). This part of the work did not advance beyond the Greeks

---

[1] I. x.   [2] I. xviii.

[3] Cf. letter to Tieck of Nov. 1792: 'Solltest du in Göttingen einmal den Professor Forkel, der eine Geschichte der Musik, eine musikalische kritische Bibliothek u.s.w. geschrieben, und ein vortrefflicher musikalischer Kritiker ist, kennen lernen, so schreib mir von ihm. Schreib mir doch ja ob er Kollegia über die Musik jetzt liest? Er ist mir ein interessanter Mann.' (*WW*. ii. 112.)

[4] Pütter, op. cit. ii. 197, Pütter-Saalfeld, op. cit. iii. 383.

[5] Op. cit., pp. 108, 125 (where vol. ii is referred to in error for vol. i).

and Romans, but no doubt the substance of the second
volume, which was brought down to the sixteenth century
and included an account of medieval church music, was
delivered in his lectures; there is no definite evidence that
Wackenroder attended them, however, probable though
it may be. But Forkel's voluminous writings,[1] valuable
as they were from the point of view of subject-matter,
contained ideas that could not but be extremely question-
able in Wackenroder's eyes. For, after complaining bitterly
about the decline of German music (he has no appreciation for Mozart, Haydn, and Beethoven), Forkel comes
to the conclusion that the key to its revival lies in a rigid
adherence to rules derived from accepted practice. No
words of his are severe enough to condemn 'die Willkühr
jener Naturalisten, die blos der gütigen Natur, aber nicht
der Übung und dem Fleiß die Gabe, einige Accorde ohne
offenbare Fehler aufeinander folgen zu lassen, zu ver-
danken haben';[2] indeed in view of the 'eigensinnige aus
einer zügellosen Phantasie entstandene Einfälle',[3] which
he sees around him, 'alle Ordnung, alle wahre Natur,
jeder edle und würdige Ausdruck, und kurz alles, was

---

[1] In addition to the *Allgemeine Geschichte der Musik*, he published
Über die Theorie der Musik, Göttingen, 1774. *Genauere Bestimmung
einiger musikalischer Begriffe. Zur Ankündigung der akademischen Winter-
Concerts von Michaelis 1780 bis Ostern 1781*, Göttingen, 1780; *Musi-
kalischer Almanach für Deutschland auf das Jahr 1782, 1783, 1784*,
Leipzig, 1781–3; *Musikalisch-kritische Bibliothek*, 3 vols., Gotha, 1778–
9; *Allgemeine Litteratur der Musik oder Anleitung zur Kenntniß musi-
kalischer Bücher, welche von den ältesten bis auf die neuesten Zeiten bey den
Griechen, Römern und den meisten neuern europäischen Nationen sind
geschrieben worden*, Leipzig, 1792; *Über Johann Sebastian Bachs Leben,
Kunst und Kunstwerke. Für patriotische Verehrer echter musikalischer
Kunst*, Leipzig, 1802. This last was translated into English by a banker,
Stephenson, in 1820; a further translation, with notes and appendixes,
has been more recently made by Charles Sanford Terry (London, 1920),
and is provided with a useful introduction on Forkel's career.

[2] *Musikalisch-kritische Bibliothek*, i. xiii f.   [3] Ibid., xiv.

dem ächten Musiker und Kenner außer dem sinnlichen, auch noch ein intellektuelles Vergnügen gewähren könnte',[1] is in acute danger of being thrust out. While agreeing with his attack on superficiality and lack of seriousness and dignity, and being doubtless highly attracted by his arguments in favour of reuniting music and religion in order to achieve greatness,[2] Wackenroder could not possibly have subscribed to the rationalistic remedy, slavery to rule and precept, that he suggested. Sentences such as the following must have caused him great pain:

Der natürliche Mensch ist ein rohes, ungesittetes Thier, und die natürliche Kunst ein regelloses und unbedeutendes Ding. Künstliche Musik, oder ausgebildete Kunst aber verhält sich gegen die natürliche, wie ein feiner Geist- und Charaktervoller Mann gegen einen Phantasievollen sich selbst immer ungleichen Schwärmer. Dort ist immer Werth: hier aber nur bisweilen.[3]

It was precisely sentiments of this kind that Josef Berglinger was to complain of so bitterly, and it is hardly possible to over-estimate Forkel's reactionary influence in this respect. But however much Wackenroder was repelled on the one hand, he must have been attracted on the other by Forkel's interest in sixteenth-century masses and motets and, in particular, by his championship of Bach, not only as a player and composer, but also as a national treasure and a maker of the modern German spirit.[4]

Such were Wackenroder's teachers. All of them, in their various ways, had inculcated a spirit of earnestness and devoted absorption in study, and all appealed especially to the historical sense within him. It remains now to consider the immediate results of their teaching. In

[1] Loc. cit.   [2] Ibid., xxi ff.
[3] *Genauere Bestimmung einiger musikalischer Begriffe*, 8. On Wackenroder's disapproval of Forkel's taste cf. *WW.* ii. 114, 140.
[4] Cf. C. S. Terry, op. cit., Introduction, esp. pp. xi seq.

particular, Wackenroder's use of the Göttingen University library is significant.[1]

On music Wackenroder borrowed very little indeed— only two works, Forkel's *Allgemeine Geschichte der Musik*, vol. i, Leipzig, 1788 (on 1 February 1794), and J. P. Kirnberger's purely technical *Kunst des reinen Satzes in der Musik*, Berlin, 1771 (on 18 February)—no doubt because of the uncertainty into which Forkel's position had thrust him.[2] To these, however, should be added Cahusac's 'Historische Abhandlung von der alten und neuen Tanzkunst', contained in the first two volumes of the *Sammlung vermischter Schriften zur Beförderung der schönen Wissenschaften und der freyen Künste* (6 vols., Berlin, 1759–63), which he took out on 9 September 1794,[3] and J. B. Dubos's *Réflexions critiques sur la poésie et sur la peinture* (3 vols., Paris, 1755)—with its section on music—of which he borrowed the first volume on 7 January. It is sufficiently clear that Wackenroder did not compose the Berglinger essays without close acquaintance with his subject, however much he reacted against the actual method which Forkel, especially, presented.

In other directions, Wackenroder was far more assiduous. On aesthetics and the history of art he took out the following books:

13 Nov. 1793, A. R. Mengs, *Schreiben an Pons*, Vienna, 1778.

[1] For information regarding Wackenroder's borrowings from the Göttingen library I am indebted to the courtesy of the library authorities, and especially to Dr. G. von Selle and Dr. W. Vogt, for their ready assistance and for generously placing at my disposal the register of borrowings of the years 1793–4. On the procedure followed by borrowers at that time see my article on 'Ludwig Tieck's English Studies at the University of Göttingen, 1792–1794' (*Journal of English and Germanic Philology*, April 1937).

[2] On these works as sources of the *Herzensergießungen* cf. Koldewey, op. cit., pp. 108, 125 ff., 131.   [3] Cf. ibid., p. 99.

7 Jan. 1794, J. B. Dubos, *Réflexions critiques sur la poésie et sur la peinture*, vol. i, Paris, 1755.

29 July 1794, C. G. von Murr, *Journal zur Kunstgeschichte und zur allgemeinen Litteratur*, Nürnberg, 1775–89, vols. i–iv.

1 Aug., Murr, *Journal, &c.*, vols. v–ix.

4 Aug., Murr, *Journal, &c.*, vols. x–xiv.

9 Aug., Murr, *Journal, &c.*, vols. xv–xvii.

19 Aug., K. H. Heinecken, *Nachrichten von Künstlern und Kunstsachen*, 2 vols., Leipzig, 1768–9.

On 8 January, Tieck borrowed the *Serie degli uomini i più illustri nella pittura, scultura e architettura*, vol. i, Florence, 1769.[1] Dessauer's statement[2] that Wackenroder used Vasari in the Göttingen library is not borne out by the evidence, although it is not unlikely that he may have consulted this writer at Fiorillo's house, in view of the latter's close attention to him.[3]

Koldewey[4] has already discussed the importance of Mengs's book as a source of the chapter of the *Herzensergießungen* entitled 'Der Schüler und Raphael', while Wölfflin[5] has revealed Wackenroder's opposition to that writer's professional abstractions. Heinecken's work, which contains miscellaneous accounts of artists and art-collections, along with a valuable section on early woodcuts and the beginning of book-illustration, is not remarkable, despite its learning, for any depth of artistic feeling, and can hardly have served Wackenroder as

---

[1] In the Göttingen copy of this book the first three of the twelve volumes are bound together, so that 'Vol. 1' must be interpreted as 'Vols. 1–3'.

[2] Op. cit., p. 249.   [3] Cf. Koldewey, op. cit., p. 7.

[4] Ibid., p. 36.

[5] 'Die Herzensergießungen eines kunstliebenden Klosterbruders' in *Studien zur Literaturgeschichte Michael Bernays gewidmet*, Hamburg and Leipzig, 1893, p. 68.

anything more than a reference book.¹ Dubos's emphasis on feeling, rather than on the understanding, as the key to artistic appreciation² must have been infinitely more welcome and have considerably assisted that spirit of adoring self-surrender which marked Wackenroder's standpoint.

But of all these works it was Murr's *Journal* that was of greatest importance. Wackenroder's personal contact with the versatile compiler has already been noted, and Fiorillo, who frequently refers to him, no doubt confirmed the very high opinion that every one held of his scholarship and influence.³ In the meantime, too, Wackenroder had been able to extend his first-hand knowledge of works of art by a visit to the Cassel gallery⁴ and was accordingly now in an excellent position to derive the utmost profit from his perusal of the *Journal*. This work noticed the latest publications on art, literature, and music, and contained useful articles on points connected with the history of art; so that Wackenroder must have come upon many new topics of interest, besides owing a great deal to its copious bibliographical references. But it was most valuable, as might be expected, on Dürer and Nürnberg, Murr's account being compiled from municipal registers and other documents from the city's archives, as well as from the works of Sandrart and Doppelmayr,⁵ which he

---

¹ On Heinecken cf. C. Justi, *Winckelmann und seine Zeitgenossen*, Leipzig, 1923³, i. 313–18.

² Cf. A. Lombard, *L'Abbé du Bos, un initiateur de la pensée moderne (1670–1742)*, Paris, 1913, and *La querelle des anciens et des modernes; l'abbé du Bos* (Recueil de travaux publiés par la Faculté des Lettres de l'Académie de Neuchâtel, 4), Neuchâtel, Paris, Leipzig, 1908; and L. Brunschvig, *L'abbé du Bos*, Toulouse, 1904.

³ On Murr, *v. supra*, p. 195, n. 5.

⁴ Cf. Grundy, op. cit., p. 43.

⁵ Joachim von Sandrart (1606–88), *Teutsche Akademie der edlen Bau-, Bild-, und Mahlerkünste*, 2 vols., Nürnberg and Frankfurt, 1675, and ed. by J. J. Volkmann, Nürnberg, 1768–75; J. G. Doppelmayr

specially recommends as leading authorities on sixteenth-century German art.[1] Dürer's diary of his journey to the Netherlands is included with his 'Reime',[2] his letters to Pirkheimer and essays on him by the latter.[3] Wackenroder did not actually borrow Sandrart and Doppelmayr from the library—he expressly mentions the former as a source of his remarks on Dürer[4]—but he may nevertheless have consulted them at Fiorillo's house; in any case he had abundant material at his disposal in order to be able to draft the Dürer chapters in Göttingen, as Koldewey suggests,[5] and perhaps a considerable portion of the *Herzensergießungen* as a whole. Murr, of course, frequently quoted from Vasari, whose book he tells us he intended to translate into German;[6] at every turn Wackenroder would realize how indispensable this author really was.

At this point we may also note that some lines on Dürer by Matthes Quad in his *Teutscher Nation Herrlichkeit*, Köln, 1609—borrowed by Wackenroder on 28 July—were made use of for the second chapter on Dürer.[7]

From Dürer to Hans Sachs—of whom Murr was a solitary and enthusiastic champion—and to the whole field of older German literature generally was but a step, and almost immediately on arrival in Göttingen Wackenroder began his keen search for information. His borrowings

(1671–1750), *Historische Nachricht von den nürnbergischen Mathematicis und Künstlern*, Nürnberg, 1730.

[1] *Journal*, ii. 39.
[2] Ibid., vol. vii.
[3] Ibid., vol. x.
[4] *WW*. i. 112.
[5] Koldewey, op. cit., p. 35.
[6] *Journal*, iv. 17.
[7] Cf. Koldewey, op. cit., p. 63; the passage referred to in the *Herzensergießungen* is *WW*. i. 118, and the source in Quad is at p. 426 seq. Quad was no doubt consulted at Fiorillo's, if not at Koch's, instance—Fiorillo himself refers to this writer in his *Geschichte der zeichnenden Künste in Deutschland*, ii. 345: *v. supra.*

from the library bear witness to his enthusiasm; they are as follows:

6 Nov. *Sammlung von Minnesingern aus dem schwäbischen Zeitpuncte CXL Dichter enthaltend durch Ruedger Manessen, weiland des Rathes der uralten Zyrich*, Zyrich, 1758–9 (2 vols., by Bodmer and Breitinger).

21 Nov. *Sammlung der zürcherischen Streitschriften*[1] *zur Verbesserung des deutschen Geschmacks, wider die Gottschedische Schule von 1741 bis 1744*, 3 vols., Zürich, 1753.

10 Dec. *Hannoversches Magazin*, Jahrgang 1767, 1768.

31 Dec. *Hans Sachsens Gedichte*, 5 vols., Kempten, 1612–1616.[2]

10 Jan. *Hans Sachsens Gedichte*, ed. cit., vols. iii, iv.

23 Jan. *Hans Sachsens Gedichte*, ed. cit., vols. i, iv.

12 Feb. *Hannoversches Magazin*, Jahrgang 1765. *Hans Sachsens Gedichte*, ed. cit., vol. v.

20 Mar. *Pegnesisches Schäfergedicht in den Berinorgischen Gefilden angestimmet von Strefon und Clajus*, Nürnberg, 1644.

23 Mar. Jacob Ayrer, *Opus theatricum*, Nürnberg, 1618.

25 Mar. (Wolfgang Helmhard von Hoh(en)berg),[3] *Lust- und Artzney-Garten des Königlichen Propheten Davids*, Regensburg, 1675.

12 May. Malory, *History of the renowned Prince Arthur, King of Britaine*, London, 1634.

---

[1] MS. 'Preißschrift'. Cf. Koldewey, op. cit., p. 34, who interprets this as *Sammlung kritischer, poetischer und anderer geistvollen Schriften*, Zürich, 1741–4 (the first edition).

[2] MS. 'Auchsburg'—the title-page reads 'Getruckt in deß Heyligen Reichs Statt Kempten durch Christoff Krausen / Bey Hansen Krügern in Augspurg zu finden'.

[3] MS. 'v. Harburg Lustgart, &c. fol. (!)'.

9 Sept. *Sammlung vermischter Schriften zur Beförderung der schönen Wissenschaften und der freyen Künste,* 6 vols., Berlin, 1759–63.

It will be seen that Wackenroder's interest in the sixteenth century reached its peak in the first of his two Göttingen terms, when the memories of Erlangen were still uppermost in his mind. In the second term it was the history of art that had his main attention. His concentration on Hans Sachs—which seems to have been almost as feverish as Tieck's on Shakespeare[1]—is remarkable, and there can be no doubt that his fragmentary essay on that poet dates from this time.[2] Once more—as in his attitude to Forkel—Wackenroder resisted strongly the majority of opinions which were presented to him: he represents the transition from the antiquarian to the aesthetic and historical approach. This does not mean that he did not condemn the crudities and improbabilities of Hans Sachs's drama, but he did approach him with some degree of sympathy because he realized his place in the growth of the German drama; and this was a real advance, in an age when only Goethe, of the great ones, and Murr had shown understanding.

Seine *dramatischen* Arbeiten, die einen beträchtlichen Teil seiner Werke ausmachen, sind freilich weder in Ansehung des Plans, noch der poetischen Behandlung, weder als Dramas, noch als Gedichte, von dem geringsten Verdienst, (einige Fastnachtspiele ausgenommen); aber sie müssen uns darum interessant sein, weil wir in ihnen unsre Bühne, von der wir so wenig frühere Proben haben, in der Kindheit erblicken. Dies muß uns anreizen, sie näher kennen zu lernen, [he wrote].[3]

It was in this application of the historical standpoint —behind which stood, of course, primarily Koch—that

---

[1] See 'Ludwig Tieck's English Studies, &c.'
[2] Cf. Köpke, op. cit. i. 176, 297.   [3] *WW.* i. 326.

Wackenroder differed from the works he read. Ebeling[1] in the *Hannoversches Magazin* had been roundly antagonistic to Hans Sachs. The *Sammlung der zürcherischen Streitschriften* included the flippant, satirical poem by Wernicke, written on the model of Dryden's Mac Flecknoe,[2] as well as Bodmer's condemnatory essays 'Von den vortrefflichen Umständen für die Poesie unter den Kaisern aus dem schwäbischen Hause', 'Von der Poesie des sechzehnten Jahrhunderts nach ihrem schönsten Lichte' and 'Von dem Zustande der deutschen Poesie bey Ankunft Martin Opitzens'. Bodmer, primarily concerned with Middle High German poetry, completely failed to appreciate Sachs, holding him largely responsible for the decline of sixteenth-century German literature because of the 'aberwitziger und kahler Inhalt seines Reimgeklappers', and pressed rather the claims of Brant and Fischart;[3] he did, however, advance a step forward towards the historical outlook when he suggested that the language of the sixteenth century should be studied, in order that a just idea might be formed of its literature, and his work was generally helpful because of the publicity it gave to this period.

On Middle High German, however, Bodmer's essays represent meritorious pioneer work,[4] recognizing as they did both the historical and the aesthetic importance of this new field. In his *Streitschriften* as well as in the pre-

[1] *V. infra.*

[2] The poem is entitled 'Hans Sachs. Ein Heldengedicht'. Cf. F. Eichler, *Das Nachleben des Hans Sachs vom XVI. bis ins XIX. Jahrhundert*, Leipzig, 1904, p. 146 (and A. Eichler, 'Christian Wernickes Hans Sachs und sein Drydensches Vorbild MacFlecknoe. Zur Geschichte deutscher Kritik', *Zs. f. vergl. Literaturgesch.*, N.F. 17, 1909).

[3] Ibid., p. 149, also S. von Lempicki, *Geschichte der deutchen Literaturwissenschaft bis zum Ende des 18. Jahrhunderts*, Göttingen, 1920, p. 282 f.

[4] Cf. K. Burdach, 'Die Entdeckung des Minnesangs und die deutsche Sprache', *Vorspiel*, ii, Halle, 1926, pp. 10 ff.

face to his edition of the *Minnesänger* he not only looked very closely at the main factors in the development of medieval poetry, indicating its reflection of medieval culture and, inversely, its value for the study of theology, heraldry, and law, but he also provided a really excellent characterization of the *Minnesang*, distinguishing between it and the *Meistergesang*, and praising its language as a potential source of refreshment and rejuvenation for modern German. According to Köpke,[1] Wackenroder also studied Christoph Heinrich Myller's edition of the *Heldengedichte*, but there is no record of his having used the Göttingen copy.

The 'Kurze Geschichte der deutschen Dichtkunst' which the *Hannoversches Magazin*—the periodical with which the unfortunate Raspe had been connected—published in the form of fourteen articles in its volumes for 1767 and 1768, was a useful, if not inspiring, guide. Koch may have originally drawn Wackenroder's attention to it. The author was Christoph Daniel Ebeling, and it was really a revision of the introduction to Michael Huber's[2] *Choix de poésies allemandes* (Paris, 1766). It is one of the first attempts to survey the whole field of German literature and, considering its date, remarkably complete and instructive. On the older period it did not go beyond Bodmer, though it was well up to date in recommending the study of Old English and Old Norse to those who desired to obtain a complete picture of Germanic culture. The author seems to have been abreast, though not ahead of contemporary criticism; he was, moreover, well aware of the novelty of his whole effort, since, as he noted, Gottsched's history of German

---

[1] Köpke, op. cit. i. 176.
[2] 1727–1804. Professor and Lector in French at Leipzig, and translator of Gessner into French.

language and literature was as yet unpublished and Neukirch's introduction to *Hofmannswaldaus und andere Gedichte* (1697) and Morhof's *Unterricht von der Teutschen Sprache* (1718) were incomplete and 'ohne Geschmack'. He had nothing but censure for the party squabbles of Klotz und Gerstenberg and the rest and looks with distinct disfavour on the 'Hamannische Schwärmereyen' of the rising school. There was indeed a Nicolai-like attitude in his comments, which could not but have aroused Wackenroder's animosity; he writes, for instance, on the *Minnesänger*, in a passage that may serve as a typical example:

Ihre Gedichte sind voll Natur, es herrscht darin viel Geist, viel feine, zärtliche, ungekünstelte und vornehmlich naive Empfindung. . . . Aber man muß bedenken, daß alles bloße Natur war, und diese weder von den Schätzen der Belesenheit, noch von der Strenge der Kritik verbessert und verschönert ward.[1]

It is almost incredible!

Of the other works that Wackenroder borrowed it would seem that some were consulted on Koch's behalf. This was no doubt the case with Hohberg's verse translation of the Psalter or Harsdörfer's *Schäfergedicht*. Jacob Ayrer, however, would interest the student of Hans Sachs, though he may really have been borrowed on Tieck's behalf, since Tieck was concerned at this time with *The Spanish Tragedy* and Ayrer's adaptation.[2] Malory no doubt attracted both of the friends; possibly, also, Nicolai's *Sammlung vermischter Schriften*, which contained, apart from Cahusac's essay remarked on above, a translation of Dryden's 'Essay on the origin and progress of satire', two essays (one by Sulzer) on the subject of genius,

---

[1] *Hannoversches Magazin*, 1767, p. 98. The 1765 volume of the *Magazin* contained an article of Kästner's 'Über die Zeiten in welche Don Quixote gehört', which may have attracted Tieck's attention, in view of his Spanish interests.　　[2] See 'Ludwig Tieck's English Studies, &c.'

and a German version of Young's 'Discourse on lyric poetry'.[1]

In view of the very close collaboration between Wackenroder and Tieck, it might be convenient at this stage briefly to note Tieck's library borrowings in this field; for while it is true that Tieck showed signs of desiring to investigate all literature of the period that included Shakespeare—a breadth of vision that no doubt owed something to Wackenroder—one cannot be absolutely certain whether his library borrowings in German literature were for himself alone or for his friend.[2] He took out Gryphius's *Teutsche Gedichte* (Breslau, 1698) on 13 December 1793 and Christian Weise's *Der grünenden Jugend überflüssige Gedanken* (Nürnberg, 1671)[3] on 19 June 1794. It is well known that he developed a keen interest in Weise, who influenced his satirical vein, especially in the *Verkehrte Welt*, *Prinz Zerbino* and the earlier *Hanswurst als Emigrant*,[4] and one might have expected that he would sooner or later plunge for Gryphius, too. C. Denina's *Révolutions d'Italie* (Tieck borrowed the French translation, vols. v and vi, Paris, 1773, on 13 December 1793) may have been consulted in connexion with Fiorillo's course: for these volumes deal with the Italian Renaissance. Crescimbeni's *Istoria della volgar Poesia* (6 vols., Venice, 1730–1), (which Tieck took out on 14 July 1794, retaining the first volume on 23 August),

---

[1] Cf. J. L. Kind, *Edward Young in Germany* (Columbia Univ. Germanic Studies, II. iii), New York, 1906, pp. 132, 144 (where 'vol. i' is given erroneously for 'vol. ii').

[2] Both Burgsdorff and Wackenroder borrowed books for Tieck (cf. 'Ludwig Tieck's English Studies, etc.').

[3] A new edition by Max Frhr. von Waldberg appeared in 1914 (Braune's *Neudrucke*, pp. 242–5).

[4] Cf. F. Riederer, *Ludwig Tiecks Beziehungen zur deutschen Literatur des 17. Jahrhunderts*, Diss. Greifswald, 1915, pp. 71–93.

provided information on the origin and growth of the
European drama and other genres. This was certainly a
most important authority for those times[1]—it had been
from this work, indeed, that Bodmer had derived his
knowledge of the Troubadours.[2] It may have been this
Arcadian satellite of Queen Christine who helped to bring
out the nationalistic, anti-cosmopolitan strain in Tieck's
criticism.[3] Wackenroder must have read with great profit
the accounts of Troubadour poetry in connexion with his
study of the *Minnesang*.

The remaining books which Wackenroder borrowed
from the Göttingen library may be dismissed without
special comment. They are:

7 Dec. J. B. F. Hennebert, *Histoire Générale de la
Province d'Artois*,[4] 3 vols., Lille, 1786–9 (of which
only vol. i was present in Göttingen).

13 Jan. Plautus, *Comédies nouvellement traduites par
Gueudeville*, vols. vii, viii, Leyden, 1718.[5]

27 May. C. W. J. Gatterer, *Anleitung den Harz und
andere Bergwerke mit Nuzen zu bereisen*, Göttingen,
1785–93.[6]

[1] It is mentioned with honour by A. Jeanroy, *La poésie lyrique des
troubadours*, Paris, 1934, i. 11, for its publication of specimens of Troubadour poetry.

[2] 'Crescimbenis Storia', remarks Burdach (*Vorspiel*, ii. 21 n.), 'ist für
die Methode literaturgeschichtlicher Betrachtung bedeutsam und hat
als Beispiel patriotisch-reformatorischer Literaturpädagogik auf Bodmer
sicher befruchtend gewirkt.'

[3] Cf. J. G. Robertson, *Studies in the Genesis of Romantic Theory in the
Eighteenth Century*, Cambridge, 1923, pp. 16 ff. and 56.

[4] MS. 'Histoire de la Provence'. What interest had Wackenroder in
Artois?

[5] Burgsdorff had already borrowed these volumes on 18 Nov. 1792,
and no doubt these two were passed on to him. Volume 10 of this edition,
in which all the improprieties are listed, does not seem to have been consulted by any of the friends!

[6] Perhaps perused in preparation for the journey home in the autumn.

22 July. *Commentationes societatis scientiarum Goettingensis*, ii, 1779, and *Novi commentarii societatis reg. scientiarum Goettingensis*, iv, 1774.[1]

Such was the immediate fruit of his teachers' influence. In this reading-list of Wackenroder's it was not so much the matter he absorbed—important as it undoubtedly was—but before all else the method of his approach that meant such a great deal during this formative period of his life. It was his resistance to the cold abstractions of analytical criticism, which he felt in his bones stood in the way of real enjoyment of works of art, and his conversion, under the guidance of such men as Koch and Fiorillo, to the historical standpoint, that made of his *Herzensergießungen*, to which everything was already pointing so clearly during these Göttingen terms, so entrancing a pendant to *Von deutscher Art und Kunst*. The insistance on faith and feeling as the real keys to artistic pleasure, the mystical reverence before the inscrutable divinity of the creative artist, made technical faultfinding and frigid systematic theorizing appear in the light of blasphemy. When Winckelmann finished his *Geschichte der Kunst des Altertums*, he wrote, in his last paragraph:

So wie eine Liebste an dem Ufer des Meeres ihren abfahrenden Liebhaber, ohne Hoffnung, ihn wiederzusehen, mit betränten Augen verfolgt und selbst in dem entfernten Segel das Bild des Geliebten zu sehen glaubt. Wir haben, wie die Geliebte, gleichsam nur einen Schatten von dem Vorwurfe unserer Wünsche übrig; aber desto größere Sehnsucht nach dem Verlorenen erweckt derselbe, und wir betrachten die Kopien der Urbilder mit größerer Aufmerksamkeit, als wie wir in dem völligen Besitze von diesen nicht würden getan haben—

a passage that might well be applied to Wackenroder's

[1] Consulted on Koch's behalf?—the latter volume contained an article by J. P. Murray on 'Antiquitates septentrionales et Britannicae atque Hibernicae inter se comparatae', the Edda being among the subjects discussed.

attitude, except that to its reminiscent sentiment must be added a note of religious fervour, which in Tieck's hands became highly catholicized, and the final observation amended to show that in Wackenroder's case the art treasures he enthused about were far from being departing shadows or inadequate copies, but originals in all their fascinating glory. Wackenroder's yearning attached itself rather to the departed age and spirituality that brought them forth.

THE CADENCE IN GERMANIC
ALLITERATIVE VERSE

By C. E. GOUGH

IN any examination of old Germanic alliterative poetry
the reader is struck by the great diversity of metrical
forms, called by Sievers 'types'. Each half-line could fall
into one of Sievers's normal types, A, C, D with *klingend*
endings and B, D 4, E with *stumpf* endings, or two
exceptional types F and G, or into the variants of these
types. Kaluza,[1] who in the main follows Sievers, further
subdivides the types into ninety sub-species, to which
two more[2] may be added. This multiplicity of forms
might lead us to suppose that the poets of the earlier
Middle Ages, in spite of their lower cultural development,
laboured under more intricate metrical rules than the
classical Greek and Latin authors or the poets of modern
times. This seems highly improbable to me, and the
object of this paper is to endeavour to discover the
essential laws of versification observed in alliterative
poetry. These in a primitive civilization should tend to
be simple; they would furthermore be evolved from the
conditions for which the poetry was composed. In an
age when a reading public did not exist, we may suppose
that practically all narrative poetry was intended for
recitation. In this case the peculiarities of Germanic
intonation would of themselves supply the rhythmic laws
to be observed.

All metricists are agreed that the Germanic *long-line*

---

[1] *A Short History of English Versification*, transl. A. C. Dunstan,
George Allen, 1911, p. 76 f.

[2] Cf. *sub* §§ 12 and 15.

consists of two short-lines, of the *on-half* and of the *off-half*, joined together by alliteration. In the on-half one or two words, the *Stollen*, commence with exactly the same sound as that possessed by the first highly stressed word, the *Hauptstab*, of the off-line. This *Hauptstab* must be placed as near as possible to the beginning of the off-line, but the position of the *Stollen* varies considerably. Since there are clearly two heavily stressed syllables in the on-half, and we find the *Hauptstab* and one other important syllable in the second half-line, it is certain that each half-line contains two main stresses.

But even within half-lines of the same rhythmical structure little uniformity is seen. Thus, whilst the half-line in its shortest form (normally) consists of *four* syllables, other half-lines contain more, sometimes even twice as many.

Since they know with certainty only of the existence of *two* highly-stressed syllables in each half-line, many metricists ignore the value of the other syllables. Their reading of alliterative verse does not differ essentially from that of prose and lacks the rhythm found in all true poetry. To primitive peoples rhythm is of greater value than melody. Other metricists base their views on the shortest form of the half-line—four syllables—and assign a secondary accent to those syllables on which the main stress does not fall. This procedure seems somewhat forced at first sight, but is more readily appreciated when the half-line consists of more than four syllables, thus containing two highly-stressed, two lesser-stressed, and some unstressed syllables. We have then the difference of a syllable in a *Senkung* (i.e. bearing a lesser stress) from one standing in a dip or *Taktfüllung* (i.e. absolutely unstressed).

Thus, whilst alliterative verse scanned by adherents of

the 'Two-stress school' lacks rhythm, in the hands of 'Four-stress' metricists it becomes a most complex matter and apparently possesses more rules and greater difficulties than does blank verse or any other form of modern poetry. It is inconceivable that a poet in primitive times could keep all these rules in mind whilst he was in the throes of composition. Did the author of *Beowulf* decide that he would open his epic with a D-type followed by a C-type? Or did he follow some simpler plan, contented when his half-lines conformed to it and rang metrically true to his ear?

A. Heussler (*Deutsche Versgeschichte*) offers another solution to the riddle of alliterative verse. He presupposes (justly?) that Type A is the basic form and that all other types are differentiations of it. By an ingenious but complicated system of adding pauses whenever required he lets every half-line be read as an A-type.[1] The drawback of this method is that it demands too delicate and exact an ear for poetry on behalf of the listeners, as well as the need of metronome for the poet or declaimer of the verse.

Practically all the old Germanic poetry which has survived was intended for recitation. Certainly the oldest epics were—they formed an entertainment after a feast— and the Christian epics surely were composed less for the enjoyment of the few who could read, than with the object of spreading religious instruction in a popular garb.

If we bear in mind that old Germanic poetry was composed for the purpose of *recitation to large audiences*, we shall find in the peculiar intonation of the Germanic languages and in the efforts of the reciter to make his voice carry far the clue to many puzzling characteristics of alliterative verse. To intonation must be attributed its chief feature—*alliteration*. In the Germanic dialects, at

[1] Cf. § 14, *infra*.

any rate after the migration of the peoples, from which time the oldest poetical documents have come down to us, the accent on each word had become stationary and could never change to any other syllable in the word, as it could in Latin, e.g. in *habere*, *habui* or *Cato*, *Catonis*. The accent rested on the first syllable, the root of the word. To the natural emphasis of language the old poets added further stress by making the most important words of the line begin with the same sound. In the on-half one or two words possessed alliteration, in the off-half the most important word. If the hearers heard the first alliterating word, they would listen carefully for the second and third, and, even if they were at a distance from the reciter, they could gather the gist of the passage by putting together these highly emphasized words, although they had not always been able to catch the unstressed syllables. This was rendered easier by another peculiarity of Germanic articulation. The expiratory current is applied with full force at the beginning of a sentence, as it is in the case of individual words. Now, after the on-half there was a pause much greater than a mere caesura. The all-important word came directly after this pause; it received alliteration, sentence-stress, and word-stress combined. It was as important as is the last word in the limerick to-day. The Germans call it *Hauptstab*, the chief stave. Of the *Stollen* or supports one only need alliterate, and it seems to have been a matter of indifference which, though normally the first highly stressed bore alliteration.

In a consideration of the kinds of words usually found in alliteration we must bear in mind that they must be the key-words of the sentence. They must give the clue to its meaning should some of the less important words not be caught. With us the verb seems to be the most important part of speech, but for the purposes of alliteration it is not. After all, in subordinate clauses in German the verb is relegated to the end, when there is scarcely any breath left for articulation. A verb only becomes emphatic when it is brought quite up to the beginning of the sentence, when it receives the full force of sentence-stress. In *Stabreim* (alliterative verse) nouns, adjectives, and even adverbs are of greater value than verbs. This can be readily understood, if we think of what happens when we listen to a speech, stand far from the speaker, and catch only a word here and there. Supposing we hear the nouns, we can with ease mentally supply the gaps in the sentence. Thus we can easily supply the verb to the words: *The man . . . beggar . . . penny* or *The man . . . beggar nothing.* It is a different matter if we hear: *The man* **gave** . . . and then a lot of mumbling. An adjective has greater stress than the noun following—þæt **wæs gōd cyning!** Think; what word would you emphasize in the sentence: '*He was a wise man*'?

But the necessity for making oneself understood by a large audience could not be limited to the stressing of the syllables bearing alliteration. Adjectives, nouns, verbs, and adverbs when inflected consisted of a heavily stressed root-syllable and an ending often containing a sonorous vowel. Since the terminations played an important part in understanding the meaning of the sentence, the reciter was obliged to articulate them very clearly. In doing so he would give them a stress greater than that to which they were entitled. In the case of poetry this tendency is enhanced; in its love for the archaic the language of alliterative verse preserved obsolescent forms and avoided the use of prepositions and the definite article already in vogue in prose. In the half-line: *suertu hauwan* the four syllables imply: hack me *with* his sword. Without a certain amount of stress on the endings the meaning might not be clearly perceived.[1] Thus the act of declamation altered the rhythmical construction of words from their prose norms, and gave a secondary stress to syllables usually devoid of stress altogether. We may notice the same process to-day, whenever a notice is given out in a loud voice, as in the toastmaster's formula:

My Lords, Ladies and Gentlemen, pray silence ...

How different in intonation to *ladies 'n gent'lm'n* of every-day speech! With such articulation words like Ladies, Gentlemen, silence become rhythmical units. We have a heavily stressed root-syllable—though sometimes two short syllables are resolved into one long one, as in Gentlemen—and a sonorous ending, which receives more stress than in normal diction. Such a unit I propose to call a *Cadence*, because a fall in stress (as well as in pitch) is characteristic of it. If a half-line ends in a long stressed monosyllable, it is said to have a *stumpf* or blunt ending, if in a *cadence*, it is said to have a *klingend* or sonorous ending. In examples of the latter taken from *Béowulf*:

lange hwīle (16 *a*)

on freān wǣre (28 *b*)

the endings are cadences of the type ⌢.

The adherents of the two-stress school deny the existence of the cadence in the *klingend* ending. But Otfrid preserved it carefully, even when he replaced alliteration by end-rhyme; it existed in MHG. poetry and does so to-day still in German folk-song and in

[1] The tendency of English philologists to adhere to the 'two-stress' school is perhaps largely due to the fact that it is hard for them to realize the importance of inflectional endings, since the latter have almost disappeared in Modern English.

English and German nursery rhymes. The refrain of Goethe's 'Heidenröslein' borrowed from a folk-song has a *klingend* ending in *Heiden*. English infants chant: 'A ring, a ring of roses, a pocketful of posies' to the same intonation as the German: 'Ringel, Ringel, Reihe, Sind der Kinder dreie'. In alliterative verse the cadence was, however, not restricted to the ending; it could occur after either or each of the heavily stressed syllables in the half-line, and in any position within it.

Before going into an examination of cadences and the part they played in alliterative poetry, I should like to discuss the question: Were the old epics intoned? The Germans say no; the adherents of the two-stress school will not admit the declamatory element even in recitation, but believe that no departure was made from the rhythm of prose. Now, if there had been given melodies for the different types, it would have been very difficult for the singer to keep all the changes correctly, especially as there were some ninety sub-species to select from, as Kaluza has shown. To-day in a music-hall *tour de force* a singer sometimes draws two lines each from a number of well-known airs and combines them into a sort of narrative. But, what if he had to change tunes after every fourth or fifth syllable and go on doing that by the hour without previous rehearsal? We may conclude that the epics were not intended for singing; indeed, the MHG. expression *singen unde sagen* makes this clear. But the recitation of epics was accompanied by much modulation and also was presumably highly declamatory for the following reasons. The tendency inherent to all to recite in a sing-song manner, is very evident among primitive individuals, children, and less educated adults. It is noticeable too among poets reciting verses, probably owing to a poet's sensitiveness to the *Stimmung* of a lyric, which reproduces itself in a sub-conscious melody. Another tendency towards declamatory effect was the need for stressing (even to excess) the alliterating words in the verse; further, the necessity for the *scop* or minstrel to make his words carry far. Presumably either the minstrel or an attendant played a soft accompaniment on the harp, but the 'singer' need not have sung the words to the notes played. On the wireless from foreign stations poems can be heard recited with much declamation to the accompaniment of a cello or violin playing music in feeling with the poem. The harp accompaniment is well attested in Anglo-Saxon poetry; the *epitheton ornans* of the harp, the *gamenwudu* implies that it took part in all social entertainment, even that of recital of narrative poetry. But it is a well-known fact that it is easier to 'catch' the spoken word than words that are sung; the *scop* would, therefore, have desired to make himself understood rather than to show off the range of his voice. Then, as now, some poetry was certainly sung, but it was of a lyrical nature, *Wini-lieder* or love-songs, none of which have come down to us. Here we are only concerned with the epic measures.

The mode of epic recitation, the necessity for declamation, for heavy emphasis on certain words and for emphasizing their endings have produced the peculiar forms of alliterative Germanic poetry. Clear accentuation was of greater importance than vowel-quantity. Most metricists have been trained in the schools of the Greek and Latin classics, and have never been able to rid themselves of classical tradition. Now it is to be doubted whether any Germans spoke Latin, though like the Sepoys and other native troops of to-day they understood the words of command used in the armies of the Empire. But their own language in its whole intonation differed from that of the Latin nations. They neither recognized in poetry the need for a fixed number of syllables to the line, nor for any regular sequence of feet containing vowels of definite length. Some of this persists to the present day, when the substitution of an anapaestic foot for an iambus is permissible even in poetry written for song. Furthermore, the sagas, and with them the Germanic form of the epic, originated in the stories of national heroes who fought and fell in the struggles during the migrations of the peoples, after the downfall of the Empire, and before Latin influence reached the Germanic nations through the christianizing efforts of Rome. Old Germanic metres are therefore a thing absolutely apart from those of the classics, and it is only confusing to use classical terms, such as tetrameters, dipodies, and feet.

It is fairly safe to follow the example of ten Brink[1] and Kaluza[2] and to accept as *Urform* of the alliterating half-line an Indo-Germanic measure:

$$1 \quad 2 \quad 3 \quad 4$$
$$\times \diagup \times \diagup \times \diagup \times \diagup$$

The stressed syllables are of unequal value; two are heavier than the others. According to their positions in the line I shall speak of them as tacts (*Takte*). It will be observed that the half-line closes with a stress. If tact 4 bears a main stress, it is *stumpf* or blunt and has the value of two moras. It may be expressed quantitatively by $\smile\smile$.

But tact 4 may bear a secondary stress only. In that case it has the value of a single mora, thus $\smile$, and forms the last element of a *klingend* or sonorous ending. Schematically this may be expressed as $\smile\smile\smile$. It is formed by

[1] *Grundriß*, 1893², II. i. 516.
[2] Cf. note 1, pp. 56 f., 65 f.

the close interlocking of tacts 3 and 4, for instance as syllables of the same word.

But a cadence of the rhythmical form of the *klingend* ending can be found anywhere within the half-line. All we have to do is to link two tacts together; thus [∕×∕] produces ⌣⌣⌢∖.

    × [∕×∕] × [∕×∕] becomes (×) ⌣⌣⌢∖ (×) ⌣⌣⌢∖

    × ∕ × [∕ × ∕] × ∕ ,,   (×)∖(×) ⌣⌣⌢∖ (×) ⌣⌣

    × [∕ × ∕] × ∕ × ∕ ,,   (×) ⌣⌣⌢∖(×)∖(×) ⌣⌣

It will be noticed that the dips marked by × in the original scheme are bracketed in that of the alliterative half-line. That is because it was optional to fill them or to omit them. At first there was a tendency to reduce the half-line to its shortest form of four syllables all stressed to various degrees. These 'emphatic syllables' now form the rhythmical framework of the half-line. Later on, as the striving after terseness in poetic diction grew less and a degeneration of alliterative versification set in, we find the initial dip (in the anacrusis or *Auftakt*) expanded inordinately.[1] The dip or dips permissible within the line are then filled in, and this *Taktfüllung* often reaches too wide dimensions.

It will be observed that the cadence ⌣⌣⌢∖ need not consist of two syllables only. If the root-vowel is short, it and the next vowel count only as one long syllable together. *făter* is impossible as a cadence, but the half-line

    fateres mînes   ⌣⌣⌢∖   ⌣_⌢∖

contains two, one in the *klingend* ending *mînes*, the other in *fateres*, where the short *a* is compensated for by the *e* immediately following.

---

[1] Cf. § 22, *infra*.

Owing to the facility with which the Germanic languages make compound words we find cadences stretching over three and even four tacts. *Beowulf* is particularly rich in them, thus:

Gār-Dena (1*a*), geārdagum (1 *b*)
æðelingas (3 *a*)
þeōdcyninga (2 *a*)

Four times in the three first lines! Examples of three-tact cadences may be found in the *Hildebrandslied* at 19*a*, 23*a*, 25*a*, 26*b*, in the *Heliand* at 4*a*, 60*a*, 100*b*. Four-tact cadences (filling the whole half-line) are not rare; they occur in *HL.* (= *Hildebrandslied*) at 4*a*, 42*b*, in *H.* (= *Heliand*) at 82*b*, 91*b*, 130*a*, &c.

In MHG. four-tact cadences are unknown, but three-stress *klingende Endungen* are plentiful, especially in the *Volksepen*. In the *Nibelungen* (*B.*) they occur as endings of first half-lines in stanzas 2 and 5 (*Burgonden*), 9 (*marcgrâven, Alzeije*), 30 (*Sîvrîde*), &c. Even a careful author like Hartmann von Aue wrote in his *Armer Heinrich*:

305.   so rehte güetlîchen.
326.   mit süezer unmuoze.
1514.   nâch süezem lanclîbe.

The occurrence of cadences at the end, in the middle, and at the beginning of half-lines may be explained by the rule that no dip or unstressed syllable was permitted after *one* of the two main stresses.

prût in bûre   (*HL.* 21 *a*)
un*tar* heriun tuēm   (*HL.* 3 *b*)
mit gēru scal man (*HL.* 37 *a*)

In fact the cadence formed an integral part of the half-line; it is really the chief rhythmic element and forms a good guide to the scansion. Thus it is necessary only to pick out the two chief stresses, both often marked by alliteration and to note the one accompanied by the cadence. Read thus the fourth syllable falls into its right place in the metrical scheme. Though there must be *two* main-stresses, occasionally a third may occur. In the lines:

welag*a nû* **w**altant got   (*HL. 49 a*)
micel **m**orgen-swég   (*B. 129 a*)

the first two main-stresses are indicated by alliteration, the third by its position at the end of the line in a *stumpf* ending.

Whilst resolution (*Auflösung*) of the main-stresses was permissible, no lesser-stressed syllable was *aufgelöst* in the cadence. For instance, in the first off-half in *Béowulf : in gēardagum* the stem *dag* is short, but bears a stress less heavy than *gēar*. It may not be resolved with the ending *-um* to form one long syllable. The cadence is ⌒⌣⌣, not ⌒ ⌣⌣.

Before passing to a closer examination of Sievers's 'types', I should like to outline my thesis. The old poets wrote for recitation, and this reacted on the metrical form. Presumably they did not recognize six 'types' (as well as several sub-species), but observed very few and simple rules. These are:

Each verse consists of two half-lines, each containing four emphatic syllables. The on-half and the off-half are joined (*gebunden*) by alliteration, which must be exact (just as in modern verse end-rime should be pure). The on-half has one or two alliterating syllables (the *Stollen*); the off-half has one alliterating syllable (the *Hauptstab*), placed as near to the beginning as possible.

After one of the main-stresses in each half a cadence must

follow. The cadence must extend over the whole dis-
syllabic (or polysyllabic) word.[1]

The cadence gives to alliterative poetry its verse-rhythm,
which is quite distinct from prose intonation. Two
cadences are permissible, but not obligatory (any
more than double alliteration, which occurs sometimes as poetic adornment).

Auftakt or anacrusis is free; that is, an unaccented
syllable (or even two or three unimportant words)
may be prefixed to the rhythmic part of each half-
line. Also within the half-line extra syllables may
be introduced (from grammatical considerations) as
long as they are not intruded into a cadence.

A. *Half-lines with 'klingend' endings*

§ 1. Presumably the oldest form of the half-line was the
type called A by Sievers. It has been evolved from the *Urform*

$$\times [\diagup \times \diagup] \times [\diagup \times \diagup] \text{ as } (\times) \, \frown \, (\times) \, \frown$$

Shortest forms:

> wuldres wealdend (*B.* 17 *a*, cf. 10 *b*, 11 *a*, 16 *a*, &c.)
> ænôn muotîn (*HL.* 2 *b*, cf. 9 *a*, 22 *a*, 25 *b*, &c.)
> lera Cristes (*H.* 6 *b*, cf. 13 *b*, 37 *b*, 46 *a*, &c.)

With *Auftakt*:

> *In* Caines cynne (*B.* 107 *a*)
> *der dir nû* wîges warne (*HL.* 59 *a*)
> *ge*corana uurđun (*H.* 17 *b*)

With *Taktfüllung*:

> folce *tó* frófre (*B.* 14 *a*, cf. 18 *a*, 29 *a*, &c.)
> alte *anti* frôte (*HL.* 16 *a*, cf. 30 *b*, 48 *b*, &c.)
> reckean *that* giruni (*H.* 3 *a*, cf. 11 *a*, 22 *a*, &c.)

---

[1] We shall see later that the cadence is apparently missing in some half-
lines; but in these cases a highly stressed syllable is always followed by an
independent syllable bearing a lesser stress. These two words are then
linked together rhythmically, and heard as one rhythmic unit, a cadence
for the ear only.

With *Auftakt* and *Taktfüllung*:

> *in* mǽgða gehwǽre (*B.* 25 *a*)
> her *was eo* folches *at* ente (*HL.* 27 *a*, cf. 65 *a*)
> *mid* uuordun *endi mid* uuercun (*H.* 5 *a*)

With resolution in tact 1:

> monegum mǽgðum (*B.* 5 *a*, cf. 27 *a*, 60 *b*, &c.)
> fateres mînes (*HL.* 24 *a*, cf. 16 *a*, 30 *b*, 6 *a*)
> Manega uuaron (*H.* 1 *a*, cf. 21 *a*, 28 *a*, 51 *b*, &c.)

With resolution in tact 3:

> ellen fremedon (*B.* 3 *b*, cf. 19 *a*, 41 *a*, 46 *b*, &c.)
> rauba *bi*rahanen (*HL.* 57 *a*, cf. 26 *a*, 30 *b*, 65 *a*)
> helpa *fan* himila (*H.* 11 *b*, cf. 34 *b*, 89 *b*, &c.)

§ 2. Breaking-up of the First Cadence. Since only one cadence was demanded, and the final cadence was essential in a half-line with *klingend* ending, it might be better to consider that the *Urform* was adhered to up to tact 3, thus

$$\times / \times / \times \; [/ \times /] \text{ becomes } (\times) / (\times) \setminus (\times) \,\overset{\frown}{\smile}$$

(*a*) The alliteration must rest on tact 1, otherwise the half-line coincides with Sievers's C-type.

> want *her* dô *ar* arme (*HL.* 33 *a*, cf. 40 *a*, 54 *a*, 61 *b*)
> uuis*a* man *mid* uuordun (*H.* 95 *a*, cf. 26 *a*, 199 *b*)

(*b*) Sometimes both stresses, separated by an un-accented syllable, occur (in OHG. and OS. poetry) in the same word, usually a proper noun:

> Hilt*i*brant *enti* Haðubrant (*HL.* 3 *a*, cf. 7 *a*, 45 *a*; 14 *a*, 36 *a*)
> hel*a*gar*o* stemnun (*H.* 24 *b*)

(*c*) Frequently tact 2 is replaced by a preposition or a prefix (usually *gi-*, *ge-*).

> geong in geardum (*B.* 13 *a*, cf. 81 *a*)
> wil-gesîðas (*B.* 23 *a*, cf. 22 *b*, 42 *b*, 45 *b*, &c.)
> prût in bûre (*HL.* 21 *a*, cf. 20 *a*)
> craft fan Criste (*H.* 12 *a*, cf. 37 *a*)

(*d*) Occasionally we find tact 2 compensated, so that a cadence of the type $\angle\widehat{\smile}$ is apparently formed. Since a lesser stress cannot be resolved, I can only account for it by supposing the last syllable to have been totally unstressed, thus $\wedge\times$, and recited as in *Nibelungen* 5 (4*b*):

sît in Étzélen lant.

Thus: ort wid*ar* orte *HL*. 38*a* leads to wuntan*e* bougâ *HL*. 33*b*. This is uncommon, but is a sign of degeneration in the metrics of alliterative verse.

> folc-sted*e* frætwan (*B*. 76 *a*, cf. 156 *a*, 193 *a*, 208 *a*, &c.)
> bêder*o* uualtan (*HL*. 62 *b*)
> marith*a* g*i*frumida (*H*. 4 *b*, cf. 50 *b*, 83 *a*, 106 *a*, &c.)

(*e*) Sometimes both main-stresses fall within the ending; the original scheme $\times\diagup\times\diagup\times\ [\diagup\times\diagup]$ is reproduced as $(\times)\diagdown(\times)\diagdown(\times)\diagup\widehat{}$. Alliteration rests on tact 3; this subspecies only occurs in on-lines and the off-line following invariably opens with the *Hauptstab*.[1]

> *þæt* hin*e* on ylde (*B*. 22 *a*, cf. 28 *a*, 43 *a*, 47 *a*, &c.)
> unt*i* im *iro* lintûn (*HL*. 67 *a*, cf. 47 *a* and 63 *a*)
> *that* sia fan Cristes (*H*. 34 *a*, cf. 74 *a*, 82 *a*, 90 *a*)

§ 3. If the *klingend* ending formed by the union of tacts 3 and 4 is preserved, but the first main-stress rests on tact 2 instead of tact 1 as before, we obtain the type called C by Sievers.

Thus $\times\diagup\times\diagup\times[\diagup\times\diagup]$ becomes $(\times)\diagdown(\times)\diagup(\times)\widehat{\diagdown}$

> on fréan wǽre (*B*. 27 *b*, cf. 4 *a*, 28 *b*, 60 *a*, &c.)
> ir*o* saro rihtun (*HL*. 4 *b*)
> an buok scrîƀan (*H*. 14 *a*, cf. 132 *a*)

An irregular cadence $\angle\widehat{\smile}$ is found in *H*. at l. 18*b*: *so uuarun* thia man hetana.

---

[1] This rule does not obtain in ON., and Koegel (*Gesch. d. deut. Lit.*, Strassburg, 1894, i. 296 f.) scans *HL*. 17 *b*—*ih heittu Hádubrànt*. Since *h* is the alliterating letter, I prefer to read *ih* heittu Hadubrant as an A-type (with double alliteration in the off-half as poetic adornment).

§ 4. *Formation of Threefold Cadences.* Whenever a cadence is preceded immediately by a main-stress, there is a tendency to widen the cadence, because the second stress is weaker than the first. From the formula ╱╱⌢╲ we get ╱⌢╲. The compound words (both nouns and adjectives) in which the Germanic dialects are so rich have mainly produced these threefold cadences. From ×╱×[╱×╱×╱] we obtain (×)╲×╱⌢╲

The following instances from *B.* will serve to illustrate the new formation:

(*a*) [Hwæt!]wé Gár-dena (1 *a*)
  in géar-dagum (1 *b*)
  of*er* hron-ráde (10 *a*)
  tó *ge*scæp-hwíle (26 *b*)

In these examples we have two words so closely connected that in English it is customary to hyphen them; in German the hyphen is superfluous. From such words it is but a short transition to *one* word only, which has falling intonation.

(*b*) hú *þá* æðelingas (*B.* 3 *a*, cf. 38 *a*, 45 *a*, 64 *a*, &c.)
  sîd Dêtrîhhe (*HL.* 23 *a*, cf. 2 *a*, 19 *a*, 25 *a*, &c.)
  und*ar* mancunnea (*H.* 4 *a*, cf. 44 *a*, 89 *a*, 99 *a*, &c.)

Occasionally the second element of the cadence (the second main-stress of the half-line) consists of a short syllable:

(*c*) þæt heal-reced (*B.* 68 *a*, cf. 37 *a*, 1 *a*, 1 *b*, &c.)
  mid *is* rokfaton (*H.* 108 *a*, cf. 44 *a*, 58 *b*, 100 *b*, &c.)

Thus quantity in this position is immaterial; it is essential that the stress on the second element should be greater than that on the last.

§ 5. In the type (*c*) described in the previous paragraph we have a half-line with apparently only one stress, since the second main-stress lies within the cadence and possesses little more strength than a secondary stress. If, instead of the weakly accented syllable in tact 1 we

found the first main-stress, we should have the type called
D by Sievers. It can easily be distinguished from C by
the alliteration resting on tact 1.

×∕×[∕×∕×∕] develops into ∕(×)‿⌣.
Auftakt is usually lacking:

> léof landfruma (*B.* 31 *a*, cf. 21 *a*, 57 *a*, 223 *a*, &c.)
> wine Scyldinga (*B.* 30 *b*, cf. 47 *b*, 58 *b*, 291 *a*, &c.)
> chind, *in* chunincrîche (*HL.* 13 *a*, cf. 5 *a*, 8 *a*, 66 *a*)
> barn unwahsan (*HL.* 21 *b*)
> allon elitheodon (*H.* 60 *a*, cf. 55 *a*, 65 *a*, 109 *a*, &c.)

§ 6. *Four-stress cadences.* The compound word, usually
a noun, fills the whole half-line. No *Auftakt* is permitted.
The transition to this form from that just described is
clearly seen in compounds like:

> wig-weorðunga (*B.* 176 *a*)
> adalordfrumo (*H.* 31 *a*),

but commonly only tact 1 has alliteration.

The scheme ×[∕×∕×∕×∕] is reduced to ‿⌣ ‿⌣ ⌣⌣:

> lind-hæbbende (*B.* 245 *a*, cf. 2 *a*, 95 *b*, 246 *a*, &c.)
> sunufatarungo (*HL.* 4 *a*, sêolîdante *HL.* 42 *b*)
> heƀancuninge[1] (*H.* 278 *b*, cf. 130 *a*)

Four-stress cadences with *Auftakt* may be found, but
need examination.

> þára ymb-sittendra (*B.* 9 *b*)

Presumably in the *Ur-Béowulf* the half-line read: *ymb-
sittendra*. In the later WS. rendering *þára* was inserted
owing to the more frequent use made of the article at a
later period.

> in folc sceotantero (*HL.* 51 *b*)

Here the *Auftakt*: *in folc* is impossible, because *folc* being

---

[1] The poet of the *Heliand* is inconsistent in his treatment of *cuning* and
boran in cadences. Here he stresses each syllable; in 159*a* and elsewhere
he resolves them into a single stress.

the first noun should bear the *Hauptstab*, but *sc* represents the alliteration. The line has been wrongly divided, it should read:

 dâr man mih eo scerita *in* folc sceotantero

and the on-half be scanned as a B-type, cf. § 8.

§ 7. Not all single words filling the half-line are to be read as four-stress cadences. Many are really A-types (cf. §§ 1, 2): ╱＼ ╱＼

 wil-gesíðas (*B.* 23 *a*, cf. 63 *b*, 209 *b*, &c.)
 earfoðlíce (*B.* 86 *b*)
 ôstarliuto (*HL.* 58 *b*)
 saliglico (*H.* 48 *b*, cf. 65 *b*, 68 *b*, 69 *b*, &c.)

In gerúmlícor (*B.* 139*a*) we have a C-type, cf. § 4. ＼╱＼

B. *Half-lines with 'stumpf' endings*

A *stumpf* ending has the form ⌣⌣, and, since it possesses the value of two moras, always represents a main-stress. In on-halves it often bears alliteration; if we find alliteration resting on tacts 1 and 2, or 1 and 3, but not on 4, we have before us an on-half with *three* main-stresses and one secondary stress instead of the usual two main and two lesser stresses. The cadence will be found inside or at the beginning of the half-line.

1. *Inner Cadences.*

§ 8. The type (called B by Sievers) in which the cadence occurs in the middle of the half-line is very common. Whenever *Auftakt* appears the tendency is to consider that the word immediately preceding the cadence bears a secondary stress. It has been evolved out of the basic scheme ×╱×[╱×╱]×╱ as (×)＼(×)⌣⌣＼(×)⌣⌣

 swá hé selfa bæd (*B.* 29 *b*, cf. 6 *b*, 7 *b*, 12 *a*, &c.)
 þær wæs mádma fela (*B* 36 *b*)

unt*ar* heriun tuêm (*HL.* 3 *b*, cf. 8 *b*, 12 *b*, 15 *a*, &c.)
enti sîn*ero* degano filu (*HL.* 19 *b*, cf. 22 *b*)
that thie riceo Crist (*H.* 3 *b*, cf. 12 *b*, 15 *b*, 16 *b*, &c.)
end*i* ferahtan hugi (*H.* 22 *b*, cf. 29 *b*)

To the examples from *HL.* I should like to add 12*a*: *ibu dû* mî ê̜nan sagês, because the scribe wrote the OHG. form *sagês* for the OS. *sagis* or *segis*. Likewise in 15*a*: dat sagêtun mî the OHG. *sagêtun* stands for OS. *sagdun*. *H.* has an irregular cadence ($\angle\cup$) in 166*a*: *fan* thin*ero* aldero idis.

§ 9. (*a*) In this type main-stresses are found in tacts 1, 2, and 4. The type has been evolved from $\times/\times[/\times/]\times/$ as $(\times)\underline{\widehat{}}(\times)\widehat{}\backslash(\times)\underline{\widehat{}}$, and is called D 4. In on-halves we usually find alliteration in tacts 1 and 2:

micel m**o**rgen-sw**é**g (*B.* 129 *a*, cf. 218 *a*, 298 *a*, 626 *a*, &c.)
w**e**st*ar* *ubar* w**e**ntilsê̜o (*HL.* 43 *a*, cf. 49 *a*, 17 *a*)
hel*ag* himilisc uuord (*H.* 15 *a*, cf. 9 *a*, 440 *a*, 92 *a*)

In *B.* 182*a* we have threefold alliteration:

né híe húru heofena helm.

In *H.* we occasionally find on-halves of this type with alliteration in tact 1 only:

Thuo ni uuas lang after thiu (243 *a*)
godes egan barn (794 *a*, 838 *a*)

Another form of this type (defined by its inner cadence) has alliteration in tacts 1 and 4 (and has often been taken for an E-type):

twelf wintra t**í**d (*B.* 147 *a*, cf. 545 *a*)
uuises mannes **uu**ord (*H.* 503 *a*, cf. 510 *a*, 47 *a*, 52 *a*, &c.)

(*b*) In off-halves alliteration can rest on tact 1 only:

bl**æ**d w**í**de sprang (*B.* 18 *b*, cf. 55 *b*, 104 *b*, 121 *b*, &c.)
chûd ist mî al irmendeot (*HL.* 13 *b*, cf. also 14 *b*)
man oðar cuman (*H.* 926 *b*)
That **uu**erod othar bed (*H.* 103 *b*)

2. *Initial Cadences.*

From the *Urform* ×/×/×/×/ the following sub-species
may be derived:

(a)   ×[/×/]×/×/ gives us (×)⌣̣⌣‿(×)‿(×)⌣̣⌣.
(b)   ×[/×/×/]×/   „   (×)⌣̣⌣⍀(×)⌣̣⌣.
(c)   ×[/×/]×/×/   „   (×)⌣̣⌣‿(×)⌣̣⌣(×)⌣̣⌣.

§ 10. *Twofold initial cadence.* The alliteration rests on
tacts 1 and 4. This form is relatively rare; its scheme is
(×)⌣̣⌣‿(×)‿(×)⌣̣⌣:

> æsc-holt uf*an* græg (*B.* 330 *a*, cf. 259 *b*, 4861 *b*)
> *mit* gêru scal man (*HL.* 37 *a*)
> uualdand gisprak (*H.* 39 *a*, cf. 267 *b*, 4861 *b*)

Among examples of this form I include

> gurtun *sih iro* suert ana (*HL.* 5 *b*). The word *suert* is not
> highly emphasized, since *sih ana gurten* implied 'to gird
> one's sword up', to get it within handy reach (of a horseman).

§ 11. *Threefold initial cadence* of the form:

$$(×)⌣̣⌣⍀(×)⌣̣⌣$$

is as common as the twofold is rare.

> Egsode eorl (*B.* 6 *a*, cf. 8 *b*, 14 *b*, 17 *b*, &c.)
> *flôh her* Ôtachres nîd (*HL.* 18 *b*, cf. 7 *a*, 44 *b*, 45 *b*, 34 *a*, 56 *a*)
> berethlico *an* buok (*H.* 8 *a*, cf. 5 *b*, 11 *b*, &c.)

§ 12. This is an unusual type; it has alliteration on
tacts 1 and 3. Probably it was taken for a D4-type
(cf. § 9), but the real cadence is found initially; the dip
after tact 3 is usually filled, but as it then contains a
totally unstressed syllable (usually a prefix), I cannot
admit this apparent cadence to rank above the real one
in tacts 1 and 2.

$$(×)⌣̣⌣‿(×)⌣̣⌣(×)⌣̣⌣$$

> scencte scír wered (*B.* 496 *a*)
> frécne fen-*ge*lád (*B.* 1360 *a*)
> Héoldon héah *ge*sceap (*B.* 3085 *a*)

§ 13. *Persistence of the types in MHG. poetry.*—The *klingend* endings, whether of two or three tacts, are a feature of MHG. verse, especially that of a narrative kind. But in the first on-halves and in the last off-half of the Nibelungen stanza we meet frequent examples of the older forms. In the first 100 stanzas of the *NL.* (in *B*) one recognizes the following rhythms:

(*a*) *Klingend* endings:

Type A.   Kriemhilt *ge*heizen 2 (3 *a*), *von* swannen *si* füeren 85 (4 *a*), Sîvrit *der* herre 61 (1 *a*).

C or D.   *Es* wuohs *in* Burgonden 2 (1 *a*), *die* zwêne marcgrâven 9 (3*a*), sam*et* Sîvrîde 30 (1*a*), hund*ert* kanzwägene 92 (2 *a*).

(*b*) *Stumpf* endings. Presumably B-types, since these were commoner than D4-types:

vil *ver*liesen *den* lîp 2 (4 *b*), *diu* was *ze* Santen *ge*nant 20 (4 *b*), si *sint* hôhe *ge*muot 85 (4 *b*), nie *mêr* recke *ge*wan 99 (4 *b*)

§ 14. *Heußler's method of scansion.*—Heußler makes all types conform to A. In the case of those half-lines ending in an accented syllable, and having *stumpf* endings, the loss of the second syllable of the final cadence of A is compensated by a pause. Thus if the type were of this form:

$$\smallsmile\smallsmile$$

he would scan it as

$$\times\diagup\diagdown\|\diagup-$$

where the dash denotes a rest.

But difficulties arise in such half-lines, where a long *Auftakt* precedes what was formerly considered the rhythmical portion of the half-line; for instance, if the half-line according to scansion of earlier metricists were of the form $\times\times\times\diagdown\times\diagup\smallsmile\diagup$. Then the first part of the older rhythmical portion has to be taken up into the *Auftakt*, thus

$$\times\times\times\times\times\wedge\|{/}{-}$$

The *Auftakt* portion requires a toneless recitation. If read aloud to a large audience, much of it would not be heard distinctly. Furthermore, the caesura after the cadence would split the half-line into very unequal parts. The rest would be added to the pause preceding the next half-line. The recitation would proceed in a series of unpleasant jerks.

Irregular Cadences

Up to the present we have dealt with cadences formed either by a word-root and its inflectional ending or by word-compounds. But in certain half-lines no true cadences are to be found. The proportion of such cases to the whole lies between 5 and 10 per cent. If we examine the following half-lines:

		1	2	3
B. 11 b.	þæt *wæs* gód cyning	$\setminus(\times)$	$\angle$	$\overset{\smile}{\smile}$
B. 90 a.	swutol sang scopes	$\overset{\smile}{\smile}$	$\angle$	$\overset{\smile}{\smile}$
HL. 49 b.	wêwurt skihit	$\overset{\wedge}{\nearrow}$		$\overset{\smile}{\smile}$

we notice that they lack a whole tact, because apparently they have a *stumpf* ending (with resolution).

But if a main-stress is followed by an independent word also bearing stress, the two may be linked together in recitation to form one rhythmic unit, a *cadence for the ear* only.

In the cases above *gód cyning, sang scopes, wêwurt skihit* are spoken as though they were *gód-cyning, sang-scopes, wêwurt-skihit*. A cadence—effect is produced, since the second word is uttered quickly after the first, and there is no gap or rest between. Although not grammatically connected such cadences sound right to the *ear*, the real judge in this matter! We can now scan the examples given:

B. 11 b.	þæt *wæs* gód(-)cyning	＼(×) ╱⌢⟍
B. 90 a.	swutol sang (-)scopes	⌣⌣ ╱⌢⟍
HL. 49 b.	wêwurt(-)skihit	╱ / ⌢⟍

Considering the frequency of their occurrence, ear-cadences should be found in all the commoner types of the half-line.

A. *Ear-cadences in Half-lines with 'klingend' endings*

§ 15. In the A-types (cf. §§ 1, 2 *ante*)

$$(\times)\overset{\frown}{\smile\smile}\searbackslash(\times)\smile\smile\searbackslash$$

we have seen (cf. § 2) that the first cadence might be broken up, but that the second cadence (in the *klingend* ending) must be preserved:

$$(\times)\smile\smile(\times)\searbackslash(\times)\overset{\frown}{\smile\smile}\searbackslash$$

It is only important to show that ear-cadences of the form ⌣⌣(-)⟍ occur in tacts 3 and 4.

But there is a form of A, in which the ending bears alliteration in on-halves, and which really contains both main-stresses (cf. § 2*e*). Ear-cadences for this sub-species occur:

hýrde *ic*, þæt Elan(-) cwén (*B.* 62 *a*)
haƀd*un* sia grama(-)barn (*H.* 5310 *b*, cf. also 5104 *a*).

§ 16. *Ear-cadences in C-types with three-stress 'klingend' endings* (cf. § 4). The scheme is: (×)＼(×)⌣⌣⟍, therefore we may expect a cadence of the form: ⌣⌣(-)⟍. This is very frequently found:

on fæder(-)wine (*B.* 21 *b*, cf. 11 *b*, 15 *a*, 23 *b*, &c.)
that sia uuord(-)godes (*H.* 2 *a*, cf. 10 *b*, 14 *b*, 23 *b*, &c.)
ibu dû dâr ênîc reht(-)habês *HL.* 57 *b*. Here *habês* = OS.
ha ƀes (?).

§ 17. *Ear-cadences in D-types with three-stress 'klingend'*
endings (cf. § 5). The scheme is (×)/(×)⌣⌣ ＼ and the
ear-cadence will be of the same form as in the paragraph
above.

> éam his(-)nefan (*B.* 882 *a*, cf. 90 *a*, 215 *b*, 1231 *b*, &c.)
> hel*ag* uuord(-) godas (*H.* 7 *a*, cf. 49 *a*)

An exceptional form of ear-cadence occurs in *B.* 272*b*:

> *þú* w*á*st, gif(-)hit(-)is,   × / (-)⍀(-)＼

§ 18. *Ear-cadences in D-types with four-stress 'klingend'*
endings (cf. § 6). The scheme is ⌣⌣ ⌣⌣ ＼ and the ear-
cadence has the form ⌣⌣ ⌣ (-) ＼.
Sievers[1] called this sub-type A 2 k (*mit kurzer zweiter*
Hebung); he scans *gúðrinc monig* (*B.* 839*b*) as ⌃＼ ⌃⌣.
There is reason to believe that many poets shared this
belief. In *B.* on-halves are frequently of this form:

> wæl-réow wiga (630 *a*, cf. 777 *a*, 787 *a*, 1016 *a*, &c.)

In the first 1,000 lines of *H.* it occurs at 792*a*: m*a*ncraft
m*i*kil.
But in that case such half-lines consist of three tacts only,
as has been shown before, ⌣⌣ ⍀ ⌣⌣. This may have led
to the construction of three-syllabled half-lines in the
Völuspa, 41, 2*b*, and *Hávamál* (frequently).[2]

Even so, after the weighty syllables in tacts 1 and 2
there would be less expiratory current to spend on the
last word; we should have falling stress throughout and
the half-line would have been heard as a four-stress
cadence.

---

[1] Cf. *Grundriß*, 1893[2], II. i. 868.

[2] Cf. *Sæmundar-edda*, Finnur Jónsson, Reykjavik, 1905. This must
be considered a metrical innovation; though the ON. tradition is conser-
vative in historical matters, the Icelandic poets were and are fond of
metrical experiments.

In off-halves alliteration rests on tact 1 only, and there is no reason to scan this sub-type otherwise than ◡◡ ⊥ ◡. Koegel, discussing this form says: 'Im Hild. ist *wêwùrt skíhìt* 49*b* das einzige Beispiel und es ist nicht einmal ganz sicher, weil es auch zu D gehören kann.'[1] Examples in on-halves:

> prȳð-word(-)sprecen (*B.* 644 *a*, cf. 658 *a*, 974 *a*, 2589 *a*)
> lofuuord(-)manag (*H.* 413 *a*, cf. 703 *a*, 759 *a*, 978 *b*, &c.)

In fact in *H.* this is the normal form even in on-halves. In off-halves it is the only form that can occur.

> Gold-fág(-)scinon (*B.* 995 *b*, cf. 1311 *b*, 1511 *b*, 1829 *b*, &c.)
> wêwurt(-)skihit (*HL.* 49 *b*)
> unrim(-)cuman (*H.* 410 *b*, cf. 978 *b*)

One would not expect an ear-cadence in a form, which is of itself an ear-cadence, yet we find

> hlǽw(-)on(-)hlìðe (*B.* 3159 *a*).

B. *Ear-cadences in Half-lines with 'stumpf' endings*

1. *Inner Ear-cadences.*

§ 19. *Ear-cadences in B-types* (cf. § 8) *of the form* (×)◟(×)◡◡◟(×)◡◡. Though none occur in *HL.* they are common elsewhere and fall into two groups: (*a*) The main-stress is followed by an independent word:

> *wæs* þæt *ge*win(-)tó strang (*B.* 133 *b*, cf. 137 *b*, 191 *b*, 426 *b*, &c.)
> *er than quami* thit uuif(-)te mi (*H.* 145 *b*, cf. 78 *b*, 117 *b*, 142 *b*, &c.)
> hú *hé* fród(-)ond gód (*B.* 279), huo liof(-) is that (*H.* 5034 *b*)
> né léof(-)né láð (*B.* 511 *a*), so liof(-) so led (*H.* 1332 *a*)

(*b*) The first main-stress is followed by the prefix of a following verb or noun:

> syðð*an* niht(-)becóm (*B.* 115 *b*, cf. 67 *b*, 107 *b*, 109 *b*, &c.)
> *the* sia *iro* mod(-)gespon (*H.* 1 *b*, cf. 39 *b*, 40 *a*, 123 *b*, &c.)

[1] Cf. p. 231, n. 1, *ante*, i, 296.

§ 20. *Ear-cadences in D 4-types* (§ 9) *of the form*

$$(\times)\underset{\smile}{\cup}(\times)\underset{\frown}{\cap}\setminus(\times)\underset{\smile}{\cup}.$$

Examples from *Béowulf*:

(*a*) Alliteration in tacts 1 and 2 (in on-halves):

Fyrst forð(-)gewát (*B*. 210 *a*, cf. 1782 *a*, 2082 *a*)

(*b*) Alliteration in tact 1 only (in off-halves):

Wá *bið* pǽm (-) þe sceal (*B*. 183 *b*, cf. 187 *b*)

2. *Initial Ear-cadences.*

§ 21. *Ear-cadences in E-types* (cf. §§ 10, 11, 12 ante). Ear-cadences have only been found in the form $(\times)\underset{\smile}{\cup}\setminus(\times)\setminus(\times)\underset{\smile}{\cup}$, but in *B*. these are as common as examples with true cadences in tacts 1 and 2 are rare. None occur in *HL*.; in *H*. I have not been able to find any.

líf(-)éac gescéop (*B*. 97 *b*, cf. 123 *b*, 274 *b*, 455 *b*, &c.)
lid(-)zi giliden (*Merseb. Zaubersp. b*, 14 *a*)

§ 22. *Schwellverse* may be easily recognized by their length. This is due to the extension of the anacrusis. The rhythmical portion, which may conform to any of the types, is normal:

þá gyt wæs hiera sib ætgædere (*B*. 1165 *b*)	D-type
dat ih dir it nû bî huldî gibu (*HL*. 35 *b*)	B-type
that ni haƀit enigan gigadon huergin (*H*. 25 *b*)	C-type

Probably in Swell-verses we may recognize the influence of the metrical structure of the psalms.

§ 23. *Lyrical elements in long-line poetry* must be supposed to have been composed for song. In this case a long-line or a group of half-lines should consist of uniform types conforming to the tune to which they were sung. In the *Merseburger Zaubersprüche* we find narrative preludes, probably recited (to win confidence in the following magic), followed by the charm proper, which was sung.

This part did not need to be so readily understood—the more mysterious it was, the greater the awe it was likely to inspire; in Charm (*a*)

we have	in*princ* haptbandun	
	in*var* vîgandun	
in (*b*)	sô*se* benrenkî	
	sô*se* bluotrenkî	
	sô*se* lidirenkî	
	lid(-)zi giliden	
	*sôse gi*lîmida sîn	

§ 24. *The Cadences tabulated:*

Group	Cadence	Metrical Scheme	Sievers	Ending	Tacts
I	final	∧ ∧ *or* ∕ ∖ ∧	A	klingend	3, 4
	„	∖ ∕ ∧ *or*	C	„	3, 4
	„	∖ ∧	C	„	2, 3, 4
	„	∕ ∧ *or*	D	„	2, 3, 4
	„	∕ ∧	D	„	1, 2, 3, 4
2	inner	∖ ∧ ∕	B	stumpf	2, 3
	„	∕ ∧ ∕	D 4	„	2, 3
3	initial	∧ ∖ ∕ *or*	E	„	1, 2
	„	∕ ∧ ∕	E	„	1, 2, 3

In conclusion. In English seminars very little time is allotted to metrical studies; certainly anything of the nature of an exhaustive examination of the existing theories is impossible. Yet university teachers naturally desire their students to read alliterative poetry rhythmically. If students are told to emphasize the main-stresses (usually conspicuous by their rime), to give full value to all syllables in cadences and to note the position of the cadences in the half-lines, they will soon realize the difference between verse and prose rhythm, even if they cannot state off-hand to which of Sievers's 'types' this or that half-line belongs.

RILKE AND RODIN

By G. CRAIG HOUSTON

TO those familiar with the life and works of Rainer
Maria Rilke, the title of the present article may,
possibly, suggest an attempt to trace the specific influence
of one contemporary art upon another. And indeed
to-day, when the serious study of literature not only
includes the far reaches of 'Geisteswissenschaft' but also
tends to embrace the many ramifications of 'Sociology',
such an attempt might seem obvious and desirable rather
than unduly venturesome. There are, however, as I
believe, valid reasons for the avoidance of any such treatment of the subject. Rilke may justly be described as the
most elusive and most fragrant poet who has ever written
in the German tongue. It would, therefore, be a matter
of unusual delicacy to speak, in his case, of influences of
any kind; to seek to establish just where and how they
were felt; or to estimate, with any helpful degree of
accuracy, their effect. Moreover, any attempt to do so
would imply a method of criticism which, of all others,
would have been most repugnant to the poet himself.
He early declared in an article on the Worpswede school
of painters[1]—and, so far as I know, never altered his
belief—that neither the artist nor his work *can* be explained
by circumstance or relationship. He is and remains a
miracle; an example of immaculate conception in the
realm of the spirit.

[1] Many of Rilke's characteristic ideas on the relationship of Art to
Nature may be found in germ in this article published in 1903. It is
regrettable it was not included in the *Gesammelte Werke*, as it is now hard
to procure.

Furthermore, to attribute to specific influences certain clearly marked advances in the history of Rilke's poetic development, as has not infrequently been done, is, I am convinced, to misunderstand altogether the real nature of that development. Attentive study of his artistic life shows that where Rilke advances along a new pathway, he has already been travelling in that direction when he makes contact with some striking exponent of the new tendency whose example, indeed, accelerates and strengthens his progress, but does not provide the initial impetus; that has its source within the poet himself. If we look at all for 'influence' in connexion with Rilke, we must expect to find the expansion of what is already present in his genius, not the imposition from without of the artistic creed of another. This fact calls for emphasis, since it is easily obscured by the poet's characteristic fashion of yielding himself completely—for the time being—to each great new experience of his artistic life.

Beyond question, the friendship with Rodin was a major experience in the life of the poet; the greatest of those due to any single factor, as he himself later declared. It dominated the most formative years of his development and established tendencies which we rightly associate with the distinctive beauty of his poetic art. Our present concern is to trace the story of this friendship and to consider some characteristic features in the work of both artists, features which seem to me to offer suggestive comparisons, the interest of which will undoubtedly be enhanced if we can see them against a background— however tentatively outlined—of a common artistic intention or ideal.

When Rilke and Rodin met, the only common ground between them would seem to have been that they were both creative artists. In almost every other respect they

differed. By race the one was German, the other French;
the one was a poet and artist in words, the other a sculptor
and moulder of clay; the one, if not rooted in ancient
aristocracy, as he believed himself to be, was at any rate
the son of a cultured home, the other, to quote his own
description, was a plebeian, born and bred in one of the
poorer quarters of Paris. The one, of delicate constitution
and self-distrusting temperament, was *sentimentalisch* in
Schiller's sense of the word, the other, rudely robust,
with an absorbing passion for work, was himself, like
Goethe, a 'piece of Nature'. And finally, Rilke, when the
friendship began, was young, romantic, and unknown,
whilst Rodin, with a life of achievement behind him, was
imperturbably self-confident and already famous.

To appreciate with justice the significance of this
friendship for the poet, we must review very briefly the
outstanding facts of his life until the date of its inception.
Born on the fourth of December 1875, in the ancient city
of Prague, Rilke was descended on his father's side of a
German family of peasant origin.[1] These Rilkes settled
in Bohemia and their descendants rose to honourable
official positions in the country of their adoption. His
mother's family belonged originally to the respected
bourgeoisie of Alsace, a fact which the poet himself considered might have some bearing on his innate understanding of French thought and art. The boy grew up
as an only child, his favourite associate being his father,
a man of typically Austrian charm and kindliness. Between the poet and his mother, who survived him, there
seems to have been no real bond of affection at any time,

---

[1] Cf. Carl Sieber, *René Rilke. Die Jugend Rainer Maria Rilkes*,
Leipzig, 1932 (p. 11), in which Rilke's son-in-law has disposed of all
uncertainty as to the poet's origins, uncertainty which has given rise to
gravely misleading assumptions on the part of some critics.

although he remained a dutiful son until his death in 1926. After five unsuccessful years at a military academy, the boy's education was carried on privately until he passed into the University. Like Kleist before him, he could find no satisfaction in university life, either at Munich or Berlin, and soon exchanged it for some years of rather lonely wandering through Europe.

His first notable, and up to the present time, his most popular work—his 'best-seller'—was written in one night of February 1899. It is the short epic in rhythmic prose, *Von Liebe und Tod des Cornet Christoph Rilke*, distinguished alike by a remarkable mastery of rhythm and an unusual power of creating emotional atmosphere. The same year saw his first important collection of verse: *Mir zur Feier*. It is the verse of a young romanticist, who sings of Longing, Childhood, Maidenhood, and Dreams, of Evening and the simplicity of Nature, of a God, 'der in Dir schafft'; for God from the first was one of Rilke's chief preoccupations.

His first great spiritual experience was a visit to Russia in the May and June of 1899. One result of this was *Das Stunden-Buch*, of which the third and last part, however, owes probably more to Paris than to Russia. Still more characteristic of the mystical Russian phase are the *Geschichten vom lieben Gott*, written on his return to Berlin. In the autumn of the same year he visited Worps-wede, where he soon felt at home amongst the group of young painters—admirers of the Barbizon school—whose works were to make the name of the little North German village famous. Here he met the young sculptress, Clara Westhoff, whom he married in the following spring. They settled in their own little home at Westerwede, close to Worpswede, where their only child, Ruth, was born and where Rilke put together his next volume of

verse, *Buch der Bilder*, the title of which indicates sufficiently clearly his poetic ideal at this time.

So far Rilke had only a fleeting acquaintanceship with
Rodin's art. He had come across a few isolated examples
of it in his travels; that was all.[1] Now his wife, an enthusiastic and accomplished pupil of the French sculptor,
initiated him into some of the greater aspects of the
master's work. And thus it came to pass that, when
Professor Muther, the well-known art historian, visited
the painters' colony in the autumn of 1901 and asked the
young poet to write a monograph on Rodin, nothing
could have given Rilke greater pleasure. He wrote forthwith to Rodin, asking if he might visit him at his studio
in Paris in order to see and to hear about his work. These
early letters,[2] written in experimental French (because
Rodin knew no German), show clearly the nature of the
younger man's expectations. 'L'occasion d'écrire sur vos
œuvres, est pour moi une vocation intérieure, une fête,
une joie, un grand et noble devoir, vers lequel mon amour
et tout mon zèle se tournent', he writes on 28 June 1902,
and again on 1 August, as the time draws near for him
to go to Paris: '. . . il sera pour moi-même, pour mon

[1] Even at this early stage Rilke would seem to have felt instinctively
that Rodin was to have a special significance for him. In an unpublished
letter to Clara Rilke, dated 27 April 1903, now in the Rilke-Archiv,
Weimar, he wrote: 'In mir war schon damals, als ich Dich fand, ein
so starker, einfach schreiender Instinkt nach ihm, ein so großes, nicht-
zubeschwichtigendes Wissen um seine Wichtigkeit. Daß wir einmal ein
Buch von ihm machen müßten, erinnerst Du Dich, das habe ich Dir
gesagt.'
[2] The French edition of Rilke's *Lettres à Rodin*, Paris, 1931, edited,
with a preface, by M. Georges Grappe, director of the Rodin Museum,
contains some ninety-five letters covering the years 1902–13. In the
German edition, published by the Insel Verlag, *Briefe* 1902–6 contains
twenty letters to Rodin and *Briefe* 1907–14 three; often in much ab-
breviated form.

travail (le travail d'écrivain ou bien de poète) un grand évènement de m'approcher de vous.'

The meeting took place on 1 September 1902, when Rodin was sixty-one and Rilke twenty-six years of age. It is clear from the poet's letters at this time that his expectations were fulfilled. He felt no trace of strangeness in Rodin's presence, he tells his wife, for they seemed to be but renewing an earlier acquaintanceship—'mir war, als kennte ich ihn immer schon. Als sähe ich ihn nur wieder'—only that Rodin appeared mightier, kindlier, more sublime than he had conceived him. He has found what he has all these years been feeling after: 'ein Mann ohne Zeitgenossen'. The master's works make a profound impression upon him. From the very first he is struck by the fragmentary nature of the execution in many instances, where only part of the subject is shown. Yet he rightly judges that such parts or fragments are in themselves wholes. Life is expressed in them with such purity and vehemence that to ask for stereotyped 'completion' would be mere pedantry.[1]

Without preliminaries, the long intimate conversations and still more intimate silences between them begin. The poet's days are spent in seeing and listening, for the master's conversation, filled with the ripe wisdom of his craft, is as enthralling to Rilke's receptive mind as are his magnificent statues. 'Hinter jedem Wort seines Gesprächs steht, massiv und beruhigend, die schlichte Wahrheit seiner erfahrenen Tage.' This intercourse quickly ripens into friendship and when Rilke puts the burning question—the question which was, he says, the

[1] This is an aspect of the master's work upon which Rilke dwells at some length in his Rodin study when discussing the *Inner Voice*, cf. *Rodin-Buch*, and also his letter to Clara Rilke dated 2 September 1902. *Briefe*, 1902–6, p. 26.

real cause of his coming—and asks: 'Comment faut-il
vivre?', the master's reply entirely satisfies him: 'En
travaillant.' From his hotel in the Rue Toullier he writes
the thanks which he had not felt able to express in conversation: 'Je le comprends bien. Je sens que travailler
c'est vivre sans mourir. Je suis plein de reconnaissance
et de joie. Car depuis ma première jeunesse, je ne voulais
que cela.'

In reality, the poet suffered acutely all his life under
the tyranny of 'inspiration', and the robust quality of
Rodin's creative genius, which repudiated dependence
upon any such fluctuating element, seems to have been,
throughout their friendship, a source of strength and
refreshment to him. He appreciates with sudden clarity,
when he first comes into contact with the master, that
dreams, plans, the capturing of a mood are not the
creative artist's chief concern; that his true function is
forcibly to reduce all these to plastic form. He learns the
artist's twofold duty: on the one hand, to make himself
profoundly familiar with the life of things as they actually
exist and, on the other, to acquire by indefatigable
industry the absolute mastery of his medium—be it clay
or language—, so that he may re-create the reality of life.

Rilke was unstinting in the acknowledgement of his
debt to Rodin in respect of this new conception of life
and work. Writing to him on 27 October 1902, he says
explicitly that the effect of Rodin's achievement will be
present in every future work of his, even where invisible
to others, and about a year later, in one of his intimate
letters to Lou Andreas-Salomé, he writes:

'[es wird] mir offenbar, daß ich ihm, Rodin, folgen muß: nicht in
einem bildhauerischen Umgestalten meines Schaffens, aber in der
inneren Anordnung des künstlerischen Prozesses; nicht bilden muß
ich lernen von ihm, aber tiefes Gesammeltsein um des Bildens
willen. Arbeiten muß ich lernen, arbeiten . . .'

The monograph was ready by 31 December 1902, in
the preparation of which Rilke had become thoroughly
saturated with the principles of Rodin's art.[1] After
visiting Genoa and Florence, and Worpswede again in
the summer, the poet spent the winter of 1903–4 in
Rome, where he began his most important prose work,
the psychological record of experiences in Paris—scarcely
to be called a novel although, doubtless, it corresponds
to much which is allowed that title to-day—*Die Aufzeichnungen des Malte Laurids Brigge*. There followed an
important visit to Sweden and Denmark and then, in the
autumn of 1905, he received an invitation from Rodin to
stay with him at Meudon and to act as part-time secretary.
Rilke accepted it with the utmost delight and there ensued
a period of great happiness and further absorption in Rodin's
work. He wrote to his wife at this time (17 September
1905) '. . . ich habe es sehr, sehr gut; wir tun alles
gemeinsam, und alles Verstehen ist ohne Ende'. And again,
a few days later: 'Es rauscht von Kräften, die in einen
einströmen, es kommt eine Lebensfreude, eine Fähigkeit
zu leben über einen, von der ich keine Ahnung hatte.
Sein Beispiel ist so ohnegleichen.' The same note of keen
satisfaction is heard in an unpublished letter, written some
weeks later to tell his friend, Lili Kanitz-Menar,

'wie es sich leise verfügt hat, daß ich ein kleines Häuschen auf den
Höhen Meudons vielleicht (und wie ich hoffe) für lange bewohne
und an Rodin nicht nur innerlich durch das Verstehen gebunden
bin, das zwischen uns immer unmittelbarer und selbstverständ-
licher geworden ist, — sondern auch äußerlich durch das Bestreben,
ihm bei seiner Correspondenz behülflich zu sein. Ich habe es gut.
Es gibt keinen besseren und sichereren Ort als das Vertrauen und

---

[1] Writing to Rodin, with reference to its appearance in March 1903
(*Lettres à Rodin*, p. 29 f.), he says: ' Avec ce petit livre votre œuvre n'a pas
cessé de m'occuper; c'est la petite porte par laquelle il est entré dans ma
vie; et depuis ce moment il sera là dans chaque travail, dans tout livre qui
me sera encore permis de finir. . . .'

die Freundschaft dieses großen unerschöpflichen Lebens, von dem Größe und Güte ausgeht ohne Ende. . . . Hier ist eine lebendige Quelle, hier ist ein Platz (mit welchen Worten soll ichs sagen?), eine Tränke, zu der alles kommt, was wichtig ist: Wahrheit um Wahrheit, Freude um Freude.'[1]

They walk together in the early morning—at sunrise— in the park at Versailles, and the poet sees new wonder and beauty in life through the practised eye of the master. We may note in passing that not a few of the most characteristic poems of this time evoke the stately beauty of park landscape.[2] But, if we see a connexion here, it must not be forgotten that Rilke had already dwelt upon this theme in his Worpswede article, and that the park of his Swedish host had been full of poetry for him.

He is impressed by the fact that nothing in Nature is too small to win the admiration of the sculptor, who stoops by the wayside to gather a mushroom, exclaiming at the miracle of the rapid workmanship, or gazes enraptured at the configurations of the empty shell of a snail, seeing in it the beauty of Grecian modelling. And Rilke, in contact with this great lover of Nature, loses much of his spiritual uneasiness and becomes filled with the positive assurance that Life—even in *all* its phases—is good. 'La vie—cette merveille!', as Rodin was wont to exclaim, undismayed by its darker aspects. The poet depicts him as having been, even in the early stages of his development, absorbed in contemplating 'alles das, was war und wehe tat und verging und wiederkam und nicht aufhörte zu sein. Und er glaubte in alledem . . . das Ewige zu erkennen, das um dessentwillen auch das Leid gut und die Schwere Mutterschaft war und der Schmerz schön.'[3] It is not without significance that, in

---

[1] In the Rilke-Archiv, Weimar.
[2] Cf. *Neue Gedichte*, ii, Leipzig, 1919, pp. 65–71.
[3] *Das Rodin-Buch*, Leipzig, 1930, p. 50 f.

the calm and profoundly sympathetic *Briefe an einen jungen Dichter*,[1] which Rilke was writing about this time, he was able to say with full conviction: 'Glauben Sie mir: Das Leben hat recht, auf alle Fälle', a saying which we do well to bear in mind when we meet with the ill-considered assertion, all too frequent in early Rilke criticism, that the poet was not equal to facing life.

We may, indeed, accept the generalization, made by Fritz Dehn,[2] that the Paris years were a time of all-pervading fear during which Rilke fell a prey to the sordid cruelty of life. There is sufficient evidence of this in the *Neue Gedichte*, not to speak of the *Aufzeichnungen des Malte Laurids Brigge* which, together with the long letter to Lou Andreas-Salomé of 18 July 1903, leaves no doubt as to the horror and 'banges Erstaunen' with which Paris inspired the poet from the very first. But we must not overlook that other statement made at the same time, when he wrote that the overwhelming impression received from Rodin's works produced in him a sense of refuge and protection: 'im Schutze eines übergroßen Eindrucks [fühlte ich] mich ein wenig geborgen vor der tausendfachen Angst, die später kam' (1 August 1903).

It is also worth noticing that, with the exception of one or two passages, the theme of Death is markedly absent from the published letters of the Paris period, although that theme forms the main subject of the third part of the *Stunden-Buch*, written in the spring of 1903, and may be said to predominate in the *Aufzeichnungen*, begun just a year later. Indeed, it is clear from these letters—particularly those of 1906–7—that the poet is sustained by a cheerful confidence in work and a profound belief in life.

[1] These letters cover the period 17 February 1903 to 4 November 1904
[2] In one of the most interesting of recent books on the subject: *Rainer Maria Rilke und sein Werk. Eine Deutung*, Leipzig, 1934.

Writing from Capri on 11 December 1906, he explains
his positive acceptance of all life's phenomena by the fact
that he has now advanced beyond the stage of appreciating
only what is obviously beautiful.

I am of the opinion that the effect of Rodin's influence,
shown in the persistence of the poet's faith in life, can be
followed out even to the final statement of that faith in
the *Elegien*. The depth of Rilke's 'discontent' has too
often been allowed, in the judgements of his critics, to
obscure the fact of his ultimate courageous affirmation.
The need to correct such misunderstanding was recognized
by the poet himself when, in giving his own interpretation
of the elegies in the important letter written from Muzot
on 13 November 1925, he said:

'In den *Elegien* .   . wird das Leben wieder möglich, ja es
erfährt hier diejenige entgültige *Bejahung*, zu der es der junge
Malte, obwohl auf dem richtigen schweren Wege "*des longues
études*", noch nicht führen konnte. Lebens- *und* Todesbejahung
erweist sich als Eines in den *Elegien*.'[1]

During the winter of 1905–6 he lectured on Rodin's
art in Dresden, Prague, and elsewhere—'Mes conférences
ont eu partout ce succès qui nous semble essentiel', he is
able to report when writing from Worpswede on 13 March.
It is the substance of the lecture thus delivered which
forms the second part of the *Rodin-Buch*, first published
in its entirety in 1907.

In May the life at Meudon was interrupted by a
sudden disagreement, and Rilke moved into rooms of his
own in Paris. Bitterly as he felt the separation, it was
advantageous for his own work. He now had time to get

---

[1] Herr Dehn recognizes this affirmative element in Rilke's philosophy
when he says: 'Diese Liebe zum Sein bleibt des Dichters unverlierbares
Thema, auch nachdem aus der positiven Mystik des Stundenbuches die
negative Mystik des 'Panther' und schließlich der Duineser Elegieen
wurde.' Loc. cit., p. 122.

ready for publication the enlarged edition of the *Buch der Bilder*, which reflects something of the new experiences;[1] the Rodin lecture; and the first volume of the *Neue Gedichte*.

In the autumn of 1907 Rodin got into touch with him again whilst he was in Vienna. It is characteristic of Rilke that throughout their estrangement his admiration of the artist and his work had never waned. He now responds with all the old warmth, promising to send him his new works completed in the meantime.[2] Of *Neue Gedichte* I he says it contains 'quelques pièces travaillées d'après nature humblement', adding 'J'espère qu'on y reconnaîtra combien votre œuvre et votre exemple m'ont forcé à des progrès définitifs, car si un jour on me nomme parmi ceux qui ont suivi dignement la nature, ce sera parce que j'étais de tout cœur votre élève obéissant et convaincu'.[3]

Their intercourse was resumed in Paris the following year, when Rilke was immersed in the second volume of the *Neue Gedichte*. In a hitherto unpublished letter of the 20 August 1908, he writes to S. Fischer: 'Ich sehe ja niemanden, außer von Zeit zu Zeit Rodin; unsere Freundschaft ist so sicher und fest geworden und steht wie ein Markstein zwischen seiner Einsamkeit und meiner.'[4] A few days later, the poet moved into rooms in the beautiful eighteenth-century mansion in the rue de Varenne, familiar to us now as the *Musée Rodin*. It was Rilke's discovery; Rodin, visiting him there, took a fancy to the stately rooms and the old-fashioned garden and moved in after him.[5]

---

[1] Cf. my note on the *Buch der Bilder* in *Modern Language Review*, xxix, 1934, pp. 333 ff.

[2] Cf. *Lettres à Rodin*, pp. 75 f.

[3] Ibid., p. 83.   [4] In the Rilke-Archiv, Weimar.

[5] There is a pleasing photograph in *Stimmen der Freunde*, Freiburg im

The following November the second volume of *Neue Gedichte* appeared with a dedication 'à mon grand ami, Rodin'. It is the last of the group of works published during these years, which give the immediate precipitate of Rilke's Rodin experience. *Die Aufzeichnungen des Malte Laurids Brigge*, which undoubtedly contains much of like provenance, was not finished until 1910. It therefore seems sufficient, for our present purpose, to quote in its connexion the poet's own witness to the help which Rodin's example afforded him in the writing of prose.

' . . . Je parviens à me servir de plus en plus de cette longue patience que vous m'avez enseignée par votre tenace exemple. . . . La prose veut être bâtie comme une cathédrale. . . . Et pensez qu'en cette prose je sais maintenant faire des hommes et des femmes, des enfants et des vieillards. J'ai évoqué surtout des femmes en faisant soigneusement toutes les choses autour d'elles, laissant un blanc qui ne serait qu'un vide, mais qui, contourné avec tendresse et amplement, devient vibrant et lumineux, presque comme un de vos marbres.'[1]

Clearly the poet saw here a certain similarity of artistic method.

Intercourse with Rodin continued, but from now onwards it offers little of immediate interest for our present consideration. The date of the last letter in the published collection is 13 May 1913. August 1914 made further communication between them impossible. Rilke was alone in Berlin[2] when the news of Rodin's death reached him on 18 November 1917. No more poignant letter of

Breisgau, 1931, opposite p. 128, showing the slim figure of the poet seated at his desk in the lofty room whose windows 'donnent prodigieuse-ment sur un jardin abandonné' (*Lettres à Rodin*, p. 99.). This and another illustration are omitted from the impression of this edition described as 'Lizenzausgabe durch Munz & Co. G.M.B.H., Leipzig'.

[1] *Lettres à Rodin*, pp. 127 ff.
[2] Not Vienna, as M. Grappe states in his preface to the letters.

grief can have been occasioned by that event than the one written by the poet to his wife:

'Ich weiß nicht,' he writes, 'was Rodin's Tod mir in normalen Umständen gewesen wäre — vielleicht etwas nach allem Versöhnliches —, jetzt überwiegt zunächst die Verwirrung in mir, daß so nahe Angehendes so wenig auslösbar und so unabgegrenzt gegen das Wirrwarr der Zeit sich vollziehen muß, daß hinter der unnatürlichen und fürchterlichen Wand des Krieges diese rein gekannten Gestalten einem wegsinken, irgendwohin, Verhaeren, Rodin, — die großen, wissenden Freunde, ihr Tod wird ungenau und unkenntlich . . ., ich fühle nur: sie werden nicht mehr da sein, wenn der entsetzliche Dampf sich verzieht und werden denen, die die Welt wieder aufzurichten und zu pflegen haben werden, nicht beistehen können.'[1]

To estimate the importance which Rodin had for the writer Rilke, we must turn to the works most closely associated with their friendship: the *Rodin-Buch*, *Neue Gedichte* I and II. In his Rodin studies (the monograph and the lecture) Rilke has given an interpretive account of the sculptor's work which has not been surpassed even by the writings of professional art-critics, such as Camille Mauclair. The artist's ideas and the secret of his technique, the nature and beauty of his innovation in sculpture, are set forth with a vivid clarity which is due, in the first instance, to intimate understanding and, in the second, to poetic power of expression where verbal expression was pre-eminently difficult.

What impresses the poet most in all the variety of Rodin's statuary, as he saw it 'like a great forest' in the studio at Meudon, is its tremendous suggestiveness. A suggestiveness which is dependent upon what Worringer has defined for us as the essential quality of Gothic: the power of expression.[2]

[1] In the Rilke-Archiv, Weimar. *Briefe* 1914–23, pp. 169 f.

[2] '*Ausdrucksmacht*.' Cf. *Formprobleme der Gothik*, München, 1930, p. 35.

The embodying of the pure idea, the presentation of a state of feeling in sculptured form, as exemplified in such pieces as the *Inner Voice*, the *Prodigal Son* or the *Convalescent*, was an innovation in statuary and peculiar to Rodin's art.[1] I see a similarity of effect, *mutatis mutandis*, in some of Rilke's most characteristic verse as, for example, in *Die Anfahrt*, from the second volume of the *Neue Gedichte*, or in the beautiful little poem, which appeared in the later edition of the *Buch der Bilder*, entitled *Herbst*. These few lines convey the essential character of the season which has given to the American language one of its rare beauties of idiom in the expression, the Fall.

We need only compare it with our English 'Season of mists and mellow fruitfulness', with Storm's *Oktoberlied* or Lamartine's *L'automne* to appreciate its purely suggestive quality—its fragmentary character. Description, common to these other poems, is absent, but does more, after all, need to be said when so much is suggested? This manner of treatment is frequent in Rilke's verse; it is also the secret of much effective writing in the *Aufzeichnungen*.

The critic Mauclair, in discussing the suggestiveness of Rodin's art, has well said that it creates an emotion before it awakens comprehension.[2] I believe the same is true of certain of Rilke's writings. Does not such a process, indeed, lie behind our enjoyment of the *Duineser Elegien*, where comprehension of the poet's intricate metaphysical thought lags far behind our emotional response to the beauty of his lines? And was not Rilke, in

[1] It is well dealt with by Geo. Simmel in his essay on Rodin (*Philosophische Kultur*, Leipzig, 1919, pp. 168 ff.), referred to by Rilke in *Lettres à Rodin*, p. 26.

[2] Camille Mauclair, *Auguste Rodin*, Paris, 1900.

some sense, conscious of this when he wrote that their meaning must be apprehended by intuition (*Eingebung des Gleichgerichteten*), rather than by what we call 'understanding'.[1]

In the case of neither artist was the suggestive power of his work due to accident or mere instinct. Rodin's secret lay in a profound obedience to Nature. Art, he declared, is only a close study of Nature, for Nature 'est la source de toute beauté, étant la source de toute vie'.[2] It was a turning-point in the poet's experience when he passed from the adoration and wistful interpretation of romantic Nature, as he knew it at Worpswede, to the unquestioning joy of practical obedience to reality, as exemplified in Rodin. In the *Age of Bronze* it was the sculptor's absolute fidelity to Nature which caused this figure to be rejected as a work of art by the authorities and its author to be accused of having reproduced every detail of the living body by illegitimate means. Even where the figure in no sense represents reality, being conceived purely as a symbol—as in the case of the *Hand of God*, which made so deep an impression upon Rilke[3]—the secret of its power lies in the artist's obedience to Nature; its symbolic force depends upon the perfect truthfulness of his depiction of a reality.

Now, we find the same thing, transferred to the sphere of poetry, in much of Rilke's work. It is the vivid realism in his imagery which so often startles us into a new understanding of the idea which it serves. Herein, as Pongs has rightly seen, lies the originality of Rilke's treatment of the 'Thing-Image'. *Die Fensterrose* and

[1] *Briefe aus Muzot*, Leipzig, 1935, p. 220.

[2] Cf. *Écrits et lettres choisies*, Paris, 1919, in which Eugène Carrière reports some of his conversations with the master.

[3] Cf. the letter to his wife after his first visit to Rodin's studio *Briefe*, 1902–6, pp. 26 ff.

Der Schwan from the first volume, and *Die Flamingos* or *Bildnis* from the second volume of *Neue Gedichte*, afford striking examples of it.

Implicit in Rodin's devotion to Nature was his reverence for the individual phenomenon in which she reveals herself. This led to an indefatigable study of the natural object, from every possible angle and in every possible phase of its life. Here, undoubtedly, Rilke learnt a great lesson. We are even tempted to think that without it we might never have had the miracle of his encaged *Panther* nor the living flesh of the mystical *Einhorn* nor, indeed, the dynamic vitality of metaphor which is constantly present in his writing. He learnt to emulate the master's untiring observation. Poetry, conceived by him formerly as the melody which the soul draws from Nature, must now, in his new conception of it, present the Thing uninterpreted—as a pure existence. He has become confident that it is possible to know the life of a thing without admixture of the personal equation.[1] With the result that his whole endeavour now is to live the life of the Thing, and to express that life in words. And, in fact, this is, in one aspect of them, what the *Neue Gedichte* give us: *the Thing become Word*, an impersonal presentation of a reality; of which such a poem as the *Römische Fontäne* affords an excellent example. In this, of course, Rilke runs directly counter to an accepted definition of lyric poetry, expressed by Otto Ludwig when he said that the lyric poet must give only his own thoughts and feelings.[2]

---

[1] The direct opposite this of the Impressionist's belief; yet there are those who have seen in Rilke's peculiar contribution to German poetry a form of Impressionism! Prof. Walzel has dealt with the point in his article in *Orplid*, IV. Jhg., 1927, 'Sonderband für Rilke'.

[2] 'In ihr (der Lyrik) will und soll der Dichter ja nur seine eigenen Gedanken und Gefühle geben.' Otto Ludwig: *Werke*, Meyers Klassiker-Ausgabe, vol. iii, p. 339. *Mein Wille und Weg*.

But to-day the impersonal lyric—the lyric from which the *I* is conspicuously absent—is scarcely felt to be a paradox; and Rilke is one of its most notable exponents.

There is, however, more in the *Neue Gedichte* than the striking presentation of natural phenomena. Indeed, at the risk of seeming contradiction, I would say that they can be most truly described as the expression of spiritual experience by means of concrete imagery. Already in these poems Rilke is approaching that *Verinnerlichung des Sichtbaren* which, in his final statement in the *Elegien*, he declares to be the whole purpose of the poet's function. Poetic transmutation seems to have taken place as follows: the observed reality having been resolved into a state of feeling, that feeling (not to be disassociated from the thing itself) has, in turn, been reclothed in language and transmitted by the realism of his imagery in poetic form. I see a process here not unlike that which the dramatist Hebbel defined, when he said that the raw material must resolve itself into an idea and the idea must, in turn, take concrete poetic form.[1] If the word 'feeling' be substituted for 'idea', I believe we shall approach most nearly to a true understanding of the poetic procedure in the *Neue Gedichte*.

That the observed reality consists frequently of the most elusive elements in experience does not lessen but rather enhances the poet's achievement. Rilke attributed the secret of Rodin's originality to the fact that he seized upon 'alles das Vage, Sich-Verwandelnde, Werdende, das auch in ihm war' and enclosed it in form. The words are singularly apt in describing one element, at least, of Rilke's

---

[1] 'In dem echten Dichtergeist muß, bevor er etwas ausbilden kann, ein doppelter Proceß vorgehen. Der gemeine Stoff muß sich in eine Idee auflösen und die Idee sich wieder zur Gestalt verdichten.' Hebbel, *Tagebücher*, edited by R. M. Werner, vol. i, p. 260.

own originality, namely, his peculiarly sensitive apprehension of what to blunter perception remains elusively vague
and fluctuating. It is one source of such a poem as *Der
Tod des Dichters*. The other is the power, which Rilke
has now acquired, to say what he will in language. The
significance of the dying face of a poet had, perhaps,
been felt before—in some region of consciousness where
formulated thought has no place. It is here for the first
time enclosed in form; in words which are weighted with
meaning and unforgettable.

In addition to such similarities of artistic procedure in
the work of the sculptor and the poet, it is legitimate,
I think, without straining comparison, to see a certain
correlation in matters of technical detail. There is, for
instance, a common use of the idea of *movement* in securing
the utmost emotional effect of which their subject is
capable. By the new emphasis which he laid upon movement in the body, Rodin was enabled to give that illusion
of spiritual intensity which seems, in certain of his figures,
to emanate from the living soul within. And in that
remarkable poem, consisting of some sixty-three lines,
which occurs at the end of the *Neue Gedichte*, entitled
Geburt der Venus, it is in and through movement that all
the beauty of the theme is revealed. We are reminded
of a passage in Rodin's *Conversations* where, discussing
the artistic significance of movement, he cites Ovid's use
of it in the *Metamorphoses*, in his descriptions of Daphne
and Procne.[1] Or, again, may we not see a counterpart to
Rodin's intensive study of the technical problem of planes
and surfaces—*le modelé*—as the key to the whole question
of sculptural beauty, in the poet's preoccupation with the
nature and use of words? It was in the Paris-Rodin years
that Rilke turned to the serious study of Grimm's great

[1] Cf. *Entretiens sur l'Art*, Paris, 1911, chap. iv.

dictionary. And I believe it could be shown that it is to
the technique of his craft, to the choice and placing of
words, that we owe a certain radiating beauty in his verse,
comparable to the luminosity which the sculptor created
by his treatment of surface.[1] It was this quality in the
Eternal Idol which so ravished the poet. He saw thoughts
passing over it like shadows; believed there were a thousand
interpretations of its meaning; and did not dare to venture
on dogmatic explanation. Is not this what we feel regarding certain passages in the *Elegien*? Explicit or final
commentary is scarcely possible; yet the lines fill the
mind with a new light and impart a strange radiance to
thought.

Identity of theme in the works of both artists must also
be noticed. Subjects treated by Rodin in his *Convalescent*,
the Prodigal Son, *Adam* and *Eve* have all a poetic counterpart in Rilke's verse. So far there is no direct evidence,
in the Letters or elsewhere, that there was any closer
connexion here than that of coincidence; yet one cannot
read *Die Genesende* (*Neue Gedichte* I) without seeing in
these strange, suggestive verses a reflection of the transparent beauty of the marble, with the hesitating gesture
of the hand feeling its way back into life. Again, one of
the finest dramatic ballads in modern German literature
occurs in the *Neue Gedichte*, entitled *Josuas Landtag*.
It is interesting to find that Léon Maillard, a personal
friend of Rodin, records that in the period 1880–85 the
latter made 'an unusual statue, destroyed by accident, which
represented Joshua causing the sun and moon to stand
still'; the identical theme, that is to say, of the poem.
Rilke had, obviously, not seen this statue; but we know,

---

[1] Cf. Rilke's letter to Lou Andreas-Salomé, dated 10 August 1903
(*Briefe*, 1902–6, pp. 117 ff.), in which he speaks of this purely technical
side of the poet's craft.

from his correspondence, that he had read and discussed Maillard's book[1] with his wife before his first visit to Paris.

I have been able to deal with only some of the more striking points of interest which the friendship between Rilke and Rodin suggests. To place even these in true perspective, it would be necessary to consider at some length other important experiences in Paris—more especially the poetry of Baudelaire and the painting of Cézanne—and then to examine the works of the post-Rodin period, each showing some modification of ideal or technique, or, of both equally. For Rilke's genius, essentially that of a Germanic poet, swung back after the writing of the *Aufzeichnungen* to its earlier, more mystical preoccupations, and it is possible to see in the Paris period, and in the works connected with it, a chapter in the story of the poet's development which is based upon an inspiration peculiar to itself.

Looking back in later life upon his association with Rodin, the poet did not minimize its importance. In an unpublished letter of 2 February 1921, writing about his incursion into the province of the art-critic, he says:

'Der Fall Rodin ist für mich völlig unvergleichlich. Rodin ist, wie ich wohl sagen darf, mein Lehrer gewesen, das Beispiel seines gewaltigen Werkes war mir, während vieler Lehrjahre, maß-gebend. . . .'[2]

and again on 26 February 1924, whilst repudiating the idea of his 'secretaryship', he acknowledges himself a pupil of the sculptor.

'Daß ich Rodin's "Sekretär" gewesen sei, ist nicht viel mehr als eine hartnäckige Legende, erwachsen aus dem Umstande, daß ich ihm einmal, vorübergehend, während fünf Monaten in seiner

---

[1] Léon Maillard, *Auguste Rodin*, Paris, 1899.
[2] A letter to Herr von Winterfeldt, in the Rilke-Archiv, Weimar.

Correspondenz behülflich war. . . . Aber sein *Schüler* bin ich viel
besser und viel länger gewesen: denn auf dem Grunde aller Kunst
wirkt die eine, gleiche Forderung, die ich nie so rein übernommen
habe, wie durch die Gespräche mit dem gewaltigen Meister, der
damals noch, obwohl im höchsten Alter, voll von lebendiger
Erfahrung war.'[1]

The Rodin experience remained, as Rilke early pro-
phesied it would, an inalienable element of his inner life.
And we know that in every period of activity he wrote
with the whole of his personality and with the whole of
the experience which was behind him. His conception
of what goes to the making of even one line of true poetry
is familiar to all readers of the *Aufzeichnungen*. It is not
enough for the poet to possess the memory of many and
great experiences. Such memories must pass into the
blood; they must become nameless, and an indistinguish-
able part of his personality. Then and only then can they
reappear as poetry. This is, I believe, a true description
of what happened in the case of Rilke and his association
with Rodin.

Nothing could be less desirable than to turn a friendship, which is of absorbing interest to students of one of
the greatest of modern poets, into a thorny and barren
problem of specific 'influence'. But the facts of this
friendship seem increasingly on closer examination to
justify the belief that the beauty of form and of thought
in the crowning work of Rilke's life—the *Duineser Elegien*
—is due, at least in part, to the sculptor Rodin.

[1] From an unpublished letter to Herrn Dr. Schaer, also in the Rilke-
Archiv.

The letters to which reference is made on p. 257, footnote 1, and
p. 264, footnote 2, will be found in the volume of *Briefe 1914–21*
(pp. 169 f. and p. 374 respectively), which is in proof as this goes to
press).

GOTTFRIED VON NEIFEN'S MINNELIEDER AND BALLADS

By R. MARLEYN

THE reprinting of Haupt's *Gedichte Gottfrieds von Neifen* by Edward Schröder (Berlin, 1932) draws attention once more to a Minnesänger whose work has been the subject of research and controversy in more than one field. From the manifold problems raised by this collection of forty-four conventional Minnelieder and six ballads, three points of interest are selected and separately treated in the following notes: the style of the Minnelieder, Neifen's use of cadences, and the authorship of the ballads.

The Style of the Minnelieder

The fact that Neifen has always been thought of as a virtuoso of metrics, as a *Formenkünstler* (W. Fischer, *Der stollige Strophenbau im Minnesang*, p. 11), in itself points to poverty of content and expression in his work; and, indeed, the monotonous vagueness of the minor Minnesänger is aggravated in Neifen by a looseness of style, a complete failure to relate the thematic material to the metrical form. The songs are individual entities in respect of metrics only, in expression they merge into a formless continuum, while no one theme is ever forceful enough to persist throughout the length of a poem, seldom of a strophe.

This disjunctive style has led to two attempts to split up Neifen's work, even down to sub-divisions of strophes, among a number of hypothetical authors. The spaces for one or more strophes left in the Heidelberg MS. after many of Neifen's poems form the starting-point for Wilhelm Uhl's arguments (*Unechtes bei Neifen*, 1888), while Walter Muchall (*Zur Poesie Gottfrieds von Neifen*, 1911) bases his theory on sound-analytical investigations. The reasoning of both is criticized in the introduction to my Göttingen dissertation, 'Die Kunst Gottfried von Neifens', to be printed shortly, and the mere fact that the two scholars divide the material into totally different groups would appear to mean that an explanation on other lines is required.

It is here suggested that Neifen's disintegrated style and the poverty of content so closely associated with it are connected with a radical transformation in the Minne *motif*, prepared by Morungen and Walther, but destined to undermine the ethos of the Blütezeit, and with it the poetic values of the Minnesang.

Of the formulae which are repeated over and over again by Neifen, with variation in detail but never in essence, three types predominate. First there are the many expressions of homage to *diu fröude*. The cult of joy as a social-ethical ideal pervades, in one form or another, the whole of the Minnesang; it is common to the 'Hohe Minne' and the Neidhart school, and the only remarkable feature in Neifen is the relative emphasis placed upon it, together with the recurrent play upon the word *fro* itself and its derivatives (in *fröiden froelich* 7, 26. *froelich fro* 10, 11 &c.).

More important is the second type of formula. In contrast with the prominence given to the cult of the abstraction *fröude*, the mood of the poet himself is never a joyful one. (This is by no means the case with Neifen's predecessors; among many examples of the contrary may be recalled:

Reimar 182, 14   Hohe alsam diu sunne stet daz herze min.
Walther 118, 24   Ich bin nu so rehte fro
                       daz ich vil schiere wunder tuon beginne).

The result of this juxtaposition of homage to joy and a
subjective state of unrelieved gloom is that the poet is
unable to find in the real world of the present a situation
infused with the spirit of *fröude* which he worships, and
must seek it in a hypothetical future.

Hence the many conditional constructions containing
the idea:

ob ich daz da funde
sone kunde mir uf erde niemer werden baz (8, 9)

or

wiltu, herzen trut, so mac min sendez leit verswinden (40, 15)

or, negatively,

tuot si des niht diu vil reine, seht, so ist mir iemer we (32, 7).

The attainment of his desire at some point in the future
is hinted at now and then by Reimar in semi-humorous
parenthesis, as:

165, 27 gewinne ab ich nu niemer guoten tac?

or when such an eventuality is entertained only as a
'miracle':

159, 14 waz obe ein wunder lihte an mir geschiht,
        daz si mich eteswenne gerne siht?

and Walther reproduces this:

(Paul 27, 18)   so mac ein wunder wol geschehen.

The crusading poet plays with the hope of a return to
his native land:

Hausen 45, 1   Gelebt ich noch die lieben zit
                 daz ich daz lant solt aber schouwen, . . .
Reimar 156, 19   Herre got, gestate mir
                 daz ich sie sehen müeze

                 .   .   .   .   .

                 so mugen wir fröide niezen.

Apart from these special instances, a list of such expressions in the major poets of the Blütezeit shows that they are rare except in Morungen and Walther:

Hausen: 43, 10 : 19. 44, 28. 51, 33.
Veldeke: 58, 23. 63, 9.
Morungen: 124, 13. 126, 14. 129, 11. 139, 16. 142, 8. 144, 31.
Reimar: 180, 31. 184, 19. 203, 4.
Walther: 6, 19. 7, 10 : 21 : 27. 8, 17 : 22. 9, 30 : 45. 11, 7.
            17, 8 : 26. 22, 9. 23, 27. 25, 47. 28, 3. 40, 5.
            48, 29. 50, 5.

Neifen's songs, on the other hand, are a veritable treasure-house of MHG. variations in the hypothetical clause. We find, for instance, the following examples with positive meaning:

Inversion: tuot mir wol diu minnecliche (21, 9)
  with *solt*   solt ich ein wip umbvahen (22, 25)
  with *möht*   möht ez so minneclich geschehen (22, 27)
  with *wil*   wil mir der von herzen lachen (9, 20)
ob   ob mir der vil guoten einiu braehte
                     mit ir güete hohen muot (4, 2).

and with negative meaning:

Inversion: tuot si des niht diu vil reine,
                    seht, so ist mir iemer we (32, 7)
ob   ob ez niht wendet
                    ir munt gar durliuhtic rot (6, 25)
en with Pres. Subj. ez enwende ir kiuscher wibes lip (4, 37)
or *ne*   sine troeste mich aleine (21, 16).

The same tendency away from the real and present seems to be manifested in the third predominant component of Neifen's style, the frequent, and sometimes comparatively lengthy passages addressed to *diu frouwe* or to *frou Minne*. Again, examples in the work of Neifen's most important predecessors are rare except for Morungen and Walther:

The apostrophe of *diu frouwe*.

Veldeke: 59, 7.
Morungen: 124, 8. 133, 2. 133, 35. 137, 10. 137, 27. 141, 7.
          146, 9. 147, 4. 147, 24.
Reimar: 176, 5. 190, 27. 194, 26.
Walther: 7, 19. 8, 33. 24, 1. 25, 25. 30, 12. 33, 1. 42, 25.
          49, 11. 50, 8.

Passages addressed to *frou Minne* are not found until
Walther, except for Hausen, 53, 23:

> Minne, got müeze mich an dir rechen! . . .

Even in Walther the instances are not nearly as
numerous as in Neifen:

Walther: 8, 13. 17, 15. 31, 8. 44, 33. 45, 8.

The effect of the unilateral apostrophe of the Minnelieder is diametrically opposed to that produced by the
dialogue characteristic of the ballad style. Whereas the
latter introduces a vivid realism, the reiterated appeal to a
frouwe who is never present, and never responds, approaches ever nearer to a liturgical formula, addressed to
an intangible, almost an abstract being. From here it is
but a short step to the apostrophe of *frou Minne*. This
hypothesis that the figure of *frou Minne*, playing an
increasingly prominent role, is genetically associated with
that of the *frouwe*, becoming more and more phantom-
like, may be strikingly illustrated by reference to the
parallel, in some cases almost identical wording of certain
passages in Neifen addressed now to the one, now to the
other:

an die frouwe: hilfa, helferichez wip 15, 3.
an die Minne: hilf mir, helferichiu süeze Minne 8, 20.
f: hilf troesterinne 22, 24.
M: sorgen troesterinne 27, 10.
f: sit er (ir lip) sich min underwant 23, 34.
M: sit du dichs hast underwunden 23, 31.
f: (unde ir roter munt)

mir tuo hilfe schin   32, 35.
M: (Minne, frouwe min)
    tuo mir helfe kunt   32, 29.
f: wie stet daz dir?   33, 32.
f and M: frouwe Minne und ir vil saelic wip,
      wie stat iu beiden daz?   20, 33.
f: ir sult iuch underwinden
    mis herzen, saelic wip   18, 1.
M: Minne, min dich underwint   5, 8.
f: (roter munt)
    wunt wart ich von dinen schulden   21, 29.
M: wan ich stan von iuwern schulden fröidelos   9, 17
f: (reine saelic wip) . . .
    sol ich niht den roten kus erwerben   39, 15.
M: owe, Minne, sol ich niht den roten kus erwerben   11, 27.
f: liebiu frouwe, ich han gedienet lange iu her von kinde 11, 17.
M: minneclichiu Minne, ich was gebunden   39, 32.
f: (saelic wip)
    ich diende ie mit triuwen dar   46, 14.
M: (frouwe Minne)
    sit ich iu han gedienet mange stunde   51, 6.
f: . . . ja du reine saelic wip
    du maht mir wol minen kumber wenden
    unde helfe senden   9, 13.
M: Minne, du kanst truren swenden
    hochgemüete in herze senden   29, 17.
f: reine saelic wip, nu troestent ir mich baz   39, 13.
M: nu troeste du mich baz,
    lieplichiu Minne.   27, 5.

This brief and partial analysis points the way to an alternative explanation of the defects of Neifen's style. The Minnesang flourished in a particular environment, its content in the Blütezeit was not merely the Minne *motif*, but, interwoven therewith, the social and, to some extent, the religious ethos of the court circle. In Neifen, this essential content has been lost, and with it some of

the Minne-genres which owed their existence to it. With
the passing of the age of the Third Crusade the Kreuzlied
disappears, and the poet who is no longer inspired by
social idealism or interested in the doings of his fellow
men no longer writes Sprüche, Minnedialoge, Tage-
lieder, Wechsel, or Botenlieder. He turns from the
present, with its problems and conflicts, to a hypothetical
fulfilment in the future, and from the real, but inaccessible
frouwe to an abstraction whom he may importune at will.

May not the loss of essential content and its replace-
ment by an uncertain groping towards a new sphere of
vague abstractions and allegorical figures explain not only
the disappearance of particular forms, but also the
looseness of style, the absence of any binding force in
song and strophe, which have been pointed out as negative
characteristics of Neifen's poetry?

Neifen's Treatment of Cadences.

Plenio has stated as a general principle for the Minnesang, 'daß der postzäsurale Auftakt nach klingendem
Ausgang diesen als schwerklingend erweist' (*PBB.* xli,
72), but this rule has been categorically rejected by
Walter Fischer in his *Der stollige Strophenbau im Minnesang* (Göttingen, 1932), p. 79. A consideration of Neifen's
treatment of cadences will show that Plenio's rule holds
at any rate as far as that poet is concerned, and will throw
light on the measure in which the lines are composed and
on the concluding bars of periods and strophes in Neifen.

In the following places a feminine cadence at the end
of one line encounters an anacrusis in the next. The
number of accents in the first of each pair of lines is added
in brackets:

3, 10 (7). 17, 19: 20 (3). 17, 27 (5). 17, 28: 31 (3).
19, 32: 36 (3). 24, 35 (3). 25, 6 (3). 25, 20 (3).

30, 1 (5). 30, 5 (5). 34, 30 (3). 44, 20 (3). 44, 32 (3).
45, 9 (3). 45, 12 (5). 45, 23 (3). 46, 31 (5) (throughout the strophe). 49, 17 (5). 49, 18 (4). 50, 7–9 (5).
50, 13 (5). 50, 14–15 (3).

(Repetitions in succeeding strophes or Stollen are, of course, not given.)

It will be seen that an even number of accents occurs in only one of the lines concerned, 49, 18, which has, however, dactylic measure, so that there is in this case no collision between feminine cadence and initial upbeat, but rather a prolongation of the dactyls. Why does Neifen admit such additional unaccented syllables only after a line containing an uneven number of accents? Must not the explanation be that the feminine cadence is treated differently at the end of such a line—is treated, in fact, in such a way that even when anacrusis follows there is no superfluous unaccented syllable? This could only be so if these cadences were taken to be *schwerklingend*. We could then state two principles of Neifen's metrics.

(*a*) A feminine cadence to a line with an uneven number of accents is *schwerklingend* (i.e. lines with an uneven number of beats do not occur).

(*b*) A feminine cadence followed by anacrusis is *schwerklingend* (Plenio's rule).

The first of these can be further demonstrated by reference to the feminine endings which occur at the conclusions of strophes or periods (including those already considered under the above category).

The following are the examples, cited as above:
Final lines of strophes: 30, 9 (3). 38, 14 (5). 40, 6 (7). 43, 8 (5). 45, 14 (5). 47, 2 (7). 49, 19 (5). 50, 16 (3).
Of Stollen (when differing from strophe-endings):
11, 9 (9). 14, 13 (5). 34, 29 (3). 45, 25 (3).

Once more there is in every instance an uneven number

of accents, and a similar explanation is suggested. A 'full' feminine cadence is indisputably less conclusive than a 'heavy' one, and it seems clear that Neifen avoids the former at the end of a strophe or period, as he avoided it, for a different reason, before anacrusis. And so, while confirming (*a*), we arrive at a third principle:

(*c*) In Neifen a feminine cadence at the end of a strophe or period is always *schwerklingend*.

This differential treatment of the concluding line has a parallel in the cases where the cadence is masculine. Here the full cadence is only used when the succeeding strophe or period has no anacrusis, clearly in order to avoid carrying the alternating rhythm over into the next metrical unit.

Initial Auftakt follows a final masculine cadence after lines:

11, 35 (7). 19, 34 (7). 22, 17 (5). 44, 21 (3). 48, 12 (3).

In all five instances an uneven number of accents occurs, and we may therefore assume that the cadences are *stumpf*, i.e. that the lines have an even number of beats.

The converse of (*a*), namely, that lines with an even number of accents end in a full cadence, is suggested by a glance at the internal feminine rhyme. On the three occasions when this is used by Neifen, it binds the last word of one line with the first of the next:

21, 3   in dem walde suoze *erklingen*
             dringen siht man bluomen durch daz gras
38, 27   walt den anger und die *heide*
             beide kleiden: dast dien kleinen vogeln not
42, 35   ich solt aber durch die *süezen*
             grüezen meigen wald heid ouwe.

If this device is to produce its full effect, the cadence concerned must be a full one. We should expect *süezĕn grüezĕn*, not *süezèn grüezĕn*.

The Authorship of the Ballads

Six of the poems associated with Neifen's name are dissimilar in general content and style to the rest, and there has long been controversy as to whether they are correctly assigned to him. They are the ballads: 34, 26 ('die Garnwinderin'), 37, 2 ('die Wasserträgerin'), 44, 20 ('das Büttnerlied'), 45, 8 ('das Pilgerlied'), 45, 22 ('die Dehserin'), 52, 7 ('das Ammenlied').

Strong specific resemblances may be traced between two of them and Neifen's regular Minnelieder. The following are the corresponding passages:

'Die Wasserträgerin.' 37, 18 : 40, 24. 24, 22.
                       24 : 40, 2.
              38, 1   : 13, 34. 22, 26.
                3   : 32, 35.
'Die Garnwinderin.' 34, 26 : 23, 16.
                28 : 27, 16. 23, 11. 23, 15.
            33–34 : 23, 35–36.
              36 : 26, 34.
          35, 11 : 17, 37.
              12 : 5, 7. 16, 6.
              16 : 36, 17.

The resemblances of the 'Garnwinderin' with the song 23,8 are particularly striking, and it should be especially noticed that the two 'rührende Reime' *winden-erwinden* (23, 15–16) and *saeldebaere-gebaere* (23, 35–36) respond to one another in the same position (the ante-penultimate and penultimate lines) of the strophe in both poems.

Is it perhaps significant that none of the passages cited from the 'Garnwinderin' appears in the third strophe, which has always offered the most important difficulties in interpretation?

In addition, there are in the Ammenlied 52, 7 the courtly expressions already pointed out by W. Behne,

Die Reihenfolge der Lieder Gottfried von Neifens, p. 98,
and in the short 45, 22 the figure of the 'Dehserin', which
Haupt considered a guarantee of Neifen's authorship, in
view of the allusions 4, 13; 5, 20; 32, 12.

Two of the four ballads we have been considering are
composed according to a metrical scheme in each case
decidedly unusual, and yet differing only in slight detail
from a tone used for a Minnelied.

37, 2	3+	3*+	3	+3:	3	3+ 3	3*+ 3	4	
compare									
32, 14	3	3	3	3:	3+	3+ 3+	3+ 3+	4	
52, 7	4		3+	4:	4	3	7		
compare									
43, 27	4+			7:	4+ 3	4+5	4+5		

In the remaining ballads, the 'Büttnerlied' 44, 20 and
the 'Pilgerlied' 45, 8, no such similarities, either of
expression or of metrical structure, to other poems of
Neifen are to be found. Is one justified, therefore, in
considering these two separately when discussing the
authorship problem? A comparison of the two groups
with one another, ignoring any other relationship,
strengthens the case for such a division. The four ballads
first considered are all 'Icherzählungen', three of them
are constructed after a common plan (a chance-meeting
between the poet-knight and a picturesque female character, Garnwinderin, Dehserin, or Wasserträgerin), and all
four commence with some sort of indication of time,

> 34, 28　　hiure in küelen winden
> 45, 24　　ez kam umb einen mitten tac
> 52, 7　　 . . . disen sumer lanc,

while 37, 2 preserves the full *Natureingang* of the Minnelieder. These features are all lacking in the 'Büttnerlied'
and the 'Pilgerlied', which are in turn characterized by
an obscene ambiguity entirely absent in the others.

There are grounds, therefore, for returning to the conclusion of Liliencron (*ZfdA*. vi. 93) that the 'Büttnerlied' and the 'Pilgerlied' have no place among Neifen's songs, and for casting doubt on the third strophe of the 'Garnwinderin', but for rejecting any other attempt to ascribe this collection of poems to a multiplicity of authors.

A NEW READING OF 'WILHELM TELL'

By W. G. MOORE

ON few great plays is less interpretation available. This drama of freedom has called forth almost more than its measure of admiration, and less than it deserved of insight. Its infectious movement, its concern with national issues, its stirring language, seem to have made it a play for the patriot rather than for the critic, and indeed its aesthetic value has never been considered apart from its national inspiration. A recent writer has used drastic words to describe the stalemate into which *Tell* criticism has fallen: 'keinem Gebildeten mehr ein künstlerisches Problem, Gegenstand der Begeisterung fast nur aus kunstfremden Gründen.'[1]

This will seem a hard judgement to those not conversant with what has actually been written about *Tell*. The most striking and disturbing fact about most discussions of the play is their uniformity. In a century which has seen the most violent changes in estimates of Schiller, that of *Tell* has, officially at least, remained constant. The author of the latest monograph thinks of the play very much in the same terms as did Carlyle or Scherer.

What are these conclusions so unanimously arrived at as to form a real tradition of interpretation? To begin with, the play is taken to be the dramatization of a national event; the nation is its hero, revolution its subject; it shows a struggle of freedom against tyranny, and within that struggle a personal case of individual determination, which, driven to violence, rids the people of their chief oppressor. *Tell* is thus a subjective play written by an

[1] H. Schneider, *Von Wallenstein zum Demetrius*, 1933, p. 74.

idealist about the virtues of that middle class from which
he comes, and in which he profoundly believes; it exalts
the simplicity and manliness and idealism which Schiller
is known to have admired, and shows how these virtues
may be preserved by a national sense of responsibility,
co-operation, and decision.

Such is, in general terms, the view of the play found in
the usual authorities. There is no need of detailed quotation, since it may be found in any one of them, in Bellermann, Bulthaupt, Kettner, Ziegler, Berger, Biese and,
moreover, in contemporary writers. For Cysarz as for
Brüggemann the play is 'das hohe Lied des deutschen
Bürgers'.[1] Carlyle wrote that 'in Tell are combined all
the attributes of a great man', and Biese, nearly a hundred
years after, writes of the moral greatness of the murder
Tell commits.[2] Scherer insists that the author is powerfully on the side of the oppressed,[3] Dilthey that the work
shows an example of 'einer ungetrübten heilsamen Revolution' and has been 'eine große Tatsache in der Erziehung der Deutschen zum politischen und historischen
Denken'.[4] Almost all the critics here mentioned agree
that the murder becomes by reason of the circumstances
a righteous act, and that the famous Parricida scene is
therefore a mistake unless intended as a final justification
of Tell.

This unanimity is at once formidable and disquieting.
It is formidable in the agreement which has maintained it
for so long, no less than by the powerful support of such
a master of criticism as Dilthey. It is disquieting because
it leaves the play exposed to some very damaging defects.

[1] H. Cysarz, *Schiller*, 1934, p. 368.
[2] A. Biese, *Deutsche Literaturgeschichte*, ii. 249.
[3] W. Scherer, *Geschichte der deutschen Litteratur*, p. 609.
[4] W. Dilthey, *Von deutscher Dichtung und Musik*, 1933, pp. 417, 419.

In the interests of a true judgement upon Schiller, these defects must be examined.

First of all, why is the central figure so perfect as to cause the dramatic illusion to be at times nearly destroyed? Is there in great drama another instance of a man so idealized, so brave, laconic, faithful, honourable, as the hero of this play? The fact that he is representative and indeed symbolic of his nation does not make him any more of a dramatic character. And it is this upright man who commits murder. This idealist is an assassin. A hero so unusual would seem assured of at least provoking discord among the critics, but so thoroughly has the author justified him that the morality of his deed has been hardly discussed. Schiller himself was surely more sensitive to moral issues. A passage in his essay 'Über das Erhabene' describes the 'realistic' achievement of freedom 'wenn der Mensch der Gewalt Gewalt entgegensetzt, wenn er als Natur die Natur beherrschet', in terms that do not agree with the supposed attitude of the author of *Tell*. Yet the protests of Bismarck, Börne, and Hettner against the assassin hiding behind the bush have been lost in a chorus of approval, and the scene where we are brought nearest to a discussion of murder has been since Iffland almost uniformly condemned. Taking account of all the authorities just quoted, it seems fair to say that German literary criticism has so far not put forward any satisfactory explanation of this most baffling of dramatic heroes.

Again, the subject of the play is not in itself dramatic, and here the critics are divided. Many of them write, understandably, of epic material and treatment. Walzel regards *Tell* as a chronicle play which keeps so close to its source that it can hardly be called a dramatic construction.[1]

[1] Schiller, Säkularausgabe, VII. xxv.

The essence of drama is conflict, and in how few great plays is the conflict brought by human integrity to a triumphant and righteous issue? If the usual reading of *Tell* be acceptable, the play is an exception in the world's dramatic literature.

No less is it an exception in Schiller's own career. He was always interested in freedom, but where else has he dramatized its successful achievement? Was he not, from *Die Räuber* onwards, and increasingly in his later plays, concerned to show the obstacles to freedom, the restrictions which life forces upon the idealist? It is possible, of course, that he was trying the experiment, that after the Greek imitation of the *Braut* he turned to depict the triumph of reason and honour and justice, but this in itself would be the most exceptional fact in his plays.

Finally, this reading of *Tell* is surely most difficult to fit in to any conception of Schiller's 'classicism'. There is little or nothing in common between art which may be called classical and this idealized and idealist revolt. The form may be explained as an experiment, the atmosphere and conception of drama are the creation of a genius other than the author of the *Braut*. The disparity between the idealism of *Tell* and the classicism of the *Braut* and *Demetrius* has been forcibly expressed by Walzel: 'Die Braut von Messina zu verstehen, muß man die Entwicklung, die Schillers aesthetische und technische Grundsätze in seiner Reifezeit durchmachen, jederzeit sich gegenwärtig halten; man muß dieselben Grundsätze vergessen, um dem Tell gerecht zu werden.'[1] This is no explanation of the relation of the two plays, but a recognition of an arbitrary experiment which apparently defies explanation. How could the poet who wrote the *Braut* as

[1] Schiller, Säkularausgabe, VII. xxii.

the culmination of years of reflection upon his art take up
and execute and be satisfied with *Tell* beyond all his other
works? How could he thereupon return to tragedy without any hint of reversal to an earlier idea? This is the
riddle of *Tell*, and within the limits of the traditional interpretation no answer seems possible.

Now, these are serious counts against a masterpiece of
classical drama, and I have made no mention of the difficulties which the critics emphasize, such as the loose
construction, the weakness of the fifth act, and so on.
On the other hand, no one would wish to deny that there
were inducements for Schiller to treat the *Tell* theme
when he did. One thinks at once of the parallel, and still
more of the contrast, with the French Revolution, or the
opportunity which the material would afford to stage the
conflict between simplicity and integrity on the one hand
and tyranny and cruelty on the other. There is more than
one passage in Schiller's earlier work where he shows his
sympathy with this conflict. In 1788 he introduces his
history of the Revolt of the Netherlands as 'ein neues
unverwerfliches Beispiel, was Menschen wagen dürfen
für die gute Sache und ausrichten mögen durch Vereini-
gung'.[1] Again, in the *Briefe über die ästhetische Erziehung
des Menschen* he speaks of the 'Versuch eines mündig ge-
wordenen Volks, seinen Naturstaat in einen sittlichen
umzuformen', a phrase which would serve as a definition
of the Tell theme. But there is a great difference, not only
between the Schiller of 1788 and of 1803, but between
the historical and the dramatic treatment of such themes.
Discussions about *Tell* really rest upon a decision as to
whether Schiller was predominantly a thinker, writing to
present an argument about freedom, or a dramatist, presenting a case of notable conflict and a revelation of the

---

[1] *Werke*, ed. Bellermann, viii. 39.

mystery of life. The traditional interpretation justifies the idealist at the expense of the dramatist.

Few readers of *Tell* can be insensible of its dramatic power, just as few students of Schiller's later years can fail to be conscious that his chief preoccupation is, precisely, not argument, whether about ideas or ideals, but drama. It is the purpose of the present essay to put the case for a revised approach to *Wilhelm Tell* in the light of these facts. It is possible to outline an alternative interpretation of the purpose, form, and nature of the play, an interpretation which, if it is to be qualified by any single word, must be termed tragic.

Ten years ago it would have seemed unusual to insist on Schiller's devotion to tragedy, but some recent studies have made it a main feature of the new approach to Schiller which seems now to be taking shape.[1] 'Das immer neu entfachte Ringen um die deutsche Tragödie, das immer heftigere Suchen nach dem Wesen des Tragischen ist das große beherrschende Thema in Schillers Leben.' These words of Werner Deubel[2] find interesting support in the penetrating analyses by G. Fricke of the *Jungfrau* and *Demetrius*.[3] They imply a reconsideration of the later dramas and make Tell as usually read more than ever an island of idealism in a sea of tragedy. Are there reasons for this isolation, or may we look in the material and treatment of the Tell theme for elements of tragedy which have so far escaped notice?

Our starting-point in answering this question must be

[1] Cf. R. Unger, *Richtungen und Probleme neuerer Schiller-Deutung.* Nachrichten von der Gesellschaft der Wissenschaften zu Göttingen, 1937.

[2] W. Deubel, 'Umrisse eines neuen Schillerbildes', *Goethejahrbuch*, 1934, p. 6. My quotation must not be taken as implying agreement with the whole essay from which it comes.

[3] G. Fricke, 'Die Problematik des Tragischen im Drama Schillers' *Jahrbuch des Freien Deutschen Hochstifts*, 1930.

Schiller's letter to Körner of 9 September 1802,[1] in which
he explains how the first idea of *Tell* came to him, apparently by a rumour that he was already writing a play upon
the subject. Tschudi's Swiss history was a revelation to
him, and induced him to work seriously at the theme.
He summarizes the difficulties of this *verteufelte Aufgabe*,
which he would not have done at the moment of writing
the *Braut* had he not been convinced it would be worth
while. He expresses what he calls the *Hauptsache* thus:
'ein ganz örtliches ja beinah individuelles und einziges
Phänomen, mit dem Charakter der höchsten Notwendigkeit und Wahrheit soll zur Anschauung gebracht werden.'
The words are precise, and contain no hint either of
passionate defence of Tell's act, nor of epic treatment.
The sentence could well describe a ballad or a drama, and
the terms *Notwendigkeit und Wahrheit* are significant in
the light of three tragedies completed within four years.

Indeed, a later letter contains the actual statement that
Schiller intended to make the new play into a tragedy.
Writing to Wilhelm von Wolzogen on 4 September 1803,
after having had the subject in mind for more than a year,
his words are:[2] 'Gegenwärtig arbeite ich an Wilhelm Tell,
woraus ich eine große Tragödie zu machen gedenke.'
The important evidence furnished here has never to
my knowledge been adequately considered. The word
Tragödie is that used on the title-page of *Die Jungfrau
von Orleans*. It is repeated with reference to *Tell* in the
letter to Iffland of 14 April 1804[3], and no later change in
Schiller's plan is known to us. Some forty years ago
Bellermann based his interpretation of the play partly on
the fact that it was a *Schauspiel*, thus:

'So tiefe Blicke ins innerste Geheimnis der Menschennatur, wie

[1] *Briefe*, ed. Jonas, vi. 414.   [2] Ibid. vii. 69.
[3] Ibid. vii. 138.

fast alle übrigen Stücke Schillers, läßt es uns nicht tun. Dies liegt
allerdings zum Teil daran, daß es keine Tragödie ist, sondern ein
Schauspiel, d.h. daß es keinen Konflikt enthält, der so tief angelegt
wäre, daß eine Lösung nur durch die Vernichtung der sterblichen
Persönlichkeit des Helden ermöglicht werden könnte.'[1]

Now Schiller himself obviously thought that the play did
contain such a conflict, and since he can hardly have
contemplated ending his play with the death of Tell, his
phrase is proof that he saw tragedy in a theme which did
not result in the physical death of the hero. He may very
well have altered the title to *Schauspiel* for the conventional reason that plays in which the hero survived were
commonly so called. If this reasoning is acceptable, we
are entitled to look for tragic issues in *Wilhelm Tell*. In
view of the traditional criticism the suggestion is surprising; we may recall that for at least one contemporary it was no suggestion but an assumption, and it is
evidently in line with the author's chief preoccupations
after 1800.[2]

A detailed examination of the play must be reserved for
another place, but considering the *Tellhandlung* for the
moment apart from the rest, may it not be said that we
are shown a good man forced to do murder in order to
free his country from tyranny? He is of a retiring nature,
laconic, simple-hearted, unwillingly and gradually brought
to his momentous decision. The circumstances which
force him to it, are, so we are told, the justification of what
is usually termed a crime. But I do not find evidence that
Schiller thought so. The play relates two other murders,
that of Wolfenschiessen and that of the Kaiser. Can

---

1 *Schillers Dramen*, iii. 133.
2 A reviewer in the *Göttinger Gelehrte Anzeigen* (Nov. 1804) writes
that 'der tragische Eindruck durch das große theatralische Aufgebot
gefährdet sei'. Cit. Schneider, op. cit., p. 94.

circumstances make two of these excusable and the other
one guilty?

This is the crucial point, where interpretations of *Tell*
diverge. Was he murderer or hero? Critics have vainly
sought an absolute answer to this question, and have
'justified' him more completely than the dramatist ever
did. We have in the play neither one-sided justification
nor condemnation, but rather, and with the greatest
clarity, the situation of a man who merits both, portrayed
as the author set out to portray it, *mit höchster Notwendigkeit und Wahrheit.*

It is no service to a great author to decide a complicated
issue which he has taken pains to state but not to solve.
By so doing we force the dramatic presentation out of the
perspective in which it is set. It is disingenuous to claim
that Tell's murder was justified because it prepared the
freedom of his people, or because he is obviously the hero
of the play. It would be equally false to consider him a
criminal shown in his true colours by Parricida. There
are other things which may more truly be said about
Tell's act than these. First, that it was necessary. There
was for such a man as he, in such a situation, no other
way out. Secondly, it was tragic, for it was the act of a
good man, peace-loving and friendly. Whether or not
we consider murder in all cases a crime, it was certainly
in this case a tragic departure from Tell's ideal. Slaying
in cold blood is the last thing which he and his friends
as here portrayed would willingly do. Readers are apt
to be scornful of the innocence and perfection of Tell and
his compatriots, but are they not an artistic necessity
here? They form the essential element in a tragic situation. Tell would have had no qualms about murder, he
would not have been stung by the comparison with
Parricida if he had been a bad or thoughtless man. It is

because he is *rechtschaffen* that murder must be for him
detestable. Yet events and his conviction force him to
act, in a situation where no action is possible other than
murder, that is, an action destructive of his whole position
as an idealist. Idealism prompts him to action which is
incompatible with an idealistic view of things.

Is not this true to type in Schiller's drama? Once
again we see the real and the ideal separated. Once again,
and more definitely than ever before, we are given a real
situation in which idealism is impossible. Schiller was
groping after this conviction in *Die Räuber*, discovered it
in the character of Philip in *Don Carlos*, and made it the
main axis of his greater dramas from *Wallenstein* onwards. It is in *Die Jungfrau* that the parallel with *Tell* is
closest. Johanna, by virtue of her humanity and its natural
affection, is denied the fulfilment of her passionate desire,
to obey the heavenly voices. Was Schiller conscious that
he had here discovered a type of fate much more appropriate to the modern age than the external inscrutable
force of *Wallenstein* or the *Braut*? The fact that brings
the ruin of a character is in the very make-up of that
character, in its idealism which appears to be the most
ethereal and untouchable thing about it. Idealism never
fits into life without tragedy, sacrifice, or death. This is
surely brilliantly shown in the case of Tell. He does not
court destruction by any appreciable sin. He is no
Wallenstein or Don Cesar, irresolute or selfish. He is if
anything too virtuous to be human. Yet he is impelled to
murder. The consequences of his act are mercifully not
shown; he is left in the glamour of popular acclaim. But
he knows that he has done, for the best reasons in the
world, what Parricida has done; his soul revolts against
his own deed performed by another. He does not know,
and we do not know, the sequel of the revolt which he

has made possible. But we know that it is not usual for violence to beget peace or mercy.

Does not this view permit a re-reading of the famous scene with Parricida? It is the only scene in which Tell is faced with the inevitable consequences of his act. Again, the question as to whether it is intended to justify him is, surely, the wrong question. It definitely shows three things: Tell's amazed discovery that he is compared with another murderer, his confidence in the righteousness of his deed, and his personal discomfiture. None of these three could have been omitted without the aesthetic balance being destroyed. Was Tell right or wrong? With superb skill the question is still posed, still unanswered, because perhaps humanly unanswerable. The tragedy is precisely that there is no answer. Is it astonishing that both Goethe and Schiller insisted against Iffland that the scene must be kept?[1]

But the play is not the private problem of Tell's conduct. It is a national action, involving several groups of people. Its loose construction has been found lacking in unity. But the unity is surely this identity of tragic situation. The play is not primarily concerned with Tell or with Switzerland, but with the various attempts made to solve one single situation. These attempts are not just compared; they condition each other. Tell only finally acts because other forces will not. The elder aristocracy is too feeble, the younger too careless, the confederates too deliberate. Every solution fails, save the violent act from which all parties, including Tell, recoil. The famous Rütli scene connects the vital threads of this process, and while showing the inefficacy of political debate, is itself a discussion of the issue before Tell. Is violence the solution or not? There are times, says Stauffacher in famous

[1] *Briefe*, ed. Jonas, vii. 138.

lines, when man must take his fate into his own hands:

> Wenn unerträglich wird die Last greift er
> Hinauf getrosten Mutes in den Himmel
> Und holt herunter seine ew'gen Rechte . . .

This speech has been taken as the motto of the play, but it reads more effectively as one position of its dialectic. Not all think with Stauffacher. Reding puts the other view:

> Schrecklich immer
> Auch in gerechter Sache ist Gewalt.

Nor does Walter Fürst really hold with a violent solution, though he does not speak his mind until later:

> Rache trägt keine Frucht. Sich selbst ist sie
> Die fürchterliche Nahrung, ihr Genuß
> Ist Mord und ihre Sättigung das Grausen. (3012)

Thus the subordinate actions strengthen and build up the whole. Its unity is strictly speaking an idea made tangible, just as the unity of Goethe's *Iphigenie* is an idea. In both cases, the idea is presented in classic form under its universal aspect. Goethe gives this effect by distance and poetic expression, Schiller by a variety of single impressions of the life pulsing through a people. The identity of situation and problem unifies the multiple parts of the action.

The dialectic of this problem, rather than any one situation or character, is the central nerve of the play. It is Schiller's own discussion of the clash between violence and ideals. Perhaps the dramatist has never been given credit for the range and objectivity with which he has conducted the argument. It is at bottom a question of theology. In no other play, with the possible exception of *Die Räuber*, is there so much implicit theology. Reliance on God, appeals to heaven, discussion of the divine will, these accompany the entire action. The tragedy of Tell is the fact that he is nerved to his deed by trust in God.

> Es lebt ein Gott zu strafen und zu rächen

are his words in the monologue as he unconsciously identifies the divine action and his own. 'Gott hat geholfen', he says later, in the conviction that he has been the divine instrument (3131). The confederates, no less than Tell himself, show Schiller's sense of the immense power, and danger, that comes to man with the conviction that the execution of God's will lies on and with him. Brüggemann's studies of eighteenth-century psychology aptly culminate in *Tell*. Here are no terrified or questioning beings awaiting a transcendental decision as in *Emilia Galotti*. Here are men imbued with the realization that they can and must express the will of God. 'Das bedeutet den vollen Sieg der immanenten Schicksalsidee.'[1]

But here a vital distinction must be made. Brüggemann considers *Tell* as a point in the evolution of an idea; he was not concerned to point out that it was a work of art. Schiller reached this new Weltanschauung by ways that we cannot know, but in *Tell* he does not so much plead for it as show it to be tragic. We may, and indeed must, give a new sense to Brüggemann's phrase, and say that Schiller has at last been able to make fate immanent in drama, inherent rather than excrescent, natural where in earlier plays it was still more or less artificial.

It is this, to my mind stupendous, achievement that links *Tell* to Schiller's last play. An analysis of *Demetrius* is unnecessary after the brilliant study of Gerhard Fricke, who shows it to be the last stage in Schiller's attempts to

---

[1] Fr. Brüggemann, 'Der Kampf um die bürgerliche Welt- und Lebensanschauung in der deutschen Literatur des 18. Jahrhunderts', *Deutsche Vierteljahrschrift*, iii. 122.

recover tragedy. I need only quote a sentence or two of his argument:

'Hier ist das Schicksal nicht mehr nur Ausdruck des Physischen, und es hat Gewalt nicht mehr nur über den, der sich der Leidenschaft hingibt und sich dadurch der Freiheit beraubt; hier zerstört es den Menschen an seiner Wurzel, an seiner moralischen Existenz, hier beweist es, was der Idealismus niemals zugeben durfte, daß echte Freiheit und reines Wollen ein Wahn und ein Werkzeug des Bösen zum Bösen sein kann.'[1]

The words might stand as a summary of the main contention of the present essay, and indeed the only point where I part company with them is that they ascribe to one play what is due to another. It is surely in *Tell*, and not first in *Demetrius*, that Schiller discovered a fate that attacks man at the root of his existence and makes of his freedom and will an illusion and an instrument of evil. It is *Tell* in which his tireless pursuit of his art brings him to the expression of a view of human nature which is deeply and inevitably tragic.

If we are to be consequent we must admit that this view also is essentially religious, but it is not the religion of Schiller's own age from which it springs, not the idealism of Humboldt, but the conviction of Luther. It is significant that a recent historian of Lutheranism finds in both Kant and Schiller 'Anklänge an das reformatorische Urerlebnis. Der Dramatiker Schiller weiß um die tragische Synthese von Schicksal und Schuld.'[2] Luther long before Schiller had seen man in a tragic situation by reason of his sense of obligation impossible to fulfil, as Elert puts it, quoting Luther's own words, 'den Widerspruch in dem sich der Mensch von Natur vorfindet: Non implesti, nec potes, et tamen debes'.[3]

[1] Fricke, op. cit., p. 65.
[2] W. Elert, *Morphologie des Luthertums*, 1931, i. 31.
[3] Ibid. i. 34.

The natural man is on the deepest analysis faced with the impossibility of doing what he would, with 'die Unvereinbarkeit unseres Könnens und Sollens'.[1] If this be a fair reading of Tell's position, the drama falls into its place not only as the ultimate stage of Schiller's classicism but as the achievement of that 'Durchbruch des deutschen Genius zur Tragödie',[2] which is from another angle a return from the positions of the Aufklärung to the powerful religious inspiration of the German people which was the main fact of the Reformation.

[1] i.e. the exact opposite of Cysarz's view: 'Schiller glaubt an die letzte Vereinbarkeit aller menschlichen Dinge und Gesetze.' Op. cit., p. 386.

[2] Deubel, op. cit., p. 7.

THE GERMANIC HEROIC POET AND HIS ART

By F. NORMAN

IN discussions of modern literature, when critics are not concerned with models, influences, trends, sources, and other even more remote constructions, they spend much time discoursing on the lives of the poets with whom they are dealing. Where biographical details are available, they are frequently utilized in explanation of the poetic work, and the analysis both of the poet's mind and of his art largely go hand in hand. Such study has its uses, and it can be profitably pursued where there is sufficient material. Not that minute details of a man's life are invariably necessary for an understanding either of his artistic development or of his work. We know far too much about Goethe, and much of what we know might just as well be forgotten. Again, critics are apt to complain that we know rather too little about Shakespeare, and our ignorance may be good and providential.

However, the biographical method has its uses, and the further we go back in time the more useful biographical details become. For the further we have to go back, the less intimate must be our feeling for the poet's culture and surroundings, and every scrap of information helps us towards building up a consistent picture. When we have to deal with poets like William Langland or Wolfram von Eschenbach, biographical details have to be culled largely from the works themselves; there is little corroborative evidence from outside. The further we go back, the less often do we know even the names of the authors. In Old High German literature we only know one name of any consequence: Otfried von Weissenburg. Apart from this solitary instance, all we have is the work, and everything has to be deduced from that.

Nowhere is this lack of information more troublesome than in a consideration of the Germanic heroic lay. We do not know a single author of such a lay, we cannot say for certain whether the language in which the lay is preserved is the original language, and we are unable to give a satisfactory literary history of the development of the genre.[1] Stray references in classical and post-classical authors, occasional fulminations of the Church,[2] some apparently reliable though highly stylized information in Old English poems: that is all the material available. If we add to this the two fragmentary southern lays, *Hildebrandslied* and the *Fight at Finnsburg*, and some of the presumably genuine lays retold by Germanic chroniclers of monkish outlook composing in Latin,[3] we have mentioned almost everything that could be of use to us in our quest in southern Germania. Scandinavia adds a little. Some of the poems preserved in the *Codex Regius*, and scraps embedded by way of quotation and elucidation in sagas recover some of the southern material. Scandinavian chroniclers also add their share, and the contribution of Saxo Grammaticus is not to be despised either quantitatively or qualitatively.

Biographical details, however, are equally hard to

---

[1] Indeed, the only serious attempt so far in this direction is a stimulating study by H. Schneider, 'Lebensgeschichte des altgermanischen Heldenlieds', *Deutsche Vierteljahrschrift für Literaturwissenschaft und Geistesgeschichte*, xii. 1–21. The author admits that his sketch of the development is to a large extent speculative. But it is a move in the right direction.

[2] These refer rarely, however, directly to the lay. The clergy could hardly have stigmatized heroic lays as *carmina obscoena et turpilena*, however little Ingeld may have had to do with Christ.

[3] Paul the Deacon, Widukind of Corvey, and a few others.

obtain in the north. What we know of the old Scandinavian poets—and we know a great deal—is of little use for
the reconstruction of earlier conditions. These poets gave
up cultivating heroic material probably not later than the
ninth century. This break with tradition may have been
due to the outstanding poetic personality and influence of
Brági the Old. In how far Brági himself was indebted
to Irish models is another matter. Henceforth the Scandinavian poets developed scaldic form and technique,[1] and
apart from a traditional interest in mythological verse, they
chiefly wrote encomiastic poetry. The heroic lay was
neglected, and, with it, the old heroic style. Yet it is
certain that the scalds knew more of the ancient simple
manner than is apparent on the surface. Many a kenning
must have been meaningless unless poet and listener were
familiar with what is called, somewhat loosely, Eddic
material.

In the north the heroic lay had had its day. We once
hear of the recitation of an heroic poem, at the battle of
Stiklastad in which King Olav was slain. But this was in
the camp, not at court. Knowledge of the lays went to
Iceland. There they were preserved, and at the beginning
of the thirteenth century a representative collection was
still to be obtained.

Where so little independent evidence is forthcoming,

---

[1] There is, of course, no clear division such as 'scaldic' and 'eddic'.
Many of the earliest poems in the *Edda* show scaldic stylistic tricks, many
of the scaldic poems work with images and metaphors derived from an
older state of affairs. And this is only what we should expect. The scaldic
development was a revolution from within, the civilization remained
homogeneous, and we should be surprised if we were to find such glaring
contrasts as in OHG. literature, for instance. In the southern example we
are dealing with imposition from without, and the contrast is sometimes
painful. There is no such thing as a moderately uniform literary culture
in early Germany. England solved the problem in its own peculiar way,
and the transition is less abrupt.

it is natural that we should interest ourselves in sub-
sidiary sources. One of these is the technical terms in use
for the poet and for the various forms of verse. This type
of investigation will yield some information, though not
as much as one might hope.

To a literary historian concerned with more modern
times, such an inquiry is hardly profitable unless he is
concerned with a circumscribed technical task. Thus
everybody knows that 'sonnet' means a certain type of
poem which became fashionable in western Europe from
the sixteenth century on, and everybody knows that the
word either comes straight from Italian or from Italian
through French. Where so many other and more in-
formative sources are to be had, it is not necessary to
reconstruct the original home and development of a
verse-form on linguistic considerations.

Yet an examination of technical terms in English and
German can teach us something. Where we say 'poet'
the German normally says *Dichter*. Both languages derive
many words from these two 'roots', though there is no
single word current in English to express the idea *dichten*.
Neither word is Germanic; the Germanic words for 'poet'
which were common to the two languages died out early,
together with the poems. In English, 'poet' is first used
of Homer round about 1300; in German, *Dichter* is
somewhat earlier. Dialectically and archaically English
preserves 'dight' which goes back to an Old English
verb *dihtan*. This is used, already in late Old English, in
a great number of different senses, and during the Middle
English period 'dight' was one of the most widely used
words. Yet the senses recorded rarely refer to writing.
The *Oxford English Dictionary* gives as the earliest example
in this sense a quotation from Ælfric: *Nu cwæþ se halʒa
Beda, ðe ðas boc ʒedihte*, and the latest reference is *c.* 1400:

A lettre has he dyght. The noun 'dighter' has a similar fate. Round about the year 1000 we find in the prologue to St. *Guthlac: Ic write swa me ða dihteras sædon ðe his lif . . . cuðon,* and a glossary of the same date gives us: 'commentator, expositor': *dihtere.* There are few later references. At no time were either verb or noun used specifically for verse-composition or versifier.

Otfried introduces the word into German. *Evangelien-buch,* 1. i. 18, he writes: *nim góuma thera dihta,* and that this *dihta* is to be understood as composition in either prose or verse is shown by the next two lines.[1] The verb *dihtōn* occurs several times in Otfried.[2] Now although Otfried was a pupil at the Anglo-Saxon foundation Fulda, it is unlikely that he brought the word away with him from there, since Old English and Old High German show different derivation.[3] He uses it in a sense not too far removed from *dictare.* Later on, *dichten* is used more widely. It can still be used for composition in prose or verse, and a modern German phrase like 'Was dichtet er sich da zusammen?' shows an even more extended significance.

Derivations from *dictare* are found in all Germanic languages, apparently of independent origin in each, except for the Danish *digte* which seems to go back to German.

A word common to English and German is 'rhyme'

[1] *Ist iz prósun slihti, thaz drénkit thih in rihti; odo métres kléini, theist góuma filu réini.*

[2] I. i. 6 *thes dihtonnes réini;* 1. i. 49 (not 42, as stated in Piper's edition): *dihto io thaz zi nóti;* Lud. 87: *Themo tihton ih thiz buah.* This is the only sense in which Otfried uses the word.

[3] OE. *dihtan* from *dihtjan,* OHG. *dihtōn.* Otfried's lack of dependence on English models should be noted. He spent most of his life west of the Rhine, and was much nearer to West-Frankish methods of composition. Most Old High German literature is directly and deeply indebted to English Christianity. Otfried is the one notable exception.

and its *nomen agentis* 'rimer'. The latter has never been respectable in German, and already Reinmar von Zweter, apparently the first German author to use the word, writes *ir hōhen rīmære* with satirical intent. In English the term was less opprobrious. Both 'rhyme' and 'rimer' are ultimately derived from Latin *rithmus, rythmus*, which had come to denote the accentuated as against the quantitative verse. Since the accentual verse allowed and later encouraged rhyme, the term became used in the sense in which it is still employed. In the form *rime* it spread from France all over Europe. Germanic languages mostly show a monosyllabic form and this may be due to the influence of an old Germanic noun *rīm*='number'.

So far we have found that the normal English and German words either differ and are of non-Germanic origin ('poet', *Dichter*), or the words are the same, are of non-Germanic origin, and have meanings that were fixed in a non-Germanic language ('rhyme', *Reim*). The Germanic languages have therefore taken over both form and content. Similar investigations could be pursued for many other technical terms (e.g. 'verse', 'strophe', 'ode', 'epic', 'lyric', 'ballad', &c.),[1] and we should discover in almost every case word-material of Graeco-Latin origin, taken over directly or through the Romance languages. Scandinavia, lying farther off from the Romance cultural sphere, has a few more modern technical poetic terms to show of Germanic origin, but in English and German hardly anything has survived. We have nowadays not one word of Germanic provenance for 'poet', no Germanic verb denoting 'to compose verse', no Germanic verb with the meaning 'to recite verse' unless we presume 'to

---

[1] The word 'lay' is of French origin as regards meaning. The etymology is not known. Following Gaston Paris, it is assumed that the OF. *lai* is somehow derived from a relation of OHG. *leich*.

sing'[1] to have had such a sense, which is almost certainly untrue. Of nouns we preserve German *Lied*, English 'spell' in certain senses hardly connected with literary composition, and, still more archaically, 'fit', 'saw', and 'yed'.

Our short survey of the technical terms in English and German for the poet and his craft has thus made clear the influences at work during the Middle Ages. In England, especially in the North, alliterative form survives for an astonishingly long time.[2] Germanic material is of less consequence. In Germany, alliterative form is completely superseded by the middle of the tenth century at the very latest, but much of the material survives. It is sufficiently alive during the thirteenth century to be worked up into long epics, and what is still more remarkable, the sixteenth century, after hundreds of years of silence on the subject, is still able to produce a poem on the death of Ermanaric.

Yet there is a clear and definite break. What was Common Germanic became, if it survived at all, ultimately English or German through Christian and classical influences, and the resulting civilizations became something radically different from what had existed before. The bridges that have been built connecting the earlier with the later have been constructed by scholars, and they will not bear too heavy a weight. However much and however eagerly we may stress the modern 'Germanic' component in our civilization, the 'Germanic' world is completely

[1] The word 'song' is used for poetry in older times, but it is used loosely, and has no specific meaning attached to it. The formula *singen und sagen*, found frequently in Middle High German, does not represent an old formula meaning 'to sing a lyric or short lay and to recite a longer poem'. The verbs appear coupled only once in early times, *Widsith* 54: *Forþon ic mæʒ sinʒan ond secʒan spell* ..., and there is no particular technical sense implied.

[2] The last alliterative poem in English is a poem on the battle of Flodden.

foreign to us. Our appreciation of the literary remains of our forefathers used to be to a large extent forced, and there have been few critics who have ventured into the realm of aesthetic criticism when discussing Germanic literature. There was too much comparing with later developments, too much apology for aspects that were barely tolerable to a modern European, too much insistence that the literature of the Germanic tribes was a beginning, and that one cannot expect too much from beginnings. Until the days of W. P. Ker hardly anybody progressed beyond admiration for the wild and rude grandeur of the heroic lay. Ker realized immediately and instinctively that the old poets were 'classic' within their own culture, that they composed according to rules that fitted into their own scheme of values, and that their rules of composition were well-defined, adequate, and needed no censure or support from any Aristotelian canon.[1] Ker's work was taken on abroad, chiefly by that brilliant exponent Andreas Heusler, and our notions on Germanic verse have altered so radically that we seem to be living in a different world when we read older literary histories by scholars like Kelle, Koegel, and even Ehrismann.[2]

---

[1] Ker's views will be found scattered throughout *Epic and Romance*, 1897. Ker propounded no doctrine. He neither systematized nor dogmatized, nor did he indulge in long learned argument and proof. He stated, casually and quietly, what were the aesthetic facts. To him the facts were obvious, and Ker was no friend of labouring the obvious. All that we know and believe now about Germanic heroic poetry goes back to Ker. Others have proved where he stated. But later proof has added nothing new and nothing material. Since 1897 our knowledge has advanced a good deal, but the fundamental, aesthetic foundations, laid by Ker, remain the same, and are likely to remain the same.

[2] J. Kelle, *Geschichte der deutschen Literatur* (1892), is still indispensable for the notes (i. 289–416, ii. 237–394) which deal very fully, always in original quotations, with the official Christian attitude. R. Koegel, *Geschichte der deutschen Literatur bis zum Ausgange des Mittelalters*, i (1894), also retains its value as a good collection of material, though the

Now that we realize that there was a break there is no
need to compare Germanic verse with a later and different
technique.[1] Since we are no longer apologetic, we can
look at what there is with less prejudice and uneasiness.
There is no necessity for walking over any unstable bridge.
We can now take a clean jump into a world that is not
our world, and we should be able to study it dispassionately
in the way in which we should study any other culture.
Let us begin with a consideration of the Germanic words
for the 'poet'.

Glosses preserve a number of words not found elsewhere. Such words are all suspicious. The translators
were attempting to gloss Graeco-Latin terms, and their
translations cannot be accepted as current coin unless
there is other evidence. Special suspicion attaches to
compounds, just as suspicion attaches to the many terms
for different types of poems in the glosses. We shall not
consider any terms for which there is no reasonable
evidence.

text is antiquated, and now largely useless. Koegel was insufficiently
familiar with the Scandinavian sources, and his remarks under this heading
are second-hand and often erroneous. He is also too fond of taking poems
back to the stone-age and the Indo-Europeans. G. Ehrismann, *Geschichte
der deutschen Literatur*, i[2] (1932), is a fully documented string of mono-
graphs, quite unreadable, and invariably wrong on matters Germanic.
For the Scandinavian material we have two excellent and reliable treatises,
F. Jónsson, *Den oldnorske og oldislandske Litteraturs Historie*[2] (1920–3),
and Axel Olrik, *Danmarks Heltedigtning* (1903–10). The best comprehensive survey is A. Heusler, *Die altgermanische Dichtung* (1923).

[1] Earlier discussions have sometimes suffered from too much attention
to the Greek parallel. In Greece, as in Germania, an earlier heroic outlook
has left its traces on later literature. But Greece remained Greece, and
thus Grecian culture developed continuously and harmoniously, whereas
southern Germania, and later Scandinavia, became Christian. This was
as violent an interference from outside with the normal development of
the culture as could well be imagined, and comparisons of Germanic and
Greek methods of dealing with the traditions and literature of the respective
heroic ages are therefore mostly futile.

Much has been written about the enigmatic character known in Old English as a *þyle*. In Scandinavia he occurs as *þulr* so that we have good grounds for believing the word to have been common Germanic. Whatever he may have been in later Scandinavian days, in the earlier records and in Old English literature he was not a poet. In *Beowulf*, Unferð is the *þyle* of King Hroðʒar. He is an unpleasant character and a quarrelsome fellow, yet he holds some position of trust. His role is similar, as far as his unbridled language is concerned, to that of Sir Kei in other and more romantic days. He does not seem to be a responsible political leader. That position was held by Æschere, whom Hroðʒar refers to as his *runwita* and *rædbora*, i.e. his confidential secretary who gives him advice and who is able to interpret runes, or, more probably, who knows all his secrets.[1] Glosses supply us with 'oratores: *þylæs*', and the noun *þelcræft* glosses 'rhetorica'. So, whatever the *þyle* may have been in England, he was no poet. In Scandinavia there are references, chiefly late, connecting the *þulr* with verse, but even there he could be considered at most the reciter of magical or legal formulae, the wise old man who remembers incantations or laws in alliterative form. In *Fáfnismál* 34 *þulr* is used of Regin, a magician possibly, but never a poet.

Scop was the West Germanic word for the poet, and here we are on surer ground. True, the etymology is uncertain. The vowel was once considered long, and that made it easy to connect the word with the gradation

---

[1] The personal name þyle in *Widsith* 24 may not be connected with the office of *þyle* at all, if Professor Kemp Malone is right, who argues that the designation given to a retainer is hardly the proper name for a king. For his connexion of the *Widsith* þyle with the þilir, cf. Kemp Malone, *Widsith* (Methuen's Old English Library A 5), 1936, p. 192.

of the root of modern German *schaffen*. The vowel is, however, undoubtedly short.[1] This has led many scholars, among them Heusler, to connect the word with the noun *scop/scof*, 'Spott, Spaß, Schimpf'. The word would then possibly be a contrafacture of Latin *ioculator*.[2] Heusler points to the Old English *ȝleoman* which is glossed as *mimus, iocista, scurra*, and which can yet, in epic poetry, be used as a variation for *scop*. The derivation is not happy. If the poet who wrote poems like the *Hamðismál* was given such a scurrilous title, the reactions of the listeners must have been quite different from what all other evidence leads us to expect. Another possibility would be that the *comicus* gradually became a *tragicus*. This is still less likely. The immediate connexion of *scop* with words of unworthy origin cannot be accepted.

In Old English we have the special term *ȝleoman*, which is not found elsewhere. In glosses this word is used to explain Latin *mimus, iocista, scurra*, and on account of its derivation from 'glee' it is almost certain that it is a contrafacture of *iocista*. In meaning it would thus appear to be strictly comparable to the German *spileman*. The only difficulty is that the word is used in *Widsith* and in

[1] The short vowel *o* could nevertheless allow a connexion with *scap/scōp* if we adopt the arguments put forward by E. Sievers, 'Germanisch *u* als Vertreter von indogerm. *ǝ*, *Paul und Braunes Beiträge*, xvi. 235 seq. Sievers did not mention *scop*, but he tried to connect, *inter alia*, *Zapfen* and *Zipfel* with *Zopf*, the Old English *scacan* with Modern English *shock*. Possibly *scop* represented a pronunciation of *scap* current among the poets themselves.

[2] A. Heusler, *Die altgerm. Dichtung*, p. 110: 'Als man für den neuaufkommenden Hofdichter eine Bezeichnung brauchte, wählte man sie in Nachahmung des römischen *joculator*; vermutlich am fränkischen Hofe in Gallien, wo man den Mimus gut kannte. Eine Ähnlichkeit der beiden Berufe hat man also empfinden müssen. Beide dienten ja der geselligen Lust, der ernste Dichter wie der Spaßmacher traten, schon vor Attila, nach dem Schmause auf, während die Becher oder Trinkhörner kreisten.' The arguments on *ȝleoman* precede the passage quoted here.

Beowulf as a variation of *scop*, moreover in contexts where *scop* should mean the heroic court-poet. Need for variation may be partly responsible for this. In any case, since the word is a loan-translation, it cannot have a very old history, and it cannot have been the original term for a heroic poet. It is probably an English coinage.

The Scandinavian term is *skáld*. The word does not appear to be older than the ninth century. On account of later developments we are apt to think of the *skáld* rather in connexion with later, complicated forms of encomiastic verse. But originally *skáld* must have meant the court-poet pure and simple without any special meaning attached to the stylized form of verse that came into vogue after the time of Brági the Old. The word cannot be derived from any Germanic root, and it is most likely connected with the Old Irish *scêlide*. If that is so, it must be a borrowing from Irish. Not only that. If the Scandinavians, during the early ninth century, borrowed the term, it is most likely that they also took over the poetic technique of the *scêlide*, and the origins of scaldic verse can then be referred with some confidence to Ireland. The *scêlide* was the Irish court-poet. It was his business to know the history and traditions of the king and his people, his stylistic tricks and allusive manner of composition are similar to the methods that suddenly appear in Scandinavia, the composition of encomia was one of his main duties. There is evidence for the presence of Scandinavians in Ireland during the ninth century, and the case seems conclusive. We may be justified in referring the special Scandinavian developments to Irish influence.

It is often stated that the *scop* is the heroic court-poet, the *skáld* the encomiastic court-poet. There is evidence to show that the *skáld* occasionally recited heroic verse. If the *skáld* had ousted the *scop* in the north, we should at least expect to meet the word *scop* now and again. But it never appears, and there is little doubt that it was never known in Scandinavia.

We must draw conclusions. The gleeman is known only in English, the *scop* only in West Germanic, the *skáld* only in North Germanic. The Germanic tribes may have had a word for 'poet'. If they did, it has not come down to us. Three different words in use for court-poet do not encourage the belief that he was a common Germanic institution. The Scandinavian evidence can teach us little, and we shall have to confine ourselves, in what follows, largely to the south.

At the end of the first century Tacitus wrote his *Germania*. He had not visited the country himself, and he was dependent on the accounts of soldiers, civil servants, possibly traders, and earlier written records no longer available to us. We are justified in treating his remarks critically.

Julius Caesar tells us that the Germanic tribes spent all their life in hunting and military affairs.[1] Of their literature he has nothing to say. Tacitus knows something of their religious poetry,[2] and his words prove alliteration and primitive religious verse, probably choral poetry. We can guess how Tacitus came to hear of this poetry. The poem gives tribal information, which is what the Romans required. Anyhow, there is no poet

[1] *Bellum Gallicum*, vi. 21: 'Vita omnis in uenationibus atque in studiis rei militaris consistit . . . .'

[2] *Germania*, ii: 'Celebrant carminibus antiquis, quod unum apud illos memoriae et annalium genus est, Tuistonem deum terra editum et filium Mannum originem gentis conditoresque. Manno tris filios adsignant, e quorum nominibus proximi Oceano Ingaeuones, medii Herminones, ceteri Istaeuones uocentur.'

mentioned, and it does not seem probable that there was a class of person specially charged with preserving the racial memories and handing them over to posterity in the form of alliterative lines. Too much has been read into these lines from Celtic parallels.

The next reference in Tacitus is to war-poetry. On the eve of battle they laud 'Hercules, the first of brave men'.[1] Again choral utterance, and no evidence for a poet. There follows the famous description of the *barditus* or *baritus*, the savage roar before the battle, in which the shields were brought to the lips, 'so that the voice may swell to a deeper and fuller note by means of the echo'.[2] Again, it is a choral effort, nor is it literature. There has been an unnecessary discussion in literary histories of these savage war-cries. They are the business of the cultural anthropologist.

Tacitus knows nothing further in the *Germania*, but in the *Annals* there is a puzzling reference to Arminius.[3] If we can trust this one piece of information that seems to point to an individual poet, we must assume that there was some verse that celebrated Arminius, who was killed about A.D. 17. And this verse must have survived until the end of the century.[4] From the nature of the case, a simple piece of encomiastic verse would best explain the circumstances. We know too little to say more. We can, however, be certain that we are not dealing with an heroic lay, and attempts to connect the fate of Arminius with later verse of the post-migratory period can be dismissed. The factual basis is slender. Arminius was slain in a feud

---

[1] *Germania*, iii: 'Fuisse apud eos et Herculem memorant, primumque omnium uirorum fortium ituri in proelia canunt.'

[2] *Germania*, iii: 'adfectatur praecipue asperitas soni et fractum murmur, obiectis ad os scutis, quo plenior et grauior uox repercussu intumescat.'

[3] Book ii, ch. 88: 'caniturque adhuc barbaras apud gentes.'

[4] The *Annals* were composed not long after A.D. 115.

with kinsmen. That is a normal way for a Germanic chieftain to meet his end.[1]

The Romans were naturally interested in the chieftain and his followers, and we can be sure that Tacitus is reliable in his details about the military organization. Yet, in the full discussion of such primitive 'courts', there is not a word about poetry or a poet. Judged by the heroic lay, the Germanic court-poet was a person of very superior intellect, and if there had been any institution of that sort, it is unlikely that the Romans would not have known about it. Such men would have been potentially dangerous, and it is not stretching legitimate argument if we draw a negative conclusion.

Even if we cannot credit that the poem on Arminius was a developed encomium, we are probably right in assuming that it was, in a way, the 'source' of later encomiastic poetry. Added to that, Tacitus gives us information that seems to prove the beginning of mnemonic verse, and he probably proves alliteration as a formal element.

For the next few hundred years we hear nothing that could relate to court-poetry. These are the centuries during which the Germanic tribes got into closer touch with civilization, and there is no means at our disposal from which we could judge what effect that had on their literature. Already in the days of Arminius, noble Germanic hostages lived for a time in Rome. Arminius himself had been there. And with the passage of time more and more barbarians came to the capital of the world. Rome could not produce anything that could account for the development of the heroic lay, but there was much in

---

[1] In his discussion of this passage, Ehrismann, op. cit., p. 18, talks of *Heldenlieder, das historische Volkslied,* and *Ballade.* Literary terms cease to have any meaning at all when they are bandied about like that.

Rome that could have influenced encomiastic poetry, and the encomium may have some classical roots.

During the fourth century there was a powerful Gothic realm on the shores of the Black Sea. Later material can again and again be proved to have been originally Gothic, and the Goths, most brilliant of all the Germanic tribes, provide us with the earliest evidence for court-poetry.

In the year 448 a Byzantine ambassador, Priscos, paid a visit to the court of Attila the Hun. Already Attila's predecessors had harassed the Ostrogoths, and, so Jordanes relates, their king Ermanaric, worn out with cares, had perished by his own hand in 375. Ermanaric's successors were unable to stem the tide of invasion. The country was gradually conquered, and the Goths were forced to recognize foreign overlords. But the Goths were by this time a moderately civilized people. It did not take long before they occupied high positions in the rather loosely organized state, and under Attila the Hunnish court was modelled on Germanic lines. Gothic was freely spoken, and Priscos tells us:

'In the evening torches were lit, and two barbarians came before Attila and recited poems they had composed, telling of his victories and of his brave, warlike deeds. The banqueters fixed their eyes upon them, some being charmed with the poems, while others were roused in spirit, as they remembered their own war-careers. Others again wept, since their bodies had become weakened by age and their martial ardour had therefore to remain unsatisfied.'[1]

This teaches us a number of things. To begin with, we are justified in assuming that the 'barbarians' were Goths. The performance takes place after the meal when the

[1] Translation quoted partly from H. M. Chadwick and N. K. Chadwick, *The Growth of Literature*, i (1932), p. 575 seq. The original text is most easily consulted in Kelle, op. cit., i. 295 or in Koegel, op. cit., i. 114. A German translation will be found in G. Freytag, *Bilder aus der deutschen Vergangenheit*, i. 168.

warriors are sitting around drinking. There are two reciters, and since there is no mention of song, we must assume that they took it in turns to recite. The poems have been prepared beforehand, and they deal with the deeds of Attila. Here we have the court-poet composing his encomia, and reciting them before his lord. There are present companions-in-arms of Attila, and they listen in rapt attention to the praise that is also a praise of their own deeds.

From other evidence we know that the court-poet produced both encomia and heroic lays, and we are justified in assuming that at this time there already existed an heroic poet, though we cannot say whether he was an 'official' poet. Priscos himself gives information that presumably goes back to a lay when he tells us that he passed through a place where formerly Vidigoia, bravest of Goths, fell through the treachery of the Sarmatians. From whom could Priscos have obtained this local information except from a Gothic guide who was taking him to Attila's court?

It would be idle to speculate about this earliest *Vidigoia* lay. It is interesting to note, however, that in Gothic-Hunnish territory the enemies are Sarmatians, whereas in another reference to early battles the antagonists are Goths and Huns.[1] References to Widia and his companion Hama seem to be of the earliest, and in some of these references the heroes are not friendly with Ermanaric. Since this enmity must be a later addition, Widia is one of the oldest heroes in the Germanic heroic lay.

Evidence for both encomium and the heroic lay is

[1] *Widsith*, ll. 119 seq.

> *Wulfhere sohte ic ond Wyrmhere: ful oft þær wiз ne alæз*
> *þonne Hræda here   heardum sweordum*
> *ymb Wistla wudu   werзan sceoldon*
> *ealdne eþelstol   Ætlan leodum.*

found in Jordanes, and the list of Gothic kings supplied
may go back to a catalogue arranged in alliterative lines.[1]
The best evidence, however, is internal, and is gained
from a study of the story-material itself. As earliest lays
we assume *Hamðismál*,[2] the *Battle of the Goths and the Huns*,
the *Vidigoia* lay, the *Offa* lay, the *Heoden-Hild* lay, the
Wayland lay. They must all have been in existence not
much later than 400. Three of them are Gothic, the other
three belong to more northern regions. If we assume that
the Goths were the first Germanic tribe to develop the
heroic lay, we must assume that this type of poem caught
on very quickly, and that poets soon arose in other parts
of Germania.

We can speak with some confidence about five of these
lays. They are concerned with personal rather than with

[1] Jordanes wrote his *De origine actibusque Getarum c.* 551. For the
older parts it is largely copied from a similar work by Cassiodorus, under-
taken at the desire of Theodoric, and finished before 533. This work is
not preserved. We do not know in how far Cassiodorus was dependent
on a still earlier work by a certain Ablabius, but we know that Cassiodorus
is not to be trusted implicitly. His work was political propaganda for the
Gothic royal house: the Goths are made an old race with a 'genuine' early
and glorious history, a most suspicious genealogy is provided for the Amali,
the ruling Gothic house, and much of the 'early history' of Cassiodorus
is his own invention. It is also unsound to presuppose encomiastic vernacular verse behind some of the fulsome flattery of this accomplished
courtier. Thus Cassiodorus (*Variae*, bk. xi, ch. i), when accounting for the
virtues of the Gothic princess Amalasuentha, writes: '*Enituit enim Amala
felicitate, Ostrogotha patientia, Athala mansuetudine, Uinitharius aequitate,
Hunimundus forma, Thorismundus castitate, Ualamir fide, Theodemir
pietate, sapientia inclitus pater.*' Since *Widsith*, l. 113 seq. refers to
Eastʒotan, frodne ond ʒodne, editors have attempted to connect this with
the *patientia* of Ostrogotha. But the evidence is poor. The virtues
enumerated may occasionally have occurred in encomiastic court poems,
but fundamentally such poetry was concerned with the deeds of the person
praised, as in the case of Attila.

[2] For the sake of convenience the *Edda* title is given. This does not
imply that the earliest version corresponded in all its details. Similar
reservations apply to other titles.

political aspects. One brings in supernatural elements, and it is no accident that this lay has classical roots. The lays are normally tragic; it is not, however, inevitable that they should be so. In the *Wayland* lay there is resolution of the tragedy, and in the *Offa* lay there is no ultimate tragedy at all. Similar reservations have to be made for later lays. It was an exaggeration to say that the lays are always tragic and fatalistic.

The question of the origin of the heroic lay is closely bound up with the question of the origin of the poets who produced them. At one time it was believed that the heroic lay had grown naturally out of the encomium with the mere passage of time. That theory is now discarded. The only poem that might conceivably have started as an encomium is the *Offa* lay, and if that were so, it would help us to understand the lack of tragedy. But for the others such a theory will not work. We have seen that there is nothing in classical antiquity that could have served as a model; indeed, the heroic lay is the one independent creation of the Germanic tribes, and it is the one fundamentally heathen contribution of any importance to the literature of western Europe. So powerful was the original stimulus that despite bell, book, and candle it kept alive in Germany until after the Reformation, then contributed its share to the chap-book literature, and from the eighteenth century on, through learned sources, again started to play its part. If we exclude learned resuscitation, it was alive in some form or other for over thirteen hundred years.[1]

The origins of the heroic lay have been sought with the Huns, the Thracians, the Armenians. We know

[1] This does not invalidate the statement that there was a complete break with Germanic traditions. The material could not have survived if it had not adapted itself, if it had not become German rather than Germanic.

nothing of heroic poetry among the first two, and in the case of the Huns it is not very likely that this barbarous people should have provided the more civilized Goths with material out of which one of the most 'classic' forms in literature was developed. It is said that there was early heroic poetry among the Armenians; we know nothing of it. Theories of origins can be pushed too far. The alliterative long line lay ready to hand, there was primitive encomiastic verse, we can assume poetic lament for the death of a chieftain, and other simple forms of composition. The Goths may well have produced the genius who invented the *genre*, and there is nothing improbable in the assumption that the *Vidigoia* lay and the prototype of the *Hamðismál* were among the first works produced either by this early Gothic genius or by one of his immediate followers.

Belief in this early Gothic genius does not mean that we have to abandon the search for origins. It must be continued, however, on a comparative basis. Only by comparing, in detail, the social structure, the aims, the expression of these aims in literary form, and other matters, in as many heroic civilizations as possible shall we be able to give a moderately correct answer to two questions. We must first of all discover what is general to heroic cultures, we must next find out in what way any particular culture differs, and it is only when this has been done that we shall be able to answer at all satisfactorily the vexed question of origins both of the heroic artist and of his work. And it is important that this should be done, for we cannot say anything definite about the originality or otherwise of the Germanic and other heroic poets until the general problem has been brought a little nearer to a solution.

Jordanes tells us nothing of the poet, and later Latin

chroniclers are equally silent. Were it not for the information we are given in Old English verse, we should not be able to reconstruct our picture at all. *Widsith*, *Beowulf*, and *Deor* tell us a certain amount, though not as much as we should like. The evidence is too late to be altogether reliable. Heroic court-poetry must have died out in southern Germania as an independent, creative art not long after 700. The latest historical hero who was celebrated in an heroic lay was Alboin the Longobard, who died in 572, and the latest heroic lay of southern origin that we know of is the *Hildebrandslied*, composed in Bavaria round about 700.[1] There can have been little after that date. *Beowulf* was written by a cleric who certainly knew heroic lays, but it is just as certain that he was not in the habit of reciting them. The same applies, with less confidence, to the authors of *Widsith* and *Deor*. It is difficult to believe that the poets are giving the repertoire from which they are willing to recite, should there be a demand. Both these poems were probably written in the first instance, and the author of *Widsith* was certainly a cleric. They knew the stories, and their audience knew the stories, but even if they could have recited some of the lays, their poems are in no sense introductions to such recitals. If we knew the date of composition of our three Old English sources, we should be in a slightly better position to judge the value of the evidence. But the dates are quite uncertain, except that all three poems, in their present form, must be later than 700.

The *scop* is an aristocratic retainer who enjoys the same social position as any other member of the king's company. In Scandinavia he is a fighting man: whether he also fought in England we cannot judge. It is, however,

[1] Cf. F. Norman, 'Some Problems of the Hildebrandslied', *London Mediæval Studies*, i. 6 ff.

inherently improbable that he should not have been a warrior, when occasion required. The fictitious *scop* in *Widsith* accompanies a royal princess to a distant court. He may have gone with a harp, it is unlikely that he went without a sword. The connexion between the artist and the audience is much more intimate than now, and no proper respect for the poet is possible unless the retainers either know him as a warrior or as an older man who has seen some active service. There is, thus, no justification for the assumption that the *skáld* fought and that the *scop* did not. The wandering *scop* in *Widsith* is richly rewarded for his art, by Guðhere, by Ælfwine, by Eormanric. The gift of the last-named is one of unheard-of generosity. When he returns to his native land, he presents this gift to his overlord in return for the land that his father had already held. So that the father of the *scop* is presented here as a man of consequence. From this it follows necessarily that it was no disgrace for the son partly to earn his living by singing the praises of princes. The *scop* has a companion, Scilling, and the two perform together. The audience is appreciative, and it is admitted —by the poet!—that nobody ever heard a better recital.

It is difficult to disentangle antiquarian fiction from possible fiction in this account. The listeners, we must presume, were as well acquainted with the possibilities of heroic life at a court as the poet, and it would therefore have been impossible for the author to depart too much from tradition. The word *scop* does not occur in the poem, *ȝleomen* (nom. pl.) in line 136.

From *Deor* we learn little more. The poem is constructed with such delicate artistry that it can never have been recited before the retainers in the hall.[1] It is an

---

[1] For its construction, cf. F. Norman, 'Deor: A Criticism and an Interpretation', *Modern Language Review*, xxxii.

intricate structure that may well have been recited before a court like that of Bishop Higebald at Lindisfarne to whom Alcuin writes, in 797, that he wishes, during the meals of the priests, *lectorem audiri, non citharistam; sermones patrum, non carmina gentilium.* However difficult it may be to credit the recitation of *Deor* before warriors, it must have been recited before people who immediately understood the heroic references, otherwise the whole poem would have been pointless. In one detail *Deor* agrees with *Widsith.* The poet is said to have had an estate. He has lost it, however, to a famous rival, Heorrenda. Deor, therefore, obtained his *londryht* originally not because it was his *fæder epel.* It provided him with a living whilst his song was acceptable, and was forfeited with his office. Another statement in *Deor* links up with *Beowulf.* Deor describes himself as formerly the *Heodeninʒa scop*, the accredited court-poet of Heoden. The *scop* in *Beowulf* is referred to as *Hropʒares scop*, again an official court-poet and reciter.

Beowulf contains a good deal of evidence, though it is not definite enough to allow of certain interpretation. Moreover, we are dealing with a poet who is far removed from the earlier court-life that he describes, and the very first introduction of the *scop* should put us on our guard. At Heorot, the retainers listen to *hearpan sweʒ, swutol sanʒ scopes* (*Beowulf*, 89 f.). What follows (lines 90ᵇ–98) is a Christian hymn of creation that closely adheres to the first verses of Genesis i. The reference to the *scop* in line 496 teaches us nothing new. A more interesting passage occurs 867 ff. After Grendel's death the country is thought to be safer, and a number of warriors ride about the country-side. The king's thane, presumably the *scop* already mentioned before, celebrates the heroic deed of Beowulf in extempore verse, and, in a rather

obscure manner, glides over into the recitation of a lay
concerning Sigmund. This extempore poem must have
been an encomium. It is significant that it is not recited
in the hall before the assembled company; that would
have required rather more careful preparation. Nor is
the harp mentioned. The poem on Beowulf is described as a *spell*, and the *Sigmund* lay is recited rather
than sung.

Later on there takes place the great victory-feast. After
a proper amount of eloquence the banquet begins, presents are given to Beowulf and his companions, there is
great joy, and then Hrothgar's *scop* sings a lay connected
with the Battle at Finnsburg.[1] At the end of the poet's
résumé we are told: *Leoð wæs asunȝen, ȝleomannes ȝyd.
ȝamen eft astah*, ... The poet clearly wishes us to
understand that the lay was sung, and *ȝamen eft astah*
tells us that the song was listened to in respectful
silence.

When Beowulf has returned home, he reports to his
overlord Hygelac. He tells of the slaying of Grendel,
and the feast that followed. During this feast there was
poetical and musical entertainment, and if we interpret
the text straightforwardly, most of this entertainment was
provided by King Hrothgar. He first told stories, whether
in prose or in verse, is not clear, probably the former.
He then played the harp, and recited *ȝyd . . . soð ond
sarlic*.[2] This may have been an elegy, and it may have
been accompanied on the harp. The poet is not precise

[1] *Beowulf*, 1068–1159. It is unnecessary to quarrel about the exact
place where the lay begins. Properly speaking, it does not begin at all.
What the poet gives is a résumé, decked out in his own elegiac fashion.
Many editions place the 'lay' between inverted commas, which is non-
sensical.

[2] In the only other occurrence of *ȝid awræcan* the reference is certainly
to a speech in prose (*Beowulf*, 1723 f.).

enough for us to be certain of what is meant. It is not to be made out, either, whether the rest of the report refers to Hrothgar's prose or to his verse.

If we accept Hrothgar as a musician and as a reciter of verse,[1] there is nothing extraordinary in that. In Scandinavia many kings were good poets, and we can find an example at home in the royal prince Aldhelm, a good vernacular poet and a good reciter. Bede's death-song is preserved. We cannot doubt its authenticity, and it is a good poem. The most famous reference to a royal singer is the one transmitted by Procopios. The Vandal King Gelimer, besieged and at the end of his powers of resistance, sends a messenger to the Roman General requesting, among other things, a harp, so that he may give expression to his sorrow in song.[2] In none of the cases of 'amateurs' are we dealing with heroic lays. These were reserved for the court-poets.

The English evidence has not taught us as much as we might have hoped, and we shall have to fall back on a literary interpretation of the actual lays preserved, if we are to gain any clear idea of the poet in early Germanic days. None of our sources refers to instruction in poetic technique, and there is no reason to assume that there ever existed a special class of poets or a special doctrine that had to be assimilated. It is unbelievable that a *skáld* should have had no training, but the training he received was no more and no less than that of a modern poet. Given the necessary gifts and cunning, it was part of the ordinary day's work of an Icelander to dabble in verse-composition, and we know the names of hundreds of *skálds*. The north preserves names of poets, there is pride in authorship. The names preserved in the south refer

---

[1] Authorship is not necessarily implied.
[2] c. 533. *De bello Vandalico*, ii. 6.

to reciters (Widsith, Deor, Scilling, Bernlef). The heroic lay was traditionally anonymous, and this anonymity adds to our difficulties of interpretation.

In the *Germania* we hear of Germanic tribes where a king has great power. This is the exception. Most tribes have a loose kind of organization comparable to that of the Frisians at the time of Charlemagne, or the Ditmarschen until the fourteenth century. It is a patrilineal clan-system based on the authority of the head of the clan. Clans are constantly quarrelling with neighbouring clans, and no clan can survive unless every member of the clan is imbued with the spirit: Right or wrong, my clan. Loyalty to the clan arises naturally. It is the only way to ensure some sort of stability. The clan is responsible for the deeds of its members, and in a blood-revenge it is not necessary to kill the original slayer. When the Germanic tribes organized themselves into larger confederations, and attacked the Roman Empire, they carried their clan loyalties with them. They were in the blood, ineradicable. To sin against the ties of blood was the great sin, and when interest clashed with interest, such a sin frequently became inevitable. The Romans lost no time in pitting clan against clan, and the Germanic tribes destroyed one another as much as they were destroyed by the legions. In the end there were too many Barbarians, and the Empire collapsed. But this collapse took hundreds of years to accomplish, and many of the tribes had in the meantime been cleared completely off the face of the earth. These are the conditions which form the main background for the heroic lay.

Germanic kingdoms of Migration days were ruled by the king and his faithful followers. Just as in later medieval romance we are moving in a world of knights, so in the heroic lay we are moving in a world of heroes. The lower orders do not occur, or if they do, they are there for contrast.[1] There is no strict division of society. True, a newcomer is asked his name, and his father's name. Heroic qualities are believed to be inheritable, and a famous father's son is accepted until he has proved himself unworthy. Honourable aristocratic descent is, however, not essential. If a man can prove himself by his deeds he is accepted as a full member of the king's household.

Every society has its code, and there must be instruction in the code. In the Germanic kingdoms religion is of secondary importance. Most of our southern heroic poets must have been Christians. But the conversion went only skin-deep, and a warrior trusted to his sword more than to Christ or Wodan. There is no religion in the lays, they are not concerned with religion. Heroic society needed an instructor, and found him in the poet. As man to man, the poet is no better than any other man of the king's household. He is in a very real sense a member of the company. What distinguishes him is his gift of words, and his ability to embody the ideals of the society in concrete examples. He is the teacher who places before the company idealized portraits, and his company is aware of the idealization. Every member in the hall wishes to become like Vidigoia, like Hamðir, like Offa.

Withal, there is an underlying sense of reality. Germanic heroes do not perform tasks that are quite impossible. Beowulf's swimming-match is late and fabulous; an early heroic court would have treated such adventures as at best a joke. If you invade your enemy's hall, you are bound

---

[1] Cf. the episode of the cowardly Hjalli in *Atlakviða*. This episode may, of course, be a Scandinavian innovation.

to suffer death: there are heroes on the other side. Nor does death matter. It should be met with fortitude if it cannot be avoided. But as long as it can be avoided honourably, it is better to be alive. The journeys of Gunnar and Hǫgni in the *Atlakviða*, and of Hamðir and Sǫrli in the *Hamðismál* were foolhardy in the extreme, and there was from the outset no possible way of avoiding death. Honour demanded that the perils should be faced, and faced they were. The moral note is quite clear in Gunnar's speech to his retainers, in which he gives the reasons why he must go. And Gunnar's household knows that the challenge must be accepted. There is, then, less stress on the heroic deed than on the heroic attitude. And this helps to explain why the deeds themselves remain comparatively sober, why fantastic feats of arms, so common in Irish material and so ridiculous in later romance, are not required. The true hero shows himself by the spirit in which he accepts victory and defeat, not by the number of enemies slain. And where the hero survives, he has frequently bought his life too dearly by slaying a near kinsman, as is the case with Angantyr and Hildebrand.

The subjects treated may or may not be historical, and there is no insistence on glorifying the tribe to which one happens to belong. There is little tribal, and no national patriotism, though it is only natural that the poet should find his material most easily amongst the people he lives with. Everything political recedes into the background. The quarrels are all personal quarrels, and this is proper and essential in a society that is held together, not by any abstract theory of state, but by personal ties. Supernatural beings play a subordinate part. Amongst the early lays the only one with such elements is the *Wayland* lay, classical in its roots. Sometimes the poet invented his main character, as is probably the case with Hildebrand.[1]

The lay is tense and concentrated from the very outset. There is never a long exposition. The problem is stated in as few words as possible. There is little description; most of the action takes place in speeches. There is also surprisingly little fighting. The reasons that impel towards the fight are more important. The *Hildebrandslied* is, of course, only a fragment, and it breaks off in the middle of the fight. But there cannot have been much more description of the actual fighting. The first sixty-two lines are exposition and argument. The fight does not begin until line 63, and at the end of the fragment (68[a], i.e. five and a half lines) we have already got to the stage where the spear-fighting is over, and where the shields have been almost hacked away by a long sword-duel. Concentration could hardly be carried further.

The heroic poet creates the heroic lay, and the heroic lay is the beginning of any real traditional story. We can no longer believe that the heroic poet was a mere versifier of events. He took events, moulded them carefully to his purpose, or, if he did not know of a suitable event, he invented it himself. All the old lays have the stamp of a genuine individual personality, their creator, even if he remains nameless to us. Popular rumour and tradition cannot produce a rounded-off and consistent plot, it can merely ruin it when the heroic courts have decayed and there is no guardian responsible for treasuring the original creation. In the end, then, the heroic poet is the real creator of what is known as 'Heldensage'. The anonymous poet of Migration days, sure of his material and certain of his art-form, eschewed mere swashbuckling and

[1] For an attempt to prove this, cf. F. Norman, *London Mediæval Studies*, i. 22 ff.

concentrated instead on the underlying ethical realities. Had he been mainly concerned with warlike adventures, the material would not have survived. It does not need poetic talent of a high order to invent fighting-contexts. Later ages could do that just as well, and their stories would have been more up to date.

The art of the heroic court-poet is intensely real, intensely felt, intensely genuine. One would like to feel that anything that springs from such depths of human emotion and endeavour must endure through the ages. Such a belief is probably illusory, but any one who cares to adopt it can cite as proof the survival and literary influence of the anonymous, unwritten lays of the Germanic heroic poet.

THE POETRY OF NOVALIS

By R. PEACOCK

IT is strange that the position of Novalis as the only creative genius of the older Romantic School in Germany should so long have been obscured. Scherer, it is true, said his poems were the only ones the school produced that were likely to last. But he fails entirely to grasp their true significance, and misinterprets them. Gervinus, before him, had been unable even to believe the evidence of the romanticists themselves that Novalis was the profoundest spirit amongst them. Probably the speculative side of romanticism, that ferment of philosophical thinking they caused round about the year 1798, and Novalis's collaboration in it, have overshadowed his poetic work and its uniqueness. For Novalis had a philosophic and scientific mind equal to that of Friedrich Schlegel in its alertness, elasticity, adventurousness, and profundity, and superior in the diversity of sciences it embraced; so that a certain degree of congeniality made for a good understanding and enjoyable co-operation in literary tasks. But Novalis was, too, a visionary, with his own life, whilst Schlegel, though brilliant and suggestive, was a critic and historian. His chief faculty was a masterful intellect; he had no soul such as Novalis possessed, deep, full, and initiate. Novalis's poems, sprung from a genuine inspiration, have a life that the critical and philosophical work of the romanticists could never have; a life, moreover, that could only come from an individual spirit and not from the kind of collaborative literary production in which the romanticists, as a 'school', indulged. The predominance of the critical spirit, and the preoccupation with a theory of poetry, might create, indeed, do create, amongst the unwary the impression that romantic critical theory produced romantic poetry; that the latter was composed according to a formula. The theories of the Schlegels, however, produced nothing whatever, unless it be the salonesque verse of August Wilhelm, or the spiritless disorder and undisciplined intellectual conceits of *Lucinde*. But they did throw light on poetry and literature that already existed and had existed for a long time before the work they all admired —*Wilhelm Meister*—appeared; and though this light may not have been pure, showing up everything in its completeness as the sun's light does, but one tinged by the colour of their own temperament, making some things stand out in relief at the cost of others, yet it did illumine much that had been obscure, and rendered critical service of a high order. There is, of course, a relationship between Novalis's poems and the criticism of the Schlegels; but it is the relationship of derived thought to the living spirit; his poems make Novalis not a mere collaborator, still less a follower, but rather the leader of the group.

An urgent disposition towards the transcendental is the common origin of those works that give Novalis a high rank as poet, though they are so few in number— two unfinished romances, one of them, indeed, only just begun, and a score of poems. The fundamental trait of them all is their preoccupation with a metaphysical world. It takes different forms in different works; or rather, Novalis finds his way to the transcendental by different approaches; now by way of nature, now through love of a woman, now by the mediation of Christ. But however unlike these various approaches may seem to be, his peculiar vision of a transcendental state remains constant; and the effect of this is to draw closer together those

various media, nature, the loved woman, and Christ, since
they are all the objects of the poet's longing, and since
their names are used as symbols of the transcendental
state. This process of *rapprochement* is a violent one for
those who distinguish between God and nature, between
love of a woman and love of Christ, however anxious they
are to see an ordered relationship in things, dependent
on a supreme Law-giver. But violence was one of the
things Novalis, and his friends, enjoyed; they liked, on
occasion, to be reckless, wilful and shameless, even
impious; they then felt that absolute freedom of spirit
they demanded and coveted. It is an element in all their
activity, even in their religion, as we see here with Novalis.
For in considering him we have to do with a trend of
religious feeling, however unusual, capricious, or irreligious
it might sometimes appear; the very paradox would please
the romanticists.

There are the clearest indications of Novalis's nature
philosophy in the early fragment *Die Lehrlinge zu Sais*.
Its theme is the search for the meaning of nature and of
human existence in its dependence on nature, and it
consists of a series of conversations between an apprentice,
his friends, and their master, in which various theories
about man, nature, and life are discussed. For these
theories Novalis draws on the thought of past and present,
and from them emerge gradually his own principal ideas.
The different, contradictory arguments confuse the
apprentice, but they are suddenly broken off and the so-
called sprightly playfellow, freeing him from the criss-
cross of opinions, tells him of feeling and love. He does
this by means of a fairy-story. Tenderly and gracefully,
and with a sweet flow of language all his own, Novalis
tells the story of Hyazinth and Rosenblüt; how Hyazinth
leaves his home and beloved playmate Rosenblüt and

goes far away to seek Isis, the veiled maiden, the mother
of things, the goddess of fertility. After a long time he
reaches the dwelling-place of the goddess; in ecstasy he
enters and then sinks into sleep—for dream alone gives
access to the holy of holies. He wanders through many
chambers, all earthly things are left behind, and at last
he stands before the heavenly maiden; he raises the veil
—and Rosenblüt sinks into his arms.

The teaching which is embodied in so pregnant and
lively a manner in this delightful story is that the force of
love stirring in one's own heart is the key to the true
being of nature. Speculation is therewith put on one side,
for final truths are communicated through other organs
than reason. This lesson is the kernel of what is now said
by a beautiful youth, in whom we hear the voice of the
poet himself. Some thoughts are retained from the earlier
conversations; they are, briefly, as follows: man and
nature are really one, and the relation between them is of
a religious kind. Nature is also intimately connected with
poetry, and thus nature, religion, and poetry are very close
together in the thought of the poet, a point to which we
shall come back. There is, further, a gradual progress
towards a new age of harmony between nature and man;
and poets are the prophets of this new age. These ideas
receive a new complexion and a more precise meaning
by now being combined with three new ones: *Liebe,
Wollust, Genuß* (love, voluptuousness, pleasure), which
recur again and again in Novalis, to the point of satiety.
They are obviously three aspects of one thing. The
beautiful youth reveals the true working of nature: in-
cessant generation, and its energizing force, voluptuousness. The most evident symbol of this process is water, as
the element infinitely capable of embracing and mingling:

Wem regt sich nicht das Herz in hüpfender Lust, wenn ihm

das innerste Leben der Natur in seiner ganzen Fülle in das Gemüt
kommt! wenn dann jenes mächtige Gefühl, wofür die Sprache
keine anderen Namen als Liebe und Wollust hat, sich in ihm
ausdehnt, wie ein gewaltiger, alles auflösender Dunst, und er
bebend in süßer Angst in den dunkeln lockenden Schoß der
Natur versinkt, die arme Persönlichkeit in den überschlagenden
Wogen der Lust sich verzehrt, und nichts als ein Brennpunkt der
unermeßlichen Zeugungskraft, ein verschluckender Wirbel im
großen Ozean übrig bleibt! Was ist die überall erscheinende
Flamme? Eine innige Umarmung, deren süße Frucht in wollüstigen Tropfen heruntertaut. Das Wasser, dieses erstgeborne
Kind luftiger Verschmelzungen, kann seinen wollüstigen Ursprung
nicht verleugnen und zeigt sich als Element der Liebe und der
Mischung mit himmlischer Allgewalt auf Erden. Nicht unwahr
haben alte Weisen im Wasser den Ursprung der Dinge gesucht,
und wahrlich sie haben von einem höhern Wasser als dem Meer-
und Quellwasser gesprochen. In jenem offenbaret sich nur das
Urflüssige, wie es im flüssigen Metall zum Vorschein kommt, und
darum mögen die Menschen es immer auch nur göttlich verehren.
Wie wenige haben sich noch in die Geheimnisse des Flüssigen
vertieft und manchem ist diese Ahndung des höchsten Genusses
und Lebens wohl nie in der trunkenen Seele aufgegangen. Im
Durste offenbaret sich diese Weltseele, diese gewaltige Sehnsucht
nach dem Zerfließen. Die Berauschten fühlen nur zu gut diese
überirdische Wonne des Flüssigen, und am Ende sind alle ange-
nehme Empfindungen in uns mannigfache Zerfließungen, Regun-
gen jener Urgewässer in uns.

In order to make clear the tendency of Novalis and the
results of his particular insight, let us recall the pan-
theism of 'Tintern Abbey', or Goethe's 'Ganymed'.
Wordsworth is aware of

> A presence that disturbs me with the joy
> Of elevated thoughts; a sense sublime
> Of something far more deeply interfused,
> Whose dwelling is the light of setting suns,
> And the round ocean and the living air,
> And the blue sky, and in the mind of man;

> A motion and a spirit, that impels
> All thinking things, all objects of all thought,
> And rolls through all things.

This passage reveals how the poet perceives a spirit that dwells in things everywhere. Or let us take Goethe:

> Und deine Blumen, dein Gras
> Drängen sich an mein Herz.
> Du kühlst den brennenden
> Durst meines Busens,
> Lieblicher Morgenwind!
> Ruft drein die Nachtigall
> Liebend nach mir aus dem Nebeltal.

Goethe feels here the unity of life, the secret bond between himself and the rest of nature. But both Wordsworth and Goethe have this in common, that the world of appearances, of bodies and forms, remains, and therewith, too, their own personality. In Novalis, however, the world of bodies and forms is dissipated; his aim is to shake off the forms of our consciousness and participate in the endless flux of universal life, to give up his own personality and sink into the voluptuous mingling process. It is not entirely clear what he really means, and that is probably because he is struggling to express himself in a medium which is inadequate. For the words he is obliged to use to describe his transcendental state are heavy with sensual, physiological, and organic associations, whereas he constantly hints at processes and organs far more refined and spiritual than earthly man knows or possesses. The mingling and embracing of fluids and essences which forms the transcendental is not an organic process, but seems to be a spiritual counterpart of the organic processes of nature. Moreover, being spiritual, it is conceived by Novalis as being conscious of itself; it is knowing. Thus Novalis seizes on the essential principle of nature, generation, and then makes it into an absolute, spiritual principle, that can be called divinity. He thinks it is possible for man to apprehend this by means of a delicate, inner organ. Here appears that element of magic in Novalis, who, by means of a mysterious power, strains beyond the ordinary experience of the human senses. The language of the fragment reflects the tendency: the prose of the first parts, although glowing with enthusiasm, is yet the language of thought, but gradually it passes into the most intense expression of an inspired vision of supra-sensuous mysteries. It is by this particular contribution that Novalis has enriched the general poetic experience of nature.

Now, an experience of this kind being religious in character, since it relates to the absolute, divine significance of things, that near connexion we have mentioned between poetry and religion in Novalis's work becomes clearer; poetry proclaims the mysteries of religion. Thus nature, religion, and poetry are bound up with one another in the most intimate manner. And this gives grounds for the belief that only poets are enabled to see and communicate such mysteries; they are therefore seers and educators. The poet writes:

Glücklich preis ich diesen Sohn, diesen Liebling der Natur, dem sie verstattet sie in ihrer Zweiheit, als erzeugende und gebärende Macht, und in ihrer Einheit, als eine unendliche, ewigdauernde Ehe, zu betrachten. Sein Leben wird eine Fülle aller Genüsse, eine Kette der Wollust und seine Religion der eigentliche, echte Naturalismus sein.

Amongst the romantic friends it was especially Friedrich Schlegel and Schleiermacher who played with the idea of a religious revival. With Schlegel this was a matter of deliberate calculation, of cool speculation, of purely intellectual lust. Novalis was less dominated than

he by that rather insolent tendency of the mind to absolute
sovereignty, which was one of the dubious results of
Fichte's philosophy. Novalis was nearest to genuine
religious experience—nearer than Schleiermacher, too,
in spite of theology—by the fullness of his emotional life,
by the heritage of pious disposition he had from his father,
by the magic contact he had with the world of influences
and secret workings behind the world of bodies and forms,
by his susceptibility to the power of love, and by his power
of surrender to higher things. With the penetrating
insight that distinguished him, Friedrich Schlegel recognized this disposition of his friend. In the well-known
letter to Novalis (2 December 1798), in which he describes
his new 'biblical', religious 'project', as he calls it, and
presumes talent enough on his part to found a new religion,
he suddenly pauses and remarks: 'Doch vielleicht hast Du
mehr Talent zu einem neuen Christus, der in mir seinen
wackern Paulus findet.' And there follow these significant words: 'Vielleicht hast Du noch die Wahl, mein
Freund, entweder der letzte Christ, der Brutus der alten
Religion, oder der Christus des neuen Evangeliums zu
sein.'

Thus we see Novalis as a man predisposed to religion
and mysticism in a rare degree, and in *Die Lehrlinge zu
Sais* we have had experience of it. But the most significant unfolding of spiritual life in him was occasioned by
the death of the girl he loved, Sophie von Kühn.

Although she was only thirteen when Novalis made
her acquaintance, and fifteen when she died, Novalis saw
in her a higher type of existence. There are other witnesses
to the personality of this extraordinary girl; Tieck, and
particularly the Kreisamtmann Just, have both written
down their impressions of her, confirming what might
otherwise appear to be the unreliable evidence of a

strangely infatuated young man. The violent shock her
death gave Novalis is seen from his diaries and letters;
and later remarks refer continually to the innate nobility
of Sophie's nature and prove the lasting influence of her
existence and being on his own life, up to the point of
death itself. After the first grief was over his spirits
brightened again, it is true, and later he loved again and
was betrothed, but in spite of this he remained in his
innermost heart true to Sophie, for, having seen and
known her, his faith in her nobility could not relax. But
her death meant nothing less than this, that the higher
life embodied in her belonged no more to the earthly
sphere but to the world of the beyond, of death. In his
attitude towards her there is combined love and reverence;
both the feeling within himself of the voluptuous creative
impulse, the longing for mingling, and at the same time
the perception of a purer spiritual life. 'Ich habe zu
Söphchen Religion—nicht Liebe,' he writes. She gives
him, then, that key to the knowledge of nature's true
being that Hyazinth discovered; but she is also a force
making for spiritual regeneration. The implications of
Die Lehrlinge zu Sais are that death is the gateway to
participation in nature's inmost being, to the dissolution
which enables one to sink into the eternal flux of life.
Moreover, some early fragments, in an apprehension of
the truth, point to death as the real life, and affirm that
the dark night of the grave is in reality the bright day-
light. Sophie's death brings these half-perceived truths
to maturity, as the sun opens the budding flower. The
Night of death which holds Sophie is the transcendental
sphere of love and true life; and whether Novalis speaks
of descending into this night or of being united and
mingling with Sophie in death, he means in both cases the
same thing, participation in the eternal process of love,

the transcendental life; he means quitting earthly life to be taken up into that true life, which he conceives as an eternal flux and as a spirit, as the eternal spiritual, from which flow lower forms of life. Night is understood, in the sense of the old Greek myth, as the pregnant sphere, the fertile chaos, the progenitress; but also, in a spiritual sense, as the absolute, all-embracing, everlasting; and in this respect the idea of the higher life embodied in Sophie helps us to understand more clearly the spiritual nature of the transcendental in Novalis's conception. The living Sophie is a sign for Novalis of a higher existence; the dead Sophie is identical with the transcendental.

Night, then, in all this complexity of meaning, is a homeland for which the poet longs; after Sophie's death his whole feeling is directed to night, in such a degree that he wished to follow her into death (though the method he contemplated—volition alone—introduces a touch of intellectual experimenting which, whilst entirely in keeping with his character, spoils the purity of his sentiment). Love and nostalgia combine and produce that state of emotional excitement in him from which sprang the *Hymnen an die Nacht.*

Preis der Weltkönigin, der hohen Verkündigerin heiliger Welten, der Pflegerin seliger Liebe—sie sendet mir dich—zarte Geliebte— liebliche Sonne der Nacht,—nun wach ich—denn ich bin dein und mein—du hast die Nacht mir zum Leben verkündet—mich zum Menschen gemacht—zehre mit Geisterglut meinen Leib, daß ich luftig mit dir inniger mich mische und dann ewig die Brautnacht währt.

The deep meaning of all these words, and from what profound recesses of spiritual experience they come, is clear from what has been said. The words of the third hymn, in which the poet relates a mystical vision of his beloved at her grave-side, are still more mysterious, weighty, and pregnant:

Einst da ich bittre Tränen vergoß, da in Schmerz aufgelöst

meine Hoffnung zerrann, und ich einsam stand am dürren Hügel,
der im engen, dunkeln Raum die Gestalt meines Lebens barg—einsam, wie noch kein Einsamer war, von unsäglicher Angst getrieben
—kraftlos, nur ein Gedanken des Elends noch.—Wie ich da nach
Hülfe umherschaute, vorwärts nicht konnte und rückwärts nicht,
und am fliehenden, verlöschten Leben mit unendlicher Sehnsucht
hing:—da kam aus blauen Fernen—von den Höhen meiner alten
Seligkeit ein Dämmerungsschauer—und mit einemmale riß das
Band der Geburt—des Lichtes Fessel. Hin floh die irdische Herrlichkeit und meine Trauer mit ihr—zusammen floß die Wehmut
in eine neue, unergründliche Welt—du Nachtbegeisterung,
Schlummer des Himmels kamst über mich—die Gegend hob sich
sacht empor; über der Gegend schwebte mein entbundner, neu-
geborner Geist. Zur Staubwolke wurde der Hügel—durch die
Wolke sah ich die verklärten Züge der Geliebten. In Ihren
Augen ruhte die Ewigkeit—ich faßte Ihre Hände, und die Tränen
wurden ein funkelndes, unzerreißliches Band. Jahrtausende
zogen abwärts in die Ferne, wie Ungewitter. An Ihrem Halse
weint ich dem neuen Leben entzückende Tränen.—Es war der
erste, einzige Traum—und erst seitdem fühl ich ewigen, unwandel-
baren Glauben an den Himmel der Nacht und sein Licht, die
Geliebte.

Let us bring out the peculiar character of this poem by
comparing it with others. In Young's *Night Thoughts*
a cult is made of night and thoughts of death, but only
out of a spirit of sentimentality, and the wish to indulge
in melancholy moods; this sets a limit to Young's influence on Novalis. Again, the enthusiasm of later German
romanticists for night and death springs rather from a
childlike, primitive awe at the secret things of nature, or
from the desire of the weary for the rest that liberates.
To understand how deep a significance love has in the
Hymnen an die Nacht, let us recall Lamartine's *Le Lac*,
a well-known and typical product of French romanticism.
It represents a despairing and sorrowful attempt to cling
to the memory of lost love in a beautiful landscape, such

memory alone being a sure possession. Novalis goes deeper than all these; he seeks not the cessation and calming of life in death, but the renewal of life, he seeks regeneration, the essential life. He is similar only to Shelley in philosophy and visionary experience.

The fourth Hymn sings the praise of night as the spiritual sphere of fertile mingling, the theatre of voluptuous creative processes. But new conceptions are brought in, for in an unexpected but most significant way the Cross of Christ appears. This occurs after an apostrophe to Light, in which the poet predicts the end of its sway: 'Unverbrennlich', he says then, 'steht das Kreuz—eine Siegesfahne unsers Geschlechts.'

This gives us the third principal element—a Christian tendency—of the background of Novalis's poems. We must be careful not to look upon this sudden turn as a straightforward confession of Christian faith. It is due to the fusion in Novalis's thought and feeling of two worlds: that of the night which holds Sophie, and the Christian beyond. For the significance of the latter dawns on him, now that Sophie, his own very life, is lost in night. It was Christ who unsealed the mystery of the grave. With that act a new era was born, a new life; it presented to Novalis, then, a parallel to his own experience, as the third Hymn records it. Sophie and Christ, and all they represent, thus blend in the imagination of the poet. This interpenetration of two originally separate spiritual spheres is seen especially clearly in the fourth of the *Geistliche Lieder*:

> Da ich so im stillen krankte,
> Ewig weint' und wegverlangte,
> Und nur blieb vor Angst und Wahn:
> Ward mir plötzlich wie von oben
> Weg des Grabes Stein gehoben,
> Und mein Innres aufgetan.

Wen ich sah, und wen an seiner
Hand erblickte, frage keiner,
Ewig werd' ich dies nur sehn;
Und von allen Lebensstunden
Wird nur die wie meine Wunden
Ewig heiter, offen stehn.

It is the double inspiration of much in the *Hymnen* and
the *Geistliche Lieder*.

The connexion between nature, Sophie, and Christ,
and the character of Novalis's religious feeling, can be
made more explicit still by reference to his conception
of 'mediation'. In a famous fragment in *Blütenstaub*
Novalis asserts that nothing is more indispensable to true
religiosity than a mediating member (*Mittelglied*), which
connects us with the divinity. Each man must be free
to choose his own mediator. That religion is the true one
which takes the mediator simply as a mediator (not as the
divinity itself), and considers it to be, as it were, the organ
of the divinity, its sensuous form. Novalis distinguishes
then between pantheistic and monotheistic mediators.
Anything, he says, can be an organ of divinity, a mediator,
by man raising it to that position; this is the pantheistic
interpretation. On the other hand, there can be a single
mediator, a God-man, for instance, like Jesus; and this
according to the belief of each individual. These apparently incompatible ideas can be reconciled, in Novalis's
opinion, by conceiving two degrees or levels of mediation;
first, things—the pantheistic degree; secondly, a single
God-man—the monotheistic degree. The God-man
mediates between things and the divinity. In the words
of Novalis: 'man kann den monotheistischen Mittler zum
Mittler der Mittelwelt des Pantheismus machen, und
diese gleichsam durch ihn zentrieren.' Religion is here
translated into a completely personal sphere by the force,

indeed, by the violence, of this one personality, Novalis.
He creates a religion for himself. It consists of pantheistic,
ideal-human, and Christian elements, which he chooses
arbitrarily, and connects by means of this idea of mediation. One asks, what is the object of such mediation?—
And the answer is: the 'divinity' (*Gottheit*), not a clear
'God'; Novalis avoids the word God in this connexion.
By 'divinity' we have undoubtedly to understand the
transcendental, that metaphysical state or existence which
occasions in him all his nostalgia. Nature, Sophie, Christ
are the mediators he chooses to link himself with that
metaphysical life which is the true reality, that voluptuous
and mysterious mingling of all things. And though these
various mediators follow after each other in the course
of his spiritual development, they do not replace each
other, but indicate a gradual widening of the possibilities
of religious experience for Novalis. Thus Sophie remains
the 'sun' of night; she is not displaced by Christ, but their
figures mingle. Thus, too, Christ is seen pantheistically
intermingled with all the fluid things of nature:

> In schweren Wolken sammle ihn
> Und laß ihn so hernieder ziehn.

> In kühlen Strömen send' ihn her,
> In Feuerflammen lodre er,
> In Luft und Öl, in Klang und Tau
> Durchdring er unsrer Erde Bau.

In this way he makes nature, his beloved, and Christ serve
his purposes. They are a trinity which have a unity only
in his consciousness, or in the use to which he puts them.
It is extremely difficult to determine whether he imagined
a personal reunion with Sophie, or Christ, in the flux and
intermingling of the beyond. But he attributed such
magic properties to the absolute spirit, such all-penetrat-

ing consciousness and all-powerful will, or caprice, that we can fairly believe he thought everything possible, both the most extreme and desirable degree of intermingling, and at the same time the ability to perceive persons at will. A related difficulty, already noticed in considering *Die Lehrlinge zu Sais*, is that of understanding the spirituality of the eternal flux he describes in such sensuous terms. For the refinement of sensuous vocabulary he uses emphasizes the sensuousness just as much as it hints at something supra-sensuous. We can conceive with ease an organic flux of things; we can grasp, too, the idea of a spiritual state; but a combination of both eludes us. And yet it is precisely the combination that is important, that is so unique; it is precisely the combination, we can be sure, that fascinated and held Novalis in its sway, as did, in a smaller way, the corresponding notion of 'thinking and feeling at once'.

The most comprehensive expression for the complex spiritual experience of Novalis and all the longing it induced in him is the so-called *Abendmahlshymne*, which, in consequence, is at the centre of his work; it begins:

> Wenige wissen
> Das Geheimnis der Liebe,
> Fühlen Unersättlichkeit
> Und ewigen Durst.
> Des Abendmahls
> Göttliche Bedeutung
> Ist den irdischen Sinnen Rätsel;
> Aber wer jemals
> Von heißen, geliebten Lippen
> Atem des Lebens sog,
> Wem heilige Glut
> In zitternde Wellen das Herz schmolz,
> Wem das Auge aufging,
> Daß er des Himmels

> Unergründliche Tiefe maß,
> Wird essen von seinem Leibe
> Und trinken von seinem Blute
> Ewiglich.

This astonishing poem shows to the full extent how
personal the religious feeling of Novalis was, to what
extent he took material and symbols from a religion of
wide appeal and used them to express feelings which only
he had; and it shows, too, in the most striking manner,
all the wildness of his transcendental thirst. Comparison
with the Christian sacrament is scarcely possible, for there
the believer participates by means of bread and wine in
the Body and Blood of Christ to refresh his spirit. But
in the poem, this act of cult is exploited by the poet in
order to represent the mystic mingling not with Christ
alone, but with nature, too, and Sophie, and all things:

> Einst ist alles Leib,
> E i n Leib,
> In himmlischem Blute
> Schwimmt das selige Paar.—
> O! daß das Weltmeer
> Schon errötete,
> Und in duftiges Fleisch
> Aufquölle der Fels!
> Nie endet das süße Mahl,
> Nie sättigt die Liebe sich.
> Nicht innig, nicht eigen genug
> Kann sie haben den Geliebten.
> Von immer zärteren Lippen
> Verwandelt wird das Genossene
> Inniglicher und näher.

Here is no celebration of Christ, the Redeemer from sin;
Christian cult is used to reveal the transcendental condition of voluptuous intermingling, of endless flux, of
chaos. The longing of the poet for eternal love and

dissolution discharges itself here with such power of
vision and force of emotion, that the very language,
strained to the utmost, almost bursts the bounds of the
possible and threatens itself to become chaotic.

All the motives we have mentioned recur again and
again in the *Hymnen an die Nacht* and the *Geistliche
Lieder* which follow them, recalling continually the
spiritual core of Novalis's life. The same words and
phrases, into which the utmost force and meaning are
pressed, are used again and again in his poems, in varied
combination, to express rapturous or consuming longing
and love-desire, or the ecstatic urge beyond earthly
bounds, or the drunken surrender of one who lets himself
sink into the eternal flood. *Wallen, wogen, saugen,
mischen, sättigen; hinüber, trunken, unendlich, gewaltig,
heilig; Glut, Wollust, Liebe, Schoß, Tod, Flut*; these are
the favourite words of Novalis. In the *Geistliche Lieder*,
it is true, there is, too, a simpler language, which lends
to them a pious, child-like quality; it is one of their
principal charms, and provides a strange contrast to the
deep spiritual turmoil of their origin.

The *Hymnen an die Nacht* have a considerable narrative and even dramatic element in them, because they
tell of the crisis which occurred in the life of Novalis.
The *Geistliche Lieder* flow from the settled emotion that
followed the crisis, from the constant nostalgia for the
home beyond life. Characteristic for the difference between them is the transition from free rhythms to fixed
metrical forms; the poet felt no restraint in the expressing
of his own intense, violent personal experience, but now
he feels and seeks a certain connexion with the Christian
community, so that he is no longer entirely free. For the
same reason further Christian motives are introduced.
Amongst his papers there is a note on the kind of religious

song he was endeavouring to produce: 'In den meisten Lavaterschen Liedern ist noch zu viel Irdisches—und zu viel Moral und *Asketik*. Zu wenig *Wesentliches*—zu wenig Mystik. Die Lieder müssen weit lebendiger, inniger, allgemeiner und mystischer sein.' It is these qualities that distinguish his *Lieder* from those of Luther, Gerhardt, or Zinzendorf. But again we see how Novalis, in spite of his intention to write for a Christian congregation, really stands alone, how he expresses not what a congregation feels when at prayer and in communion with its God, but his own metaphysical needs. Hence his *Lieder* are far more independent as poetry, compared with the subservient position of ordinary religious songs or hymns. The religious feelings of the latter are general, though the poet, in the role of spokesman, may express them more delicately or forcibly than others could; the poems of Novalis are the result of the unique religious experience of a single man. Novalis owes the greater liveliness, intensity, fervour, and mysticism of these *Lieder* to his love experience. The fourth *Lied* and its connexion with the third hymn are a proof of this. Let us recall the kernel of the Christian faith, the redemption of sins, and ask where it is to be found in the work of Novalis. It is nowhere mentioned; neither are repentance, humility, charity, spiritual virtues without which Christianity is inconceivable. Some poems of Brentano provide examples of a true Christian attitude of repentance and humility, contrasting strongly with that of Novalis.

Finally, then, these *Lieder* fail as a 'Probe eines neuen geistlichen Gesangbuches' for congregational use. Novalis planned to publish them along with sermons; it is important to note that the sermons were never written, and the plan, in consequence, not carried out. Moreover, the songs, it is true, have been sung as hymns in the course of

Holy Worship, but not before their text had been suitably revised.

A rapid glance at *Heinrich von Ofterdingen* will be enough to show how this romance, too, receives its substance from the same sources as the poems. The transcendental world, the vision of which is communicated by these poems, is called by Novalis 'poetic', and his conception of poetry is determined by it; poetry is simply the revelation of it by means of words. Poetic revelation communicates to earthly men the eternal life of the beyond. The poet, then, is a mediator (in the religious sense of Novalis), a seer and teacher, as we have already seen in considering the *Lehrlinge zu Sais*. The romance *Heinrich von Ofterdingen* represents the development of a poet, seer, teacher of this kind. We recognize Novalis himself. Time and milieu are provided by the Middle Ages, a poetic age in the imagination of Novalis, since they stand under the sign of Christian otherworldliness. The youth Heinrich is led through different spheres of the 'poetic' —the mystic Orient, the religious wars, nature, and history—to the decisive meeting with the poet Klingsohr and his daughter Mathilde. Love for her opens his eyes to the truth of things, she awakens the poet in him. We need only mention two things to illustrate what this means. Firstly, Heinrich's remark: 'Sie wird mich in Musik auflösen.' For Novalis, music is simply movement, spiritualized movement, a symbol, therefore, of the transcendental state of flux; it is, too, the most adequate, intense expression of infinite longing. For that reason he introduces *Lieder* into his romance; they are an approach to music, for the meaning of the words is less important than the *Stimmung* they provoke, than the longing they convey. Secondly, Heinrich's dream, that he is immersed with Mathilde in the flowing of those eternal waters he so often mentions. It is clear, from what has been said, how it comes about that love and Mathilde give Heinrich the key to the poetic world. Klingsohr, the poet, shows him this world, and in the form of a fairy-tale (*Märchen*). The fairy-tale is Novalis's ideal of poetry, because it gives free rein to fantasy, because all limits and restrictions are broken down, because chance reigns supreme; in other words, it is the image of chaos, of a state of flux. But Klingsohr's *Märchen* contains a moral which corresponds to the whole tendency of the book: that poetry liberates, or redeems, the world. We saw how in the *Lehrlinge zu Sais* the fairy-tale of Hyazinth and Rosenblüt was a revelation that liberated the apprentice from his doubts. The peculiarity of Klingsohr's *Märchen*, compared with this and others, is that it is poetic representation, and at the same time shows the will to poetry, the conviction and teaching that poetry is an instrument of revelation. The very point, wrapped up as it is in the most extraordinary and complicated trappings, is a demand it makes that poetry should fulfil a certain function; but, being poetry itself—according to the poet's own ideal of poetry —it is itself fulfilling that function whilst teaching it. Add to this that an author, a poet, within the larger framework of his romance, makes a mature poet use this *Märchen* to teach a young one what poetry should be:—in what folds of that notorious romantic irony we are being wrapped! In spite of his independence and his superior creative genius, there were elements in his temperament that Novalis had in common with his witty friends. The romance was thus in danger of the capricious play of sovereign and absolute mind; it shows a tendency to the chaos Novalis loved, the chaos which is conscious of itself; and Novalis himself says of *Ofterdingen*, it was gradually to become a *Märchen*. It reflects the transcendental of Novalis's conception.

What is our reaction to these poetic works, the unity of which we have tried to demonstrate and explain? Whatever graces *Heinrich von Ofterdingen* has, the poems, and especially the *Hymnen an die Nacht*, scarcely occasion the serene joy, or the warm and pleasurable excitement, or the still satisfaction that poetry generally gives; but they disturb profoundly, as everything must do that opens up, whether to enjoy or to conquer, recesses of life into which the good light of day never penetrates. One reads these poems with admiration, no doubt, still more with astonishment, and recoiling from the abysses they reveal. Only those who in themselves feel the same urge as Novalis will be able to surrender completely and really 'enjoy' them as Novalis might wish them to. But whoever adheres to an ideal of human and earthly life, will reject the fundamental tendency of Novalis to dissolution and chaos, in however spiritualized a form he may conceive it. And yet his poems are so significant, the poetic diction so compelling in its magic quality, that they must be considered by all who are concerned with poetry at all.

In the light of Goethe's work—and let Goethe be taken as representing the whole of humanist culture—that of Novalis with its mysticism, its emotionalism, its strange, 'magical' control of sensuous and spiritual experiences, its urge to dissolution, to eternal movement and chaos, is a reaction. For it offended Goethe's ideal of human mastery within the bounds of moderation, it destroyed the ideal of form. His work is the negation of the values and art-standards won by Goethe from the Greeks. But in spite of the fact that Novalis joined with his romantic friends, and, in a common intoxication of thought and feeling, nailed Christianity to his banner, his work indicates by no means a simple, clear reversion to Christianity, as is sometimes affirmed of him as well as of the whole romantic movement. It puts forward new values, in the formation of which old, Christian ones have been used; but the new values are of so peculiar and personal a kind, and the old Christian ones are so adapted to personal ends, and in consequence deprived of their significance for the general run of Christians, that Novalis appears in a solitary position. He is neither the Brutus of the old religion, nor the Christ of a new gospel.

His connexion with that general revival of the poetry of Christian chivalry, especially amongst his successors, is thus seen to be anything but direct and simple. For his work went much deeper; it was a poetry devoted to the transcendental and having roots in his own entirely personal spiritual experiences. And the romanticism of night and death in poems that followed cannot be compared in intensity with his feelings, whether or not one sees his influence, or a similar emotional tendency. He was, too, far superior to his successors in breadth and force of intellect. Novalis as poet is as solitary as that contemporary of his who was of such different composition, Hölderlin, the representative of the Hellenic ideal. Judged by their inmost kernel, his poems seem to us to spring from such unique earthly and spiritual circumstances that they neither come from a past nor point to a future, but stand alone, with their strangeness and force, their fervent and fantastic vision.

FRIEDRICH VON MATTHISSON ON GIBBON

By L. F. POWELL

FRIEDRICH VON MATTHISSON'S account of his visit to Gibbon at Lausanne in the autumn of 1789 appears to be unknown to the biographers and editors of the great historian, even to the devoted General Read;[1] it is time that the narrative, which adds to our knowledge, be given a wider publicity than it at present enjoys. Matthisson first wrote it in a letter to his friend Charles de Bonstetten, well known to students of Gray, and after-wards published it in his *Briefe*,[2] from which it is here reprinted. Matthisson's letter is dated from Lausanne, '11 Okt. 1789'.

'Ich war gestern bei Gibbon. Sein Aeußeres hat viel Auffallendes. Er ist groß und von starkem Gliederbau; dabei etwas unbehülflich in seinen Bewegungen. Sein Gesicht ist eine der sonderbarsten fysiognomischen Erscheinungen, wegen des unrichtigen Verhältnisses der einzelnen Theile zum Ganzen. Die Augen sind so klein, daß sie mit der hohen und prächtig gewölbten Stirn den härtesten Kontrast machen; die etwas stumpfe Nase verschwindet fast zwischen den stark hervorspringenden Backen, und die weit herabhangende Unterkehle macht das, an sich schon sehr längliche, Oval des Gesichts noch frappanter. Ungeachtet dieser Unregelmäßigkeiten hat Gibbons Fysiognomie einen außerordentlichen Ausdruck von Würde, und kündigt, beim ersten Blicke, den tiefen

[1] The fruits of General Meredith Read's research, protracted over eighteen years, were published in his *Historic Studies in Vaud, Berne, and Savoy* (1897, 2 vols.).

[2] *Briefe von Friedrich Matthisson*, Erster Theil (Zürich, 1795), pp. 117 ff.

und scharfsinnigen Denker an. Nichts geht über das geistvolle Feuer seiner Augen.[1]

Gibbon hat ganz den Ton und die Manieren eines abgeschliffenen Weltmannes; ist kalthöflich; spricht das Französische mit Eleganz und hat (ein wahres Fänomen bei einem Engländer) fast die Aussprache eines Pariser-Gelehrten. Er hört sich mit Wohlgefallen und redet langsam, weil er jede Frase sorgfältig zu prüfen scheint, ehe er sie ausspricht.[2] Mit immer gleicher Miene unterhält er sich von angenehmen und unangenehmen Dingen, von frohen und tragischen Begebenheiten, und sein Gesicht verzog sich, so lange wir beisammen waren, ungeachtet er veranlaßt wurde, eine sehr drollige Geschichte zu erzählen, nicht ein einzigesmal zum Lächeln. In seinem Hause herrscht die strengste Pünktlichkeit und

[1] Gibbon, who at this time was writing his own Memoirs, describes his 'frame' as 'of the common shape' (*Autobiographies*, ed. Murray, 1897, p. 112), but he was in fact grotesquely corpulent. Horace Walpole speaks of his 'ridiculous face and person' (*Letters*, ii. 377), and Boswell, who disliked him, never missed an opportunity of sneering at his ugliness (*Life of Johnson*, 1934, ii. 443, iv. 73, 484). It is stated that one of his nicknames was 'Monsieur Pomme de Terre' (G. M. Young, *Gibbon*, 1932, p. 102). It is pleasant to read Mlle Curchod's description of him as a young man: 'Sa physionomie est si spirituelle et singulière, que je ne connois personne qui lui ressemble. Elle a tant d'expression, qu'on y découvre presque toujours quelque chose de nouveau. . . . En un mot, c'est une de ces physionomies, si extraordinaires, qu'on ne se lasse presque point de l'examiner, de le peindre et de le contrefaire.' D'Haussonville, *Le Salon de Madame Necker*, 1885, i. 35.

[2] Miss Holroyd, who knew Gibbon intimately, confirms Matthisson's account. She says of Gibbon that 'when "the King of the Place", as he is called, opens his mouth, which you know he generally does some time before he has arranged his sentence), all wait in awful and respectful silence for what shall follow'. *The Girlhood of Maria Josepha Holroyd*, ed. J. H. Adeane, 1896, p. 77. On the other hand, Fox, who visited Gibbon at Lausanne in 1788, told Samuel Rogers that he 'talked a great deal, walking up and down the room, and generally ending his sentences with a genitive case'. *Recollections of the Table-Talk of Samuel Rogers*, 1856, p. 77.

Ordnung. Seine Leute müssen ihre Geschäfte beinahe
zur bestimmten Minute verrichten, oder sie laufen Gefahr
verabschiedet zu werden. Er giebt ihnen aber auch selbst
das Beispiel. Sein Tag ist eingetheilt, wie der Tag des
angelsächsischen Königs Alfred. Mit dem Klockenschlage geht er an die Arbeit, zu Tische und in Gesellschaft, und bleibt in keiner von ihm abhangenden
Lebenslage eine Minute länger, als die festgesezte Tags-
ordnung es gestattet. Ein Friseur wurde verabschiedet,
weil er einige Minuten nach 7. Uhr kam. Sein Nach-
folger stellte sich, um mehrerer Sicherheit willen, etwas
früher ein und hatte gleiches Schicksal. Nur der dritte,
der mit Klockenschlage in die Hausthür trat, wurde
beibehalten.

Gibbon arbeitet gegenwärtig am Katalogus seiner
Bibliothek, die sehr reich an kostbaren Werken, besonders
aber an treflichen Ausgaben der Klassiker ist, und überhaupt für eine der vorzüglichsten Privatbibliotheken
gehalten wird, die je ein Gelehrter zusammenbrachte.[1]

[1] Gibbon transported his library to Lausanne in 1784 and left it there
when he returned to England in 1793. After his death in the following year
it was bought by William Beckford, the author of *Vathek*, so that he might
have 'something to read' when he passed through Lausanne. Beckford gave
nearly the whole collection to his physician, Dr. F. A. Scholl, who in 1832
sold a large part of it to an Englishman, J. W. Halliday, who lived near
Geneva. This portion of the library passed successively to M. Charles
Bedot, his son Maurice, and finally to M. Bader, who in 1933 offered it
for sale. The books were brought to England and on 20 Dec. 1934 put up
to auction at Sotheby's: thirty-eight volumes now rest on the shelves of
Magdalen College Library, the key of which was given to Gibbon when
he became a Gentleman Commoner. See Gibbon's *Memoirs*, ed. G. Birk-
beck Hill, 1900, p. 338, General Meredith Read's *Historic Studies*, ii.
506, *The Times*, 14 Jan. 1933, and the Sotheby sale catalogue, 1934.

Two manuscript catalogues of Gibbon's library have survived, both,
I suspect, incomplete: the one that Gibbon himself compiled consists of
playing-cards, on the backs of which the titles were entered. *Proc. of
Gibbon Commemoration, 1794–1894*, p. 47. General Read reports that
on one of these catalogue cards Gibbon also wrote a tribute, in French verse,

Das erste Werk, womit er als Schriftsteller auftrat, schrieb
er, noch sehr jung, in französischer Sprache. Er sagte
mir, es sei so selten geworden, daß man diese wenigen
Bogen kürzlich in einer Aukzion bis auf zwei Guineen
heraufgetrieben habe.[1] In den Ruinen des Kapitols faßte
er zuerst den Gedanken, die Geschichte des Verfalls und
des Umsturzes der römischen Monarchie zu schreiben;[2]
und er hat mit männlicher Beharrlichkeit eine der müh-
vollsten Laufbahnen zurückgelegt, die jemals ein Schriftsteller betrat.

Unser Gespräch gieng bald von der altenglischen
Literatur, worin er eine vorzügliche Stärke besizt, zur
deutschen über. Gibbon, einer der größten Literatoren
unsrer Zeit, dem nichts entgangen ist, was England,
Frankreich, Italien und Spanien, fast in jedem Fache des
menschlichen Wissens, vorzügliches oder merkwürdiges

to a lady friend. Read, op. cit. ii. 449. Among the volumes offered for
sale at Sotheby's in 1934 was Christian Ludwig's *Teutsch-Englisches
Lexicon*, 1763–5, so that Gibbon did possess at least one German book.

[1] Gibbon began to write his first work, the *Essai sur l'étude de la littéra-
ture*, at Lausanne in 1758, when he was 21, and finished it in England in
1759: it was published in London in 1761. He states in his autobiography:
'The publication of my History fifteen years afterwards revived the
memory of my first performance, and the Essay was eagerly sought in the
shops . . . ; and when a copy of the original edition has been discovered
in a sale the primitive value of half a crown has risen to the fanciful price
of a Guinea or thirty shillings.' *Autobiographies*, ed. Murray, 1897,
p. 171, see also ibid., p. 256. A copy was sold at auction in Sotheby's
rooms on 16 July 1934 for £12 10s. The copy that Gibbon presented
to Horace Walpole was sold for £50 on 26 June 1933. 'Such is the power
of a name.'

[2] 'It was at Rome, on the fifteenth of October, 1764, as I sat musing
amidst the ruins of the Capitol while the barefooted fryars were singing
Vespers in the temple of Jupiter, that the idea of writing the decline and
fall of the City first started to my mind.' Gibbon's *Autobiographies*, ed.
Murray, 1897, p. 302. Matthisson could, however, have learned the
fact from the concluding paragraph of Gibbon's great work, the last
three volumes of which were published on his 51st birthday, 8 May 1788.

aufzuweisen haben, verrieth von der Geschichte unsrer
Sprache und Literatur nur sehr eingeschränkte Kenntnisse.
Von den deutschen Nachbildungen alter Sylbenmaße
hatte er nie etwas gehört. Bei dieser Gelegenheit führte
er Algarottis Abhandlung über den Reim an, worin, mit
gänzlicher Uebergehung der Deutschen, nur die verun-
glückten Hexameterversuche der Engländer, Franzosen
und Italiäner aufgezählt werden. Dies veranlaßte mich
zu einem kurzen Abriß der Geschichte der deutschen
Sprache und ihrer schnellen Ausbildung, den ich mit der
Nachricht von einer deutschen Odyssee schloß, wo der
Uebersezer[1] nicht nur das Metrum und die Verszahl des
Originals, sondern in vielen Hexametern sogar die Sylben-
füße desselben wiedergegeben habe. Mein Gedächtniß
war mir getreu genug, um die beiden berühmten Verse[2]
vom Steinwälzen des Sisyfus, aus dem eilften Gesange der
Odyssee, griechisch und deutsch hersagen zu können,

Λᾶαν βαστάζοντα πελώριον ἀμφοτέρῃσιν:
Einen schweren Marmor mit großer Gewalt forthebend.

Αὖτις ἔπειτα πέδονδε κυλίνδετο λᾶας ἀναιδής:
Hurtig mit Donnergepolter entrollte der tückische Marmor.

Troz seiner Unkunde der deutschen Sprache, mußte
er doch, durch das bloße Gehör, vom Meisterbau dieser
beiden Hexameter überzeugt werden. Ich bin nicht im
Stande, sein Erstaunen, nach mehrmaliger Anhörung
derselben, zu schildern. Er bekam plözlich eine so hohe
Meinung von der Ausbildung unsrer Sprache und den
Riesenschritten unsrer Literatur, wie er sich ausdrückte,
daß er den Entschluß faßte, bei mehrerer Muße, so-
gleich deutsch zu lernen.[3] Ich hoffe, Du werdest, bei

---

[1] J. H. Voss, 1781.   [2] 594 and 598.

[3] Gibbon apparently invited Matthisson to teach him, but he, for
excellent reasons, chose a less honourable office and a more tractable pupil.
There is no evidence for this in Gibbon's own letters and journals,

erster Gelegenheit, diesen merkwürdigen Mann persön-
lich kennen zu lernen suchen. Bei ihm sieht man die
ausgewählteste Gesellschaft und die interessantesten
durchreisenden Fremden.'

La Grotte, the ancient and spacious mansion in which

but Matthisson supplies it: he writes in his *Selbstbiographie* (Wien,
1818):

'In Lausanne wünschte der daselbst angesiedelte Engländer Gibbon
ihn zum Hausgenossen, hauptsächlich der deutschen Sprache wegen,
welche dieser berühmte Gelehrte noch zu lernen wünschte, und von
Lyon aus machte Herr Scherer . . . ihm den Antrag, die Erziehung eines
kaum siebenjährigen, hoffnungsvollen Sohnes zu übernehmen. Er ent-
schied sich für das Letztere: denn der biedere und joviale Scherer sprach . . .
sein Gemüth mit ungleich wärmerer Beredsamkeit an, als der kalt höfische
und nicht selten ein wenig despotische Gibbon' (p. 73). This is, I suspect,
the source of Alois Heers's more highly coloured version; he writes in his
Das Leben Friedrich von Matthissons (1913): 'Unter den Anerbietungen,
die er [Matthisson] erhielt, reizte ihn anfangs besonders die Stellung als
Privatsekretär bei Gibbon . . ., den er für die deutsche Literatur zu
interessieren gewußt hatte, und der jetzt von ihm zugleich Deutsch lernen
wollte. Doch ließ er sich durch den außerordentlichen Jähzorn dieses
Mannes abschrecken und nahm dafür das Angebot des Bankiers Scherer
aus Lyon an, eines Freundes von Bonstetten, der ihn als Hauslehrer für
seinen 8jährigen Sohn Adrian gewinnen wollte' (p. 48).

It may be doubted whether Gibbon made any further effort to obtain
a teacher: it is certain that he never learnt German. Early in life he was
obliged to abandon his design of writing 'The history of the liberty of the
Swiss' because the materials of it were inaccessible to him, being 'fast
locked in the obscurity of an old barbarous German dialect' of which
he was totally ignorant. *Autobiographies*, 1897, p. 197. Referring to the
same projected work he wrote *c.* 1789: 'By the assistance of Mr. Deyverdun
I obtained many extracts and translations from the German originals of
Tschudi, Stetler, Schilling, Lauffer, Leu, etc.; but I soon found, on a
tryal, that these materials were insufficient. An historian should command
the language, the libraries, and the archives of the country of which he
presumes to write.' Ibid., p. 301 note. In the same memoir he expressed
a wish that it had been in his power to read the German translation of his
Decline and Fall, 'which is praised by the best judges'. Ibid., p. 339 note.

It is of interest to note that William Law, who taught himself German
'on purpose to know the original words of the blessed Jacob [Böhme]',
was tutor to Gibbon's father. J. H. Overton's *W. Law,* 1881, p. 181.

this interview took place, was Gibbon's third and last home in Lausanne. It was the property of Georges Deyverdun, and in it the two friends lived from 1783 to 1789, when Deyverdun died: he left Gibbon the option of purchasing the house and garden, or of possessing them during his life: Gibbon chose the latter alternative and remained in possession till 1793. The house no longer exists.[1]

13 *March*, 1937.

[1] The history of the house, which was demolished in 1896, is told by General Meredith Read in his *Historic Studies*. The Hôtel des Postes now occupies its site.

NOTE

Mr. D. M. Low in his *Gibbon* (Chatto and Windus, 1937, p. 2) quotes and translates Matthisson's description of Gibbon's face, and Mr. J. W. Thompson in *The Library Quarterly* (vol. vii, July 1937, pp. 343–53) gives an account of Gibbon's library.

SOME ADVENTURES OF 'PAMELA' ON THE CONTINENTAL STAGE

By E. PURDIE

'I BELIEVE I set out about eight o'clock in the morning; I wondered, when it was about two, as I saw by a church-dial in a little village, as we passed through, that I was still more and more out of my knowledge. "Hey day!" thought I, "to drive this strange pace, and be so long a going a little more than twenty miles, is very odd! But, to be sure," thought I, "Robin knows the way."'

So wrote Pamela Andrews of her forced journey to her master's house in Lincolnshire, when she had thought to be returning to her parents. She would no doubt have agreed with the heroine of a later English novel in thinking that Mrs. Collins, settled in Kent, was a long way from her family and her friends in Hertfordshire. She was, in all that period of her life which is important for the history of literature, a little stay-at-home, endowed by nature with a passion for detail and inclined by training to a peaceful domesticity. 'I am as much frighted as were the city mouse and country mouse, in the same book of fables, at every thing that stirs. I have a power of these things to entertain you with in winter evenings, when I come home. If I can but get work, with a little time for reading, I hope we shall be very happy, over our peat fires,' she writes in the initial stages of that long-drawn-out attempt upon her virtue which is recorded so exhaustively in the pages of her innumerable letters. And when, having at length compassed the reformation of her rake, she enters into a model marriage with him, her ideals are unchanged; she looks forward to the end of 'these tumultuous visitings', in order that her mind may 'subside into a family calm', and she may make herself a little useful to the household.

There is thus a pleasant touch of irony in the swift triumphal progress of *Pamela, or Virtue Rewarded* across the continent of Europe. For this precocious English servant-girl, who recorded every minutest detail of her daily experience and her personal feelings, swept the European stage; she was hardly eclipsed even by the much greater heroine of Richardson's second novel, *Clarissa*, eight years later. *Pamela*, indeed, seems to have been a kind of spiritual rain-gauge; its popularity may serve as an index to more than one of the changes in sentiment of eighteenth-century Europe. Critics such as Diderot might acknowledge the perfect art of *Clarissa* and state a personal preference for that work;[1] but *Pamela* was compared with it in no unfavourable sense: 'Pamela est un ouvrage plus simple, moins étendu, moins intrigué; mais y a-t-il moins de génie?'[2] And Diderot links all three novels in a general term of praise: 'Pamela, Clarice et Grandisson sont trois grands drames.'[3] If *Clarissa* dominated the finer spirits of the age in virtue of its tragic greatness, *Pamela* had the advantage, for many other readers, of a happy ending. And if Lovelace and Clarissa both left a more lasting imprint on European literature, Pamela had for her own age the greater touch of novelty.

[1] Cf. Diderot's 'Éloge de Richardson' in *Journal étranger*, January 1762, p. 35.

[2] Ibid., p. 27.

[3] Ibid., p. 14. In a review for the *Hamburgische Neue Zeitung*, 5 September 1768, Gerstenberg praises the 'diderotschen Enthusiasmus' of the writer of *Polycletus und Critos Briefe über Clarissa* (1750) and adds: 'Man kann kein schlimmeres Merkmaal vom Mangel an Genie und an Herz geben, als wenn man Richardsons Meisterstücke tadelt oder gar kaltsinnig lobt.' (*H. W. v. Gerstenbergs Rezensionen* . . . ed. O. Fischer, *Deutsche Literaturdenkmale des 18. und 19. Jahrhunderts*, 128, p. 92.)

All her piety and consciousness of lowly birth could not obliterate the revolutionary element in her surprising marriage; little as her creator may have intended it, she made a significant contribution to the changes in social values which mark the later eighteenth century.

The two aspects of her story—Virtue, and Virtue's reward—seem to have imposed themselves in varying degrees upon the readers and the critics of the age. The differing emphasis was responsible for differing judgements; the book was alternatively regarded with suspicion or hailed with exultation. But in either case, it was a phenomenon that could not be disregarded. The early eulogies of German writers such as Brockes, or Gellert, stress the element of virtue. Brockes considers the teaching of the novel an adequate substitute for the doctrines of 'popular' philosophy.[1] Gellert makes Simon, in *Die Betschwester*, protest to Frau Richardinn: 'Die Pamela ist ein sehr guter Roman, der die Unschuld und Tugend liebenswürdig zu machen sucht.'[2] In 1757 Lessing alludes to the book in similar terms;[3] four years earlier he had referred to its striking popularity.[4]

On the other hand, Goldoni, when he wished to adapt Richardson's novel for the Italian stage, found the moral

---

[1] *v.* B. H. Brockes, *Lobgedichte auf die Pamela*; *Irdisches Vergnügen in Gott*, Hamburg, 1721–48, ix (1748), p. 556. Cf. L. M. Price, 'On the reception of Richardson in Germany' (*Journal of English and Germanic Philology*, xxv (1926), pp. 7 ff.)—an article to which all students of Richardson's influence abroad must be deeply indebted. The critic's contention that Brockes's references to *Pamela* prove that the book was accorded, in general, a cool reception in Germany (pp. 13 ff.) seems, however, open to question.   [2] Act ii, sc. i. *Gellerts Lustspiele*, Leipzig, 1748, p. 177.

[3] In his Preface to *Sittenlehre für die Jugend*, translated from Richardson and published at Leipzig in 1757 (*Sämtliche Schriften*, ed. K. Lachmann and F. Muncker, 3rd ed., Stuttgart, 1886–1924, vii. 75).

[4] In a review of *Felicia* in the *Berlinische privilegirte Zeitung*, 17 May 1753 (*Sämtliche Schriften*, ed. cit., v. 165).

purpose of the author unsuited to the customs of his country:

'A Londres un Lord ne déroge pas à la noblesse en épousant une paysanne; à Venise un patricien qui épouse une plébéienne, prive ses enfans de la nob[l]esse patricienne, et ils perdent leurs droits à la souveraineté. La Comédie, qui est ou devroit être l'école des mœurs, ne doit exposer les foiblesses humaines que pour les corriger, et il ne faut pas hazarder le sacrifice d'une postérité malheureuse sous prétexte de récompenser la vertu.'[1]

Goldoni, however, since he was only concerned with the problem of his comedy, soon found a solution 'plus agréable et plus intéressante'[2] in the eventual revelation of Pamela's noble birth. But this device did not always meet with approval elsewhere. The Viennese critic Josef von Sonnenfels compared it very unfavourably with Richardson's reward of virtue alone, ending his comparison with the protest: 'ist die Tugend ausschlüssend ein Erb des Adels?'[3] Yet this same critic, in the previous year, had published comments in his journal *Theresie und Eleonore* which stressed the dangerous implications of the English novel, and were pervaded by a note alike of social and of moral indignation.[4] The dangerous social implication is also the subject of the Gräfin La Roche's sermon to Marie Wesener in Lenz's play *Die Soldaten*, published

---

[1] *Mémoires de M. Goldoni, pour servir à l'histoire de sa vie, et à celle de son Théâtre*, Paris, 1787, ii. 63 f.   [2] Ibid.

[3] *Briefe über die wienerische Schaubühne*, ii. viii, 20 May 1768 (*Wiener Neudrucke*, vii, Wien, 1884, p. 146).

[4] Cf. Josef von Sonnenfels, *Gesammelte Schriften*, Wien, 1783–7, iv. 147. Cited in an article by L. M. Price, 'Richardson in the Moral Weeklies of Germany' (*University of Wisconsin Studies in Language and Literature*, xxii, Madison, 1925, p. 177) which contains much interesting material gathered from eighteenth-century German periodicals. The difference of view in Sonnenfels's two publications is not noted in this article; but it may well reflect a conflict in contemporary opinion in Vienna, where Goldoni's plays were frequently performed (*v. infra*, pp. 379 ff.)

nine years later. She links *Pamela* with the common theme of the *bürgerliches Trauerspiel* when she reproaches Marie with having disregarded social differences:

> Ihr einziger Fehler war, daß Sie die Welt nicht kannten, daß Sie den Unterschied nicht kannten, der unter den verschiedenen Ständen herrscht, daß Sie die Pamela gelesen haben, das gefährlichste Buch, das eine Person aus Ihrem Stande lesen kann.

But that Lenz's purpose was not devoid of irony may perhaps be inferred from Marie's naïve reply: 'Ich kenne das Buch ganz und gar nicht.'[1]

The fluctuations of opinion in respect of *Pamela* may thus be explained, at least in part, as the reactions of different minds, on the one hand to the explicit, on the other to the implicit teaching of the novel. Few of its critics were as clear-sighted as Diderot, who, with all the exaggerated fervour of his praise, yet seized on the essential point of Richardson's artistic achievement:

> J'ai entendu disputer sur la conduite de ses personnages, comme sur des évènemens réels, louer, blâmer Pamela, Clarisse, Grandison, comme des personnages vivans qu'on auroit connus et auxquels on auroit pris le plus grand intérêt.[2]

Translations of *Pamela* began to appear very early. The first was a French version, *Paméla, ou la Vertu récompensée*,[3] of which the first two volumes appeared in London in 1741; the complete translation, in four volumes, followed in 1742. A Dutch version also began to appear

---

[1] Act III, sc. x; *Gesammelte Schriften*, ed. E. Lewy, Leipzig, 1917, i, 201.

[2] 'Éloge de Richardson', *Journal Étranger*, January 1762, p. 21.

[3] Attributed commonly to the Abbé Prévost (in whose *Œuvres Choisies* of 1783 it was included), but possibly by another hand, or in collaboration. Cf. F. H. Wilcox, 'Prévost's Translations of Richardson's Novels' (*University of California Publications in Modern Philology*, xii, no. 5 (1927), pp. 351 f.).

in 1742,[1] and in the following year the first German translation was published at Leipzig.[2] The work was translated into Italian in 1744–5,[3] and into Danish in the years 1743–6.[4] Abridged versions were also current; and an enterprising German editor, Friedrich Wilhelm Streit, even published a translation of an English extract-book of virtue: *Die Wege der Tugend oder die Geschichte der berühmten Pamela, der Clarissa Harlowe und des Ritters Carl Grandisons, ins Kleine gebracht. Aus dem Englischen übersetzt.*[5]

[1] *Pamela of de beloonde deugd*; the translation appeared in the years 1742–4, and was perhaps by Johannes Stinstra. Cf. Jan te Winkel, *De Ontwikkelingsgang der Nederlandsche Letterkunde*, Haarlem, 1908–21, iv (1), p. 133.

[2] *Pamela oder die belohnte Tugend.* Aus der sechsten vermehrten Englischen Auflage in das Deutsche übersetzt und mit Kupfern gezieret. Leipzig, 1743. (Cf. J. Beckstein, *Richardsons Pamela nach ihrem Gedankengehalt betrachtet*, Bremen, 1929, p. 7, and L. M. Price in *Journal of English and Germanic Philology*, xxv, 7 (note 2)). Goedeke lists two translations: one by Johann Mattheson, *Pamela, oder die belohnte Tugend.* Aus dem Englischen Richardsons. Leipzig, 1742; the other anonymous, *Pamela oder die belohnte Tugend.* Aus dem Englischen. Leipzig, 1750 (*Grundriss*, 3rd ed. IV, i, 576). A version with the same title appeared at Leipzig and Liegnitz in 1763, and a third (also at Leipzig and Liegnitz) in 1772 (cf. L. M. Price, loc. cit.). This last version is recorded by Goedeke as *Pamela, oder die belohnte Tugend eines Frauenzimmers.* Aus dem Englischen. Liegnitz, 1772, and the translator's name is given as Friedrich Schmit (*Grundriss*, ed. cit. IV. i. 97, 576). Kayser (*Vollständiges Bücher-Lexicon*, Pt. vi, Leipzig, 1836) records the Liegnitz edition of 1772, and also a French translation, *Histoire de Pamela*, published at Frankfurt in 1771 (*v.* under *Romane*, pp. 112 f.).

[3] Three volumes of the translation were published at Venice in 1744, the fourth in 1745. (Cf. *Opere Complete di Carlo Goldoni*, Venice, 1907–35, v. 101.)

[4] *Pamela eller den belønnede Dyd*, først skrevet i Engelsk, og nu i Dansk oversat af L. [Barthold Joh. Lodde], Copenhagen, 1743–6 (*v.* C. V. Bruun, *Bibliotheca Danica*, iv (Copenhagen, 1902), 484).

[5] This was published at Altenburg in 1765, and was followed by another version 'im Kleinen entworfen', also published at Altenburg, in the years 1769–76 (*v.* Goedeke, *Grundriss*, ed. cit. IV. i. 576). *The Paths of Virtue*

But there was also a less direct form of influence exerted through dramatic adaptations, during the period of Richardson's popularity abroad;[1] and it may be of interest therefore to consider in greater detail the fortunes of Pamela on the continental stage.

Her dramatic adventures may be said to begin with a version made by the actor James Love [James Dance], which was performed in London in 1741.[2] This version, however, in spite of some dramatic qualities, seems to have exerted little or no influence on subsequent dramatizations abroad. Indeed, even had it been sufficiently well-known, it conformed perhaps too closely to older traditions of English comedy; its technique of exposition through conversation in the servants' hall in the first act, its lively picture of the villainous French valet, its caricature of the young London rake, would scarcely have contributed to a wider popularity. Yet the dramatic conflict in Belvile's mind emerges with some vividness; and the portrait of Mr. Williams in Act IV, where he is first the target of Belvile's jealous rage and then the agent of his timely repentance, shows a slight family likeness to that painted by Nivelle de la Chaussée in his *comédie*

---

delineated; or, the History in miniature of the celebrated Pamela, Clarissa Harlowe, and Sir Charles Grandison. Familiarised and adapted to the capacities of youth appeared in London in 1756.

[1] L. M. Price, in the later of the two articles already referred to, traces a rise in Richardson's popularity in Germany until the 'sixties, and a subsequent decline (*Journal of English and Germanic Philology*, xxv. 27); in the first article he adduces evidence from the German Moral Weeklies to show an earlier decline of Richardson in public favour (*University of Wisconsin Studies*, xxii, 170, 180).

[2] *Pamela, A Comedy. As it is Perform'd Gratis*, at the Late Theatre in Goodman's-Fields. London, 1741. According to a pencil note in the British Museum copy of the play, Garrick played Jack Smatter, Lady Davers's nephew—a role marked in the list of *Dramatis Personae* as played by 'A Gentleman' (p. [6]).

larmoyante of 1743. It is clear that in each case the dramatist felt the need of endowing the character of Richardson's clergyman with greater independence.

But if in some respects James Love compares favourably with adapters of Richardson abroad, he was hardly more successful than they in solving the chief problem confronting all who attempted to dramatize the novel: the presentation of the completely virtuous heroine, and this without the aid of those detailed accounts of her feelings and experiences which alone gave life to the original character. This was a problem inherent in the nature of Richardson's whole artistic achievement. It was clearly recognized by that acute critic, Moses Mendelssohn, who in a review of Wieland's *Clementina von Porretta*—a dramatic adaptation of *Grandison*—seized on the essential point:

Dem ersten Anblicke nach sollte nichts leichter scheinen, als die Verwandlung einer rührenden Episode in ein bürgerliches Trauerspiel; und der Vortrag des Hrn. Richardson kommt hier diesem Betruge sehr zu statten. Denn da er so natürlich dialogirt, und so sorgfältig die Geberden seiner unterredenden Personen beschreibt; so wird man verführt zu glauben, er habe nicht nur die Erfindung, sondern auch den größten Theil der theatralischen Ausführung, bis auf die Pantomime sogar, die der Schauspieler zu beobachten hat, über sich genommen. . . .[1] Aber wie soll der dramatische Dichter. . . die *Clementina* auf die Schaubühne bringen, ohne den Zuschauer bedauern zu lassen, daß er nicht lieber zu Hause den *Richardson* liest? . . .[2]

Few, if any, of the dramatic adapters of *Pamela* found an adequate answer to this question; and to some at least Mendelssohn's judgement on Wieland's attempt applies

---

[1] *Briefe, die neueste Litteratur betreffend*, no. cxxiii, 21 August 1760; Mendelssohn, *Gesammelte Schriften*, Leipzig, 1843–5, iv. 2, pp. 141 f.

[2] *Briefe, die neueste Litteratur betreffend*, no. cxxiii (Beschluß), 28 August 1760; *Gesammelte Schriften*, ed. cit. iv. 2, p. 148.

in equal measure: 'Wenn er das Glück hat, Zuschauer
zu finden, welche niemals die Geschichte beim Richardson
gelesen, so kann er vielleicht auch Beifall hoffen.'[1]

Pamela's Grand Tour of the European stage began in
France, where Nivelle de la Chaussée produced a dramatic
version in 1743, and Louis de Boissy a burlesque in the
same year. Boissy's play,[2] which had nothing in common
with Richardson's novel but the name and figure of the
heroine and a few stray allusions to her history, was
performed at the Théâtre Italien thirteen times; La
Chaussée's *Paméla* was given once only, at the Comédie
Française.[3] In 1743 also there appeared a parody, *La
Déroute des Paméla*, by Godard d'Aucour, which was
performed with some success.[4] La Chaussée treated the
story in the new fashion of pathetic comedy. Choosing
the moment of Milord B——'s final attempt to conquer
Pamela's resistance, he set the scene in Lincolnshire, and
opposed to the plot between Lord B—— and Mrs. Jewks
a counter-plot dependent on the activities of Mr. Williams,
introducing the figure of Pamela's mother, who arrives
in time to support her daughter's spirits and preserve
decorum. The author clearly felt the need for supplying
incident and an element of surprise in the action; but in
fact he does little more than supply a series of coinci-
dences. Wishing to evoke a sentimental sympathy for the
chief characters, he succeeds merely in diluting their

---

[1] *Briefe, die neueste Litteratur betreffend,* no. cxxiv, 28 August 1760;
Gesammelte Schriften, ed. cit. iv. 2, pp. 151 f.

[2] *Paméla en France ou la Vertu mieux Éprouvée.* Comédie en Vers et
en trois Actes. Représentée pour la premiere fois . . . 4 Mars 1743. (*Œuvres
de Théâtre de M. de Boissy* (nouvelle édition), Paris, 1758, ix. 1 ff.).

[3] *v.* A. Léris, *Dictionnaire portatif historique et littéraire des Théâtres,*
2nd ed., Paris, 1763, pp. 330 f. Cf. also B. A. Facteau, *Les Romans de
Richardson sur la Scène française,* Paris [1927], pp. 23, 25 f.

[4] *v.* Léris, *Dictionnaire,* ed. cit., p. 140 (cf. also p. 549, under Daucour);
B. A. Facteau, op. cit., pp. 27 f.

strength. Milord B—— is less of a rake than Mr. B——; his conscience is livelier, and his behaviour less violent. Pamela is less priggish—less irritating, even—than Richardson's heroine, but she is a much more ordinary person. Her feelings are mixed in more usual proportions, and there is none of the excitement of discovery which the reader feels when he finds Pamela writing: 'Thus foolishly dialogued I with my heart; and yet, all the time, this heart is Pamela.' La Chaussée converted the English waiting-maid, with her limited and literal conception of virtue and her passionate interest in her own reactions to life, into the heroine of a *comédie larmoyante*, decorously concerned to preserve her innocence, but unable to resist for a moment any appeal to her sensibility. The French Paméla may be the pleasanter creature; but as far as literature is concerned she does not compare with her English original.

'La Chaussée', Voltaire said, 'avait bien fait cinq actes de sa *Paméla*, dans laquelle il n'y avait pas une scène.'[1] This criticism at least could not be levelled at the play in which Voltaire himself borrowed his subject from Richardson. *Nanine, ou le préjugé vaincu*, which was played at the Théâtre Français on 16 June 1749,[2] wrapped the basic theme of the English novel in a vesture of intrigue which transformed it almost completely. 'Die Geschichte der Nanine', Lessing wrote in the *Hamburgische Dramaturgie*,[3] 'ist die Geschichte der Pamela'; but it is likely that he was mainly concerned to diminish the credit

---

[1] Letter to M. le Comte d'Argental, 24 July 1749 (*Œuvres Complètes de Voltaire*, Paris, 1877–85, xxxvii (Correspondance v), p. 34).

[2] *Œuvres Complètes de Voltaire*, ed. cit. v, p. [4].

[3] St. xxi; *Sämtliche Schriften*, ed. cit. ix. 271. Gottsched had made a similar comment in 1750 (*Neuer Büchersaal der schönen Wissenschaften und freyen Künste*, x. 72). Lessing goes on to refer in disparaging terms to the plays by Boissy and La Chaussée.

of Voltaire by suggesting that he had only written another *Pamela* play. The intrigue and the solution of *Nanine* are in fact of Voltaire's invention; and the resemblance to *Pamela* is no more than superficial. The Comte d'Olban has none but virtuous intentions towards Nanine; the complications of the plot are solely due to the intervention of the jealous Baronne de l'Orme and the intercepting of a letter addressed by Nanine to Philippe Hombert, who is represented to the Comte as being her lover. With the discovery that this Philippe Hombert is in fact her father, and the Comte's consequent resolve to marry Nanine in spite of the Baronne, the very slight action is concluded. But the parallel suggested by Lessing was further pursued by his Viennese imitator C. G. Klemm.[1] In reviewing the plays performed in Vienna during the year 1769–70 this critic took the opportunity of comparing Voltaire's comedy with *Die ledige Pamela* (a translation of Goldoni's first *Pamela* play) and in anticipation of this described *Nanine* as 'eine französische Pamela',[2] praising the logical development of the French play and the dramatist's attention to detail. Goldoni's play, he maintains, is far below *Nanine*; but, on the other hand, it is more entertaining.[3]

The drama by Goldoni which was the occasion of Klemm's comparison dates from 1750, when it was performed, with great success, at Mantua. It is clear from the author's own statement that *Pamela Nubile*, or *Pamela Fanciulla*,[4] was written because Richardson's novel was in

---

[1] Cf. C. G. Klemm, *Dramaturgie, Litteratur und Sitten*, Wien, 1769, pp. 269–89.   [2] Ibid., p. 161.   [3] Ibid., pp. 285 f.

[4] At its appearance the comedy was entitled *Pamela*; in the first volume of the Pasquali edition of Goldoni's works (Venice, 1761) it was called *Pamela Fanciulla*, in order to distinguish it from the sequel, *Pamela Maritata*. In the edition published at Venice in 1788 the title was changed to *Pamela Nubile* (possibly by Goldoni's desire), and this title reappears in many later editions. (Cf. *Opere Complete di Carlo Goldoni*, ed. cit. v. 106.

fashion: 'Il y avoit quelque tems que le Roman de Pamela faisoit les délices des Italiens, et mes amis me tourmentoient pour que j'en fisse une Comédie.'[1] Although he insisted that his play was a *drame* in the French sense,[2] Goldoni in fact showed considerable skill in reshaping the story of Pamela to a conventional comedy-pattern. In the three acts of his play he develops a more lively action than La Chaussée had compassed in the space of five. Discarding the figure of Mr. Williams, since the scene is set in London, he introduces two new characters of some importance: Milord Artur, a man of reason and reflection and a friend of Milord Bonfil, and the Cavaliere Ernold, nephew to Miledi Daure, a scatter-brained young man whose head has been turned by travel.[3] Milord Artur plays the part of counsellor to Milord Bonfil, and helps to set the latter's character in a more favourable light; the young nephew, with his interminable accounts of foreign parts, provides an element of comedy and at the same time complicates the plot by his gallantries towards Pamela. A new turn is given to the story in the last act by the opportune arrival of Pamela's father and by the disclosure that he is in reality Count Auspingh, a proscribed Scottish rebel. Thus Bonfil's hesitations are removed and Pamela's conflict is solved. The play ends with a general reconciliation and a speech by Pamela, containing the assurance of her continued humility and celebrating the triumph of virtue.

[1] *Mémoires*, ed. cit. ii. 63. [2] Ibid., p. 68.
[3] In Richardson's novel one of Mr. B.'s friends is called Mr. Arthur, but his character is only very slightly sketched and does not correspond to that of Milord Artur; Lady Davers's 'rakish nephew', on the other hand, may have provided more than a hint for the character of the Cavaliere Ernold. Cf. more particularly his behaviour to Pamela during his aunt's visit in the First Part, and the description of his demeanour abroad in the Second Part (especially in Letter xcix).

Goldoni might well congratulate himself on having adapted the 'graziosissimo Romanzo Inglese'[1] to the taste of his public. There is little indeed to remind one of Richardson's real achievement, in the Griselda-like figure of Pamela and the fundamentally amiable character of Milord Bonfil, for whose conflicting feelings so opportune a solution is found. Of the startling novelty of the situation only an echo remains; enough, no doubt, to give the flavour of strangeness without undue sacrifice of the conventions. The story has become prettily romantic; the passionate Bonfil possesses essential nobility, and Pamela's resistance to his passion proceeds almost as much from her love for him as from her principles. There is little calculation in her feelings; the fineness of her sensibility is as marked as the rigidity of her virtue. Such differences did not wholly arise from the essential distinctions between novel and drama, although Goldoni was well aware of the difficulties of transferring the story of a novel to the stage;[2] they also reveal a difference in artistic outlook and in national taste.

Dialogue and action in Goldoni's comedy have a characteristic liveliness. Act I contains indeed three monologues by Pamela, which form an essential part of the exposition of her feelings; but apart from this, long speeches by any of the characters are rare. The quick tempo of the dialogue contrasts strongly with that of the French dramatizations; but Goldoni was doubtless right in thinking it impossible to reflect, in the comedy of his day, the impression of time in the original story. Moreover, with the fresh dénouement, this point became much less important for the course of the action.

[1] Preface to *Pamela Fanciulla* (*Pamela Nubile*); *Opere Complete di Carlo Goldoni*, ed. cit. v. 13.

[2] Ibid., p. 14.

Pamela Nubile won immediate and widespread popularity. It was translated into German in 1756,[1] and again in 1758,[2] into English in 1756,[3] and into French in 1759;[4] Spanish versions both of this play and its sequel appeared as late as 1796.[5] A play entitled *Paméla, ou la Vertu Récompensée*, written by François de Neufchâteau in 1788, and performed in Paris in 1793, was, in its first form at least, a fairly faithful version of Goldoni's drama.[6] The author read his play to Goldoni in 1788,[7] and prefixed to it some verses acknowledging its parentage, and indicating the varied fortunes of his theme.[8] Interest of an unusual kind attaches to this version of *Pamela Nubile*. For a short period of time it cost its author his liberty;

---

[1] *Pamela, oder: Die belohnte Tugend.* Ein Lustspiel in drey Handlungen, aus dem italiänischen des Herrn D. Carl Goldoni übersetzt. Danzig, 1756. A copy of this translation is in the British Museum.

[2] *Die Engeländische Pamela*, ein Lustspiel von drey Aufzügen; dem Italienischen des Herrn Karl Goldoni nachgeahmet, und für die k. k. privilegirte Deutsche Schaubühne zu Wien eingerichtet von Friedrich Wilhelm Weiskern. Wien, 1758. A copy is in the Stadtbibliothek, Vienna. According to Goedeke (*Grundriss*, 3rd ed. IV. i. 147) the translator's name was Weisker; but the form Weiskern, with the inflectional *n*, occurs constantly in repertory lists, &c., in Vienna, and has been adopted in this article.

[3] *Pamela.* A Comedy. By Charles Goldoni. Translated into English with the Italian Original. London, 1756. A copy of this is in the British Museum.

[4] By Du Bonnel de Valguier (Paris, 1759). *v.* B. A. Facteau, *Les Romans de Richardson sur la Scène française*, Paris [1927], pp. 38, 126.

[5] *Comedia famosa. La bella Inglesa Pamela en el estado de soltera....* Primera parte. Valencia, 1796; and *Comedia famosa. La bella Inglesa Pamela en el estado de casada.... Segunda* parte. Valencia, 1796. A copy of each of these translations is in the British Museum.

[6] *Paméla, ou la Vertu Récompensée*, Comédie en cinq Actes, en vers.... Par le citoyen François (de Neufchâteau). Paris, III [1795]. A copy of this play is in the British Museum.

[7] Cf. *N. François (de Neufchâteau), Auteur de Paméla, à la Convention Nationale* [Paris, 1793], p. 12. (*v. infra*, p. 366, note 1).

[8] *Paméla, ou la Vertu Récompensée*, ed. cit., pp. 6 f.

and only after an appeal to the National Convention was his innocence of aristocratic and anti-revolutionary tendencies established.[1]

Like Richardson, Goldoni found himself pushed, with some slight reluctance, into writing a sequel. *Pamela Maritata* was composed at the express desire of the actors at the Capranica theatre in Rome, where *Pamela Nubile* was being performed with great success during Goldoni's visit in 1759.[2] The account in his *Memoirs* shows that he was fully aware of the difficulties inherent in such a proposal. With so virtuous and prudent a wife, so happy and reasonable a husband, how could an occasion of discord—and thus a subject for comedy—be found?[3] He confessed that it was a hard task to fashion a plot, based on deceptive appearances, and to develop it without changing the characters of his principal personages and without violating the laws of probability; he flattered himself, however, that he had succeeded in finding a subject of great interest and delicacy.[4]

Pamela Maritata is, in fact, a comedy of jealousy founded on a misunderstanding. Only a few days after their marriage, Bonfil is persuaded all too easily, by the suggestions of the Cavaliere Ernold and Miledi Daure, that an understanding exists between Pamela and Milord Artur. The development of this suspicion occupies the first and second acts; in the third, a solution is brought about by the action of Pamela's father, who, although he has not

---

[1] Cf. B. A. Facteau, *op. cit.*, pp. 46–8. The author's defence of his play to the National Convention, 21 September 1793, was printed as a *mémoire apologétique* with *pièces justificatives* attached (a copy of this publication is in *Justifications* 1–3 of the *Bibliothèque Historique de la Révolution* in the British Museum; *v.* Catalogue under François de Neufchâteau). In this defence he stressed the republican principle in the play.

[2] *v. Mémoires*, ed. cit. ii. 305.

[3] Ibid., pp. 306 f.   [4] Ibid., p. 307.

yet obtained his pardon, risks his liberty by an appeal to the King to inquire into his daughter's innocence. The private inquiry into the grounds for the accusation of infidelity, which is conducted by an assistant to the Secretary of State in Milord Bonfil's house, makes up in speed for what it lacks in probability. In one lengthy speech Pamela establishes her complete innocence and explains that her conversation and correspondence with Milord Artur were solely concerned with the negotiations for her father's pardon. The Cavaliere Ernold ends the sorry part which he has played throughout by leaving for South America, and, as in *Pamela Nubile*, Miledi Daure seeks, and obtains, Pamela's forgiveness. The latter's happiness is completed by the news of Count Auspingh's pardon, and she does not fail, in her last words, to point to the sweet uses of adversity.

Like most sequels, *Pamela Maritata* lacks the interest of its predecessor. The subject is slighter, the action less rapid; the characters, whom we already know, offer little interest of development. It is not surprising to learn that this comedy had a less brilliant reception, when it was performed in Rome in 1760, than *Pamela Nubile*; Goldoni himself comments on the fact, though perhaps in terms that favour the sequel over-much: 'Il y avoit plus d'étude et plus de finesse dans la seconde [pièce]: il y avoit plus d'intérêt et plus de jeu dans la premiere. L'une étoit faite pour le Théâtre, et l'autre pour le cabinet.'[1] The idea of *Pamela Maritata* was no doubt partly derived from the existence of Richardson's unfortunate sequel, dealing with 'Pamela in her exalted condition', and the play shares some of its defects.

Goldoni had, however, another motive for writing his second play. The Abate Pietro Chiari, whose rivalry

[1] *Mémoires*, ed. cit. ii. 307.

with Goldoni took the curious form of producing comedies on similar subjects, with slightly varying titles,[1] had already produced a *Pamela Maritata*, which was played in 1753 in its original prose form, and published, in verse form, in 1759.[2] The solution invented by Goldoni in *Pamela Nubile* suggested to Chiari the main lines of his plot. He complicates the story of Pamela's married life by introducing an intrigue —dependent on a forged letter—which is evolved in order to discredit both the memory of Pamela's father, now dead, and Pamela herself. Miledi Davre, enraged by Bonfil's refusal to allow her projected marriage with Lord Portland, is actually responsible for this plot, and calls in the aid of her nephew, the Cavaliere Ernold, in its execution. It succeeds in deceiving Bonfil, whose rage drives him to offer Pamela, with violent brutality, the alternative of confessing her guilt or seeing her child killed. At this point Pamela receives an anonymous warning against poison; but she resolves to drink the tea which she believes to be poisoned, in the hope of thus saving her child. The unravelling of this fresh complication, revealed as the work of Miledi Davre and her nephew, softens Bonfil's heart to some extent; by the end of the fourth act he is willing to commute the sentence to one of separation. A happier solution, however, is rapidly evolved in the fifth act, where a mistake in the date of the forged letter enables Pamela to discover the plot. Bonfil, who in his rage had overlooked this detail, now reinstates his wife and banishes his sister; and Pamela in a final speech again demonstrates her magnanimity.

[1] Cf. G. Sommi Picenardi, *Un rivale del Goldoni: l'Abate Chiari e il suo Teatro comico*, Milan, 1902, p. 22.

[2] *La Pamela Maritata*, Commedia del Sig. Abate Pietro Chiari . . ., Bologna, 1759; in *Commedie in Versi del Sig. Abate Pietro Chiari Bresciano*, vol. iv (Bologna, 1760).

The more violent and complicated action of Chiari's *La Pamela Maritata* does not give it any advantage over Goldoni's sequel. The characters move, but do not live; their actions make up no coherent picture; their motives, in so far as they appear, are crude and uninteresting. And although Goldoni's dialogue in his second Pamela comedy does not possess the liveliness of that in the first, it still surpasses by far the verses in Chiari's play.

The dramas dealing with Pamela's married life were no less widely known in translation than those which treated of her earlier adventures. Two free translations and an adaptation of Goldoni's sequel appeared in France between 1792 and 1804.[1] Two German versions were made by J. G. Laudes in Vienna, in 1763[2] and 1768,[3] the former of which was performed on a royal name-day. And in the translation of Goldoni's plays which began to appear in 1767 both *Die ledige Pamela* and *Die*

---

[1] Cf. B. A. Facteau, op. cit., pp. 49 f. This critic also records the various French versions of Goldoni's opera, *La Buona Figliuola*, and of its sequel, *La Buona Figliuola Maritata*, based on the material of *Pamela Nubile* and *Pamela Maritata* (ibid., pp. 41 ff.). H. S. Canby, in an article on 'Pamela Abroad' in *Modern Language Notes*, xviii (1903), pp. 206 ff., discusses some French and Italian dramatizations of the story.

[2] *Die verehlichte Pamela*, ein Lustspiel in drey Aufzügen. An dem Glorreichen Allerhöchsten Namensfeste Ihrer Königlichen Hoheit der Durchlauchtigsten Frauen FRAUEN Isabellen Kronprinzessinn zu Hungarn und Böheim etc. Aufgeführt zu Wien auf der kais. königl. privilegirten Schaubühne den 19. des Wintermonats. Aus dem Italiän. des berühmten Dr. C. Goldoni übersetzt von J. G. v. L——s. Zu finden in dem Krausischen Buchladen nächst der k. k. Burg, 1763. This translation was included in the Viennese *Neue Sammlung von Schauspielen*, iii (Vienna, 1764). A copy of the 1763 edition is in the Theatersammlung of the Nationalbibliothek, Vienna.

[3] *Pamela als Frau*. Ein rührendes Stück nach dem Italienischen von J. G. Laudes. 3te veränd. Auflage. Wien. . . . Nach der neuen Veränderung vorgestellt im Jahre 1768. A copy of this translation is in the Theatersammlung of the Nationalbibliothek, Vienna. On performances of Goldoni's two plays in Germany and Austria, *v. infra*, pp. 377 ff.

verheyrathete Pamela are to be found.[1] Short extracts translated from *Pamela Maritata* had already been included in a criticism of that play in the *Bibliothek der schönen Wissenschaften*,[2] when the first four volumes of the Pasquali edition of Goldoni's works (published at Venice in 1761) were reviewed. There was also a German translation of Chiari's play by Anton von Riegger, published in 1764.[3]

The existence of these various translations would in itself seem to indicate that plays on the subject of *Pamela* enjoyed considerable popularity in Germany and Austria.[4] The versions, though often enough inaccurate in details, were in general reasonably faithful, if seldom inspired.

---

[1] In Pt. vi, published at Leipzig in 1770. Cf. H. O. Reichard's *Theater-Kalender auf das Jahr 1775*, Gotha, p. 151, where a notice of this translation appears, with the comment: 'Der Uebers[etzer] ist H. Saal, und seine Uebers[etzung] wird unter den bisherigen für die beßre gehalten.' Unfavourable criticisms of the translation appeared, however, in Klotz's *Deutsche Bibliothek*, vii (1768), pp. 444 ff. and xvi (1770), pp. 716 ff. Cf. also L. Mathar, *Carlo Goldoni auf dem deutschen Theater des XVIII. Jahrhunderts*, Montjoie, 1910, pp. 189 ff.

[2] *Bibliothek der schönen Wissenschaften und der freyen Künste*, x (1), Leipzig, 1763, pp. 13 ff.

[3] *Pamela als Mutter*. Ein rührendes Lustspiel in drey Aufzügen. Nach dem Italiänischen des Abbts Chiari. Von einem Oesterreichischen Ritter. An dem Glorreichen Geburtsfeste Ihrer Röm. Kais. Kön. Ap. Maj. aufgeführet. Wien, 1764. This translation was included in the sixth volume of the Viennese *Neue Sammlung von Schauspielen* (1765). A separate copy (of a later edition published at Vienna in 1771) is in the Stadtbibliothek, Vienna.

[4] There was even a German translation of La Chaussée's *Paméla*, published at Bremen in 1768. A copy of this play is in the Theatersammlung of the Nationalbibliothek, Vienna (Thimig Collection 4214[II]); it is contained in the *Zweyte Sammlung einiger französischen Lustspiele für das deutsche Theater* (Bremen, 1768), and the name of Gottl[ieb] Walz as the translator is added in pencil on the title-page of the volume. This corresponds to the indication given by C. H. Schmid in his *Chronologie des deutschen Theaters* (ed. P. Legband, *Schriften der Gesellschaft für Theatergeschichte*, i, Berlin, 1902, p. 177, under the year 1768). A separate copy of the translation is in the British Museum.

The first German translation—that of *Pamela Nubile*
dating from 1756—was made by a member of Ackermann's company of actors, expressly for the purposes of
the stage, and had already been used in performances.[1]
Apart from a few errors due to faulty understanding of
the original it is a fairly literal version—more so, indeed,
than the anonymous translator's preface would suggest.[2]
The very few points in which it differs from Goldoni's
play are trifling, but nevertheless interesting, signs of the
times. The translator observes that certain passages in
the original would be 'bey uns Deutschen auf der Bühne
läppisch oder possierlich'; out of respect for his author he
would not omit them from the published version, but he
had them printed in smaller type.[3] His rendering of
'una che non sia nobile' as 'eine Bürgerliche' (i. xiii) was
no doubt only to be expected in 1756; but the addition of
'Ein ehrlicher Kaufmann ist nicht veranlasset sich diesfals
verachten zu lassen' in the discussion concerning *mésal-
liances* (i. xiii) may well reflect the social experience of
Ackermann's company in such towns as Hamburg or
Lübeck. The description by Mylord Arthur of the social
slights that will fall to Pamela's lot is enlarged by one
emphatic detail: 'Sie wird ausgesondert seyn wie eine
Magd' (ii. ii); and in the same scene he adds: 'In ganz
London, Mylord, werden Sie zum Mährchen dienen.'
The substitution of the name 'Bedford' for Goldoni's

---

[1] Cf. *Pamela, oder: Die belohnte Tugend*, Danzig, 1756, p. 4 (Vorbericht).
[2] L. Mathar, in his dissertation *Carlo Goldoni auf dem deutschen
Theater des XVIII. Jahrhunderts* (Montjoie, 1910, pp. 12 f.), censures
the author of this version both for the occasional mistranslations and for
the lack of any attempt to abridge or curtail the original; but the translation
is rather better than his comments suggest.
[3] *Vorbericht*, p. 4. The passages are few and short; they occur in
i. xvii (p. 42); ii. iv (p. 71); ii. xiv (p. 88); iii. iv (p. 97); iii. xiv (p. 120).

'Bonfil' may have arisen from the desire to use English rather than Gallicized names—'Bedford' echoes the 'Squire B—— of Bedfordshire' of Richardson's novel. So, too, when Pamela in her final speech addresses her future husband as 'geliebter Bedford' (where Goldoni still writes 'signore') there is a perceptible difference in atmosphere. But the German actor was as much at a loss as his contemporaries—in Germany and elsewhere—in dealing with English titles; although he substitutes the original Lady (Mylady) Davers for Miledi Daure, he uses the term Lady—in the manner of many German domestic tragedies in the eighteenth century—as an equivalent for *die gnädige Frau*.[1]

Weiskern's version of *Pamela Nubile*, two years later, betrays in some respects a more definite adaptation to local conditions. While the designation of Bonfil's major-domo as Herr Hanns, instead of Herr Longmann, may only indirectly suggest a comedy role, the substitution of the 'Chevalier Bernardon' for the 'Cavaliere Ernold' was a characteristically Viennese touch. In the name of Bernardon there was at once for the original audience a flavour of caricature; and indeed in this part Weiskern showed himself an adapter as well as a translator. In the figure of the young jackanapes who had made the Grand Tour of Europe, Goldoni had created a comedy role; but the Chevalier of *Die engeländische Pamela* is a fully developed figure of fun. The additions which he makes to the travel descriptions are in the tradition of extemporized comedy; and echoes of that great controversy can be heard in the comparison of the comedies of England, Italy, and Vienna:

Zu Wien machen sie auch oftmals Comedien, welche so

---

[1] 'Wenn ich zu Lady Ihrer Schwester ziehe' (i. vi); 'Bey Lady, liebe Pamela, da werden Sie nicht bleiben' (i. xviii), &c.

schmerzhaft wie die engeländischen, und weit blutiger, als alle
französische Tragödien sind; aber das geschieht nicht alleweile. Sie
wechseln ab, bald mit Baletten, Maschinen und Decorationen für
das Auge; bald mit einem lustigen Liedel für das Ohr; bald mit
einem lächerlichen Schnirkel für den Verstand. Da sie fast alle
Wochen etwas neues auf das Theater bringen, so haben sie auch
allerhand neue Autores von unterschiedlichem Caliber. . . (I. xviii).

The new Viennese comedy-writers do not exert themselves
unduly in the creation of characters, as do those in
London; they are content to piece together shreds from
operas, tragedies, comedies, or burlesques by others.
Only one thing is lacking in this 'Ollapotrie'—the Italian
Harlequin. And the ludicrous mask and many-coloured
jacket of Goldoni's description of this same Harlequin are
then amplified into

Ein kleines Kerlgen, lebhaft wie Quecksilber, mit einem kleinen
weißen Chapeau, einem von tausend bunten Flecken zusammen
gesetzten Kleide, in einer schwarzen Larve mit zwey kleinen
runden Augen, daß er beständig schielen muß: voller Männergen,
Quinten und Posituren. . .

—a picture which bears the marks of a portrait from the
life. Nor did Weiskern neglect the opportunity of flattery.
Where Goldoni's traveller merely alludes to the reputation
of Vienna 'per i gran trattamenti', the Chevalier Bernardon
gives preference to its cuisine above all others:

Jedoch gebüret Wien vor allen der Vorzug, so wohl was die
Menge von Tractamenten, als die Kostbarkeit der Speisen betrifft.
Alle Delicatessen, die man anderwärts nur Stückweise findet, trifft
man hier beysammen, wie in einem Centro an. O che gusto!
Da lebet sichs vortreflich. So gar den Punsch habe ich da so gut
als in London getrunken. . . . Ma foi, das sind die besten Menschen
von der Welt.

To Lord Artur's quiet comment: 'So viel ich merke, seyd
ihr selbst ein ganzer Wiener geworden', the Chevalier
returns an answer which is clearly of topical interest:

'Point du tout! Die Herren Wiener haben sich au Con-
traire nach mir gerichtet. Wie habe ich da brilliret! . . .
Ich habe fast die halbe Stadt in Engländer verwandelt. . .'
Whereas the anonymous translator in 1756 had contented
himself with an occasional addition of 'Messieurs', 'Vani-
glia', 'en merveille' (I. xvi) to underline the cosmopolitan
mania of the Ritter Ernold, the Chevalier's conversation
in Weiskern's version is interlarded with French and
Italian phrases. In the Francophile Vienna of the mid-
eighteenth century, where the German theatre was so
much less fashionable than its French rival, the caricature
must have been popular with the audience for German
plays at the Kärnthnerthor theatre.

Apart from such topical additions and alterations, and
some occasional curtailments, Weiskern's translation is in
general both faithful and fluent; and colour is given to the
language by the use of Viennese forms, which sometimes
reflect very aptly the diminutives of the Italian original.

The first of the two versions of *Pamela Maritata* made
by J. G. von Laudes bears traces of the rapidity with which
it was completed. The play had to be ready for a gala
performance on 19 December 1763; and the translator
assures us that he had only ten days for his work, and was
thus compelled to make a slavishly literal version.[1] Except
for a number of mistranslations (some of which are of an
elementary character) and the omission of a few isolated
sentences, his rendering indeed follows the original closely.
Even the role of the Chevalier Ernold is here embellished
only by a few French tags, and by an additional sentence
in Herr Longmann's description of the triangular combat
('Er trillert kleine französische Liederchen *für Freuden,
daß er aus diesem Handel mit ganzen Gliedern heraus
gekommen ist*', II. xi).

[1] *v. Pamela als Frau,* 3te veränderte Auflage, Wien [1768], p. [5].

For the third edition, however, the translation was revised. Some alterations and additions were made, and the new version was performed in Vienna in 1768. The most important change was the omission of the state official Herr Mayer, whom Laudes describes in the preface to this edition as a quite superfluous character. The knot is cut instead by Pamela's father, who insists on the discussion of the situation in private and so becomes a much more important and individual character. Thus the improbable scene of the inquiry conducted by the envoy of the Secretary of State is avoided. A similar desire to give a greater appearance of probability to the action is discernible in slight changes of wording, notably in the rendering of Pamela's letter to Milord Artur, and in her husband's comments upon it.[1] There is a noticeable difference in the tempo of the dialogue; numerous small alterations and omissions quicken its pace in *Pamela als Frau*, the translator curtails more frequently, and makes almost too liberal a use of broken sentences. The general result is to make the characters as a whole more lively and convincing. Pamela is less inclined to virtuous statements, and her husband is more obviously a prey to conflicting feelings.

It is interesting to note that Laudes changed the names of three characters in the revised edition, adopting the 'Bedford', 'Davers', and 'Jervis' which had already been used in *Pamela, oder: Die belohnte Tugend*. The role of the Chevalier, too, approximates more closely to that already established by Weiskern in *Die engeländische Pamela*. His conversation once more abounds in French phrases;

---

[1] Act 1, sc. xv. e.g. for ' . . . daß ich in London den kostbarsten Antheil meines Herzens zurück lasse' the 1768 edition reads: 'daß ich in London den einzigen Gegenstand aller meiner Wünsche zurück lasse' ('la miglior parte di me medesima'); other changes are of a similar kind.

but while there is a greater element of caricature here than in Laudes's first version, there is at the same time a more human mixture of qualities in his portrait. The substitution of 'Wien' for 'Venedig' (I. iv) and an allusion to Frenchified habits (I. i) indicate that Laudes too had an eye to his Viennese audience.

The third translation of a *Pamela* play which was produced in Vienna was *Pamela als Mutter*, and this too was given at a gala performance—for Maria Theresia's birthday in 1764.[1] The preface sought to justify the appearance of yet another play on this subject:

> Wie? schon wiederum eine Pamela? Auch eine Pamela als Mutter?—Eine jede Sache scheinet ihre gewissen Perioden zu haben.—Itzt schreibt man nichts lieber, als Pamelen—als von Pamelen.—Fast sollte man glauben können, unsre heutige Welt sey mehr für die Tugend und Unschuld eingenommen, als man sonst gemeiniglich dafür hält. Und das schöne Geschlecht ... von den zärtlichen Leidenschaften der Pamela hingerissen—weinet mit ihr—erfreuet sich mit ihr—bewundert sie. ...[2]

The translator—or, as he calls himself, the imitator—of Chiari's play promised his audience nothing either from his original or from his copy, but everything from the actors and their admirable technique:

> Sollte man es nicht ihrer vorzüglichen Geschicklichkeit zuschreiben können, daß man nach den zwey Goldonischen ... auch diese Chiarische Pamela, auf unsrer Schaubühne zu sehen verlangt hat? ...[3]

His disclaimer is perhaps more fully justified than he knew; for the translation is even more diffuse and unimpressive than Chiari's play. But he did not hesitate to

[1] Cf. *supra*, p. 370 (note 3), and also the letter from Laudes to Riegger attached to the translation in the *Neue Sammlung von Schauspielen* (vi), p. 127.

[2] *Pamela als Mutter*, Wien, 1764, pp. [3] f.

[3] Ibid., p. [5].

alter, curtail, or expand his original; by these means he reduced the five acts of the Italian drama to three (the number in the other Pamela plays). The son of Pamela and Bonfil—a mute character in *La Pamela Maritata*—appears in the German version as a rather unconvincing stage child, adding his tearful appeals to the lamentations of his mother; the Chevalier Ernold, who in the earlier part of the translation borrows one or two embellishments from his Viennese predecessors, is sentimentalized in the final scenes into an ardent disciple of Pamela and is adopted by young Bonfil as a brother. The already crude action of the original play becomes still more sensational and more lachrymose in a translation which cannot even claim the merit of fidelity.[1]

While these translations in themselves bear witness to the popularity of the Pamela plays in Germany and Austria, there is further evidence for this popularity in repertory lists and contemporary records during the latter half of the eighteenth century.

The first version, *Pamela, oder: Die belohnte Tugend*, was in Ackermann's repertory. Performances of this play by his company were clearly given before its publication in 1756;[2] it is then recorded as having been played by them in Hamburg in 1756[3] and on tour in 1759;[4] in

---

[1] Josef von Sonnenfels, in a very unfavourable review of the play (*Briefe über die wienerische Schaubühne*, x, xl., 7 October 1768, ed. cit., pp. 237 ff.), expresses a wish that 'der deutsche Dichter hätte sich erlauben wollen, den unförmlichen Klumpen noch freyer zu behandeln, da er schon so viel gethan hatte' (ibid., p. 238); but the comments that he goes on to make on Riegger's version suggest that this wish was rhetorical.

[2] Cf. *Vorbericht*, ed. cit., p. 4: 'bereits . . . auf verschiedenen ansehnlichen Bühnen'.

[3] Cf. F. L. W. Meyer, *F. L. Schröder*, Hamburg, 1819, ii. ii. 52.

[4] Schröder played 'Johann in der Pamela' as one of his roles in the summer of 1759. *v.* Meyer, op. cit. i. 84, and ii. ii. 140. L. Mathar (op. cit., pp. 46 f.) states that *Pamela* was first played by Koch's company

Strassburg in 1760[1] and 1761;[2] in Hamburg again in 1764[3] and 1765,[4] and in Braunschweig in 1769.[5] *Die verehlichte Pamela* is listed among Ackermann's performances in Hamburg in 1764,[6] while *Pamela als Mutter* was produced there by his company in 1771.[7] *Pamela, oder: Die belohnte Tugend* was played as far east as Königsberg (in October 1767),[8] and Schuch's company

in Hamburg, 16 February 1759, and that between this date and 4 October 1763 it was given eighteen times in all by this company.

[1] Cf. Meyer (op. cit. i. 86): 'Das Jahr 1760 begann in Strassburg mit Pamela.'

[2] L. M. Price (*University of Wisconsin Studies*, xxii. 173 ff.), quotes extracts from a correspondence in the Strassburg periodical *Der Sammler* of 1761 concerning a play which is cited as *Pamela oder die bekrönte Unschuld*, performed by Ackermann's company in Strassburg. It seems likely that this was the play to which Meyer refers as above. The last of the three letters summarized by Price alludes to the favour enjoyed by the play in Strassburg and elsewhere.

[3] Madam Ackermann played the role of Lady Davers in *Pamela* in 1764 (and also in *Die verehlichte Pamela* in that year. Cf. Meyer, op. cit., II. ii. 122). L. Mathar (op. cit., p. 84) states on the evidence of playbills that Ackermann produced the play on 9 October 1764.

[4] According to L. Mathar (loc. cit.) on 3 May 1765.

[5] Meyer (op. cit. i. 204) records that on 18 August [1769] Madam Kessel made her début as Lady [Davers] in *Pamela* under Ackermann, and that Madam Schuch at the same performance played Pamela.

[6] Ackermann himself played the role of Mayer. *v.* Meyer, op. cit. II. ii. 116 and II. ii. 54; between 1764 and 1769 Ekhof played Lord Bedford in *Die verehlichte Pamela*, as also in *Pamela* (Meyer, op. cit. II. ii. 15) and Schröder that of Isaak in *Die verehlichte Pamela* in 1764 (ibid., p. 143). Mathar (op. cit., p. 84) lists a performance of *Die verehlichte Pamela* on 16 October 1764, and states that there were six performances during this period of Ackermann's management in Hamburg, the last being on 25 September 1766.

[7] *v.* Meyer, op. cit. II. ii. 57. Schröder played the role of Isaak in this play in 1771 (ibid., p. 147), whereas in 1767 he had played Ernold in all three plays (ibid., p. 145).

[8] Kirchhoff played Bedford when the play was performed in Königsberg. Cf. E. A. Hagen, *Geschichte des Theaters in Preußen*, Königsberg, 1854, p. 259 (citing the *Königsbergsche Gelehrte und Politische Zeitungen* of October 1767).

performed a play entitled *Die Pamela* there in 1772.[1] That the first (Danzig) version was played by Koch's company as late as 1773 in Berlin is indicated by the sub-title 'oder die belohnte Tugend' in a record of a performance of *Pamela* on 4 June 1773.[2] Seyler's company played a *Pamela* in Hanover on 31 May 1771.[3] In 1769 Wäser had opened his performances in Leipzig with *Pamela als Mutter*.[4]

But although it is clear that the Pamela plays, since they formed part of the repertory of more than one travelling company, were frequently performed throughout Germany, it is in the records of the Viennese theatre that their titles are most continuously found. It was not for nothing that three translations issued from Vienna; nor is it surprising that a city so markedly subject to the influence of Italian players should have been particularly open to the influence of an Italian playwright.

Pamela is recorded as one of the few 'regular' comedies given in Vienna between 1754 and 1759.[5] The version

[1] Mathar (op. cit., p. 119) gives the date 21 February 1772, from the evidence of the repertory lists from December 1771 to February 1772, in *Billette über die Schuchische Schaubühne*.

[2] v. C. M. Plümicke, *Entwurf einer Theatergeschichte von Berlin*, Berlin und Stettin, 1781, p. 407. Mathar (op. cit., p. 110) states, on the evidence of Koch's repertory list from June 1771 to April 1775, that *Pamela* was given three times, all the performances being in the year 1773.

[3] Cf. R. Schlösser, *Vom Hamburger Nationaltheater zur Gothaer Hofbühne 1767–1779 (Theatergeschichtliche Forschungen*, xiii), Hamburg and Leipzig, 1895, p. 70.

[4] On 27 December. v. C. H. Schmid, *Chronologie des deutschen Theaters* (1775), ed. P. Legband (*Schriften der Gesellschaft für Theatergeschichte*, i), Berlin, 1902, p. 186.

[5] Cf. *Geschichte des gesammten Theaterwesens zu Wien, von den ältesten, bis auf die gegenwärtigen Zeiten*, Wien, 1803, p. 147, where it is listed with seven others as a 'new' production; also Reichard, *Theater-Kalender auf das Jahr 1776*, Gotha, p. 155, where *Pamela* is mentioned as one of the regular pieces performed in Vienna before 1759.

used at first was probably that published at Danzig in
1756; later on, no doubt, Weiskern's took its place. The
actor J. H. F. Müller, who made his first appearance in
a Viennese company in 1763 in *Polyeucte*, soon afterwards
took the part of the Chevalier Ernold in the *Pamela* plays;[1]
for both Weiskern's version of the earlier *Pamela* and
Laudes's translation of Goldoni's second play were given
in that year.[2] *Pamela als Mutter* is recorded as having
been performed in 1764.[3] From the title-page of Laudes's
revised translation, *Pamela als Frau*, we know that this
version was performed in 1768;[4] and in the following
year other evidence for performances of Pamela plays is
forthcoming. That they were a popular attraction is borne
out by a passage in a Pro Memoria of 16 December 1769
by Afflisio, the Italian director of the French theatre in
Vienna, in which he tried to discredit the German theatre

---

[1] Cf. C. H. Schmid, *Chronologie des deutschen Theaters*, ed. cit., p. 141;
v. also *J. H. F. Müllers Abschied von der k. k. Hof- und National-
Schaubühne*, Wien, 1802, p. 47: 'Durch die Rolle des *Chevalier* in der
ledigen und *verheurathen Pamela*, und in der *Pamela als Mutter*, erwarb
ich mir die Gunst des Publikums von Tag zu Tag immer mehr.'

[2] The performances are recorded in the handwritten *Repertoire des
deutschen Schauspiels in Wien, ein alphabetisches Register sämmtlicher
Aufführungen deutscher Schauspiele in den Wiener Hoftheatern von dem
Erscheinen regelmäßiger Stücke im Jahre 1748 bis zum Schlusse des
Jahres 1880*, which is in the Stadtbibliothek, Vienna (40428. Jc.).
Pamela, 'eine Dramatisirung des gleichnamigen englischen Roman's,
daher auch "die engelländische Pamela" genannt, oder auch "Pamela als
Mädchen" . . . in der Bearbeitung von Weiskern', is recorded as having
been given on 15 November 1763, 12 October 1776, and 21 July 1779
(pp. 137–8); '*Pamela als Frau*; (auch "die verehlichte Pamela") . . .
übersetzt von Laudes' is recorded as having been given on 19 November
1763, and in '1768 etc.' (ibid., p. 138). But cf. also the title-page of
Die verehlichte Pamela of 1763 (*v. supra*, p. 369, note 2).

[3] *Repertoire*, p. 138: '*Pamela als Mutter* . . . nach dem Ital. des Abbate
Pietro Chiari von Riegger, 12 Mai 1764 und 15 Apr. 1777'. *v. supra*,
p. 370 (note 3).

[4] *v. supra*, p. 369 (note 3).

and to obtain permission to reintroduce extemporized comedy. To this end he presented a list of the German plays in the Viennese repertory, attaching to each play a summary comment. Only to nineteen of them did he attach the word 'Gefällt'; but both *Pamela als Frau* and *Die ledige Pamela* were included in this select list.[1] His verdict is supported by the critical register of performances of German plays in Vienna from 1769 to 1770 given by Klemm in his *Dramaturgie, Litteratur und Sitten. Pamela als Frau* was given on 29 April and 1 May;[2] *Die ledige Pamela* (Weiskern's version) on 20 and 21 May,[3] on 28 June,[4] and on 21 September[5] 1769. It is true that Klemm, analysing the plot of *Nanine* in order to compare it with *Die ledige Pamela*, observes: 'Ueberhaupt hätten die Theatraldichter eben so wohl gethan, wenn sie alle Pamelenhistörchen von der Bühne ausgeschlossen hätten.' There is no 'fruchtbare Moral' in the story—on the contrary, there are many inconveniences in a *mésalliance*: 'Der Bürger soll ein Bürgermädel . . . der Edelmann ein Fräulein heurathen, so bleibt alles schön in seiner Ordnung.'[6] Yet he hardly approves of Goldoni's 'love-sick' Pamela, who seems to know all through the piece that she will be a *Gräfin* at the end;[7] and is inclined to attribute her popularity to the admirable acting of Mamsell Jaquet.[8] He commends the ironic portrait of the Chevalier Ernold—by this time the name 'Bernardon'

[1] Cf. J. H. F. Müller, *Geschichte und Tagbuch der Wiener Schaubühne*, Wien, 1776, p. 34. It may be noted also that among the attractions offered by the Cinquanta company in March 1769 were Italian comedies by Goldoni and Chiari (together with acrobatics and new pantomimes). Cf. *Wienerisches Diarium*, 18 March 1769.

[2] C. G. Klemm, *Dramaturgie, Litteratur und Sitten*, Wien, 1769, p. 182.

[3] Ibid., p. 269.	[4] Ibid., p. 365.
[5] Ibid., p. 456.	[6] Ibid., pp. 274 ff.
[7] Ibid., p. 281.	[8] Ibid., p. 289.

seems to have been abandoned—and adds a word of praise for Müller's acting of the part.[1]

Performances of the various Pamela plays continued to be given in Vienna as late as 1775,[2] 1776,[3] 1777,[4] and 1779.[5] Elsewhere, however, where they had not the same local interest, they faded earlier from the repertory. There is no record of them in the lists of plays performed by Seyler's company in Thüringen and Saxony between 1772 and 1775, and in Gotha from 1775 to 1779.[6] Nor do the lists of Schröder's roles and repertory contain records of them after 1771.[7] While it is clearly impossible to assert that they were not performed at all, the contrast with the earlier evidence for their popularity is plain enough. Then, actors such as Ekhof and Schröder,

[1] C. G. Klemm, *Dramaturgie, Litteratur und Sitten*, p. 287.

[2] *Pamela als Mägdchen*, in the Burgtheater, on 12 June 1775. *v.* J. H. F. Müller, *Geschichte und Tagbuch der Wiener Schaubühne*, Wien, 1776, p. 138.

[3] *Pamela als Mägdchen*, in the Burgtheater, on 12 October 1776 (Playbill in the Theatersammlung of the Nationalbibliothek, Vienna). In the *Versamlungs-Prothocol von den Jahren 1776 und 1777* in the Wiener Haus- Hof- und Staatsarchiv Madam Sacco was cast for Pamela at the session of 4 October (f. 29^r). Her name appears on the playbill, but the other actors are not mentioned. A performance of *Pamela als Frau* was to have followed on 10 December, but this was cancelled owing to the absence of Müller (ibid., ff. 32^v and 33^v).

[4] *Pamela als Mutter*, in the Burgtheater, on 15 April 1777. *v. Repertoire*, p. 138. Cf. also *Versamlungs-Prothocol*, f. 44^v.

[5] *Pamela als Mädchen*, in the Burgtheater, on 21 July 1779 (Playbill in the Theatersammlung of the Nationalbibliothek, Vienna). Pamela was played by Mlle Jaquet die ältere, the Chevalier by Herr Weidmann.

[6] Cf. R. Schlösser, op. cit., pp. 72 ff., 75 ff.

[7] Cf. F. L. W. Meyer, *F. L. Schröder*, ed. cit. ii. ii, 147 ff., 57 ff. Similarly, the *Litteratur- und Theater-Zeitung* (Berlin, 1778), which contains lists of plays performed in Berlin, and news from theatres in Breslau, Hamburg, Leipzig, Mannheim, and elsewhere, has no record of any performance of Pamela plays, although other comedies of Goldoni are listed, and some other old favourites occur amid the large number of newer dramas.

Madam Ackermann and Madam Brandes, had made some of the parts in these plays their own. Schröder, it is true, commented on Ekhof's playing of Lord Bedford in *Pamela* and *Die verehlichte Pamela* as 'grob'; [1] but his verdict on Ekhof was not always flattering.[2] Schröder himself, after acting in a minor part, took over the more grateful role of the Chevalier when he was playing for a short time under Kurz in 1767:

Da bei dieser Bühne nur wenig eingelernte Stücke im Gange waren, die bedeutende Dienerrollen hatten, so spielte Schröder alles was Chevalier hieß, oder dahin gerechnet wurde, die in den Pamelas, den le Blau in der schlauen Wittwe u.s.w.[3]

Madam Sacco is stated to have made her début at the early age of eleven at Dresden in *Pamela als Mädchen*.[4] But a more lasting memorial to the impression made by the dramatic figure of Pamela on the age is perhaps the passage in *Anton Reiser*, where Anton looks back on his experience of the theatre:

Vor zwei Jahren hatte er schon den Herkules auf dem Oeta, den Grafen von Olsbach, und die Pamela spielen sehen, wo *Eckhof, Böck, Günther, Hensel, Brandes nebst seiner Frau*, und die *Seilerin* die vorzüglichsten Rollen spielten, und schon von jener Zeit her schwebten die rührendsten Scenen aus diesen Stücken noch seinem Gedächtniß vor, worunter *Günther* als Herkules, *Böck* als Graf von Olsbach und *die Brandes* als Pamela, fast jeden Tag wechselweise einmal in seine Gedanken gekommen waren. . . [5]

The autobiographical character of *Anton Reiser* lends a special interest to this reflection of the tastes and feelings

[1] F. L. W. Meyer, op. cit. ii. ii. 15.

[2] Ibid., pp. 14–21, *passim*.

[3] Ibid. i. 164.

[4] *v. Gallerie von Teutschen Schauspielern und Schauspielerinnen*, ed. R. M. Werner (*Schriften der Gesellschaft für Theatergeschichte*, xiii), Berlin, 1910, p. 120.

[5] C. Ph. Moritz, *Anton Reiser*. Ein psychologischer Roman. Pt. ii (Berlin, 1786), pp. 164 f.

of his early youth. The novel looks back to the 'sixties and 'seventies, and this mention of the impression made by Madam Brandes as Pamela thus supports the more specific evidence of the repertory lists. By the time it was published, however, fashion had changed. The stream of sentiment was flowing in a different direction; virtue rewarded had ceased to be so enthralling a spectacle as virtue betrayed. As the tragedy of common life flourished increasingly in Germany, the appeal of the plays adapted from *Pamela* seems to have grown less; *Clarissa*—which did not acquire a new ending—was perhaps by then more in line with popular feeling. But above all, theatrical managers could no longer complain of a lack of original plays. The age of imitation and adaptation was over, and with its passing, the adventures of *Pamela* in Germany and Austria also came to an end.

KLINGER'S MEDEA DRAMAS AND THE GERMAN FATE TRAGEDY

By F. E. SANDBACH

THAT remarkable phenomenon in German literature known as the Fate Tragedy has had its full share of attention from academic investigators, and little remains to be added to the results of their labours—at any rate so far as the history of this genre in the narrow and technical sense of the term 'Fate Tragedy' is concerned. Leaving out of account the comments and judgements of contemporary critics during the Romantic period, and of literary critics and historians during the next two generations, the serious study of the Fate Tragedy set in fifty-four years ago when Minor published his *Die Schicksalstragödie in ihren Hauptvertretern* (Frankfurt a. M., 1883) and followed up this survey by editing a selection of these tragedies in the Deutsche National-Literatur series (1884). Since then there has been an intermittent stream of publications dealing specifically with or throwing useful sidelights on this topic; and a few years ago, in Merker and Stammler's *Reallexikon der deutschen Literaturgeschichte* (vol. iii, 1928–9), P. Hankamer very efficiently—though influenced, of course, by his own preferences and convictions—harvested, selected from, and blended the total crop produced by the labours of himself and others.

Readers of Hankamer's article will find in it no mention of Klinger's *Medea in Korinth* (1786) and *Medea auf dem Kaukasos* (1790), which appear to have been neglected or given very short shrift by writers on the Fate Tragedy; perhaps because Fate appears in person on the stage instead of remaining an unseen mysterious force; and because, in spite of her appearances, she has very little direct share in the real action of the plays. K. A. Rosikat, in his *Über das Wesen der Schicksalstragödie* (Jahresbericht des städtischen Realgymnasiums zu Königsberg i. Pr., Königsberg, 1891–2), simply mentions these two plays (p. 11) along with other works cited to illustrate the various conceptions of Fate in relation to human freedom of action; and M. Enzinger, in his *Das deutsche Schicksalsdrama* (Akademische Antrittsvorlesung, Innsbruck, 1922), which offers a very comprehensive survey of the whole subject and suggests lines for further investigation, remarks merely (p. 15) that here Fate appears personified, but belongs only to the 'Rahmenhandlung' in *Medea in Korinth* and is a 'frostige Allegorie' in *Medea auf dem Kaukasos*.

They are, of course, not technically 'Fate Tragedies' themselves. They do not express a gloomily fatalistic outlook on life; they do not dramatize the fulfilment of an ancestral curse; and they do not, by insistence on a fateful place, or day, or weapon, or other inanimate object, put petty limits on Fate's opportunities of intervention.[1] But they do stand in the same general relation to the Fate Tragedies as do *Iphigenie, Die Braut von Messina*, and a number of other plays in which, during approximately the last fifteen years of the eighteenth century and the first five of the nineteenth, a supernatural power, whether a pagan Destiny or a Christian Providence, is represented as controlling the affairs of men. All these plays are products of attempts to adapt to the modern tragedy of character, written for modern audiences and readers, the impressive Fate motive of Greek tragedy. They are, so to speak, the offspring of an unnatural union between classical and

---

[1] Klinger, as H. Zempel emphasizes in *Erlebnisgehalt und ideelle Zeitverbundenheit in Fr. M. Klingers Medeadramen* (Halle, 1929), was no more of a fatalist than Goethe or Schiller.

modern dramatic art; and the 'Fate Tragedies' are a group
of spiritually degenerate offspring of the same union,
degenerate both in their conception of Fate as a sort of
cruel, vindictive, destructive bogey, and in their appeal
to primitive superstitions that regained much of their
old power during the period of romanticism. In all
probability the Fate Tragedies would never have seen the
light of day but for the prior appearance of the healthier
members of the same family. Klinger's Medea tragedies
and Goethe's *Iphigenie* (1787) appeared shortly before
Tieck in 1793 planned the first of the Fate Tragedies
proper, his *Karl von Berneck*, significantly referred to by
his friend Wackenroder as an 'Orest in Ritterzeiten',
and later by Tieck himself as 'dieser deutsche Orestes'.
This work, however, which was published in 1797, neither
achieved nor deserved much success, and it had no
immediate successors. It was not until Schiller's experiments with the Fate motive—*Wallenstein* (1800), *Maria
Stuart* (1801), *Die Jungfrau von Orleans* (1802), *Die
Braut von Messina* (1803)—gave a new impetus that the
production of Fate Tragedies recommenced. Tieck's
example was now followed by Kind, whose *Schloß Aklam*
was planned in 1803, recast in 1804, and eventually
published as *Der Ministrel* ten years later, at the height
of the Fate Tragedy vogue. It was in 1803, too, that the
sequence of plays began to appear in which Werner
utilized the Fate motive, culminating in his genuine
Fate Tragedy *Der 24. Februar*, which was written, as is
well known, with Goethe's approval, and really set the
Fate Tragedy fashion. And in 1803 appeared Kleist's
Familie Schroffenstein, worth mentioning here because,
though not a Fate Tragedy proper, it does represent
human life as a 'Marionettenspiel' with Fate pulling the
strings, and therefore belongs to the same genus.

It can hardly be doubted that Klinger's two Medea dramas contributed to the genesis of the Fate Tragedy in at least the same general way as did *Iphigenie* and Schiller's experiments. In spite of the rather crude introduction of Fate in person they are by no means contemptible as literature. Their plots are sound; they contain effective scenes and good character drawing; Medea's killing of her children is led up to skilfully without making her appear either an inhuman monster or a savage—in fact she holds our sympathy throughout the two plays; and in *Medea auf dem Kaukasos* Klinger breaks away from Greek sources and shows his heroine inspired by a lofty humanitarian idealism: in spite of Fate's warning she renounces her supernatural status and powers, and finally herself falls a victim to Fate, in a vain attempt to civilize a primitive community whose religion is one of fear and human sacrifices. Klinger was, after all, one of the better as well as one of the better-known authors of his time, and these two dramas, like his *Damokles* (1788), were in line with the literary trend of the day—the change-over from Storm and Stress to modernized classicism. They were certainly known to Tieck,[1] are quite likely to have been known to Werner, were probably known to Grillparzer, and may well have been known to other writers of Fate Tragedies and similar works. The question therefore arises whether they did more than merely share in providing the general stimuli which called the Fate Tragedy into existence; whether they are remarkable enough or contributed anything definite enough to entitle them to special mention.

[1] E. H. Zeydel, in his *Ludwig Tieck, the German Romanticist* (Princeton University Press, 1935), shows (p. 19) that Tieck composed an early 'rhetorical Jason and Medea tragedy' in prose under the influence of Klinger's *Medea in Korinth*.

It seems to have been overlooked that Klinger's Medea dramas actually have more in common with the Fate Tragedies than have any of the other dramatic experiments with the Fate motive. Most of the features characteristic of or constantly recurring in the Fate Tragedies can be recognized (though some of them only in embryo) in Klinger's two plays. Even his introduction of Fate as a *dramatis persona* is worth noticing in this connexion. The most essential characteristic of the Fate Tragedies proper is, in fact, the treatment of Fate as a supernatural *dramatis persona*, an avenger of guilt, who, though unseen, lurks threatening in the background, awaits her opportunity, and when it comes ruthlessly destroys her victims. Klinger's 'Schicksal' plays almost exactly this role, except that she appears on the stage. She is, however, neither visible nor audible to the purely human characters; for them she is just as much an unseen and dreaded supernatural being as she is in the Fate Tragedies proper. In *Medea in Korinth* she opens the play with a speech beginning: 'Leise sei mein Gang; mein furchtbarer Tritt erweckt die Sterblichen aus dem sicheren Schlafe, in dem sie Wahn gefesselt hat. Schicksal nennen mich die armen Erdensöhne; sie geben Allem Namen, sie mögen's fassen oder nicht; nach ihrem beschränkten Sinne bin ich noch weit von ihnen, wenn ich schon auf ihrem Rücken würgend schwebe.' A little later comes the sentence: 'Arme Sterbliche! ihr reißt kein Glied aus der Kette, in welche ich euch eingeschmiedet habe'; and again: 'Spielt, Arme, euer Spiel; ich hülle mich in undurchdringlich Dunkel, stoß euch fort und fort und immer in den Wirbel fort.' The rest of the speech refers to the situation of Medea as well as of the purely human characters as objects of Aphrodite's vengeance, to their relations with each other, their guilt, and the sufferings they are destined to bring upon themselves. Fate herself does not appear again in *Medea in Korinth*, but her minions, the Eumenides, open and close the fifth act, in which they accuse and torture Jason and Kreon and carry them off to Erebus. In *Medea auf dem Kaukasos* she appears three times. She opens the first act, tells in general terms what is in store for Medea, and says: 'Bald wird ein täuschender Traum ihr Herz entflammen, und dann fange ich sie mit dem Netze, das ich um den Ball der Erde gezogen, und drücke sie unter mein eisernes Joch.' In the last scene of the same act she appears again, this time to participate in a small way in the action of the play. She warns Medea (whose descent from Helios raises her above the normal human plane and has so far placed her beyond Fate's reach) of the consequences of the vow she is about to take: a vow to renounce for ever her mysterious powers, and never again to use her magic against mankind; if she breaks this vow she too will become Fate's victim. And in the last scene of Act III she appears for the last time, when Medea has broken the vow, to remind her of the murders of which she has been guilty, and to announce that the Eumenides are already preparing to rise from Tartarus and fall upon her. From this point to the end of the fifth act only Medea's words depict how the Eumenides torment her till she kills herself.

The difference between Klinger's treatment of the Fate motive and that adopted by the writers of Fate Tragedies is attributable to the fact that while he had based his two Fate dramas on Greek legend, they chose more modern settings. He was the first to use Fate as a *dramatis persona*, and he went about it in the most obvious and direct way (for which he had no precedent even in Greek tragedy). But this way of his was clearly neither very effective nor at all applicable to tragedies set in medieval or modern milieus. His Medea dramas may, therefore, well have acted both as a stimulus and as a warning to Tieck and later dramatists experimenting with the Fate motive. Of these, Tieck first, and after him Werner and the other authors of Fate Tragedies did actually achieve with some success what Klinger had attempted less skilfully: they made Fate a *dramatis persona*, but they employed a more subtle technique, a technique of suggestion. Dreams, prophecies, and curses are fulfilled; one member after another of a doomed family perishes till the whole family is annihilated; death after death is caused by the same fateful weapon; disasters occur on the anniversary of a fateful date; and various devices (ghost appearances, descriptions of weather or scenery appropriate to the circumstances, gloomy introspective broodings and forebodings, &c.) are employed to produce an emotional atmosphere favourable to the reader's or spectator's surrender to the repeated suggestion that some supernatural force, Fate, is shaping man's destiny.

In the introduction of such features as these, however, and to some extent even in their employment to produce a suitable emotional atmosphere, the writers of the Fate Tragedies proper had again been anticipated by Klinger. The Greek legend on which he based his two tragedies involved the complete extermination of Jason's family, of Kreon's, and of Medea's except for Medea herself; Klinger, as we have seen, depicted the death of her too as a victim of Fate. It is of interest also, in view of the frequency with which the death of children of tender years recurs in the Fate Tragedies and kindred works (e.g. in Kleist's *Familie Schroffenstein*, Werner's *Der 24. Februar*, Müllner's *Der 29. Februar*, Houwald's *Das Bild*), to note that Klinger had deliberately and with considerable effect exploited this motive. In his hands the

two young sons of Jason and Medea are no mere lay
figures; they are well drawn; they differ both in age and
in temperament; their childish reactions and ways of
expressing themselves attract our interest; so that the
scene in which they are killed becomes all the more
moving. Not content with that, however, Klinger also
introduces repeated references to, and bewailings by
Medea's mother of, yet another child victim, an unnamed
infant in arms, 'der Säugling', who had perished of neglect
caused by his mother's grief at the death of her husband
and son when Medea betrayed them for Jason's sake.
It is difficult to believe that Klinger's example contributed
nothing to the later popularity of this motive.

Turning now to that group of favourite Fate Tragedy
motives comprising an ancestral curse, a fateful weapon, prophetic utterances, warning dreams, and ghost appearances,
we again find them all represented—some of them, it is true,
in simple or rudimentary form—in Klinger's two plays.

There is no ancestral curse; but in the Fate Tragedies
this was a modern romantic substitute for the classical
vengeance of an angry god; and this we do find as a
leading motive in Klinger's Medea dramas; there is
repeated mention of Aphrodite's wrath as the prime
cause of the destruction of Medea's and Jason's families,
the human victims of the goddess's feud with Helios,
from whom Medea's father traced his descent. There is
no fateful weapon; but the germ of this motive is there:
Medea kills her children with the dagger that slew her
brother. And, as in Tieck's *Karl von Berneck*, the weapon
is used on this second occasion to expiate the former
crime committed with it; for Medea acts under the
prompting of her mother's voice demanding vengeance
against Jason and offering to forgive Medea her former
guilt if she will do this deed. 'Versühne meines Lieblings

Absyrtos Blut durch das seine. Versühne mir den
schmachtenden Säugling, du raubtest dem Säugling die
Mutter, dem Bruder das Leben! Versühne meines Sohnes
Blut durch das seine, das in ihren Adern fließt!' says the
voice; and in its next speech: 'Diese Rache versühnt dir
deine Mutter!'; and again: 'Steige in den Erebos! zu
deiner Mutter! zu deinem Vater, den der Gram hinunter stieß! zu meinem Sohn, den dein Dolch hinunter
förderte! zu dem Säugling, nach deiner Flucht geboren,
den ich aus Schmerz verschmachten ließ. Ich will der
Schläfer Blut! Stoß in ihr Herz den Dolch!'

Prophetic utterances, put, as one would expect, into the
mouth of Fate herself, are well represented. Most of them
are in general terms: (with reference to Kreon) '[er] brütet
nur in Sorg und Angst das Ungeheuer früher aus, das
ihn erdrücken wird'; (referring to Jason and Medea) 'Ach,
der Wankelmüthige bereitet sich und seinen zarten
Söhnen schrecklich Weh. Schrecklicher Weh bereitet
sich die kühne Mörderin in der fernen Zukunft'; (addressing Medea) 'Wisse, unaussprechliche Qualen erwarten
dich'. But in one instance Fate foretells the future more
definitely. In the opening scene of *Medea in Korinth*
she explains the meaning of the words 'Bald wird ein
täuschender Traum ihr Herz entflammen' by saying:
'Thöricht wird sie sich den Menschen abermals vertrauen. In der Hoffnung, durch gute Thaten die bösen
zu versöhnen, wird sie in der süßen Täuschung nicht
fühlen, daß der schwache, blinde Sohn des Staubs
leichter auf das Böse als das Gute horcht. Rasch wird sie
vollziehen wollen, was in Jahrtausenden kaum reift', thus
prophesying the failure of Medea's attempt to civilize the
savages.—The warning dream motive occurs in a rudimentary form only. Fate says of Kreon: 'Furchtbare
Träume schickt Zeus dem grauen, sorgerfüllten Alten';

and Kreon himself says to Jason: 'Ich ahne Weh von
dem Morgen bis zum Abend; von meinem Lager jagen
mich böse Träume auf; Furcht vor der Zukunft füllt die
Gegenwart mit herber Angst.' This motive is, however,
not developed as in the Fate Tragedies, and in the *Braut
von Messina*, to serve as evidence of the intervention of
Destiny; such evidence would, of course, have been
redundant in Klinger's pieces.

Of the ghost motive, on the contrary, he makes full use,
both in its simplest form—when Medea sees, or thinks she
sees, the ghosts of her brother and the 'Säugling' shortly
before she murders her children—and in a more highly
developed form, the ghost voice of Medea's mother Hekate,
which has the part of an important *dramatis persona*.
In *Medea in Korinth* this voice takes a large share in the
dialogue of two of the scenes of Act IV. It upbraids Medea
for the deaths of her father, her brother, the babe in arms,
and Hekate herself; it goads her on to avenge these deaths,
expiate her guilt, and take revenge on Jason by killing
the children; and finally it rejoices savagely over the
accomplished vengeance. Essentially its role is that of the
ancestral ghost in *Karl von Berneck* and Grillparzer's
Ahnfrau, a spirit unable to rest until former crimes are
expiated by a final crime which completes the destruction
of the guilt-laden family. Tieck may well have derived
his use of the ghost motive, at any rate partly, from Klinger;
Grillparzer's use of it is still more like Klinger's, in that
his Ahnfrau, like Klinger's Hekate, intervenes positively
and effectively to complete the family annihilation. That
Grillparzer knew Klinger's Medea dramas when he wrote
his *Ahnfrau* is at any rate highly probable. In his *Der
Traum, ein Leben*, which in its origins belongs to almost
the same time as the *Ahnfrau*, he was certainly influenced
by Klinger's novel *Geschichte Giafars des Barmeciden*; and

he appears to have been influenced by Klinger a few years later in his treatment of Medea's murder of her children in his own *Medea* (1822). It therefore seems not unreasonable to suspect, in spite of the fact that he undoubtedly read many of the third-rate thrillers of the time, that his ghostly Ahnfrau may owe something, perhaps even the very conception of her general role, to 'Hekates Stimme' in *Medea in Korinth*.

We come finally to those devices in the Fate Tragedies used primarily to create a suitable emotional atmosphere, to induce in the spectator a 'Stimmung' receptive to suggestions or representations of the supernatural. Again we find that Klinger had pointed the way, though using these devices on the whole somewhat less persistently than is common in the Fate Tragedies; that is to say, using them freely, and often in combination, in some scenes, but little or not at all in others. His chief characters, like those of the Fate Tragedies, tend to be gloomily introspective, to brood over the past, and express forebodings of the future. Jason's first words, for instance, are: 'König von Korinth, schone meiner nicht. Ich bin nicht mehr jener Jason, einst der Argonauten stolzer Führer. Mit Scham gesteh' ich dir: Gram, des Mannes unwürdiger Feind, zehrt an meinem Innern'; and further examples might be quoted from his speeches. That Kreon has dark forebodings we have already seen. And many of Medea's speeches, especially her soliloquies, with their repeated mention of the 'düsterer Dämon', 'giftiger Dämon', 'wilder Geist', 'finstrer Geist' that besets her, provide further illustrations of this tendency.

Klinger's style, too, as is also the case in the Fate Tragedies, frequently contributes to the evoking of the required 'Stimmung'. This is especially noticeable in the speeches of Fate and the Eumenides, in the dialogues

between Medea and her mother's spirit, and in other
speeches by Medea when the semi-divine side of her
nature asserts itself; rhythmical cadence, lyrical phras-
ing, the recurrence at longer or shorter intervals of
touching or telling expressions, combine to exercise a
subtle influence beguiling the reader to accept more
easily the supernatural.

A third device employed by Klinger is the introduction
of instrumental music behind the scenes. In each of the
two plays one of the episodes in which the emotional
tension reaches a high point is accompanied by music.
In *Medea auf dem Kaukasos* this music, the 'wilde rau-
schende Musik, die nur aus blasenden Instrumenten
besteht' and the 'Klagemusik' of Act III (in which the
Druids attempt to carry out a human sacrifice) are introduced mainly for realistic effect. But in *Medea in Korinth*
its purpose is largely to induce 'Stimmung'. Act V opens
with the stage direction: 'Noch Nacht. Man hört in
Aphroditens Tempel Musik der Flöten und hochzeitliche
Lieder. . . . Gegen dem Tempel über liegen die Körper
der Jasoniden, mit einem Teppich bedeckt. Die Eumeniden treten aus dem Hain.' They demand vengeance
on the murderess of the children. As the scene proceeds
the direction 'Flöten und Gesang' recurs three times; and
when a procession, including Jason, Kreusa, and Kreon,
comes out from the temple there are two further stage
directions, separated by a few words from one of the
Eumenides: 'Die Musik dauert. Dann tritt der Zug aus
dem Tempel, mit Fackeln und Gesang. Jason, Kreusa,
Kreon folgen', and 'Die Eumeniden ziehen den Teppich
von den Leichen der Knaben weg und stehen zu ihrem
Haupte. Ein Schrei des Entsetzens Aller. Alles flieht,
außer den Dreien, die die Gewalt der Eumeniden fesselt.
Kreusa sinkt leblos auf die Stufen des Tempels nieder.

Die Scene wird von dem düstern Scheine der Fackeln der Eumeniden erleuchtet.' There is a good deal of similarity between this stage setting and that of the opening scene of Kleist's *Familie Schroffenstein* where, by torchlight, in the castle chapel, the choruses of youths and maidens, grouped round the corpse of a child assumed to have been murdered, chant their songs of lament and revenge to an accompaniment of music behind the scenes. And in Act V of Grillparzer's *Ahnfrau* there occurs another somewhat similar use of music. The background shows the exterior of the castle chapel by night, illuminated within. In it lies the body of Jaromir's father, killed by him, and the sound of music and chanting is heard. Jaromir climbs up to a window, and then describes what he has seen in a speech containing the lines:

> Und aus schwarzverhülltem Chor
> Wanden Töne sich empor,
> Die um Straf' und Rache baten
> Über ungeheure Taten.
> Und am öden Hochaltar,
> Ringsum eine Dienerschar,
> Lag, umstrahlt von dumpfen Kerzen,
> Eine Wunde auf dem Herzen,
> Weit geöffnet, blutig rot,
> Lag mein Vater bleich und tot.

In the other Fate Tragedies instrumental music is introduced for the most part merely for realistic effect or embellishment. In *Karl von Berneck*, for instance, 'Chöre von Musikanten blasen laut' and 'Die Pauken wirbeln, die Trompeten schmettern' at appropriate moments in the action; in *Die Schuld* the harp accompanies song, and the horns of a hunting party are heard; in Houwald's *Der Leuchtturm* we have again singing to the accompaniment of a harp. But sometimes it is used suggestively: in

Karl von Berneck the returning Walther's brief meeting
with the mysterious figure (the ancestral ghost) is interrupted by the stage direction 'Trompetengetümmel in der
Burg'; in *Die Schuld* and *Der Leuchtturm* the harp itself
is used to reinforce the other fatalistic suggestions: in
the opening scene of the former 'Eine Saite springt.
Elvire fährt erschrocken auf, die Harfe sinkt dröhnend
zu Boden', and in the final scene 'Sie sinkt sterbend auf
die Harfe zurück, die Hand gleitet dabei matt über die
Saiten, und man hört einen leisen verhallenden Ton'; in the
latter, during a soliloquy by the heroine, who has taken
over her father's duty, 'Man hört durch Sturmessausen
und durch das Getöse des Donners die Harfe klingen',
apparently in answer to her prayer for God's help to those
in peril on the sea, while later on the destruction of the
harp and the death of its owner are connected together.

Lastly, it is interesting to note that Klinger had already
made considerable use of the devices mentioned by
Hankamer as being more particularly Tieck's own
contribution to the characteristic features of the Fate
Tragedy. In his article in the *Reallexikon* he writes:

(Dadurch und) durch die Einbeziehung der Landschaft, Zeit
und Witterung als Stimmungsmittel wirkt Tieck auf Werner und
dadurch auf die späteren Dichter. Die Umwelt wird fast zum Mit-
spieler, wie Karl bekennt. Die Eroberung der sinnlichen Umwelt
als Schicksalsatmosphäre wird von nun an ein bezeichnender Zug
der Sch.; allerdings zeigt sich die Tendenz dazu aus gleicher Quelle
(dem Drama des Sturms und Drangs) wenigstens für die Zeit schon
bei Moritz, ohne aber die Landschaft einzubeziehen.

In fact, Klinger had shown the way in this direction too,
and much more comprehensively and intensively than
Moritz or any other Storm and Stress dramatist. In
Medea in Korinth the whole of Act IV, the act in which
Medea's mother appears to her and the children are killed,

has for its stage setting 'Ein düstrer Platz. Im Grunde ein Cypressenwald'; and the dialogue indicates the lighting and other effects required. Evening is closing in. Medea, at first the loving mother, speaks of the damp cold and noxious vapours that might harm her children during the dark night. When they have fallen asleep, her words show how the cypresses glow red in the sunset, how the sun is lost behind a cloud, and sinks, so that full night begins. After a pause she continues: 'Die Nacht, die Tochter des Chaos senkt sich hernieder. Ihr schwarzer Mantel verhüllt die unendliche Erde. Schärfer bläst der Wind durch den Baum, düstrer fühl' ich mich schon. Geheimer Schauder zittert durch die Natur, als sei sie ihrer Vernichtung nah. Dem Tartaros entsteigen die Eumeniden und fallen über die Schuldigen!' The supernatural side of her nature gains the upper hand, and when even the stars disappear she cries: 'Ha, in diesem schwarzen Dunkel fühl' ich mich ganz Medea! Durchbrochen haben meine finstren Kräfte!' and calls up her mother's spirit. When Jason's men come to take the children from her, all is dark and eerie sounds are heard. 'Es heult im Walde, ächzt in den Klüften Weh! Unweit heulen die Erinnen in ihrem furchtbaren Hain. Den Menschen ist nicht wohl in schwarzer Nacht', and 'Des Erebos Schwärze liegt auf der Erde; ich sehe nicht! Nun hör' ich ihren leisen Athem hier!' says one of the men. Later on Medea herself cannot see the children: 'Die dicke Nacht verbirgt sie mir', she tells Hekate. And the act closes with her words: 'Hier steh' ich im Dunkel der Nacht, fürchterlich groß!' In Act V it is still night time, as the stage direction indicates. A thunderstorm works up, prepared for by Kreon's words: 'Ach blase, Sturm aus Norden! Blase durch mein Gehirn, durch mein Herz, das die Erinnis umschlungen hat', and breaks in thunder

that interrupts a speech by Jason; whereupon he cries:
'Die Vernichtung rollet einher! Oeffne die Brust dem
verzehrenden Blitze! Schlage! zerschmettre! vernichte,
daß ich der Erinnis entfliehe!' *Medea auf dem Kaukasos*
opens with a romantic mountain landscape as its setting—
as does also Werner's *Der 24. Februar*, but in view of a
note in Werner's diary this may be a mere coincidence;
he had actually passed through Schwarrbach, 'das einer
Mörderhöhle ähnliche Schwarrbach', the scene of his
Fate Tragedy. Klinger's stage direction runs: 'Auf den
Höhen des Kaukasos. Im Grunde eine Felsenhöhle, mit
wildem Gesträuche umwachsen. Die ersten Strahlen der
Sonne erleuchten nach und nach die Scene.' As before,
the dialogue from time to time refers to this setting in
such phrases as: 'In jener düsteren Felsenhöhle trauert
sie ihr einsames Leben hin' and 'Sie floh aus Korinth auf
diese nackten Felsen des Kaukasos'. And in the third
scene the superstitious coupling of destructive natural
phenomena with the anger of a god is illustrated by the
Chief Druid, who, taking Medea for a deity, describes
the havoc wrought by the storms, floods, earthquakes, and
drought he believes her to have sent down upon his
people. In Act II the stage scenery again makes an appeal
to the spectator's romantic and superstitious emotions:
'Ein großer mit Bäumen besetzter Platz. In der tiefen
Ferne wird man rohe, zerstreute Hütten gewahr. Im
Grund ein großer Altar, der aus einem einzigen rohen
Felsen besteht. Auf demselben liegt ein Mordhammer,
zum Opfer bestimmt.' Act III, in which the Druids
attempt to carry out their human sacrifice, but are foiled
by Medea's intervention, again takes place by night, a
night quite dark at first, with moonlight later. In his first
speech the Chief Druid says: 'Bald wird der Mond an
jenem dunkeln Wolkensaum hervorglänzen; diese ist

die Stunde des nächtlichen Opfers!' Shortly afterwards
the moon does shine out; the Chief Druid begins the
sacrificial ceremony by a prayer to a god whom he
addresses as 'Würger! Zerstörer! Furchtbarer! Namen-
loser!' and again describes the destruction by natural
forces which he ascribes to the god's wrath. Medea,
however, determined to prevent the sacrifice, makes a
last use of her supernatural powers. In a speech too long
to quote in full she says: 'Herauf aus dem Tartaros,
Dämonen, Geister der Nacht! Hervor, alle meine zer-
störenden Kräfte! rüstet euch zur Rache! Gürtet euch
zur Vernichtung! Schwingt zu den schwarzen Wolken
der Stürme empor, entreißt ihnen die verzehrenden
Blitze, daß ich meine Hände fülle und noch einmal
jauchze in Vernichtung—Hekate! Hekate! düstre
Mutter, steige herauf mit all den Ermordeten . . . .
Der Erebos bewegt sich, sie fahren herauf; die blassen
Schatten rauschen durch die Wipfel der Tannen. Mein
Zauber beweget die Erde, rollet die Wolken, rollet die
Wogen des Meers.—Auf! blase, Sturm! heulet, tobende
Winde! Medea gebietet! Hülle dich in Schrecken,
Natur!', and so on. The dialogue and stage directions
continue to show how the moon is alternately clear and
overclouded, while the wind howls and the storm comes
on, until, at the very moment when the Druid is about
to slay the victim, Medea 'schleudert Blitze auf den
Priester und den Altar'; 'Der opfernde Priester fällt
erstarrt nieder. Der Felsenaltar zerspringt in Trümmer.
Das Feuer bricht unter ihm hervor. Schrecken und
Beben. Sausen und Heulen. Geschrei.'

. . . . . .

Of all the German forerunners of the Fate Tragedies
proper Klinger's two Medea dramas are—along with
Iphigenie, which appeared after the one but before the

other—the earliest of consequence as works of considerable literary merit. Lessing's *Das Horoskop* is only a fragment; Moritz's *Blunt, oder der Gast* is a trashy production
of hardly any interest beyond the fact that by its plot it
provides a link between Lillo's *Fatal Curiosity* and Werner's
Der 24. Februar. Besides being the earliest, they are by far
the most noteworthy on account of the extent to which
they anticipate or foreshadow so many of the characteristic
features of the Fate Tragedies. Not even Schiller's *Braut
von Messina*, however much more strongly it may have
acted as a stimulus, shows so many points of similarity with
the Fate Tragedies as do *Medea in Korinth* and *Medea auf
dem Kaukasos*. In their representation of Fate as a *dramatis
persona* waiting in the background (so far as the merely
human actors are concerned) as an inexorable and ruthless
avenger of guilt, in many of their motives, and in their
technique, these two plays come nearer than any others to
being Fate Tragedies themselves. If Klinger had kept
Fate and the Eumenides off the stage they would have
been the first two Fate Tragedies in the narrower sense.

In view of the many other factors which contributed
to the appearance and cult of the Fate Tragedy proper,
and of the many other sources (the Greek drama, Shakespeare, the Storm and Stress drama, Romantic fiction, &c.)
which might have provided the writers of these tragedies
with inspiration and with motives and technique such
as are used by Klinger, it is impossible to assess con-
fidently his contribution to the later developments. But it
seems reasonable to conclude that his influence was in fact
very considerable, passing first to Tieck, and from him—as
well as directly—to Werner and the others; originating
or encouraging the use of certain types of motive and
technique and occasionally suggesting effective detailed
treatment of individual episodes.

THE GENESIS OF SCHILLER'S THEORY
OF TRAGEDY

By E. L. STAHL

IN the present undertaking no attempt is made to give
a new interpretation of Schiller's theory of tragedy,
beyond establishing the genesis of his ideas. If it may for
this reason seem superfluous, mention must be made of
the tendencies at the present time to re-interpret Schiller's
dramas by abstracting from his theories or at least
stressing them as little as possible.[1] Other conceptions
of tragedy are adopted in this process of revaluation,
leading to complete condemnation or only partial appreciation of Schiller's dramas, according to the measure of
agreement with the conceptions adopted. Schiller's theory
is thus rejected as the product of a merely intellectual
exercise and as of no considerable importance in a definition of his real *Weltanschauung*, which is determined from
a reading of the dramas only.

It is certainly true that theories can vary in importance
in the work of a poet and must be valued accordingly

[1] Cf. notably G. Fricke, 'Die Problematik des Tragischen im Drama
Schillers', *Jahrb. d. Freien Deut. Hochstifts*, 1930, pp. 3–69; H. Gumbel,
'Die realistische Wendung des späten Schiller', ibid., 1932/3, pp. 131–
62; W. Deubel, 'Umrisse eines neuen Schillerbildes', *Jahrb. d. Goethe-
Gesellschaft*, 1934, pp. 1–64. For a similar tendency cf. H. Rempel,
'Tragödie und Komödie im dramatischen Schaffen Lessings', *Neue
Forschung*, xxvi, 1935. There is much in these essays that is unusually
suggestive and stimulating. Disagreement with their general tendencies
must nevertheless be expressed, except in the case of Gumbel, who does
not underestimate the significance of Schiller's theoretical pronouncements
and avoids the pitfall of one-sidedness, while offering valuable new interpretations. It is only his view of Schiller's conception of Fate that cannot
be fully accepted.

in any attempt to interpret them. Theory can be mere speculation on intellectual or aesthetic matters. Much of the theory of tragedy as developed in the *Hamburgische Dramaturgie* is of this kind, because Lessing was not always so concerned to give his own definition of tragedy, as to expound Aristotle. Even so, however, the principles of his philosophy are not altogether absent from his observations.[1] To disregard them in an interpretation of his dramas would lead to many errors.

This principle of interpretation must be urged even more strongly for any examination of Schiller's tragedy, in view of present-day tendencies. Schiller's theory is essentially not speculation, but the expression of his *Weltanschauung*. It would be misleading to disregard the fact that preoccupation with theoretical problems was of formative value to him, not merely as an artist. When he incorporated Kant's conception of sublimity in his definition of tragedy, he did so for no external, intellectual reasons. The philosophy of Kant did not influence him in an exoteric manner. Schiller had been prepared for it from his own development before he came into contact with it. He accepted philosophical categories and principles without having in the first place a philosophical interest in them. The *Kritik der Urteilskraft* remained the basis of his indebtedness to Kant, and he always left aside what did not come within his proper scope. It is therefore unjust to deny to Schiller what is so readily granted to Hebbel, and to reject his theoretical work as 'insignificant for his drama'. Not that the dramas should be entirely or even mainly interpreted from the theory; as works of art they have a life of their own. But when the theory is left out of account altogether, the interpretation is prone to become historically distorted and purely subjective.

[1] Cf. especially Stück 79.

The aesthetic theory of poets of the eighteenth century like Lessing and Schiller is as important a feature of their *Weltanschauung* as are their views on religious and philosophical problems. To deny the value of the theories in Schiller's *Die ästhetische Erziehung des Menschen* for the rest of his work, is to fail to distinguish between productive and reproductive criticism. Schiller's criticism is productive in a very complete sense, creative criticism. He laid the foundation of his own classical tragedy by pondering the theory of tragedy generally.

In Schiller's theory of tragedy there are several noticeable stages of development. It will be seen that his theory in its final form is a synthesis of elements from Lessing and Kant. In effect, however, it is an original view, expressing his own attitude to life. It was not until he had evolved this theory that he felt free to return to the production of drama. Nevertheless, it cannot be said that there was a complete cessation of interest in the creative production of drama during his philosophical period. There are changes of outlook in the body of his classical drama, which can be linked chronologically with the changes in his theoretical pronouncements. It is therefore reasonable to assume that Schiller was working out his theory of tragedy with intimate reference to his own dramatic plans. He did not evolve his theory in an aesthetic void, though complete and constant preoccupation with the production of drama did follow upon the philosophical period. The rapid manner in which he wrote his classical plays would indicate that there had been some previous conceptual shaping of the material. This is borne out by the genesis of the plays, as far as it can be traced.

In the following pages the main stress will be laid on the development of Schiller's theory of tragedy against the background of certain aspects of his *Weltanschauung*. The problems involved cannot be dealt with in any detail, nor can the application be made to an interpretation of the tragedies.

.   .   .   .   .   .

By comparison, Schiller's pronouncements on the nature and purpose of tragedy in his pre-classical period are less important for a proper understanding of his creative work, than those belonging to his classical period. They are more apologetic of his already published work than preparatory for future dramas. He is also at first seen to be more obviously dependent on the views of others (notably Corneille, Diderot, and Sulzer). This is true, however, in a comparative sense only, for there are certain views even in these early writings, which are fundamental to Schiller's nature and can be said to have been fully expressed only at the height of his classical period.

Such are above all his views on the educative value of art, which according to Schiller even at this stage, effects in us a harmony of our intellectual and sensual natures. *Die Schaubühne als eine moralische Anstalt betrachtet* contains the following statement:[1]

Unsre Natur, gleich unfähig, länger im Zustande des Tiers fortzudauern, als die feinern Arbeiten des Verstandes fortzusetzen, verlangte einen mittleren Zustand, der beide widersprechende Enden vereinigte, die harte Spannung zu sanfter Harmonie herabstimmte und den wechselweisen Übergang eines Zustandes in den andern erleichterte. Diesen Nutzen leistet überhaupt nun der ästhetische Sinn oder das Gefühl für das Schöne. (xi. 89.)

This view is the theme of the *Briefe über die ästhetische Erziehung des Menschen* and, with reference to tragedy, of *Über das Erhabene.*

---

[1] References are to *Schiller's Sämtliche Werke*, Säkularausgabe, vols. xi, xii, xvi.

In the early period, however, this principle is not stated in its later purity. It is linked with another thought, which could have been called antiquated even at that date, since Lessing had denied its validity in the *Hamburgische Dramaturgie*. This is the view that tragedy effects its moral purpose by teaching a direct lesson. The dramatist is said to warn his spectators against the particular aberrations displayed by his characters. Schiller justifies his first tragedies by the immediate moral effect which they are intended to produce, and thus he can defend the introduction of criminals and the depiction of vice in his tragedies:

Wer sich den Zweck vorgezeichnet hat, das Laster zu stürzen und Religion, Moral und bürgerliche Gesetze an ihren Feinden zu rächen, ein solcher muß das Laster in seiner nackten Abscheulichkeit enthüllen und in seiner kolossalischen Größe vor das Auge der Menschheit stellen. (xvi. 15; cf. xi. 91.)

The choice of criminal instead of virtuous heroes is also justified from the true nature of drama, which must have labyrinthine complications. Schiller argues that

im Schicksal des großen Rechtschaffenen, nach der reinsten Moral, durchaus kein Knoten, kein Labyrinth stattfindet, daß sich seine Werke und Schicksale notwendiger Weise zu voraus bekannten Zielen lenken, welche beim ersten (sc. der erhabene Verbrecher) zu ungewissen Zielen durch krumme Mäander sich schlängeln (ein Umstand, der in der dramatischen Kunst alles ausmacht).
(xvi. 24.)

Crime running its tortuous course is thus the theme of tragedy. But such crime must be of a 'certain magnitude', the criminal must be 'sublime'. In this connexion there exists a difference between Schiller's earlier and his later periods. In the first period it is forcefulness and not goodness that is the mark of sublimity. Sublimity is shown more in tragic conflict than, as later, in tragic

redemption. There is an implicit difference between the
conceptions of morality and sublimity, which later, under
the influence of Kant, merge into one concept. In the
earlier period the hero embodies the moral principle only
negatively, so that it is the purpose of tragedy to arouse
pity and *terror* ('Rührung und Schrecken', xi. 93). When
sublimity is defined in terms of morality, the hero becomes
a direct and positive exponent of the moral principle, and
the purpose of tragedy is to arouse pity and *admiration*.

This difference is connected with the change which
Schiller underwent in Bauerbach and Dresden. In its
widest implications it is a change of philosophic outlook,
which we may define in terms of optimism and pessimism,
distinguishing with Schiller between the universe and
our human world. In his first period Schiller identified
himself with the view which interpreted the universe as
governed and harmoniously organized by one divine
principle, Love. This old belief, Neo-Platonic in origin,
is frequently found in English and German philosophy
in the seventeenth and eighteenth centuries, and no less
in the poetry of both ages and countries. It recurs, for
example, with particular frequency in German Baroque
poetry and is also found in Bürger's poem 'Die Nachtfeier
der Venus'. It is the basis of Schiller's early philosophy
and is best expressed in his lyric poetry at that time:

> Sonnenstäubchen paart mit Sonnenstäubchen
>   Sich in trauter Harmonie,
> Sphären ineinander lenkt die Liebe,
>   Weltsysteme dauern nur durch sie.
>
> Tilge sie vom Uhrwerk der Naturen —
>   Trümmernd aus einander springt das All,
> In das Chaos donnern eure Welten,
>   Weint, Newtone, ihren Riesenfall!
>
> *(Phantasie an Laura.)*

In contrast to this optimistic view of the organization of the universe, there exists in Schiller's early (as indeed in much of his later) work the well-known pessimistic interpretation of life in our human world. But in spite of occasional melancholic reflections on the theme of death, this pessimistic view applies to our social and physical existence, our 'material' fate only, and not to our ultimate destiny. It is important to point out this distinction here, in view of possible changes of outlook in the last stages of Schiller's development and of certain trends in the nineteenth century. At the same time the differences between the pre-classical and the classical periods of Schiller in this connexion must not be obscured. In both eras his optimism subsists and determines the moral purpose of drama, but not without considerable modifications, as far as the principle and the dramatist's work are concerned.

In his early period Schiller requires the dramatist to demonstrate the ultimate harmony and justice, which are designed, but are patently lacking in this world. His work must be a theodicy. This is clearly stated in *Über das gegenwärtige teutsche Theater* (xi. 84):

Wir Menschen stehen vor dem Universum wie die Ameise vor einem majestätischen Palaste. Es ist ein ungeheueres Gebäude, unser Insektenblick verweilet auf *diesem* Flügel und findet vielleicht *diese* Säulen, *diese* Statuen übel angebracht; das Auge eines bessern Wesens umfaßt auch den gegenüberstehenden Flügel und nimmt dort Statuen und Säulen gewahr, die ihren Kamerädinnen hier symmetrisch entsprechen. Aber der Dichter male für Ameisenaugen und bringe auch die andere Hälfte in unsern Gesichtskreis verkleinert herüber; er bereite uns von der Harmonie des Kleinen auf die Harmonie des Großen, von der Symmetrie des Teils auf die Symmetrie des Ganzen und lasse uns letztere in der ersteren bewundern. Ein Versehen in diesem Punkt ist eine Ungerechtigkeit gegen das ewige Wesen, das nach dem unendlichen Umriß der Welt, nicht nach einzelnen herausgehobenen Fragmenten beurteilt sein will.

There is a discrepancy between Schiller's theory and his practice of tragedy at this time, if we accept his views literally. As love is held to be the determining force in the universe, it is the triumph of this force that we should expect to admire in tragedy. This observation is made only in order to point out the divergent tendencies in Schiller's early speculation. No strict coherence can be claimed for his fortuitous theoretical pronouncements at this stage. The experiences which effected in him the change towards classicism, also produced greater speculative accuracy, as a result of which his interpretation of the universe was revised. At the same time the subjective and emotional basis of his previous attitude tends to disappear. Finally, though the relation between optimism and pessimism in his thought remains the same as before, the accents are placed quite differently. This change, now to be briefly described, has important results for his theory of tragedy.

Under the critical influence of Körner, Schiller begins to modify his attempt to discover the organizing principle of the universe. In the earlier sections of the *Philosophische Briefe* love is still seen to be a cosmic principle:

> Die Anziehung der Elemente brachte die körperliche Form der Natur zustande. Die Anziehung der Geister, ins Unendliche vervielfältigt und fortgesetzt, müßte endlich zu Aufhebung jener Trennung führen, oder (darf ich es aussprechen, Raphael?) Gott hervorbringen. Eine solche Anziehung ist die Liebe. (xi. 127.)

In the last letter Körner's influence is evident. Raphael points out to Julius that the true nature of the universe cannot be discovered by man:

> Das Universum ist kein *reiner* Abdruck eines Ideals, wie das vollendete Werk eines menschlichen Künstlers. (xi. 137.)

The interpretation of the universe by means of the principle of love is clearly one that originates in subjective personal feeling. In an age that was gradually finding its way to an objective view of the world, such theories became suspect. Schiller's classical period therefore begins with his abandoning subjective philosophical and poetical principles. He renounces his earlier cosmic speculation and substitutes the presentation of objective reality, not, however, without a new idealistic basis of transcendental morality.

There is at first an intermediate stage, seen in the ode *An die Freude*:

> Freude heißt die starke Feder
> In der ewigen Natur.
> Freude, Freude treibt die Räder
> In der großen Weltenuhr.
> Blumen lockt sie aus den Keimen,
> Sonnen aus dem Firmament,
> Sphären rollt sie in den Räumen,
> Die des Sehers Rohr nicht kennt.

Joy is a less subjective principle than love, but it is not an objective one, because it is still founded on personal feeling. The change is complete only when Reason becomes the link between man and the universe, as in the philosophical essays. With the disappearance of subjective personal feeling as the basis of cosmic speculation, and the moderation of the earlier attitude of indignation, the purpose of art is defined in less extravagant terms, though essentially it is the same as before. The new position becomes clear when we compare the following statement from the essay *Über die tragische Kunst* with the passage from *Über das gegenwärtige teutsche Theater* quoted above:

Die Kunst erfüllt ihren Zweck durch Nachahmung der Natur, indem sie die Bedingungen erfüllt, unter welchen das Vergnügen in der Wirklichkeit möglich wird, und die zerstreuten Anstalten der Natur nach einem verständigen Plan vereinigt, um das, was diese bloß zu ihrem Nebenzweck machte, als letzten Zweck zu erreichen. (xi. 161.)

The use of *Universum* on the one hand and of *Natur* on the other, constitutes one sign of the change. Another is the importance of the pleasurable quality of poetry for Schiller in his classical period. Poetry is intended to please no less than instruct.[1] The pleasurable quality of poetry is, however, no contradiction of its moral purpose. The pleasure which we derive from poetry, particularly from tragedy, is in itself ethical. Schiller can maintain this to be the case, because he thinks of the hero as a sublime figure in his newer sense. In the course of the tragedy, sublimity is seen in action; this gives us moral pleasure. The end of tragedy is not catastrophe, but redemption. True tragic pleasure is aroused by a display of human suffering followed by an act of human 'freedom'.

Schiller develops this 'classical' conception of the nature and purpose of tragedy in his essays *Über das Pathetische* and *Über das Erhabene*. Before he reached his final conclusions (if we are to regard them as such), basing his views on the teaching of Kant, he passed through a stage at which Lessing's doctrines noticeably influenced him. The influence is clearly seen in two essays: *Über den Grund des Vergnügens an tragischen Gegenständen* and *Über die tragische Kunst*.

The definition which Schiller gives in the latter essay is as follows:

Die Tragödie wäre demnach dichterische Nachahmung einer zusammenhängenden Reihe von Begebenheiten (einer vollständigen Handlung), welche uns Menschen in einem Zustand des Leidens zeigt und zur Absicht hat, unser Mitleid zu erregen. (xi. 173.)

[1] Cf. especially the essays *Über den Grund des Vergnügens an tragischen Gegenständen* and *Über die tragische Kunst*.

The agreement with Lessing is clear. In the *Hamburgische Dramaturgie* (77. Stück) Lessing states that 'die Tragödie, mit einem Worte, ein Gedicht ist, welches Mitleid erreget'. Schiller in much the same way as Lessing defines tragedy by its purpose—to arouse pity and pity only.[1] Even the form of tragedy is explained by both from this purpose. Schiller:

Wenn der Zweck der Tragödie ist, den mitleidigen Affekt zu erregen, ihre Form aber das Mittel ist, durch welches sie diesen Zweck erreicht, so muß Nachahmung einer rührenden Handlung der Inbegriff aller Bedingungen sein, unter welchen der mitleidige Affekt am stärksten erregt wird. Die Form der Tragödie ist also die günstigste, um den mitleidigen Affekt zu erregen. (xi. 178.)

Lessing:

Aristoteles bemerkte, ... daß es ... notwendig sei, die Handlung, durch welche wir Mitleid erregen wollen, nicht als vergangen, das ist, nicht in der erzählenden Form, sondern als gegenwärtig, das ist, in der dramatischen Form, nachzuahmen.

The differences between Lessing and Schiller are no less important. The former adhered to Aristotle's definition of tragedy by interpreting the final purpose of tragedy as a catharsis. He retained the element of fear in the constitution of the tragic economy, though he made fear an integral component of tragic pity. Pity and fear are the instruments as well as the ends of the ultimate cathartic purpose of tragedy: 'Mitleid und Furcht sind die Mittel, welche die Tragödie braucht, um ihre Absicht zu erreichen.' 'In diesem ganzen Umfange soll das Mitleid und die Furcht, welche die Tragödie erweckt, unser Mitleid und unsere Furcht reinigen; aber auch nur diese reinigen und keine andere Leidenschaften' (77. Stück).

[1] In his review of Goethe's *Egmont* Schiller had maintained that the arousing of 'Furcht und Mitleid' was the 'letzte Zweck der Tragödie' (xvi. 180).

Though it was Lessing's tendency to identify the purpose of tragedy with the arousing of pity only, his respect for Aristotle led him to retain the notion of fear and thus save the rider on catharsis, in this way making of pity an instrument as well as an aim. Schiller at this time did not share Lessing's reverence for the Aristotelian word. He could thus resolutely abandon the idea of catharsis and with it the notion of fear and postulate the arousing of pity (and pity only) as the true purpose of tragedy. It will be seen that he adopts these notions later, though in a much altered form.

There is in Schiller's definition another thought not found in Lessing's. Tragedy, according to Schiller, is the imitation of an event which presents 'Menschen in einem Zustand des Leidens'. The difference between Lessing and Schiller here is a very decided one. The idea that tragedy presents a picture of human suffering colours the meaning of the term pity itself, which both prominently stress. A large part of Schiller's essay is in fact concerned with the definition of the connexion between tragic suffering and pity. This theme is also dealt with in Schiller's earlier treatise *Über den Grund des Vergnügens an tragischen Gegenständen*, to which reference is made in *Über die tragische Kunst*. Our pleasure in a tragic spectacle is proper only when the suffering presented and the pity thereby aroused, have a *moral* basis:

Dies tut vorzugsweise die Tragödie, und ihr Gebiet umfaßt alle mögliche Fälle, in denen irgend eine Naturzweckmäßigkeit einer moralischen, oder auch eine moralische Zweckmäßigkeit der andern, die höher ist, aufgeopfert wird. (xi. 146.)

The purpose of tragedy, to arouse pity, is thus interpreted in a very different way from that of Lessing in the *Hamburgische Dramaturgie*. The moral issue which Kant had stated is now included in the interpretation. Tragedy must present the spectacle of a man sacrificing his life for a higher purpose. But Kant's principle of sublimity, which Schiller is here seen to introduce into the theory of tragedy, appears imperfectly as yet, because the full meaning of the sublime act is not clearly stated. For the time being he combines it with Lessing's principle of pity. Only in the later essays can sublimity be said to have become the dominant theme of Schiller's theory of tragedy. Before discussing these essays, the effect of his transitional point of view on some other elements of tragedy must be considered, particularly with reference to the earlier attitude.

In the essay *Über das Vergnügen an tragischen Gegenständen* the criminal is still seen to be the better subject for tragic treatment:

Ob der Tugendhafte sein Leben freiwillig dahingibt, um dem Sittengesetz gemäß zu handeln—oder ob der Verbrecher unter dem Zwange des Gewissens sein Leben mit eigner Hand zerstört, um die Übertretung jenes Gesetzes an sich zu bestrafen, so steigt unsre Achtung für das Sittengesetz zu einem gleich hohen Grad empor; und, wenn ja noch ein Unterschied stattfände, so würde er vielmehr zum Vorteil des letztern ausfallen, da das beglückende Bewußtsein des Rechthandelns dem Tugendhaften seine Entschließung doch einigermaßen konnte erleichtert haben und das sittliche Verdienst an einer Handlung gerade um ebenso viel abnimmt, als Neigung und Lust daran Anteil haben. Reue und Verzweiflung über ein begangenes Verbrechen zeigen uns die Macht des Sittengesetzes nur später, nicht schwächer; es sind Gemälde der erhabensten Sittlichkeit, nur in einem gewaltsamen Zustand entworfen. (xi. 149.)

This view is not very different from that which Schiller held in his first period. Only a little later, however, in the essay *Über die tragische Kunst* it is being modified. The moral interpretation of tragic suffering now leads

naturally to the rejection of criminal qualities as the
chief cause of tragic suffering:

Ein Dichter, der sich auf seinen wahren Vorteil versteht, wird
das Unglück nicht durch einen bösen Willen, der Unglück
beabsichtigt, noch viel weniger durch einen Mangel des Verstandes,
sondern durch den Zwang der Umstände herbeiführen. Entspringt dasselbe nicht aus moralischen Quellen, sondern von
äußerlichen Dingen, die weder Willen haben, noch einem Willen
unterworfen sind, so ist das Mitleid reiner und wird zum wenigsten
durch keine Vorstellung moralischer Zweckwidrigkeit geschwächt.
Aber dann kann dem teilnehmenden Zuschauer das unangenehme
Gefühl einer Zweckwidrigkeit in der Natur nicht erlassen werden,
welche in diesem Fall allein die moralische Zweckmäßigkeit retten
kann. Zu einem weit höhern Grad steigt das Mitleid, wenn
sowohl derjenige, welcher leidet, als derjenige, welcher Leiden
verursacht, Gegenstände desselben werden. . . . Diese Gattung
des Rührenden wird noch von derjenigen übertroffen, wo die
Ursache des Unglücks nicht allein nicht der Moralität wider-
sprechend, sondern sogar durch Moralität allein möglich ist, und
wo das wechselseitige Leiden bloß von der Vorstellung herrührt,
daß man Leiden erweckte. (xi. 163, 4.)

Schiller's tendency in this period to exonerate both the
world and his hero of tragic guilt, is here evident in his
theory. Above all he does not wish tragic suffering,
though based on force of circumstances, to derive from
any fated order of things. 'Zwang der Umstände' points
to no belief on the part of Schiller in any 'pantragic'
system. Fate in his estimation ranks with the physical
forces ('Naturkräfte', xi. 146) and man submitting to fate
lacks the sublimity and independence which is now the
mark of the tragic hero: 'Eine blinde Unterwürfigkeit
unter das Schicksal (ist) immer demütigend und kränkend
für freie, sich selbst bestimmende Wesen'. (xi. 165.)

In addition to the spectacle of suffering, the display of
such moral superiority to physical forces, the assertion

of sublime will-power is the central theme of tragedy
according to Schiller's later essays: *Über das Pathetische,
Vom Erhabenen, Über das Erhabene*. The hero's *resistance*
to the source of his suffering has become an increasingly
important feature of the tragic art. Suffering is now a
mere means to the end of tragedy, which is the display
of sublimity in action, moral independence and freedom
in distress:

Darstellung des Leidens—als bloßen Leidens—ist niemals
Zweck der Kunst, aber als Mittel zu ihrem Zweck ist sie derselben
äußerst wichtig. Der letzte Zweck der Kunst ist die Darstellung
des Übersinnlichen, und die tragische Kunst insbesondere bewerk-
stelligt dieses dadurch, daß sie uns die moralische Independenz von
Naturgesetzen im Zustand des Affekts versinnlicht. Nur der
Widerstand, den es gegen die Gewalt der Gefühle äußert, macht
das freie Prinzip in uns kenntlich. (xi. 246.)

Die beiden Fundamentalgesetze aller tragischen Kunst. Diese
sind erstlich: Darstellung der leidenden Natur; zweitens: Darstellung der moralischen Selbständigkeit im Leiden. (xii. 320.)

A sublime act, i.e. the choice of duty in preference to
inclination, is one that best reveals human freedom:

Wir fühlen uns frei beim Erhabenen, weil die sinnlichen Triebe
auf die Gesetzgebung der Vernunft keinen Einfluß haben, weil
der Geist hier handelt, als ob er unter keinen andern als seinen
eigenen Gesetzen stünde. (xii. 268.)

There are two ways in which man can display his moral
freedom:

Entweder mittelbar und nach dem Gesetz der Freiheit, wenn
er aus Achtung für irgend eine Pflicht das Leiden *erwählt*. Die
Vorstellung der Pflicht bestimmt ihn in diesem Falle als *Motiv*, und
sein Leiden ist eine *Willenshandlung*. Oder unmittelbar und nach
dem Gesetz der Notwendigkeit, wenn er eine übertretene Pflicht
moralisch *büßt*. Die Vorstellung der Pflicht bestimmt ihn in
diesem Falle als Macht, und sein Leiden ist bloß eine Wirkung.
(xi. 264.)

Schiller's classical tragedies (with the exception of *Wallenstein* and *Wilhelm Tell*) are written according to the second alternative: suffering is consequent upon an act of guilt, which is redeemed by a deed of self-sacrifice. This has important consequences for the choice of the hero. He cannot be a morally perfect man. Schiller returns to a defence of the criminal. He is the fittest subject for tragic treatment, because in his case the purpose of tragedy, the display of moral freedom, can be realized most impressively:

Offenbar kündigen Laster, welche von Willensstärke zeugen, eine größere Anlage zur wahrhaften moralischen Freiheit an als Tugenden, die eine Stütze von der Neigung entlehnen, weil es dem konsequenten Bösewicht nur einen einzigen Sieg über sich selbst, eine einzige Umkehrung von Maximen kostet, um die ganze Konsequenz von Willensfertigkeit, die er an das Böse verschwendete, dem Guten zuzuwenden. (xi. 273. Cf. *Vom Erhabenen*, xii. 270.)

'Moral' pity is still the primary emotion which tragedy must arouse. But important qualifications are made. The principle of resistance demands that pity should border neither on compassion nor on abhorrence.

Die schmelzenden Affekte, die bloß zärtlichen Rührungen, gehören zum Gebiet des Angenehmen, mit dem die schöne Kunst nichts zu tun hat (xi. 250).[1]

Auf der andern Seite sind aber auch alle diejenigen Grade des Affekts ausgeschlossen, die den Sinn bloß quälen, ohne zugleich den Geist dafür zu entschädigen. Sie unterdrücken die Gemütsfreiheit durch Schmerz nicht weniger als jene durch Wollust und können deswegen bloß Verabscheuung und keine Rührung bewirken, die der Kunst würdig wäre. (xi. 251.)

We can take this to mean that neither tearfulness nor terror should be aroused. Terror is no proper tragic

---

[1] Cf. Letter to Goethe 18. 6. 1799: 'Meine Maria wird keine weiche Stimmung erregen; es ist meine Absicht nicht.'

emotion to Schiller as to Lessing. There is, however, in
the impression which tragedy makes on us, a basis of *fear*.
Schiller in his previous essays had taken no account of
this emotion, confining his attention to pity. Now fear
returns as a necessary constituent of tragic emotion. It
returns in the theory of tragedy, because it is an element
contained in the experience of the sublime. Sublimity is
manifested only where objects of fear exist. But this does
not mean that fear is an emotion immediately to be aroused
and maintained. It must be aroused only to be conquered:
the resistance and independence of man in distress is
precisely the conquest of that which is the object of his
suffering or his fear. To be sublime man must be seen to
fear physically and triumph morally:

So eine wesentliche Erfordernis es dazu (zum Begriff des
Erhabenen) ist, daß wir uns als Sinnenwesen von dem Gegenstand
abhängig fühlen, so wesentlich gehört auf der andern Seite dazu,
daß wir uns als Vernunftwesen von demselben unabhängig fühlen.
Wo das erste nicht ist, wo der Gegenstand gar nichts Furchtbares
für unsre Sinnlichkeit hat, da ist keine Erhabenheit möglich. Wo
das zweite fehlt, wo er *bloß* furchtbar ist, wo wir uns ihm als
Vernunftwesen nicht überlegen fühlen, da ist sie ebenso wenig
möglich. Innre Gemütsfreiheit gehört schlechterdings dazu, um
das Furchtbare erhaben zu finden und Wohlgefallen daran zu
haben; denn es kann ja bloß dadurch erhaben sein, daß es unsre
Unabhängigkeit, unsre Gemütsfreiheit zu empfinden gibt. Nun
hebt aber die wirkliche und ernstliche Furcht alle Gemütsfreiheit
auf. Das erhabene Objekt muß also zwar furchtbar sein, aber
wirkliche Furcht darf es nicht erregen. (xii. 301; cf. xii. 275.)

Such objects of fear are death (xii. 304) and our fate
in this world. At this stage therefore Schiller again
expresses the pessimistic view of his first period. He
speaks of the 'Abfall der Natur' and the 'Tücke der
Verhängnisse'. But once again the necessary counterpart
to such pessimism is reassurance as far as our human

destiny is concerned. For the intellect, an inferior human faculty, the disorder in our lives is an insuperable fact. For the reason, however, that faculty of man, which links him with the divine principle of the universe, disorder in this world is merely incidental. (Cf. especially xii. 275.)

It is precisely in a world of this distressing aspect that true human independence and freedom can be displayed. Tragedy therefore, once more, must reveal man in distress and yet morally triumphant. In doing so it fulfils the high purpose of steeling us against these very attacks of fate when we meet them in our lives. (Cf. xii. 279.)

This educative function of tragedy is thus cathartic in the general sense established by Lessing. The use of the word 'Fertigkeit' by both Schiller and Lessing indicates the measure of agreement in the general principle. But the difference must once again not be underrated. For Lessing the cathartic effect of tragedy was a training in pity ('der mitleidigste Mensch ist der beste Mensch'[1]), for Schiller it is a schooling in stoicism. Schiller advocates precisely what Lessing opposed. Nevertheless, Schiller can be said to have recalled Lessing's principles of fear and catharsis, which he had previously not adopted.

The highest aim of art, and of the tragic art in particular, is the presentation of freedom in action, which produces in those who behold it a freedom of mind ('Gemütsfreiheit') that is both moral and aesthetic. This is the moral purpose of tragedy, as Schiller formulates it in his last reflections upon the subject. The earlier definitions are considerably modified in this newer formulation. The moral purpose is no longer conveyed in direct teaching, nor is it even the duty of the poet to present a theodicy. Schiller now fully accepts calamity and

[1] Letter to Nicolai, November 1756.

distress as a matter of ineluctable fate ('unvermeidliches Schicksal'), and any attempt to substitute for it an ideal world of harmony is rejected as a sign of weakness. With the passage from *Über die tragische Kunst* quoted on p. 409 should be compared the last paragraph of *Über das Erhabene* or the following from the preface to *Die Braut von Messina*:

> Jeder Mensch . . . will, wenn er von ernsthafterer Natur ist, die moralische Weltregierung, die er im wirklichen Leben vermißt, auf der Schaubühne finden. Aber er weiß recht gut, daß er nur ein leeres Spiel treibt, daß er im eigentlichen Sinn sich nur an Träumen weidet, und wenn er von dem Schauplatz wieder in die wirkliche Welt zurückkehrt, so umgibt ihn diese wieder mit ihrer ganzen drückenden Enge, er ist ihr Raub wie vorher; denn sie selbst ist geblieben, was sie war, und an ihm ist nichts verändert worden. . . . Die wahre Kunst aber hat es nicht bloß auf ein vorübergehendes Spiel abgesehen: es ist ihr ernst damit, den Menschen nicht bloß in einen augenblicklichen Traum von Freiheit zu versetzen, sondern ihn wirklich und in der Tat frei zu *machen*, und dieses dadurch, daß sie eine Kraft in ihm erweckt, übt und ausbildet, die sinnliche Welt, die sonst nur als ein roher Stoff auf uns lastet, als eine blinde Macht auf uns drückt, in eine objektive Ferne zu rücken, in ein freies Werk unseres Geistes zu verwandeln und das Materielle durch Ideen zu beherrschen.

The immediate and direct transformation of the spectator is the true purpose of tragedy. This influence should be neither transitory nor indirect, but *real* ('wirklich'). The *Briefe über die ästhetische Erziehung des Menschen* had shown the full significance and extent of the transformation. Art not merely exemplifies (moral) freedom, it also produces (aesthetic and moral) freedom. Art, in Schiller's words 'läßt auch das Gemüt des Betrachters frei, weil sie nur den Schein und nicht die Wirklichkeit nachahmt' and it supplies 'eine Inokulation des unvermeidlichen Schicksals' (*Über das Erhabene*).

It has been argued[1] that Schiller's optimism waned at the end of his life. This view is hardly borne out by the evidence of his philosophical essays, nor by that of his dramas, if they are read judiciously in conjunction with his theoretical pronouncements. Schiller's conception of the relation between fate and freedom as expressed in the essays will be found adequate to explain the purpose of each of his tragedies, even of *Die Braut von Messina* and *Demetrius*. That there are indications of change in the last stage of Schiller's development cannot be denied. But whether this change was in the direction of romanticism[2] or of realism,[3] the optimistic basis of his philosophy was left untouched materially. It was perhaps made more secure. Schiller's later trust in a 'moralische Weltregierung' is expressed in the words of Demetrius, which invite comparison with similar statements from the pre-classical period:

> Gerechtigkeit
> Heißt der kunstreiche Bau des Weltgewölbes,
> Wo Alles Eines, Eines Alles hält,
> Wo mit dem Einen Alles stürzt und fällt.
>
> (Act I, lines 333 *and pass.*)

The organizing principle of the universe at the time when this play was being written, is securely rooted in objective truth, no longer in subjective personal feeling. Such an objective, 'realistic' philosophy has often led to the dissolution of a tragic view of life. It is not impossible that Schiller himself was moving in this direction. In *Über naive und sentimentalische Dichtung* comedy is ranked above tragedy because it pursues the nobler aim:

Diese Freiheit des Gemüts in uns hervorzubringen und zu

[1] Notably by G. Fricke, W. Deubel, and H. Gumbel, loc. cit.
[2] Cf. H. H. Borcherdt, *Schiller*, Wissenschaft und Bildung.
[3] Cf. H. Gumbel, loc. cit.

nähren ist die schöne Aufgabe der Komödie, so wie die Tragödie
bestimmt ist, die Gemütsfreiheit, wenn sie durch einen Affekt
gewaltsam aufgehoben worden, auf ästhetischem Weg wieder-
herstellen zu helfen. . . . Wenn also die Tragödie von einem
wichtigern Punkt ausgeht, so muß man auf der andern Seite
gestehen, daß die Komödie einem wichtigern Ziel entgegengeht
und sie würde, wenn sie es erreichte, alle Tragödie überflüssig und
unmöglich machen. Ihr Ziel ist einerlei mit dem Höchsten,
wonach der Mensch zu ringen hat, frei von Leidenschaft zu sein,
immer klar, immer ruhig um sich und in sich zu sehen, überall
mehr Zufall als Schicksal zu finden und mehr über Ungereimtheit
zu lachen als über Bosheit zu zürnen oder zu weinen. (xii. 197.)

No pantragic view of life can form the basis of this
conception of the dramatist's art. It is, on the contrary,
the product of a philosophy which is tragic in no radical sense. Schiller therefore does not develop towards a
denial of an earlier idealism, but progresses from subjective to objective idealism. It is in accordance with this
development that the genesis of his tragedy must be interpreted and for this purpose a knowledge of the genesis
of his theory of tragedy must be considered essential.

A VARIATION ON THE THEME OF HEUSLER'S FIRST LAY OF BRÜNHILD

By R. A. WILLIAMS

THE moving story of Brünhild, perhaps in its inherent potentialities the most striking character study in Germanic heroic literature, suffers for the modern reader from the weakness of its main premiss. It may well be that the deception practised by Sigfrid on its heroine was not felt by the original poet or his audience to convey any suggestion of moral obliquity. For us, however, it is a factor making for a certain pettiness which rather disagreeably clashes with the heroic atmosphere of the tale.

But the premisses of a story are, after all, only a challenge to the imagination, and if what ensues is entirely satisfactory the reader may well be content, and in this case may even smile half-enviously over a *naïveté* which *our* squeamishness has lost. *All* the consequences are not, however, satisfactory in the Lay of Brünhild. The deception which can bring Brünhild's heroism into magnificent relief, reacts very disadvantageously on Sigfrid, for he follows up his first step, which is only doubtful, by a further step which is not doubtful at all. However it is glossed over in the texts—nowhere less successfully than in the *Nibelungenlied*—the fact remains that Sigfrid betrays the confidence reposed in him by Gunther when he delivers to Kriemhild the proof that Brünhild has been deceived. It is of no consequence, compared with this, that the deception reduces Gunther to a miserably passive role: the king on a chess-board is still the king even though he be checkmated by a pawn. But Sigfrid, forced to retreat behind his wife's petticoats in order to shelter his honour, may produce the gesture of a hero in the hour of tragedy, in point of fact we have learned that the skin of horn rings hollow. This story of the fatal wound to Brünhild's confidence in her world demands undoubtedly for its full poignancy that Sigfrid should not have added disloyalty to deceit.

Viewed thus the saga raises the question: is Sigfrid's disloyalty a necessary consequence of the premiss of his deceit? Was there no other way out for the poet who introduced this trait and for those who followed him? And pondering this question we notice the powerful instinct awakening, which bids us, in studying the heroic traditions, to seek for *das Echte*, with the expectation of finding it in an original, whose virgin purity will be innocent of all the blemishes due to lapse of time, and chance. For this expectant attitude there is, if anywhere, full justification in the history of the tradition of Brünhild, since the brilliant researches of Heusler have established that its development through the ages was, in Germany at least, a rather wretched tale of degeneracy, the tragedy of a 'Stoff' which lost its soul and its heroine! But, as regards the point I have raised, expectancy does not receive much encouragement from Heusler's masterly reconstruction of the First Lay, for there Sigfrid's disloyalty, not exactly prominent, is yet apparent.

I confess that, impressed by Heusler's example, for long I believed that the dilemma I have indicated was insoluble. The famous quarrel of the queens, the 'senna', has so much the semblance of a permanent element in the tradition, that he would be daring indeed who would attempt to discard it from a reconstruction of the original lay. And the 'senna' certainly demands that Kriemhild should have knowledge of the deception to which she was not a party, and from what source could she derive this knowledge if not from Sigfrid? That seemed to settle the question of whether the original version contained the trait of Sigfrid's disclosure of the deceit. Sigfrid *must* have given Kriemhild the fatal ring, as we read in Heusler.

And yet my mind refused to come to rest on this point. I felt that Sigfrid's disloyalty (in act if not in intention) made him at best a silly blunderer, such as he could not possibly have been if he had belonged to the true race of heroes, whose instinctive sense of seemliness must surely protect them against such lapses. Nor could I persuade myself that a poet of the heroic age who was capable of conceiving Brünhild would be satisfied with *this* Sigfrid. Surely he would have had at least an opportunity of leading up to the 'senna' by a different path? But where did that lie?

At long last an accident gave me a hint. Idly turning over the leaves in Raßmann's *Deutsche Heldensage*[2], i, I hit once again at p. 301 on the account of the 'Senna' in his translation of the Danish ballad of Sivard and Brynild, Version D, in which Signild (= Kriemhild) has the following words:

> Hör' du, stolze Brynild, und liebste Schwester mein:
> Wie gewannst du die Goldringe, die du trägst am Finger dein?

The incriminating ring not in Kriemhild's but in Brünhild's possession! With what eagerness I turned once more to compare Heusler's reconstruction of this scene (*Nibelungensage und Nibelungenlied*[2], p. 11). There Kriemhild annihilates Brünhild with the words:

> e r hat . . . dir diesen Ring genommen.

Quickly I made a small alteration in the wording, which now read:

> e r hat . . . dir den Ring gegeben (den du am Finger trägst).

My dilemma was solved.

Of course that is not quite all. Before the 'Senna' Heusler recounts how on the third morning after the *keusche Beilager* Sigfrid drew a ring from Brünhild's hand. Rather should I read that (as an earnest of her husband's return) he *gave* Brünhild a ring before leaving her. The *robbing* of the ring (plus the girdle) is explained by the poet of the *Nibelungenlied* as due to Sîvrit's *übermuot*,[1] and this, though not altogether satisfactory, is the only possible explanation and not out of harmony with the exultation felt as a natural, largely physical reaction by the victor in an all-in wrestling match with a doughty opponent. But in Heusler's reconstruction such *übermuot* is a crying contradiction of the self-restraint exercised by the hero through three nights, his blood unheated by any undue physical exertion. And even if we let that pass, the internal logic of the situation is entirely against Sigfrid's handing on Brünhild's ring to Kriemhild. For in *this* situation we cannot picture a cold-blooded theft practised on Brünhild while she sleeps. She must be fully conscious of Sigfrid's action. She will therefore expect to see her ring *again*—on the finger of her *husband*, and if Gunther is unable to produce it, then woe to Gunther! It is plain that common, obvious prudence demands that, when Sigfrid goes back to Gunther and they swop disguises once more, he shall hand over to his friend the ring acquired from Brünhild. His not doing so, far from leading up to the 'Senna', really makes it superfluous, for Brünhild will soon discover from Gunther, an obvious impostor without the ring, how matters lie, and she will

---

[1] 'ine weiz ob er daz tæte durh sînen hôhen muot'. *Nibelungenlied* (Bartsch), 680². *hôhen muot* is here clearly an apologetic euphuism for *übermuot*! For the poet's reliance on the latter quality in difficulties, see Neumann, *Mogk Festschrift*, p. 135.

have more serious business in hand than bickering with Kriemhild.

One rubs one's eyes when one realizes that the coarse bridal night with its wrestling match in the later German tradition is actually in one respect an improvement on Heusler's 'Urlied', for it escapes to a considerable extent from this illogicality of the ring. If only the *Nibelungenlied* had dropped the ring! Hebbel, however, did that and shows us how the girdle carried off by Siegfried leads to a moving dilemma for the hero, torn by the warring demands of marital confidence and loyalty to his friend. A pity that that could only be done by an appeal to the long arm of chance, so that at bottom Siegfried falls a victim to the *Tücke des Objekts*. Still, his absent-mindedness is a great improvement on the *übermuot* of the *Nibelungenlied*.

Does this valiant proposal to improve on Heusler's account of the original 'senna' fail in being over-subtle for heroic times? I hardly think so. For firstly, Kriemhild is supposed with good reason to be already married to Sigfrid, before he sets out with Gunther on the wooing expedition. She is therefore certainly able to recognize Sigfrid's ring when she sees Brünhild wearing it. And since she is also able to draw a contrast between her husband and Gunther (*Svá var minn Sigurðr hiá sonom Giúka, sem væri geirlaukr ór grasi vaxinn*) and knows about the dangers of that expedition, a glance at Brünhild's ring must bring her a flood of realization. She has no need to ask Sigfrid for an explanation, no need to mention the matter at all, until Brünhild's overbearing conduct calls forth scorn and contempt for such blindness. Furthermore, Brünhild's position at Worms is so false that *her* feminine intuition must have made her uneasy long before the 'senna'. She also can compare Gunther with the dragon-slayer and her sensitiveness about precedence, that gives rise to the quarrel, is only the sign of this deep-seated uneasiness. In such circumstances the bare assertion 'Sigfrid gave you that ring' must cause her to grow pale: apart from the unlikelihood that Kriemhild could have invented it, if it were untrue, it only speaks the thought stirring in her own breast. She goes away silent. She has now to deal with others than Kriemhild.

Kriemhild flourishing her ring in the face of Brünhild is just such a theatrically telling gesture as the German 'Spielmann' loved, and such a one might well have been tempted to substitute it for something less obviously suitable to melodrama. So also does Sigfrid's *übermuot* in annexing and retaining the ring after the *keusche Beilager* —if it ever could have derived from any other version than that with the wrestling match—savour of that recklessness in regard to details of composition, which was characteristic of the 'Spielmann's' art. Does it not look rather suspicious that the texts know two traditional forms of the deceptive wooing, *keusche Beilager* and 'wrestling match', but only one of the 'senna'? Might not the 'senna' have survived in its vulgate version as a result of competition between the two traditions of the wooing? Its absence from the 'Short Lay of Sigurd' may be significant.

The poet of the Short Lay had indeed good reason to discard the 'senna' if it came to him in the form reconstructed by Heusler. For firstly, Brünhild's ring, as proof of the seduction, proves also Sigfrid's disloyalty (in contradiction of the underlying assumption that his deception springs from loyalty to his friend); for only if Sigfrid told her so, can Kriemhild know that the ring once belonged to Brünhild. Secondly, as we saw, the basis of the story, the deception practised on Brünhild, did not make it necessary to incriminate Sigfrid in order to lead up to the 'senna'. Feminine intuition working in both women was sufficient for that. The discarding of the 'senna' in the Short Lay might therefore be accounted for on any of three hypotheses. Either, the poet knew a version such as Heusler constructed, and he objected to it because it incriminated Sigfrid. Or, he knew a version which did not incriminate Sigfrid, yet thought it superfluous, because he felt that Brünhild was capable of solving the riddle without any assistance. Or,—just as in the field of textual criticism a lone manuscript may preserve a true reading against a host of witnesses—the Short Lay may be the *Kronzeuge* for an *Urlied* without any 'senna' (whence would follow that the 'senna' in the Scandinavian texts is due to influence from the German tradition of *Kampfspiele* and wrestling match); for, be it noted, the jealousy of Brünhild emphasized in the Brot (*Fyrman hon Guðrúno góðra ráða*) is in her false position at Worms a psychologically adequate lever to produce all that ensues.

Of course no claim is made, for this version of the original 'senna', of greater historical probability than for Heusler's. Cautious scholarship will rightly claim that the real existence of such a construction cannot be proved if it go beyond the testimony of the texts. But the only form of the 'senna' to which the texts bear witness is that in which the fatal ring belonged to Brünhild. Not even the Danish ballad, which presented me with the idea that the ring belonged to Sigfrid, is testimony to my version. For in that ballad—alas!—to Signild's query 'Who gave you the rings you wear?' Brynild replies, *not* 'Nileus (= Gunther) gave them to me', but 'Sivard gave them to me'! That is, the version of this late source is apparently due to a contamination of two (literary) traditions, the vulgate version of the 'senna' and Sigurd's visit to

Brünhild *prior* to the deception. The ballad, however, shows that the notion of a ring presented to Brünhild by Sigfrid naturally associates itself with a modification of the dialogue in the 'senna'.

Heusler's version remains the historically probable one. But a probability does not altogether exclude a possibility, and I hold it to be worth-while to recognize that the authors of the preserved texts could have made even better use of the 'Stoff' that came to them, and may even have been excelled in this respect by the first poet of all, for whom I have always had a great respect since he was first introduced to me by Heusler! Yet, alas, an unlucky star seems to have ruled over the historical progress of the 'matter of Brünhild', with its fine *motif* of confidence abused and a central figure potentially fit to rival Heinrich von Kleist's Penthesilea; and so in the end we may have but one more example to illustrate a melancholy truth:

> Dem Herrlichsten, was auch der Geist empfangen,
> Drängt immer fremd und fremder Stoff sich an.

Even our friend, the creator of the First Lay, may have been unable to resist the operation of that inscrutable law!

WORDSWORTH AND GERMANY

By L. A. WILLOUGHBY

'WE have a delightful scheme in agitation,' William Wordsworth writes from Alfoxden on 11 March 1798, with Coleridge prompting him at his elbow, 'we have come to a resolution, Coleridge, Mrs. Coleridge, my Sister and myself of going into Germany, where we purpose to pass the two ensuing years in order to acquire the German language, and to furnish ourselves with a tolerable stock in trade of information in natural sciences. Our plan is to settle, if possible, in a village near a university, in a pleasant, and if we can, a mountainous, country; it will be desirable that the place should be as near as may be to Hamburg, on account of the expense of travelling.'

The main outlines of the voyage of the Wordsworths and Coleridge to Germany (Mrs. Coleridge was eventually left behind with the children) have been told many times already, and nowhere more entertainingly than in the appendix to the *Biographia Literaria*, *Satyrane's Letters*. The recent life of Dorothy Wordsworth,[1] and the issue of the first volume of the *Early Letters* by Professor de Selincourt[2] provide additional and interesting particulars. The English visitors were disappointed with Hamburg as a city, but found much to admire in the picturesque dress and habits of its citizens. They made good use of the introductions the Wedgwoods had given them, and were hospitably entertained by Victor Klopstock in whose

[1] E. de Selincourt, *Dorothy Wordsworth. A Biography*, Oxford, 1933.
[2] *The Early Letters of William and Dorothy Wordsworth* (1787–1805), Oxford, 1935.

house they met his brother, the poet. Dorothy has left a lively account of the meeting in the extracts from her *Journal* recently published.[1] The poets carried on an imperfect conversation in French (of which language Dorothy assures us Klopstock had less than herself) But she was agreeably struck by 'his great cheerfulness, even liveliness under the burthen of old age and many diseases', whilst the poet's lady made an unfavourable impression of vanity and unpleasant manners.[2]

No doubt it was Klopstock, whose partiality for his native Harz is well known, who was responsible for the unfortunate choice of Goslar. The Wordsworths' chief quarrel with this 'lifeless town' was the inhospitality of its inhabitants, 'all petty tradespeople'. They found it impossible 'to see anything of the manner of the more cultivated Germans or of the higher classes', but the reason they allege is strange: 'we are not rich enough', Wordsworth writes, 'to be introduced into high or even literary society, for a man with a woman with him, is expected to return any hospitality he receives.' Coleridge was nearer the mark when he answered from Ratzeburg: 'You have two things against you: your not liking smoke[3] and your sister', and he adds in a letter to Poole: 'His taking his sister with him was a wrong step . . . sister here is considered as only a name for mistress.'[4] There is no doubt that the free and easy behaviour of Dorothy, her

---

[1] *Dorothy Wordsworth,* op. cit.

[2] Cf. her letters of 1805 (*Early Letters,* pp. 432, 481).

[3] 'I have a horror of smoking,' Wordsworth was still writing in 1829. Cf. *Memoirs of W. Wordsworth,* by C. Wordsworth, London, 1851, ii. 22. Coleridge, on the other hand, enjoyed it: 'I smoke four times a day.' *Letters* (E. H. Coleridge), i. 277.

[4] Goethe, in the *Italienische Reise* (22 Oct. 1786), affords interesting confirmation: 'Heute gesellten sich, reitend, ein Herr und eine Dame zu uns, ein Engländer mit einer sogenannten Schwester.'

'warm and ardent manner', her 'wild eyes', the lover-like terms on which she stood with her brother,[1] must inevitably have given rise to misconceptions as to their real relations in a country which was only just recovering from its literary wild oats. The love of brother and sister, it is well known, was a favourite *motif* with the 'Sturm und Drang', and Schiller's mind, in particular, was continually running upon it. And had not Goethe, whose affection for his sister bears a close parallel to that of William and Dorothy, brought Cornelie into connexion with his passion for Frau von Stein?

> Ach, du warst in abgelebten Zeiten
> Meine Schwester oder meine Frau.

And so it came about that they were dependent upon their landlady—the widow of a linen-draper—and her family and an apprentice for such practice in German as they obtained. But I suspect that Wordsworth's fluent French drove him rather to the company of an emigrant priest, just as already in Hamburg he had consorted chiefly with the French *émigrés* of which the city at this time was full.

A hard winter, the hardest of the century, had caused them great suffering, in spite of the furs in which they enveloped themselves, and they left Goslar without regret. It is typical of Wordsworth's indifference to historical monuments that he should have no praise for the historical antiquities of the place. A kingfisher flashing across his path, or, more permanently, the glorious view of pasture-land and wooded hills visible from the city's

---

[1] Mr. H. Reed and Mr. H. I. Faussett in their recent biographies both suggest that their mutual affection, never fully conscious of itself or its motive, was abnormal. There is a curious remark of Coleridge to Crabb Robinson which seems to bear on the subject: 'Coleridge envied Wordsworth his sister, his own character had suffered from the want of a sister. To-day he also spoke of incest.' *Blake, Coleridge, Wordsworth,* &c., by E. J. Morley, Manchester, 1922, p. 38.

walls on which he took his daily walks, these are the
recollections he has enshrined in his verse:

> A glimpse of such sweet life
> I saw when, from the melancholy walls
> Of Goslar, once imperial, I renewed
> My daily walk along that wide champaign,
> That, reaching to her gates, spreads east and west,
> And northwards, from beneath the mountainous verge
> Of the Hercynian forest.[1]

And even then his thoughts turned back at once to the
'Moors, mountains, headlands, and ye hollow vales' of
his native Westmorland, powers which seized his heart
with firmer grasp than the softer wooded uplands of the
Harz. It was with relief that the Wordsworths turned
from the confinement of the town to the open country.
'The brilliant green of the earth-moss under the trees',
Dorothy writes to Coleridge, 'made our eyes ache after
being so long accustomed to the snow. . .'. And they were
overjoyed 'to be saluted with the song of the larks, a pair
of larks, a sweet liquid and heavenly melody heard for the
first time after so long and severe a winter.'[2] It is a
wonderfully vivid description that she draws of their four
days' tramp through the Harz in the last week of February
1799. It has all that rigid accuracy of vision and of
colouring which makes Dorothy Wordsworth's *Journals*
the admiration of the critics, and her observations the
source of so many of her brother's poems. The sights
then enjoyed lingered long in her recollection, and during
the tour in Scotland with Coleridge in 1803 she is
constantly reminded of scenes and incidents which have
haunted her memory since Goslar days.[3]

[1] 'Prelude', viii. 209.
[2] *Early Letters*, p. 217.
[3] *Journals*, ed. Knight, 1897, i. 193, 208.

Writing to Coleridge from Nordhausen on the southern slopes of the Harz on 27 February, they meditate further excursions 'for a fortnight or three weeks'. Where they went does not appear; they had letters of introduction to Weimar, but other places promised equal advantages, and living in Erfurt and Eisenach, they had heard, was cheaper. They still hoped, apparently, to make up for the deficiencies of Goslar by finding some German household with young people 'where they could be chattering and chattered to, through the whole day'. But whether they actually took Thüringen in their stride, as Professor de Selincourt thinks, does not appear.[1] But that they definitely travelled to the South is clear from a letter of Coleridge recently published.[2] The fact remains that they turned up in Göttingen two months later, and spent some few days with Coleridge before proceeding homewards about 23 April. By 13 May they were back in Yorkshire with the Hutchinsons, having, as they told Cottle, spent their time pleasantly enough in Germany, but being right glad to find themselves in England, 'for we have learnt to know its value'.

Pleasant enough the German sojourn might seem in retrospect, but, viewed practically, it was a failure. Wordsworth had not achieved the purpose with which he set out and was forced to admit that his 'progress in German, considered with reference to literary emolument, is not even as dust in the balance. . . . I acquired more French in two months, than I should acquire German in five years, living as we have lived. In short, sorry as I am to say it, I do not consider myself as knowing anything of the German language. Consider this not as spoken in modesty

---

[1] Inquiries at Nordhausen elicited the answer that no official records of travellers were kept at this time.

[2] *Letters* (Griggs), i. 164.

either false or true but in simple verity.'[1] 'Wordsworth
seems to have employed more time in writing English
than in studying German', Coleridge wrote from Göttingen,[2] and indeed, however disappointing the five
months in Goslar may have been in other respects, it was
actually one of the most fruitful periods of his poetic
activity, which saw the production of the finest portions
of *The Prelude* and some of his most precious lyrics.

The Wordsworths' interest in the German language
was henceforth desultory, though Dorothy, with the encouragement of Coleridge, who sent her German books,
did make fitful attempts to keep it up.[3] She still desired
to make money by translation (it had actually been the
chief object of their journey to Germany), but her hopes
were not high, and 'if William's name rises among the
booksellers we shall have no occasion for it'. In 1802 she
was still translating 'two or three of Lessing's Fables and
a good deal of Lessing's Essay'. The references to her
German reading are numerous in that year,[4] but they soon
cease. Yet she was still able to converse with the peasant
folk during the continental tour of 1820, when Mary
Wordsworth was lost in admiration at the way her sister-
in-law dashed at her German. 'Dorothy', she says, 'is an
adept at making her way, for she never hesitates—off
into the kitchen, talks to everybody there, and in the
villages, on the roads, makes friends and gains information, and jabbers German everywhere. She astonishes us

---

[1] *Early Letters*, p. 221. Dora Wordsworth reports in 1828 (*D. Wordsworth. A Biography*, p. 375) that her father's half-dozen words of German stood him in better stead than all Mr. Coleridge's insight into
German literature', but by 1837 Wordsworth had apparently forgotten
even these 'half dozen words'. Cf. Knight, *Works*, xi. 295.

[2] *Letters* (ed. E. H. Coleridge), i. 272.

[3] *Early Letters*, pp. 237, 253.

[4] *Journals*, 1802, *passim*.

all.'[1] And she even acted as courier to the Monkhouses
when they made their independent excursion to Baden
Baden, to the satisfaction of all concerned. The Swiss
dialects, however, routed her, and she was vexed to find
that she could understand little of a conversation over-
heard at Altdorf.[2]

Wordsworth had already made the acquaintance of
Germany seven years previously whilst he was still an
undergraduate at Cambridge. At the end of the Swiss
tour with his college friend, Robert Jones, he had pur-
chased a boat at Basle, and 'so taken advantage of the
river down to Cologne', on the way to Ostend and
Margate.[3] He had gone to Switzerland prepared to find
the perfect patriarchal and political conditions which his
Rousseau-inspired guide-book had led him to expect.
And though in his *Descriptive Sketches* he adheres to the
literary tradition which represents the Swiss as the free
children of nature, 'unstained by envy, discontent and
pride', in his more veracious letters home to his sister
he gives free rein to his disappointment and contrasts the
rudeness of Swiss manners with the polish and elegance
of the French and Italians.

As rewritten by the Alsatian, Ramond de Carbonnières,
the severely practical guide to Switzerland of the Rev.
William Coxe, Archdeacon of Wiltshire,[4] had been
turned into a vivid, impassioned description of natural
beauties. But Ramond was more than a pioneer of Alpine
climbing; as a student of Strassburg and a friend of Lenz

---

[1] E. de Selincourt, *Dorothy Wordsworth*, p. 338.
[2] *Journals*, ii. 212, 218.   [3] *Early Letters*, p. 33.
[4] *Lettres de M. W. Coxe à M. Melmoth sur l'état politique, civil et
naturel de la Suisse, traduites de l'anglais et augmentées des observations
faites par le Traducteur dans le même pays*. Paris, Berlin, 1781, 1782[2].
Wordsworth also knew Ramond's *Pyrénées* (cf. his note to the sonnet on
'Aix la Chapelle').

he was a fervent adherent of the 'Sturm und Drang'. And as the author of *Les Dernières Aventures du jeune d'Olban* (1777), a patent imitation of *Werther*, he was one of the first to spread the vogue of *les âmes sensibles* in France.[1]

It was probably from Ramond that Wordsworth first heard the chief names of German literature, for the Frenchman has much enlarged on the literary notices of the Archdeacon. A visit to Zürich affords the occasion for references to Salomon Gessner, to the celebrated Lavater, to Bodmer, the Nestor of German literature, to the immortal Klopstock. Bodmer presented Ramond on leaving with a copy of his *Proben der alten schwäbischen Poesie des dreizehnten Jahrhunderts* (1748), and it was to this book that Dorothy referred Coleridge in Göttingen for information concerning the earlier poets of Germany, a book which Coleridge then proceeded to get out of the University Library.[2] But it is a pathetic confession of the poverty of their literary resources in Goslar that the Wordsworths should still refer to their old Swiss guide-book as their authority for German literature.[3]

At Cambridge Wordsworth had read books of travel, ancient history, and, above all, English poetry. He showed, in addition, a definite preference for modern languages, in spite of the presence of the great Porson, then still in residence at Trinity. Wordsworth, on his own admission, 'knew little of Latin and scarce anything of Greek',[4] and

[1] Cf. F. Baldensperger, *Goethe en France*, Paris, 1920, p. 17. On Ramond see A. Monglond, *Jeunesses. Les Amours de Carbonnières*, Paris, 1933. M. Legouis (*La Jeunesse de Wordsworth*, Paris, 1896, p. 117) believes that it was from Ramond that Wordsworth first heard of Rousseau. He certainly drew on him for the *Descriptive Sketches*.

[2] Cf. A. D. Snyder, 'Books borrowed by Coleridge from the Library of the University of Göttingen, 1799' in *Modern Philology* (1928), xxv. 377.

[3] *Early Letters*, p. 203.

[4] Ibid., p. 61.

devoted himself rather to reading French, Italian, and
Spanish, learning the two latter languages from Agostino
Isola, who had previously numbered among his pupils
Thomas Gray and Mr. Pitt. Was Wordsworth following
the secret precepts of the great Grecian, who declared to
Samuel Rogers that, had he a son, he should become
familiar with French and English authors rather than
with the classics, 'for Greek and Latin are only luxuries'?[1]
There seems to be a similar 'open slight of College cares
and study' in the lines of *The Prelude* where Wordsworth
condemns

> The dangerous craft of culling term and phrase
> From languages that want the living voice
> To carry meaning to the natural heart;
> To tell us what is passion, what is truth,
> What reason, what simplicity and sense.[2]

There is, however, no mention of German among the
modern languages which Wordsworth studied at Cambridge. Nor, indeed, is it clear whether the Rev. William
Render, who in a translation from Kotzebue of 1798[3]
describes himself as 'teacher of the German Language in
the University of Cambridge', was actually in office by
1791. If it offered, then Wordsworth missed the opportunity, for he was still complaining in June 1794 that he
was 'not acquainted with the German language, a circumstance which I greatly regret, as the vast tract of
country where that tongue is spoken cannot but produce
daily performances which ought to be known amongst
us'.[4] It was not until 1795, when through Coleridge he
came into contact with the German enthusiasm of the

---

[1] Samuel Rogers, *Table Talk* (1856), p. 325.
[2] vi. 110. Cf. edition by E. de Selincourt, Oxford, 1926, p. 537.
[3] *Count Benjowsky.*
[4] *Early Letters*, p. 125.

Beddoes circle in Bristol,[1] that the wish to learn the
language revived, and was eventually gratified by the
trip to Germany.

This ignorance of the language does not imply entire
ignorance of the literature, for by 1798 the chief German
authors were in the process of being translated into
English, and there is good reason to believe that Wordsworth was acquainted with some of these.[2] He had not
been neglectful, he informs Coleridge from Goslar, of the
different fragments of Wieland and Goethe which he had
seen in England.[3] It is easy to believe, with M. Legouis,
that the *Descriptive Sketches* and 'The Evening Walk' owe
some of their 'tender melancholy and fond conceit of
sadness' to Goethe's immortal work.[4] Was not Wordsworth himself addicted, like Werther, to hypochondria?—

> Having two natures in me, joy the one,
> The other melancholy.[5]

And whilst it is difficult to agree with Coleridge's description of 'The Borderers' as 'absolutely wonderful', and to
discover in it 'those profound touches of the human heart',[6]
yet the play admittedly owes something to Schiller's
Robbers (as Coleridge had himself hinted), although
more, no doubt, to the anarchism of Godwin. Wordsworth
tells in *The Prelude* how he heard fashionable preachers
in London deck out their sermons with 'ornaments and
flowers' from the poets, including him 'who penned the
other day "The Death of Abel"'[7] (the book incidentally
which served Byron as German text when he started

[1] Cf. C. A. Weber, *Bristols Bedeutung für die englische Romantik*,
Halle, 1935, p. 105.

[2] K. Lienemann, *Die Belesenheit von W. W.*, Berlin, 1908, has a fairly
full chapter on W.'s relations to German literature.

[3] *Early Letters*, p. 221.   [4] *Prelude*, vi. 366.

[5] Ibid. x. 869 (1805).   [6] To Cottle, June 1797.

[7] *Prelude*, vii. 563.

learning the language as a boy of eight). Professor Brandl asserts that Wordsworth made use of Gessner for 'Guilt and Sorrow'.[1] Wieland's *Oberon* Wordsworth had read in the translation of Sotheby as he was on the point of leaving for Germany, and he had discussed it adversely with Klopstock. It was, he maintained, a story based on 'animal gratification'.[2] Voss's *Luise*, which Coleridge was translating in 1796[3] as an exercise in German, was also known to Wordsworth, who placed it above *Hermann und Dorothea*[4] (though he thought less highly of Voss's rendering of some of the earlier poems of Milton).[5] It is obvious that the splendid reality of the characters in *Luise*, of its pastors and schoolmasters living very close to nature, but ennobled by learning and piety, should have appealed to Wordsworth, suffused as the poem is with the love of the simple and small and a pious belief in the all-goodness of the Creator. Bürger he knew from William Taylor's translations in the *Monthly Magazine* (1796), and, through them, had been attracted to the ballad as a poetic form. He was sufficiently impressed, at least, to buy Bürger's *Gedichte* almost as soon as he landed in Hamburg.[6] Klopstock commended him as 'a true poet' in preference to Schiller, 'who would soon be forgotten'.[7]

Bürger formed the subject of a most interesting epistolary discussion with Coleridge in Göttingen, of which only

---

[1] *S. T. Coleridge und die englische Romantik*, Strassburg, 1886, p. 206.

[2] *Satyrane's Letters* (Shawcross), ii. 177.

[3] *Letters*, ed. E. H. Coleridge, i. 203.

[4] Crabb Robinson, *Diary* (Sadler), i. 170.

[5] *Essay Supplementary*. They were 'L'Allegro' and 'Il Penseroso'. Voss, *Gedichte*, 1802, iv. 189, 205.

[6] 'Bought Bürger's poems, the price 6 marks and Percy's ancient poetry, 14 M'. *D. W.'s Journal*, i. 27.

[7] *Satyrane's Letters*, ibid., p. 177.

Wordsworth's letters have been preserved. It is only natural that Wordsworth should have been attracted to Bürger and his poetry for, mistaken as his ideas of *Popularität* may have been,[1] the preface to the *Gedichte* of 1789 must have contained much that was congenial to Wordsworth. But on comparing him with Burns, he deplores his lack of manners, 'whereas in Burns you have manners everywhere. Not transitory manners reflecting the wearisome, unintelligible obliquities of city life, but manners connected with the permanent objects of nature, and partaking of the simplicity of these objects.'[2] He is even more explicit in a second letter in which he bewails the lack of character in Bürger's personages; 'you have incidents and a spirited and lively style, but none of those higher beauties which can entitle him to the name of a *great* poet'. He was disappointed in 'Lenore', which he thought inferior to the English translation, and, like Coleridge, considered 'Susan's Dream' ('Des armen Suschens Traum') the most perfect and Shakespearian of his poems. 'Bürger is the poet of the animal spirits. I love his Tra ra la dearly; but less of the horn and more of the lute—and far, far more of the pencil!'[3] He censures him again severely for his deviation from the simple pathos of Percy in his 'Entführung'.[4]

In these letters Wordsworth betrays a critical attitude very close to Schiller's in his famous review of Bürger of

---

[1] Cf. E. S. Blenkinsop, *Bürger's Originality*, Oxford, 1936, where a plea is made for a reconsideration of his claims.

[2] *Early Letters*, p. 221 seq.

[3] From Coleridge's *Unpublished Letters* (ed. Griggs), i. 133 (to William Taylor of Norwich). Coleridge is quoting from one of Wordsworth's letters to him.

[4] *Essay Supplementary to the Preface.* References to Shenstone here and in the Goslar letter (*Early Letters*, p. 221) suggest that Wordsworth is again making use of German material.

1791, where he similarly deplores the banality of much of Bürger's work, ascribing it to the author's lack of balance and moral principle. Schiller, as a true child of the eighteenth century, was chiefly concerned with the moral effect of the beautiful. It is the poet's task, he maintains, so to idealize nature that its beauty may fill the reader with moral exaltation. Idealization—or, as Wordsworth would have said, selection[1]—is a prime necessity, and the poet must never descend to the level of the crowd. One passage in this review is verbally suggestive of Wordsworth's famous definition of poetry as 'emotionrecollected in tranquillity', although there is in Schiller only a hint of the third and most important stage of the creative process, that this emotion must be reconstructed in excitement:[2]

Ein Dichter nehme sich ja in Acht, mitten im Schmerz den Schmerz zu besingen. So, wie der Dichter selbst bloß leidender Teil ist, muß seine Empfindung unausbleiblich von ihrer idealistischen Allgemeinheit zu einer unvollkommenen Individualität herabsinken. *Aus der sanftern und fernenden Erinnerung mag er dichten*, und dann desto besser für ihn, je mehr er an sich erfahren hat, was er besingt; aber ja niemals unter der gegenwärtigen Herrschaft des Affekts, den er uns s c h ö n versinnlichen soll.

Schiller rarely invented, and both he and Wordsworth may, independently, be drawing on the same source; they had both, in their time, been ardent disciples of Rousseau, and the latter's 'rêverie' may have offered a suggestion.[3] Wordsworth himself owed much, as has been shown recently, not only to Hartley and his theory of the association of ideas,[4] but also to the *Discourses* of Sir Joshua

[1] Cf. 'A selection of the real language of man in a state of vivid sensation.'
[2] H. W. Garrod, *Wordsworth*, Oxford, 1927. Cf. especially Chapter XI.
[3] Cf. G. M. Harper, *William Wordsworth*, London, 1929, p. 85.
[4] A. Beatty in *University of Wisconsin Studies*, no. xxiv, 1927.

Reynolds.[1] But the general similarity of thought between
Schiller and Wordsworth, and the like occasion (Bürger's
poetry) which gave rise to it, suggest something more than
mere affinity.[2]

During the Goslar period Wordsworth took his cues
on German literature from Coleridge: 'Let me know
what you think of Wieland, You make no mention of
Klopstock; and what is the merit of Goethe's new
poem?'

From his academic vantage-point Coleridge replies with
'two valuable letters on the German poets'. They com-
prised detailed references to Lessing, Wieland, Goethe,
and Voss. Goethe's new poem, obviously *Hermann und
Dorothea*, which had appeared in October 1797, had
inspired Coleridge with the desire to emulate Goethe's
hexameters. The very name Dorothea reminded him so
forcibly of Wordsworth's best-beloved sister, and he
addresses her in verses which are certainly no worse than
Goethe's:

William, my teacher and friend! William and dear Dorothea!

[1] O. J. Campbell and P. Mueschke, 'Wordsworth's Aesthetic Development 1795–1802', in *University of Michigan Publications*, x, Ann
Arbor, 1933.

[2] Schiller's review first appeared in the *Jenaische Allgemeine Literatur
Zeitung* on 15 and 17 Jan. 1791; in book form not until 1802 in vol. iv of
the *Kleinere Schriften*; Wordsworth's second *Preface* at the end of 1800.
It is scarcely likely that Wordsworth, in his isolation at Goslar, should
himself have caught sight of this back number of a Journal. But it is more
than probable that his attention was drawn to it by Coleridge in one of
those 'valuable letters' from Göttingen (see *infra*). Coleridge, it will be
noted, was in and out of Dove Cottage in the autumn of 1800, while the
Preface was being written. Was it in this double sense that he told Southey
in 1802 that it was 'half a child of my own brain'? But in any case, the
point I would make is that it was only after his return from Germany
that Wordsworth insisted on the selective and universalizing element in
the creative process, which was absent from the cruder experiment of the
Advertisement of 1798.

William my 'head' and my 'heart', dear Poet that feelest and
thinkest;
Dorothy, eager of soul, my most affectionate sister!

. . . .

You have all in each other, but I am lonely and want you!

And inspired by his model, Coleridge translated from
Schiller (and later printed without acknowledgement) the
famous distich describing the hexameter and pentameter,
for which (amongst other plagiarisms) the captious critic
of *Blackwood's* took him so severely to task in 1840.
It is good to hear Wordsworth defending his dead friend
so warmly in a letter to Crabb Robinson:[1] As though
Coleridge was 'indebted to Germans for the brightest gems
of his poetic crown' indeed! Why, they would be much
honoured to be called 'farthings in his pocket.' 'I feel
free to affirm', Wordsworth continues in his generous
wrath, 'that Coleridge had carefully studied, and successfully practised, English hexameters before he knew a
word of German . . . but if he had stolen ten times as
freely I would have added in explanation, and partly in
exculpation, that he gave to Schiller fifty times more than
he took, without thinking worth while to let the world
know what he had done!'

It would appear from the above reference to *Wallenstein*
that Wordsworth rated his friend's translation higher than
the original, and from the former, indeed, he had borrowed
one or two motives for his own work. But in condemning
Coleridge's sonnet on *The Robbers* as a 'rant',[2] he was
at the same time condemning the play which he had laid
under contribution for his own *The Borderers*. It was
unfortunate that in Wordsworth's mind Schiller's name
should have been associated with his estrangement from

---

[1] E. J. Morley, *The Correspondence of H. C. R. with the Wordsworth
Circle*, Oxford, 1927, i. 401.   [2] *Memoirs*, loc. cit. ii. 284.

Coleridge. An unguarded remark concerning the state of Schiller's entrails when the body was opened was misrepresented by Montagu and applied to Coleridge and his addiction to drugs, with the ensuing breach between the two friends which lasted from October 1810 to May 1812.

'Of the excellence of Lessing', Wordsworth wrote to Coleridge, 'I can form no distinct idea.'[1] It is scarcely possible, however, that Coleridge should have allowed him to remain long in this state of ignorance. Coleridge, as we know, had gone to Germany with the avowed intention (inspired, no doubt, by his Unitarian patrons, the Wedgwoods) of writing a Life of Lessing.[2] It is plain that, for Coleridge, Lessing was primarily a theologian, and yet he realized his importance as a critic, although he thinks *Laokoon* 'unequal and in parts contradictory'.[3] He apparently passed on his information (and his copy) to the Wordsworths, for Dorothy (as we saw) was still using Lessing's *Fables* as a text-book and reading Lessing's 'Essay' on her return from Germany in 1802. It is difficult to imagine what 'essay' of Lessing's other than *Laokoon* she can have had in mind. It is still the work by which Lessing is traditionally known to the cultured Englishman.

It is clear that this essay with its condemnation of painting in poetry (and if Dorothy was reading it, we may be sure her brother knew about it too) must have awakened a sympathetic chord in Wordsworth, whose avowed aim was to break with the notorious *ut pictura poesis* of the Renaissance. It is tempting to see in Dorothy's famous description of the daffodils, written a few days after this reading of Lessing, the practical effect of his

---

[1] *Early Letters*, p. 221.   [2] *Letters* (E. H. C.), i. 321, 338.
[3] Morley, *Blake, Coleridge*, &c., op. cit., p. 64.

admonition to turn description into movement: 'I never saw daffodils so beautiful. They grew among the mossy stones about and above them; some rested their heads upon these stones as on a pillow for weariness; and the rest tossed and reeled and danced, and seemed as if they verily laughed with the wind that blew upon them over the lake.'[1] It remained for her brother to view the daffodils 'as something more', and for his heart to dance in rhythmic unison with them. But there is no doubt that, whether intuitively or by deliberate intention, Wordsworth does follow Lessing's precepts for the dynamic expression of poetry, and that he avoids the lifeless description which had run riot in the nature poets, and from which his own early poetic diction, derived from Erasmus Darwin,[2] had by no means been free. In the best poetry of his middle years it is the verb, not the adjective, which predominates, and all is suffused with the inward conviction that the poet's mind is in harmony with the creative urge of the universal soul, the root of poetry being emotion, not the imitation of 'beautiful nature', as the seventeenth century had taught. Everywhere is movement, rhythm, progressive action; all external objects are described by a single touch, nowhere the cloying satiety of stationary landscape painting: 'Brook and road were fellow travellers in this gloomy pass' ('The Simplon Pass'); his love is 'a phantom of delight, a dancing shape, an Image gay, sporting as the fawn, that wild with glee across the lawn and up the mountain springs'. Or, to take a poem at random, in the lines 'Written in March' (1802) we have seven adjectives in the whole poem, but double that number of verbs. It is perhaps not too fanciful to see in this tendency the

[1] *Journals*, i. 106.
[2] W. L. Sperry, *Wordsworth's Anti-Climax* (Harvard Studies in English, xiii), Cambridge, Mass., 1935, p. 136.

influence of Lessing's famous dictum. Wordsworth describes and does not seek to paint, conscious that his art differs from that of the painter who is tied to the 'pregnant moment':

To one brief moment caught from fleeting time.[1]

Years later Wordsworth would seem to acknowledge at least a portion of his debt when, long before Macaulay, he styles the Germans the best critics in Europe.[2]

If Wordsworth felt attracted to Lessing, to Goethe, on the other hand, he was definitely hostile, and not all the blandishments of Crabb Robinson (whose temper he often tried by his derogatory remarks about his hero!) could induce him to see in Goethe anything more than 'an overrated talent'. He was not one of those select few 'whose universal minds are able to reach every variety of thought and feeling without bringing their own individuality before the reader'. Such were Homer and Shakespeare, but in what Goethe writes 'you find the man, the artificial man ... aiming to be universal, and yet constantly exposing his individuality, which his character was not of a kind to dignify. He had not sufficiently clear moral perceptions to make him anything but an artificial writer'.

I have tried to read Goëthe, I never could succeed,' he continues.[3] 'Mr. Robinson refers me to his *Iphigenia*, but I there

---

[1] 'Upon the Sight of a Beautiful Picture.' Although he occasionally indulged in a *Gemäldesonnet* (cf. 'The Song at the Feast of Brougham Castle'), Wordsworth was distinctly conscious of the boundaries between poetry and painting. In the sonnet 'To a Painter' he bemoans the fact that he can only hold fast the present, not suggest the past, for he lacks the poet's 'inward eye'. Was this why he found looking at pictures so restful to the 'outward eye', to mind and senses? It did not involve the immense effort of the reconstruction of emotion. Cf. *Memoirs*, ii. 117.

[2] *Letters* (Knight), ii. 175. In the *Essay Supplementary* he has also a word of appreciation for their feeling for Shakespeare.

[3] 'Reminiscences of Wordsworth's Neighbours' in *Memoirs*, ii. 478.

recognise none of the dignified simplicity, none of the health and
vigour which the heroes and heroines of antiquity possess in the
writings of Homer. The lines of Lucretius describing the immola-
tion of Iphigenia are worth the whole of Goëthe's long poem.
Again, there is a profligacy, an inhuman sensuality in his works
which is utterly revolting. I am not intimately acquainted
with them generally. But I take up my ground on the first
canto of *Wilhelm Meister*, and as the attorney-general of human
nature, I there indict him for wantonly outraging the sympathies
of humanity.

The book 'was full of all manner of fornication', he
declared to Emerson, and to show his contempt he 'flung
it across the room'. To T. C. Grattan he once compared
the *Sorrows of Werther* with Ossian's *Poems* and 'such
worthless work'.[1] And yet he was insincere enough to
join in the address of congratulation of the fifteen English
friends on the occasion of Goethe's last birthday![2]

We can now understand something of the contemptuous
indifference to the presence of four of the greatest writers
of Germany within easy reach. But perhaps the poets of
the *Lyrical Ballads* were as yet scarcely ripe to appreciate
the great achievements of Weimar. Coleridge, it is true,
later attained to some comprehension of their importance;
Wordsworth obstinately shut his eyes and his ears. And
yet had either of them ventured to cross those few miles
which separated them from Weimar (and at Nordhausen
Wordsworth was actually within fifty miles and even
bore letters of introduction!) they would have found much
to profit and delight. The *Balladenjahr* had provided

[1] *Beaten Paths and those who trod them*, ii. 129.
[2] Cf. R. G. Alford, *Goethe's earliest critics in England*, in Publications
of the English Goethe Society (Old Series), vii. The question of the
connexion between genius and irregularity of conduct occupied Wordsworth's mind intermittently. He is much more tolerant of Burns than of
Bürger or Goethe, and thought he 'had been cruelly used, both dead and
alive'. (To John Scott, 11 June 1816.)

its harvest of ballads, by the side of which some of their own would have seemed trivial in comparison; and among Goethe's lyrics were many distinguished by that naïve simplicity which Wordsworth only occasionally achieved. Goethe and Schiller had already discussed, and partially solved, those problems of poetic diction which were to occupy the English poets for so many years to come. *Wallenstein* was being produced on the Weimar boards, and *Faust* was on the stocks once more. And in the neighbouring Jena were Schiller, Schelling, Fichte, the elder Schlegel, and Steffens and Novalis not far away, and Goethe hovering to and fro; names which appear on almost every page of Coleridge's later works, here a living reality, to be known for the asking. The stage could scarcely have been set more auspiciously for the meeting. What would we not give for Dorothy's impressions of a visit to Goethe, or for her opinions of Weimar and especially of the brilliant Jena circle, for with Caroline Schlegel she would surely have found herself in spiritual communion.

'Philosophy', we have it on Coleridge's authority, 'is the friend of poetry.'[1] In a brilliant paper written nearly thirty years ago A. C. Bradley[2] has shown how close was the parallel between English poetry and German philosophy during the age of Wordsworth. Coleridge had already been introduced to the transcendental philosophy of Kant by Thomas Beddoes, before even he left England, and through Coleridge Wordsworth must have been supplied with at least the basic ideas of German transcendentalism. And the later Romantic philosophers, with Schelling at their head, had identified the soul of man with nature and found in both the same revelation of God.

---

[1] *Anima Poetae* (ed. E. H. C., Heinemann, 1895), p. 78.
[2] *English Poetry and German Philosophy in the Age of Wordsworth*, Manchester, 1909.

And though Wordsworth might later have decried
German transcendental philosophy as the supreme cause
of his friend's fall from poetic grace[1], it is certain that,
deprived of Coleridge's inspiring presence, his own genius
died, as Professor Garrod puts it, 'of a metaphysical
atrophy'.[2]

In view of those obvious affinities it seems strange that
the reputation of Coleridge and Wordsworth should have
been so long in establishing itself in Germany, whilst that
of Byron spread like wildfire.[3] Even in the late forties the
Prussian minister in London, von Bunsen, was forced to
admit to Sara Coleridge that her father and Wordsworth
were of no account in Germany.[4] Crabb Robinson, it is
true, had made propaganda for Wordsworth. Whilst in
Germany in 1802 he had received and acclaimed the
Lyrical Ballads and reports that Friedrich Schlegel 'seemed
much pleased with one or two pieces by Wordsworth'.[5]
He had lent the volume to Herder who, so it seemed,
agreed with Wordsworth as to poetical language. 'Indeed,
Wordsworth's notions on that subject are quite German.'
He also took pains to impress his friend Knebel with
Wordsworth's importance and records an appreciative
remark. Coleridge records that he read some of Words-
worth's poems to Wilhelm von Humboldt when in Rome
in 1805 and found in him an appreciative listener.[6] When
Tieck visited England in 1817 Crabb Robinson read to

---

[1] *Memoirs*, ii. 289. Cf. his letter to Reed of 23 Dec. 1839 (*Wordsworth
and Reed. The Poet's Correspondence with his American Editor*), p. 14:
'German transcendentalism would be a woeful visitation to the world
were it not sure to be as transitory as it is pernicious.'

[2] Garrod, loc. cit., p. 30.

[3] K. Bömig, *W. W. im Urteile seiner Zeit*, Leipzig, 1906.

[4] Sara Coleridge, *Memoir and Letters*, ii. 319.

[5] *Correspondence with Wordsworth Circle*, i. 44.

[6] *The Friend* (Shedd), p. 461.

him two of Wordsworth's sonnets, and Tieck exclaimed: 'Das ist ein englischer Goethe!'[1] But the American, George Bancroft, noted in 1819 that Goethe himself knew nothing of Southey and Wordsworth, of Coleridge the name.[2] It was not until F. J. Jacobsen published the selections in prose in the *Briefe an eine deutsche Edelfrau über die neuesten englischen Dichter* (1820)[3] that Goethe obtained any insight into our Romantic school. Even so, Goethe was so taken up with Byron that Crabb Robinson did not venture to mention Wordsworth during his second visit in 1831. But he had more success with Ottilie, and hoped through her 'to convert Goethe himself to the just faith'.[4]

Goethe's attitude to his English contemporaries had been prejudiced by the hostility of *English Bards and Scotch Reviewers*, and Byron's letter from Ravenna of 14 October 1830, in which he dedicates *Marino Faliero* to him, confirmed Goethe in his opinions: 'You do not know, perhaps,' Byron mocked, 'that this gentleman [Wordsworth] is the greatest of all poets past, present and to come . . . his principal publication is entitled *Peter Bell* which he had withheld from the public for one and twenty years—to the irreparable loss of all those who died in the interim—and will have no opportunity of reading it before the resurrection.'[5] And not all the efforts of Freiligrath to popularize Wordsworth in Germany by

[1] *Correspondence*, op. cit., i. 230.

[2] *Goethes Gespräche* (Biedermann), ii. 448.

[3] It was not, apparently, the German 'magazine' in which Dorothy was pleasantly surprised to find a reference to William's poem on the *Duddon* whilst at Lucerne in 1820? Cf. her *Journals*, ii. 214.

[4] Cf. F. Norman, *Henry Crabb Robinson and Goethe*, ii. 20 (Publications of the English Goethe Society, viii), 1931.

[5] Cf. J. Boyd, *Goethe's Knowledge of English Literature*, Oxford, 1932, p. 185.

admirable translations from his shorter poems[1] have been able to eradicate entirely the animosity of this judgement.

Yet Crabb Robinson, like Tieck, thought that Wordsworth and Goethe had many high powers in common,[2] and later critics have not been slow to point out the likenesses and the contrasts. Both poets, according to Coleridge,[3] remain master of their subjects, treat them objectively: 'Although Wordsworth and Goethe are not much alike, to be sure, upon the whole; yet they both have this peculiarity of utter non-sympathy with the subjects of their poetry. They are always, both of them, spectators *ab extra*, feeling *for*, but never *with*, their characters.' Yet objectivity, as far as it conditioned their attitude to nature, was by no means identical in each case. Goethe *is* nature, and when he creates has but to be himself to merge himself in his environment and produce automatically, subconsciously, to 'let himself go'. It is in this sense that he could speak of his most genuinely poetic work as a *Gelegenheitsgedicht*, meaning that it was poetry that was the inspiration of the moment and came of itself: 'That undisturbed direct manner of working, almost like a sleep-walker, which alone can lead to greatness', as he defines the creative act in a well-known passage to Eckermann.[4] And though this method of direct composition may be applicable to the 'divine somnambulist', the author of *Kubla Khan*, it is certainly not true of Wordsworth, for whom poetry, 'recollected in tranquillity', was the result of intensive, continuous, and exhaustive effort to recapture the original emotion. Dorothy's journals

---

[1] *Englische Gedichte aus neuerer Zeit*, 1846.

[2] *Correspondence with Wordsworth Circle*, i. 111.

[3] *Table Talk*, 16 Feb. 1833. Cf. C. H. Herford, *Goethe and Wordsworth* in P.E.G.S. vii, 1930; Barker Fairley, ibid. x, 1934 and an earlier paper by Meusch in the Old Series, vii, 1893.

[4] *Goethes Gespräche* (Biedermann), iii. 57, 1824.

and letters are filled with references to her brother's weariness and exhaustion from the effects of poetic composition.

Nor does Wordsworth experience nature in the same way as Goethe. Like all true poets, he is conscious of the realm of universals which lies at the back, and beyond the experience, of the senses. He saw things with the inward eye when perception became thought and thought perception. But as has been pointed out recently,[1] for Wordsworth it was, as often as not, a visionary recollection, a joy of memory which is wanting in Goethe, who interprets all nature in terms of the present, not of the past like Wordsworth. Moreover, Goethe needed to visualize a scene concretely in a picture for the eye where Wordsworth was satisfied with a verbal image of the mind. An instance—topical in its subject-matter—will illustrate this difference: both poets had read with interest James Bruce's *Travels to discover the sources of the Nile* (1794). To Wordsworth the book merely suggested a few lines of description in *The Prelude*:

> like the mighty flood of Nile
> Poured from his fount of Abyssinian clouds
> To fertilise the whole Egyptian plain—[2]

But Goethe must needs visualize Lake Tana, the source of the Blue Nile, and draw an imaginative pen and ink sketch of it which is not at all unlike the pictures reproduced in the daily papers when the Italians occupied its shores a few months ago.[3]

There remains the question of Wordsworth's relations to Germany and the German people as a whole and apart from their literature. The Germans as experienced at

---

[1] Fairley, loc. cit.   [2] vi. 614.

[3] Cf. O. Kletzl, 'Ideale Landschaften des Zeichners Goethe', in *Jahrbuch des Freien deutschen Hochstifts*, 1932–3, p. 304.

first hand in Goslar were rather repugnant to Wordsworth;
he found them coarse, brutal, dirty, inhospitable, and
dishonest. The contrast, or supposed contrast, with his
own people cured him of his predilection for foreign
peoples and turned him into a lover of his own country:

> Nor, England! did I know till then
> What love I bore to thee.

He was generally indifferent to German affairs and was only
roused by the heroism of 'brave Schill' and Andreas Hofer,
in whom he saw the revival of 'Tell's great spirit'.[1] For
twenty years Wordsworth felt no urge to return to Germany, and even then he only took it as a necessary pre-
liminary in 'his habitual eagerness to be in Switzerland'.[2]
It needed Coleridge's company and encouragement to take
him in 1828 on the excursion to their friends the Aders
at Godesberg on the Rhine, although in retrospect it
seemed, as Dora wrote, 'a pleasant time',[3] and a few
years later both the Wordsworth boys were sent to learn
the language.[4] But the German tour with Crabb Robinson
appended to the Italian journey of 1837 was definitely
a failure, for Robinson would linger in bustling cities
when Wordsworth would have stayed peacefully at
the Bavarian lakes. Already in 1832, when threats of
revolution became insistent in England, he had visions
of retiring to 'a quiet nook in the centre of Austria'.[5]

Crabb Robinson kept him in touch with the political
situation in Germany, and Wordsworth considers the high
character of the Prussian administration, in spite of its
being a despotism, as satisfactory when compared with
the subversive democratic tendencies at home which

---

[1] See his Sonnets on 'Independence and Liberty'.

[2] De Selincourt, *Dorothy Wordsworth*, p. 325.

[3] *Correspondence with Wordsworth Circle*, op. cit. i. 265. He met
A. W. Schlegel on this occasion. (Cf. also p. 259.)

[4] Ibid., pp. 192, 222, 226.   [5] Ibid., p. 231.

threatened to destroy 'the ancient Constitution of England in Church and State'.[1] He has the Englishman's dislike, however, for the feudal aristocratic class-consciousness of the military monarchies, and considers that the more perfectly graded society of England makes for greater character and higher habits of mind: one need but compare, he says, the officers of the English army with those of Prussia. How superior they are as gentlemen![2] And he is particular to distinguish greater intelligence and beauty among the Jews of the Rhineland as compared with the wretchedness of the German peasantry.[3]

When we think of Wordsworth, apart from the poet, we are apt to think of the older, disillusioned Tory, the selfish and prudent Wordsworth, bitterly opposed to the reforming tendencies of the time, and curiously aloof from the sufferings of God's creatures, whether man or beast. But there is another Wordsworth, not the Jacobin, indeed, who had almost perished on the scaffold in the Place de la Révolution, but the Wordsworth of the middle period to whom the imperialist aggression of Napoleon had brought the consciousness of his English nationality, as it was to do for the Germans a decade later. Indeed, one of his chief objections to Goethe, apart from his lack of religion and moral character, was his indifference to the political welfare of his country: 'Goethe was amusing himself with fine fancies when his country was invaded', he remarked to Caroline Fox in 1844, 'how unlike Milton, who only asked himself whether he could best serve his country as a soldier or as a statesman, and decided that he could fight no better than others, but he might govern them better. Schiller had far more heart and ardour than

---

[1] Ibid., p. 269.
[2] *Memoirs* (C. Wordsworth), ii. 130.
[3] Ibid. ii. 128. Cf. the poem 'A Jewish Family'.

Goethe, and would not, like him, have professed indifference to Theology and Politics, which are the two
deepest things in man—indeed, all a man is worth,
involving duty to God and to man.'[1] One must read the
impassioned vindication of nationality in *The Convention
of Cintra* to realize the depths of Wordsworth's patriotic
feeling.[1] 'The man who in this age feels no regret for
the ruined honour of other nations', Wordsworth writes
in this great manifesto, 'must be poor in sympathy for the
honour of his own country.' We see how the rights of
Man for which he had fought in his republican youth,
have made way for the Rights of Nations. He has a
prophetic vision of a Europe balanced by the recognition
and fulfilment of just territorial and cultural aspirations,
and he writes in 1808, at a time, it will be noted, when the
French Usurper was at the summit of his power: 'It will
be a happy day for Europe when the natives of Italy and
the natives of Germany shall each dissolve the pernicious
barriers which divide them and form themselves into a
mighty people.'

[1] Cf. A. Dicey, *The Statesmanship of Wordsworth*, 1916.

GRILLPARZER'S 'SAPPHO'

By DOUGLAS YATES

GRILLPARZER'S *Sappho* is a work which, in spite of all that has been written about it, and for all its apparent simplicity of action and outline, still presents certain unsolved difficulties which stand in the way of its satisfactory interpretation and appreciation. An attempt is made in the following pages to furnish an acceptable account of it in its main features by regarding it as a composition that reflects, in a completer sense than has hitherto been shown, its author's intentions, his mind and feeling, and his actual observations and experiences at the time of its creation. It differs as an account of this kind from a previous attempt of mine[1] mainly in three respects: in regarding *Sappho* as an artist-tragedy (not merely a tragedy of jealousy) from the very moment of its conception (*Sec.* 2); in assessing anew the influence of Goethe's *Tasso* (*Sec.* 3); and in considering a source for *Sappho* of a kind that has not so far been seriously examined (*Sec.* 5).

Like *Sappho* itself, the work preceding it, *Die Ahnfrau*, was based on a profound inner conviction of the author. He always resented criticism which described it as being merely sensational. At the time of the first bitter attacks upon it he determined, in vindication of his injured pride, that his next work should afford no excuse for criticism on similar grounds. He would choose a subject permitting

---

[1] In *Der Kontrast zwischen Kunst und Leben bei Grillparzer*, Berlin, 1929, pp. 17 ff. A recent visit to Vienna, facilitated by the generosity of the Carnegie Trust for the Universities of Scotland, led to the discovery of material which prompted the present article.

entirely objective and dramatic, as opposed to subjective and theatrical treatment, one which did not depend on robbers, ghosts, and bangs for effect, 'die Räuber-Gespenster- und Knall-Effekte' of his *Ahnfrau*. It was his wish to prove to himself and the world that he was capable of relying solely on the poetic quality of his products.

The wisdom of Grillparzer's determination to avoid in future the crude theatrical effects of his *Ahnfrau* is self-evident. His distrust of his own feelings and his wish to keep them out of his next work may perhaps appear to be less well founded. A passage in recent musical criticism, however, fits Grillparzer's case exactly, when Mr. W. J. Turner writes of Stravinsky: 'His desire to achieve the impersonal is undoubtedly genuine, but I believe it is because he is a good and serious enough artist to have real ambitions and to be conscious of his special weakness—which is to be too personal and primarily emotional.'[1] Yet we must remember that Grillparzer's works, like those of the artist to whom these words refer, nevertheless derive their real interest and value from this weakness duly controlled; only then shall we be suitably prepared for considering the good intentions with which he took up his work on *Sappho*.

I

On 29 June 1817 Grillparzer met an acquaintance, Dr. Joël, who proposed to him that he should write an opera libretto for the composer Weigl on the subject of Sappho. Grillparzer's reply was that the subject was suitable for a tragedy. The story attracted him because it seemed particularly well adapted to the simple kind of treatment he had in mind; the more so as, according to the aesthetic convention of Grillparzer's day, classical

---

[1] *New Statesman and Nation*, 22 Feb. 1936, p. 262.

antiquity was the domain of nobility, simplicity, and objectivity in art.

Ich ... suchte ... nach einem Stoff, der es mir möglich machte, in der Behandlung eine Ruhe walten zu lassen, die mich vor der Gefahr des Selbstmitspiels bewahrte, die mir des Strebens um so würdiger schien, je fremder sie meiner Individualität ist, und je mehr ich verzweifelte sie je zu erreichen. Schon in früher Zeit hatte mich Sappho's Ende begeistert. . . .

At the time when these lines were written to Müllner,[1] who considered the first acts of *Sappho* unsatisfactory, as being written without enthusiasm, Grillparzer was still in a mind to defend his new work on the strength of the first two acts. In doing so he was quite sincere, and not merely concerned to refute Müllner's criticism. He deplored the fact that he had not been able to sustain the effort of remaining entirely objective in his treatment, that is to say, objective and dramatical as opposed to subjective and lyrical, or theatrical, perhaps. 'Ich konnte mir nicht verhehlen, daß dasjenige, was die Ahnfrau für die Meisten anziehend gemacht hatte, gröstentheils rein subjektive Ausbrüche, daß es immer mehr die Empfindungen des Dichters als die der handelnden Personen gewesen waren.'[2] Further on he writes of *Sappho*: 'Es stand übrigens schon vom Anfange her zu befürchten, daß diese, durch ein wirkliches Heraustreten aus mir selbst bewirkte Stimmung, bei der krankhaften Reitzbarkeit meines Wesens von keiner gar langen Dauer seyn würde.'[3] He then gives his account of the change which took place as the result of an averred interruption through

---

[1] *Werke* (Hist.-kritische Gesamtausgabe), iii. 1, no. 104 (Erster Entwurf), p. 97, ll. 15–24. Müllner had written from Weißenfels about a fortnight earlier, on 14 Feb. 1818: 'Sie fingen an ohne Begeisterung; aber sie kam Ihnen im Fortgang. Ist es nicht so? Darum ist der Anfang schlecht, Mittel und Ende göttlich', ibid., p. 91, ll. 8–10.

[2] Loc. cit., p. 97, ll. 9–13.   [3] Loc. cit. (Zweiter Entwurf), p. 103, ll. 1–4.

illness near the middle of the piece, and adds: 'Ich sah
sehr wohl den Kontrast ein, in dem die beiden Hälften
des Stücks gegen einander standen, aber ich war immer
bereit die Parthie der geliebten ersten Hälfte gegen die
letzte zu nehmen.'[1] This document informs us of Grillparzer's point of view at a time before *Sappho* had actually
been produced. The evidence so given of his original
intention, more especially his recognition that he had
failed to fulfil this intention, is of an importance which is
independent of the fact that he may have been wrong in
preferring the first part of his play to the more spontaneous and unpremeditated second part, or that he may
have subsequently somewhat modified his opinion as the
result of *Sappho*'s unforeseen success.

There is, in principle, no doubt that Grillparzer was
mistaken in this preference. If he had actually been
successful in carrying out his original intention, his work
could hardly have commanded the interest that it does.
'Der Vorsatz auch des größten Meisters kann immer nur
der Anstoß, nie der Inhalt und Umfang eines echten
Dichterwerks sein', as Gundolf says in reference to *Sappho*,
adding the significant words: 'Wer die Idee eines Werks
mit seinem Bewußtsein durchdringen könnte, wäre ein
flacher Poet, und wessen Werk nicht mehr ist als sein
Dichter davon weiß, lebt nicht über die kurze Dauer
seiner Theorien hinaus.'[2] It is instructive to observe that
originally Grillparzer seems to have thought differently
as regards the composition of his *Sappho* and that in the
letter to Müllner he made excuses for it in the sense in
which, if it was to be considered the work of a genuine
poet, it least needed to be excused.

[1] Loc. cit. (Zweiter Entwurf), p. 103, ll. 21–24.
[2] *Jb. d. Freien Deutschen Hochstifts*, Fr. a. M., 1931, Fr. Gundolf,
Fr. Grillparzer, pp. 9–93, cf. p. 34 f.

Perhaps it is an understanding of this truth, and not merely reserve, that fortunately prevents the greatest poets, as a rule, from volunteering information about their original intentions, as well as about the personal experiences, the real origins, the private thoughts, associated with what is expressed in their works. For when they observe the inevitable modification and transfiguration which these elements have undergone, the wider significance which through poetic treatment they have acquired, these poets must feel that whatever they might attempt to confess of the process by which this took place could only limit the potential implications of what they have expressed. An attractive, characteristic, though isolated, example of this attitude is found in Goethe's reply when, pressed for an interpretation, he opened wide his eyes and echoed mysteriously Faust's words: 'Die Mütter! Mütter! 's klingt so wunderlich!', or in his declaration that his *Faust* was 'incommensurable'. On how many matters, profound as well as intimate, did he not prefer to remain silent, when he could have helped if he would, even regarding the main purport of his *Faust*, wisely leaving his readers to imagine and his critics to explain, if they could, what he really might have meant to express!

Grillparzer's admissions about his original poetic intentions in *Sappho* are of importance, therefore, because of the unexpected light they throw on the history of its composition and the guidance they afford towards a just analysis and interpretation of the work. He knew that in some manner beyond his actual control the development of his idea had insensibly changed. What he failed to realize at the time of writing his letter to Müllner was that this was not in itself undesirable. He naïvely supposed that the distraction of an aching tooth had been

responsible for the change, not that his original conception
had been itself in some way inadequate. He was certainly
not aware of the truth that if his work was ever to transcend
mediocrity, it had to shape itself to some extent differently
under his very hands.

2

It is commonly held that the short time which elapsed
between Grillparzer's conception of *Sappho* and his setting
to work upon the play, itself virtually excludes the possibility of his having planned his material with a view to
bringing out what we now regard as the teaching of the
finished work. On the very evening of the day of his
conversation with Dr. Joël he set down his scenario, and
on the following day he was at work upon his play. With
regard to the scenario Sauer writes in his Introduction
to *Sappho*:

Aus dem Szenarium folgt aber weiter, daß Grillparzer zunächst
nur die rein menschlichen Züge des Stoffes anzogen, daß sich ihm
das Liebes- und Eifersuchtsdrama zuerst gestaltete, ohne daß ihm
die tieferen Grundideen des Werkes bereits ganz deutlich gewesen
wären . . . . Das Werk vertiefte sich mehr und mehr erst während
der Ausarbeitung. Sappho zog ihn zuerst als Weib und später als
Künstlerin, als Dichterin an. Zum Künstlerdrama wurde das
Werk erst allmählich ausgestaltet. Das Künstlerische ist das
Sekundäre.[1]

The extent to which the fact that Sappho was a poetess
may be regarded as secondary or incidental to Grillparzer's
original plan is, however, debatable. The scenario, a mere
sketch of the projected action of the play, does not suffice
to establish Sauer's contention. Grillparzer's words in
the letter to Müllner convey the impression that even in
his original conception he regarded the fact as one of
prior and not secondary importance: 'Ich verfiel auf

---

[1] *Werke*, i. 1, p. lxxxiv.

Sappho . . . Ein Charakter, der Sammelplatz glühender
Leidenschaften, über die aber eine *erworbene* Ruhe, die
schöne Frucht höherer Geistesbildung, den Szepter führt,
bis die angeschmiedeten Sklaven die Ketten brechen und
dastehen und Wuth schnauben. . . .'[1] A number of
Grillparzer's sayings afford a kind of commentary to this
conception of his heroine's character. It is essentially his own
conception. As far back as 1808 Grillparzer had expressed
in his diary the conviction that a poet must possess
violent passions: . . . 'ich *habe* heftige Leidenschaften
. . . und gewiß das muß ein Mensch besizen, der nur
einigermaßen Anspruch auf den Namen eines Dichters
machen will.'[2] A little earlier he had written the following
words, which are invariably associated with his portrayal
of Sappho: 'Ich bin *rachgierig*, und zwar so, daß ich
außer mir selbst komme, wenn ich diese Leidenschaft
nicht in vollem Maaße befriedigen kann. . . . Diese
Leidenschaft äußert sich besonders wenn die *Eifersucht*
ins Spiel kömmt.... Eifersucht schließt bei mir ganz den
Gebrauch der Vernunft aus. . . . Ich bin überzeugt, daß
ich eine Untreue der Geliebten blutig . . . rächen würde.'[3]
If these passages throw light on the phrase 'Ein Charakter,
der Sammelplatz glühender Leidenschaften', the words
'über die aber eine *erworbene* Ruhe, die schöne Frucht
höherer Geistesbildung, den Szepter führt' recall the concluding words of a diary note written while he was composing *Sappho* during the summer of 1817. The passage
affords strong evidence of Grillparzer's practice of identi-
fying himself with his central characters. And since he
invokes Shakespeare in justification of his own implied
procedure (in respect here to the passion of jealousy), it

[1] Loc. cit., p. 97, ll. 25–28.
[2] *Werke*, ii. 7, no. 32, p. 18, ll. 2–5.
[3] Ibid., no. 17, p. 8, ll. 1–30.

is of interest to observe that modern criticism of Shakespeare tends to endorse Grillparzer's remarkable insight into Shakespeare's living art. Running through almost everything that Shakespeare wrote after 1600, Mr. J. Dover Wilson detects a strain that he associates with 'the commonplace derangement known as jealousy, jealousy of the same kind as, if not identical with, that described so savagely in the Sonnets', an excessive human passion which the poet exorcizes, 'confesses' (in Goethe's meaning), interprets, or reveals, in works like *Troilus and Cressida*, *Othello*, *The Winter's Tale*, *Cymbeline*, and *Hamlet*.[1] And before quoting Grillparzer (with his reference, among other things, to Shakespeare's 'madness') it may also be appropriate to recall a judgement of Mr. T. S. Eliot's, which Mr. Dover Wilson supports: 'The "madness" of Hamlet lay to Shakespeare's hand.'[2] Grillparzer's passage about his own and Shakespeare's procedure seems to establish on his own confession what we observe in Sappho as an example of his practice in character delineation:

Man hat sehr viel über die Gabe großer Dichter gesprochen, die verschiedenartigsten, ihrem eigenen Selbst fremdartigsten Leidenschaften und Charaktere zu schildern, und Manche haben gar viel von Beobachtung und Studium des Menschen gesagt und gemeint, Shakespeare habe in Bierhäusern, unter Karrenschiebern und Matrosen die Züge zu seinen Macbeths und Othellos zusammengesammelt, und dann wenn das Bündel voll gewesen, sich hingesetzt und ein Stück d'raus zusammengesetzt. Ganz gut
   'Das rühmen die Schüler aller Orten
   Ist aber noch keiner ein Weber geworden!'
Ich glaube, daß das Genie nichts geben kann, als was es in sich selbst gefunden, und daß es nie eine Leidenschaft oder Gesinnung schildern wird, als die er selbst, als Mensch, in seinem eigenen

---

[1] Cf. J. Dover Wilson, *The Essential Shakespeare*, Cambridge, 1932, p. 118 f., and *What Happens in Hamlet*, Cambridge, 1935, p. 306 f.
[2] T. S. Eliot, *The Sacred Wood*, London, 1920, p. 93.

Busen trägt; daher kommen die richtigen Blicke, die oft ein junger
Mensch in das menschliche Herz thut, indeß ein in der Welt
Abgearbeiteter, selbst mit schärferm Beobachtungsgeist Aus-
gerüsteter nichts als 100mal gesagte Dinge zusammenstoppelt.
Also sollte Shakespeare ein Mörder, Dieb, Lügner, Verräther,
Undankbarer, Wahnsinniger gewesen seyn, weil er sie so meister-
lich schildert? Ja! Das heißt, er mußte zu dem allen Anlage in
sich haben, obschon die vorherrschende Vernunft, das moralische
Gefühl nichts davon zum Ausbruch kommen ließ. Nur ein
Mensch mit ungeheuren Leidenschaften kann meiner Meinung
nach dramatischer Dichter seyn, ob sie gleich unter dem Zügel
der Vernunft stehen müssen und daher im gemeinen Leben nicht
zum Vorschein kommen.—Ich wollte, irgend ein Dichter läse das![1]

That these concluding words have a bearing upon
Grillparzer's personal conception and presentation of
Sappho is clear. She, the poetess, was to be revealed in
circumstances in which her pent-up passions should
actually break forth. She was to be shown as discontented
with her lonely lot as a poetess, just as Grillparzer was
discontented, and seeking belatedly to partake of 'life' in
a specific manner, thus exposing herself (through the
inevitable thwarting of her desires) to the risks and consequences of such an outburst. For the same inherent
passions which, held in restraint, are a qualification for art,
prove, in real life, because of their very violence, a danger to
the happiness and well-being of the poet, because contact
with life so readily affords situations which greatly excite
them. Grillparzer considered this to indicate the special
need for restraint on the poet's part and to be an example
of the hardship attendant upon poetic endowment. This
consideration and no other was the one to which Grillparzer originally intended to give expression when he
planned his *Sappho*. It hardly seems to justify the judgement that it was planned to be an *Eifersuchtstragödie*

[1] *Werke*, ii. 7, no. 221, p. 101.

rather than a *Künstlertragödie*. For it was Sappho, the poetess, who was involved in this tragedy, and her fate was to be an original interpretation by Grillparzer of the *malheur d'être poète* in an aspect revealed to him in the first place by observation of his own nature.

The phrase *malheur d'être poète* occurs in the letter to Müllner, immediately following upon the words last quoted, and the context supports the present argument:

... Dazu gesellte sich, sobald das Wort: *Dichterin* einmal ausgesprochen war, natürlich auf der Stelle der Kontrast zwischen Kunst und Leben (wenn die Ahnfrau unwillkürlich gewissermaßen eine Paraphrase des berüchtigten d'Alambertischen *malheur d'être* geworden ist, so dürfte wohl die Sappho ein in eben dem Sinne wahres *malheur d'être poète* in sich fassen). Mit einem Wort, der Gedanke ergriff mich und ich war, als ich zur Ausführung gieng, begeisterter, als je in meinem Leben.'[1]

Influenced, no doubt, by Grillparzer's supposed change of plan, Sauer seems to assume that Grillparzer in fact added this motive of the contrast between art and life to his original conception, almost imperceptibly forgetting his first intention of showing that Sappho incurred guilt merely through her passionate character and despotic behaviour. But we have seen that in Grillparzer's original conception the cause for this behaviour actually lay within her as a poetess. In spite of Sauer's judgement, based on the scenario, the original plan must therefore, no less than the finished work, be regarded as that of an artist-tragedy.

A pencil drawing of the final scene made by Grillparzer presumably on the morning after meeting Joël, before the work was commenced, depicts Sappho with averted gaze bidding farewell to the kneeling pair.[2] It seems permissible to interpret this as showing that the poetess is

[1] Loc. cit., p. 97, l. 29–p. 98, l. 6.

[2] *Werke*, i. 17 (Apparatband), p. 174, and Tafel I, Zeichnung zum V. Akt der *Sappho*.

about to commit suicide, not blaming any one else for her fate, but recognizing that her own nature, that of a poetess, has betrayed her into behaving unworthily.

3

This aspect of the *malheur d'être poète* is paralleled in Goethe's *Tasso*, undoubtedly the most important literary influence discernible in Grillparzer's work. This influence was present (as Grillparzer knew)[1] from the start, and it affords the aptest explanation of Grillparzer's expression in the Selbstbiographie when he says of Goethe (in words that have generally so far escaped precise explanation): 'Er erwähnte meiner "Sappho", die er zu billigen schien, worin er freilich gewissermaßen sich selbst lobte, denn ich hatte so ziemlich mit seinem Kalbe gepflügt.' His theme, he says in effect, was one that the young Goethe had made use of before him. More than twenty years later he used almost the same words in a conversation with Zimmermann, and it is justifiable to assume that Grillparzer was aware of having been in part influenced by *Tasso* to treat the *malheur d'être poète* theme from the point of view natural to himself.

Grillparzer was equally aware, however, that his treatment of the *Tasso* theme fell short of Goethe's and that he was not so fitted for the task of representing in his heroine a poetess by nature, nor in his drama an example of the tragic contrast between genius and the world. 'Ein Meister hätte vielleicht verstanden', he explains to Müllner, 'Sappho'n selbst im Sturme der Leidenschaften die Farbe, die die Dichtkunst ihrem *Charakter* gab, sichtbar zu machen; ich, weniger geschickt, mußte *vor*

---

[1] Cf. *Brief an Müllner* (I. Entw.), p. 100, ll. 1–3, where Grillparzer refers to *Tasso* (and *Correggio*), insisting on his own conviction that there is 'eine natürliche Scheidewand zwischen Kunst und Leben'!

dem Sturme eine Kraft anschaulich machen, die mit unter die erregenden Kräfte des Sturms selber gehört.'[1] This passage explains that though Grillparzer's intention was similar to Goethe's in *Tasso*, he felt that he had to content himself with a treatment of the contrast between 'art' and 'life' (not genius and the world); a treatment, moreover, which presents 'art', then 'life', then 'art' again, alternately.

In view of this we might be disposed to agree with Petsch when, speaking of the opening acts, he says: 'die Sappho des ersten Entwurfes ist im Grunde gar keine wahre Künstlernatur; als ein sinnlich veranlagtes, leidenschaftliches Wesen hat sie sich vorschnell einem Beruf gewidmet, der die volle Hingabe des Menschen verlangt.'[2] But it is hardly an opinion that Grillparzer would himself have endorsed, except perhaps (after completing *Sappho*) as regards the complete self-sacrifice which is here alleged to be demanded by the poet's profession. Grillparzer was himself so preoccupied with the thought of this sacrifice that from now on it becomes in different aspects and presentation almost involuntarily the underlying theme of all his works. This conviction was founded, with Grillparzer, as it was with Beethoven, on 'the profound instinctive knowledge of genius that solitude (withdrawal from the world, or what Grillparzer calls "Sammlung") was necessary to the highest development of his creative power'.[3] If, however, this requirement is understood to imply as much as it seems to imply in Grillparzer's final treatment of Sappho, the complete renunciation of contact with life, the virtual divorcement of art and life, it is clearly invalid. The finished work

---

[1] *Brief an Müllner*, p. 99, ll. 11–16.

[2] O. E. Lessing, *Gr. u. d. neue Drama*, reviewed by R. Petsch in *Euphorion*, xiv (1907), p. 163.

[3] Cf. J. W. N. Sullivan, *Beethoven*, London, 1931, p. 183.

seems to express as its teaching this extreme view, with
the difference that for the later Sappho the world is well
lost. The original conception, however, even apart from
this difference, does not necessarily imply so much. It
may be interpreted as conveying no more than the
author's conviction that the poet's nature renders him
peculiarly apt in contact with life to offend against convention; and that consequently he must restrain his own
impulses (not specifically on behalf of his art) more than
ordinary people need to do. This again is (superficially
appraised) the 'teaching' of *Tasso*, and we must regard it
as the lesson which Grillparzer derived from the work;
it corresponded to his own conviction before *Sappho* was
commenced.

4

If it becomes clear in this way that Grillparzer's original
plan for *Sappho* grew out of a personal conviction thus
strengthened, the question arises as to what foundation
existed for his belief that the work was objectively conceived, and that it was in part so executed, until a change
in the train of his thoughts caused the introduction of
what he felt to be subjective elements.

The letter to Müllner commences with a statement that
Grillparzer originally had a twofold object: 'Erstens lebte
der Stoff wirklich in mir und zwang mich ihn nach
außen hinzustellen, zweitens wollte ich mir dabei selbst
eine Aufgabe machen.'[1] The first of these reasons must
be understood to refer not only to the mere 'material',
but also (perhaps primarily) to the conviction we have
discussed.[2] Grillparzer had no reason to suspect that it
was peculiar to himself, or in any way subject to qualification. He had found it expressed in *Tasso*. In numerous

---

[1] Loc. cit., p. 97, ll. 6–9.
[2] Cf. Sauer's comments in *Werke*, i. 1, lxxxiii f.

'artist-plays' and 'education- or vocation-novels', too, deriving their inspiration from *Tasso* and *Wilhelm Meister* (which like *Sappho* itself they 'dilute or parody'[1]), the romantics had given it wide currency. Grillparzer regarded it as a proper (a 'natural') theme for the kind of work he had intended.

In addition to this 'objective' motive regarding Sappho's nature, Grillparzer's play contains two others which have indeed an air of being calculated, and which presumably contributed to the poet's persuasion that he had conceived the work objectively.

The Sappho legend, as it presented itself to Grillparzer, told how the poetess Sappho fell violently in love with Phaon; she was supposed to have persecuted the innocent youth with her attentions and finally to have taken the plunge from the Leucadian rock into the sea in sheer despair.

The two remaining principal motives which may be regarded as supplied by Grillparzer are his introduction of Melitta, and his stress on the disparity between the ages of Sappho and Phaon.

It has frequently been claimed for Melitta that she is introduced to create a situation which is considered to be a favourite one with Grillparzer, that of a man between two women. She has also been described as embodying Grillparzer's ideal at the time (and attempts have been made to identify her with one or other of his acquaintances). Both these views are beside the mark: the central figure is Sappho, not Phaon; and Melitta has, in stage parlance, only the *naives Fach*.[2] She owes her presence primarily to dramatic necessity.

---

[1] Gundolf, loc. cit. (*Jb. d. Fr. Dt. Hochstifts*), p. 36.

[2] If she embodies Grillparzer's ideal of womanhood, the same is true of other comparatively negative characters such as Bertha (in *Melusina*) and

The importance which attaches to Melitta in *Sappho*
is best shown by Grillparzer's own words to Frau v.
Littrow-Bischoff: 'Sappho springt ins Meer, weil Phaon
ihr die Gegenliebe weigert; das konnte keinen triftigeren
Grund haben, als weil er eine Andre liebte, und damit ist
alles gegeben.'[1]

Tempting as it is to suggest, as Sauer does, that Melitta
existed in Grillparzer's mind in contrast to Sappho as
Lottchen Pichler did to the *femmes savantes* of her
mother's literary salon, such as Mme de Staël and
Dorothea Schlegel, or that she derives from some particular literary source, these conjectures can have little
bearing on the interpretation of the main theme of the
work. It is, indeed, not improbable that in his portrayal
of this 'liebes Mädchen mit dem stillen Sinn' Grillparzer
had some one in mind, possibly a figure of flesh and blood,
in accordance with his usual practice and the whole nature
of his dramatic art. It is true, too, that some such contrast
as Sauer refers to had struck Grillparzer, as the poem
'Das Urbild und die Abbilder' shows. That he was
mildly attracted to Charlotte Pichler is known. And
lastly it may be conceded that this girl's character as
depicted in the poem 'Frühlingsgedanken' and in her
mother Caroline Pichler's correspondence with Therese
Huber does show certain affinities to Melitta's. On the

Kreusa, who also occupy secondary roles. These characters do reflect,
incidentally, Grillparzer's (intermittent) *ideal of quiet happiness*, but they
fall properly to be considered in this respect only in relation to figures like
Mirza, along with certain characters in the youthful works, which seem to
reflect a prevailing 'ethical conviction' of Grillparzer's in favour of this
ideal within the works in which they appear. A lucid account of these is
contained in Ilse Münch, *Die Tragik in Drama und Persönlichkeit
Fr. Grs.*, Berlin, 1931, pp. 8–19 (Jugenddichtungen), though she quite
fails to point out the subjective nature of this defeatist mood of Grillparzer's.

[1] A. v. Littrow-Bischoff, *Aus dem persönlichen Verkehre mit Fr. Gr.*,
Vienna, 1873, p. 79 f.

other hand, the reader of what follows in this study may be equally prepared to entertain the conjecture that Melitta was modelled, as far as we can speak of modelling in reference to a figure so slight, on one of Sophie Schröder's daughters, Minna perhaps.

But this brings us no nearer to an understanding of Grillparzer's motive for insisting as he actually does, that Sappho's relation to Phaon, which is more central, is that of 'ein Weib, das einen *jüngern* Mann liebt'. Late in life Grillparzer complained that Sophie Schröder (the actress who took such an interest in the young poet and made the success of his *Ahnfrau*, in the double role of Bertha and her ghostly ancestress) was much too old for Sappho's part.[1] Actually she was nothing of the kind, and Grillparzer was only moved to this complaint when he met the youthful Charlotte Wolter and learnt the effect of her performance in the role of the poetess. This effect had been to correct outwardly, from the audience's point of view, an inherent defect in Grillparzer's treatment. The Sappho of mature age generally failed to win sympathy. In fairness to Sophie Schröder it must be affirmed, however, that she, 'Germany's greatest tragedienne',[2] triumphantly

----

[1] Cf. A. v. Littrow-Bischoff, *Aus dem persönlichen Verkehre mit Fr. Gr.*, pp. 102 ff., 109 ff. The time referred to is 1866. Many critics of *Sappho* have welcomed the statement. Grillparzer's judgement in the same year, however, expressed to Zimmermann, *Gespräche*, Abtlg. ii (vol. 5, 1863–71), p. 106 f., is as follows: 'Die Wolter ist eine Sappho fürs Auge, sagen Sie. Gut wär's; die Schröder war's auch. . . . Der Abstand soll zu klein sein zwischen der Sappho und der Melitta; den kann ich nicht groß genug haben. . . . Die Melitta ist ein albernes Mädel. Das begreift sich, die Sappho muß ein gut Stück älter aussehen, und doch nicht übel sein.' It is true that by continuing to appear in the role of the poetess long after she had passed her prime Sophie Schröder somewhat exceeded this demand.

[2] As Ludwig I of Bavaria described her. Cf. Wurzbach, *Biogr. Lex. d. k. Österr.*, xxxi. 325.

overcame the poet's deliberately introduced handicap and was by no means outshone by Mme Korn as Melitta, when the work was first presented with such astonishing success. Grillparzer assured Atterbom, the Swedish poet who was in Vienna with Rückert at the time, that her performance was a revelation to him and that she interpreted his Sappho to the last inflexion of her voice.[1] She had such sentiments to express to Phaon as that in bidding him follow her and in bestowing the favour of her devotion upon him, an obscure youth, she, who was already famous when he was still but a child, was conferring a distinction upon him which he could not reasonably expect to have deserved (l. 112)—though she does not put it so bluntly as that. It is clear that she has taken advantage of his innocence. He modestly represents himself as an instrument on which she plays (l. 158). An indication, moreover, of her age in relation to his and Melitta's is conveyed in her reference to the fact that a number of her former protégées are now counted among Mitylene's *beste Bürgerinnen*.

In the passages near the end of Act I commencing with the words: 'Was kann ich Arme denn dem Teuren bieten?' (l. 370), Sappho feels that she no longer merits nor can claim the bounty of youth and love in Phaon's person; she longs to unlive the past, obliterate even the memory of its joys and woes (including: 'Der Freundschaft und der—Liebe Täuschungen', l. 120), in order to enter a strange untrodden fairyland of love with Phaon. In reality, she declares:

Da steh' ich an dem Rand der weiten Kluft,
Die zwischen ihm und mir verschlingend gähnt (ll. 395–6).

For in her youth Sappho had renounced all quiet happiness and domestic joys in her pursuit of ambition, when (like

[1] *Gr. Gespräche*, Abtlg. ii. 1, p. 89.

Grillparzer himself) she experienced 'des Beginnens schwankendes Bestreben', 'des Vollbringens Wahnsinn-glühende Lust' (ll. 49–50); and now that she longs to return and partake of what might formerly have been hers, she fears that it is too late, because she is no longer young and fresh and innocent. The withered laurel is a symbol of her state.

Then, turning, she reflects that for the riches which Phaon offers she can recompense him, in different kind, by the achievements of her art, her past and future songs:

> Seinem Reichtum
> Kann gleichen Reichtum ich entgegen setzen,
> Der Gegenwart mir dargebotnem Kranz
> Die Blüten der Vergangenheit und Zukunft (ll. 419–22).

She then invokes, in Grillparzer's rendering of Sappho's famous ode, the aid of Aphrodite (as often in the past) towards the realization of her amorous desires.

However much he may subsequently have regretted it, Grillparzer deliberately established this disparity between Sappho and Phaon, and it was for this reason that he sought to give compensatory stress to Sappho in her quality as a poetess in her first appearance on the stage. 'Sappho ist in der Katastrophe ein verliebtes, eifer-süchtiges, in der Leidenschaft sich vergessendes Weib; ein Weib das einen *jüngern* Mann liebt,' he says in the letter to Müllner: 'In der gewöhnlichen Welt ist ein solches Weib ein eckelhafter Gegenstand. . . .' He insists, we observe, at this time, on the *alternde Frau* and on the questionableness of her attitude towards Phaon, viewed from the conventional standpoint.

War es nicht durchaus nothwendig, sie noch vor dem Sturm der Leidenschaften so zu zeigen, wie sie in ihrem gewöhnlichen Zustande war, damit der Zuseher die Arme bemitleide, statt sie zu verabscheuen? Wenn es mir gelungen ist, den Zuschauer, so sehr er in der Mitte des Stücks geneigt seyn muß, die Parthie des unschuldigen Paares zu nehmen, dennoch mit seinem Interesse auf Sappho'n fest zu halten, so gebührt ein Theil des Verdienstes vielleicht auch dem ersten Akt.[1]

The assumption that Sappho's fame and achievement as a poetess would compensate for a multitude of personal faults was a natural and characteristic one for the romanticism of Grillparzer's time.

5

But, we ask ourselves, in view of the fact that Grillparzer imposed upon himself an almost insuperable handicap by introducing a motive so damaging to the character of his heroine as that of the obvious disproportion between her own and Phaon's age, what prompted him to do so? It was not a salient feature in the legend, nor does it appear as a motive in any one of the works that have so far been generally accepted as influencing Grillparzer in the conception and execution of his tragedy.[2] This surely

[1] *Brief an Müllner*, loc. cit., p. 99.

[2] Grillparzer went to work without consulting any previous treatments of the same subject-matter, unless Backmann is right in supposing that he read Gubitz's monodrama, deriving from it perhaps the suggestion for Sappho's apotheosis (cf. 'Zur Entstehungsgesch. der "Sappho" ' in O. Katann, *Grillparzer-Studien*, Vienna, 1924, pp. 122 ff.).

Sauer shows, in *Werke*, i. 1, that reminiscences of Wieland's *Agathon* and *Aristipp*, as of Mme de Staël's *Corinne* may well have associated themselves with Grillparzer's original plan. Backmann supports Sauer's notes regarding the possible influence of Ovid's *Heroides*, particularly on account of the motive of age-disparity here under consideration (loc. cit., pp. 118ff.). He considers Fénelon's *Télémaque* as influencing Grillparzer (chiefly in the same direction), ibid., pp. 98 ff. He also seems to favour (cf. *Werke*, i. 17, p. 141) G. M. Howe's theory regarding the importance of Am. v. Imhoff's *Schwestern von Lesbos* as 'A Probable Source of Grillparzer's *Sappho*', *Journal of Eng. & Germ. Phil.* xxii (1923), pp. 503 ff.

The impression which remains when all these suggestions have been considered is that they range too far in search of literary sources and explanations for what may equally well be presumed to have lain immediately to Grillparzer's hand.

is a significant circumstance.—It is perhaps a somewhat startling conjecture, but it nevertheless seems probable enough that the idea of representing Sappho as an almost middle-aged woman resulted from Grillparzer's immediate experience, his knowledge of Sophie Schröder's notorious liaison with the young Daffinger. Astonished as we may be at the suggestion that Grillparzer should have introduced such a personal and commonplace motive into an intentionally 'classical' work, we may find it confirmed by the conclusion that his own and Sophie Schröder's contemporaries were certainly no less astonished at its introduction than we are; and that this same incongruous motive is chiefly responsible for what is unsatisfactory about the piece.

A valuable though neglected contribution to criticism of *Sappho* is contained in Alex. v. Weilen's *Geschichte des Burgtheaters*.[1] The following passage from it, not otherwise readily accessible, is quoted in full and will serve to advance the present argument:

Indem Grillparzer in Form und Geist der Dichtung nach klassischem Ausdrucke ringt, wählt er einen Stoff, den er selbst als eine 'Fiakeridee' bezeichnet hat, ganz aus dem Leben Wiens und seiner Zeit heraus erfaßt. Das alternde Weib, das mit einer jüngeren Nebenbuhlerin um den Geliebten streitet—man findet es wieder in Bäuerles Memoiren . . . man findet es wieder in Possen, welche die mannstolle alte Schachtel der mitleidlosen Lächerlichkeit preisgeben. Ein Neuling auf dem Wiener Boden, wie Costenoble, hat ganz richtig gesehen, wenn er schreibt: 'Die Liebesgeschichte und Eifersucht könnten ebenso gut zwischen einer Wiener Putzmacherin, einer ihrer Mamsellen und einem

---

[1] E. Reich, *Fr. Grillparzers Dramen*, Dresden, 1909³, p. 62, under this inadequate and faulty reference (see next note), reluctantly concedes what he describes as v. Weilen's claim that Grillparzer was 'halb unbewußt durch Sophie Schröder zur "Sappho" mit angeregt worden'. My own claim goes much further than this. It was formulated independently of v. Weilen's.

Ladendiener vorgehen—es würde nicht an Wahrheit verlieren.' Und die Bedenken, welche gegen den tragischen Schluß laut wurden, sie wurzeln in dem erstaunten Gefühle der Zuseher, eine volkstümliche, lustspielmäßig anmutende Begebenheit auf eine Höhe geschoben zu sehen, auf die ihr nicht jedermann zu folgen vermochte.

Kaum ein anderes Werk Grillparzers ist so ganz auf den Boden bestimmter theatralischer Verhältnisse gestellt wie dieses. Die künstlerische Vereinsamung Sophie Schröders, wo findet sie höheren Ausdruck als in der Gestalt Sapphos? In dem mächtigen Pathos der Rede, in dem vernichtenden Liebesbedürfnis lebte das theatralische und persönliche Wesen dieser Frau, die sich mit verzehrender Leidenschaft in die Arme nichtiger junger Burschen stürzte. Gar mancher Phaon hat in ihrem Leben eine bedeutsame Rolle gespielt, und auch von Melittas, die ihr den Freund entrissen, wußte ihr vielgeprüftes Herz zu erzählen.[1]

It will be observed that there is no mention of Daffinger in this, and there would be no need to mention him, perhaps, if we did not require evidence to confirm v. Weilen's assurances. Moreover, the work of Grillparzer's under discussion reflects the beginning only of his relations to Daffinger: in their development they are of profound importance for an understanding and interpretation of later works. At the same time it is with the actress Sophie Schröder and the way in which her circumstances came to be reflected by Grillparzer (and acted by her) in the person of Sappho that we are at present chiefly concerned.

The attitude of Sophie Schröder's contemporaries, that of the Viennese public in particular, to her person and her art was exactly Grillparzer's when he assumes that Sappho's unconventional action was compensated for by her artistic achievements. On the strength of her reputation as an artist of genius, Sophie Schröder could behave

---

[1] Alex. v. Weilen, 'Das K.-K. Hofburgtheater seit seiner Begründung' in O. Teuber, *Die Theater Wiens*, Wien, 1906, ii, 2. Halbbd., 2. Teil, p. 30.

in her private affairs very much as she pleased, without scandalizing her admiring public and intimate acquaintances. They were more solicitous for her welfare than censorious of her conduct, when in the year 1816 the famous and gifted actress, at the age of thirty-five, formed an illicit union with a young Viennese painter who was nine years her junior.[1]

It is reasonable to assume that this affair with Daffinger engaged Grillparzer's interest and concern. The intimate friendship formed between him and Sophie Schröder since the *Ahnfrau* days, based upon mutual esteem for each other's art, and gratitude on Grillparzer's part, presupposes this. Nor is it perhaps irrelevant to observe that Grillparzer found Daffinger, with whom he now became acquainted through Madame Schröder, in a relationship to her which he knew he might have occupied himself.

Apart from the fact that Daffinger was so much younger than Sophie Schröder, being but one year older than Grillparzer himself, this youthful portraitist (who had acquired a considerable reputation through the opportunities afforded him at the time of the Congress of Vienna) was thought to be unsuited to her in other respects. He was of low origin, uneducated, and unmannerly, 'ein Kind des Volkes, ein Urwiener vom Liechtentalgrund'. It appears to have been overlooked that Phaon is conceived along almost parallel lines, and in fact

---

[1] Even M. G. Saphir, who gives an intimate account of Sophie Schröder, his acquaintance, among his 'Lineamente zu Schauspieler-Bildnissen', dedicated to her, in his *Berliner Theater Almanach für 1828*, pp. 259 ff., declines to take advantage of the tempting opportunity for scurrilous comment afforded by the actress's sensational and unfortunate third marriage to a young actor named Kunst in 1825, one of her many lovers, who was nearly twenty years her junior (a step from which, according to Wurzbach, not even the personal intercession of Kaiser Franz could dissuade her). This consideration from M. G. Saphir is the strongest evidence for the kind of respect which Sophie Schröder inspired.

used originally to be so presented on the stage.[1] His 'würdelose Scheltworte' in Act III (like his 'Schmähungen' in Act V) which Kleinberg mistakenly regards as 'eine Entgleisung des Dichters (wenn man nicht zu gekünstelten Deutungen greifen will)'[2] are evidence of this conception of Phaon's character. L. Grünstein describes Daffinger's relationship to Mme Schröder, who had been twice married (for the first time at the age of fourteen) and was the mother of a son twenty years old, three daughters in their 'teens (on the elder of whom Daffinger soon forced his attentions) and a young boy, in terms remarkably reminiscent of Grillparzer's treatment: 'eine seltene und seltsame Verbindung, . . . die im Zeichen einer eruptiven Sinnlichkeit einsetzt und nach einer mehrjährigen, durch Haß und Eifersucht getrübten Gemeinschaft, zuletzt noch in der ungebundenen Leidenschaftlichkeit des Weibes und dem jähen Überdruß des Mannes, ihren schmerzlichen, in seiner Auswirkung nahezu tragischen Ausklang findet'.[3]

In a letter written on 19 January 1817 to Rahel Varnhagen (who was fortunate in her fourteen years younger mate) Sophie Schröder describes her vain search for true happiness in love, and she does so in terms which remind us of Sappho's regrets: 'Ach . . . wenn ich ein stilles häusliches Glück an der Seite eines mir *ganz*

[1] In C. L. Costenoble's excellent diaries: *Aus dem Burgtheater 1818–37, Tagebuchblätter*, 2 vols., Vienna, 1889, the following interesting comment appears: 'Fichtner (a young actor who wanted to marry [Melitta] Betty Schröder) war ein noch roherer Phaon als der *Lümmel* Grillparzers', Vol. ii, p. 75, 10 Sept. 1831 (Costenoble's italics). This points to an original conception of Phaon's role, quite different from the prevailing one, which Costenoble would have described as 'unerträglich flau' (cf. vol. i, p. 148).

[2] A. Kleinberg, *Fr. Grillparzer*, &c., 'Aus Natur u. Geisteswelt', no. 513, p. 37.

[3] Leo Grünstein, *M. M. Daffinger und sein Kreis*, Vienna, Leipzig, 1923, p. 14.

gleichgesinnten, gleichfühlenden Wesens verleben könnte...'
In this letter, which has been described as a 'Herzens-
dokument der Frauen der Romantik',[1] she speaks further
of her separation from her second husband and her union
with Daffinger. In the misgivings which she entertained
with regard to the result of this effort to win happiness
we may discern an indication that she had perused
'Sappho' (as she had actually done by this time) with
unusual interest, recognizing in it a prophetic reflection of
her own approaching disillusionment:

Ich will es Ihnen nicht leugnen, daß ich in diesem Augenblick
in einem Verhältnisse stehe, wo ich mich bemühe dieses Glück
aufzufinden—aber gelingen, ach gelingen, wird es glaube ich
kaum. Ein junger guter hübscher für alles Gute und Schöne
empfänglicher Mann hat sich mit vieler herzlichen Innigkeit an
mich geschlossen—er sucht alles auf, mich davon zu überzeugen,
er sieht meinen Augen meine Wünsche ab, und erfüllt sie, soviel in
seinen Kräften ist—das alles ist gut, *sehr* gut—aber dennoch, dennoch
stoße ich zuweilen auf Härten in diesem wirklich vortrefflichen
Gemüt, die mich verwundern, die mich fester überzeugen—es
gibt kein *ganz vollkommenes* Glück zwischen Mann und Weib....

She entertains a further cause for anxiety, one which
Grillparzer had foreshadowed, and she does so again in
terms which echo Sappho's extravagant railing against
der rauhe Phaon for his *Undank*,[2] his inconstancy:

... Doch gesetzt auch, ich irrte, gesetzt auch, es gelänge mir,
was bei einem *guten, gefühlvollen* Menschen vielleicht nicht ganz
unmöglich ist, diese Härten durch Beharrlichkeit und Sanftmut
auszugleichen und mich so dem Ziele meiner Wünsche zu nähern,
würde ich auch verhindern können, daß ein *Ungeheuer* welches
jetzt die Welt beherrscht—Unbestand—sich zwischen mich und
mein Glück stellt? Und wenn es auch nur Furcht davor ist...[3]

---

[1] Hn. Stümcke, Introduction to *Die Briefe von Sophie Schröder
1813–68* in *Schriften der Gesellschaft für Theatergesch.* xvi, xxvi, Berlin,
191–16.   [2] l. 1281, ll. 1204 ff., 1290 ff.
[3] Loc. cit., vol. i, Brief 98, pp. 144 ff.

One thing is certain, the writer of this letter was singularly well adapted for the role of Sappho. And she continued to be so qualified, long after this experience. As late as 1831 Immermann learns in Munich, where she was at that time, 'daß die 50jährige Sappho noch immer ihren jugendschönen Phaon verlange'.[1] At the time when Grillparzer's play was being written and prepared for the stage Sophie Schröder was absent from Vienna on tour. The fact that she was not considered in the first place for the role of Sappho is really eloquent, for there was obviously no one better suited, as an actress and by experience, for the part. In his *Selbstbiographie* Grillparzer, for reasons we can well understand, declares that she, 'in deren Fach die Sappho gehörte', was not reckoned on to take the part, because she was at that time not merely on tour, but 'abroad', that is, in Germany, having quarrelled with the theatre authorities in Vienna and threatened not to return; and that for this reason the role of Sappho had to be given to Mme Löwe, who was unsuited to it. We have evidence of Sophie Schröder's periodic differences with the Hofburgtheater authorities, but none to show that any existed during her *Kunstreise*, as it is correctly described, in 1817. Schreyvogel and Grillparzer probably assumed that if they delayed the production of the play till she returned, she would resent its implications, or at least refuse to expose herself to the risk of being vulgarly identified in her person with Sappho, or of seeming to exploit the undesirable notoriety which she had gained. On 26 September 1817 Schreyvogel wrote to Böttiger in Dresden about the new play: 'Die Rolle ist nicht für Mad. Schröder bestimmt, wovon sie jedoch vorderhand nichts zu wissen braucht.'[2] Why

---

[1] Cf. *Allg. deutsche Biog.* xxxii, p. 527.
[2] *Gespräche*, II. Abtlg. (vol. i, 1791–1831), p. 37.

the concealment, we ask, if as stated in the *Selbstbiographie* she was not expected to return?[1] Surely, if there had been any fear that she would not return, Schreyvogel would normally have wanted Sophie Schröder to hear that the young Grillparzer had written a new play, a *Sappho* tragedy, in the hope of enticing her back. It seems indeed likely that Grillparzer and Schreyvogel were anxious to cast and, if possible, produce *Sappho* before Sophie Schröder could return and for the reasons mentioned frustrate or complicate matters for them.

On her return to Vienna at the beginning of December 1817, however, Sophie Schröder immediately took possession of the role.[2] Yet it cannot be supposed that she failed to recognize the obvious parallel between her own and Sappho's experience. Late in life she admitted to Emilie Ringseis that she identified herself with Grillparzer's Sappho, whose fate had once been her own.[3] This admission on her part, coupled with our knowledge of Grillparzer's intimacy with her, and associated with his own and Schreyvogel's misgivings, tends to confirm the

[1] E. Reich, loc. cit., p. 59, believes that Schreyvogel's letter proves that he thought Sophie Schröder too old for the part. There is no authority for this. It is significant too that this is not the reason for excluding her which Grillparzer himself alleged.

[2] 'Die energische Frau hat ihre Rolle vor sich auf dem Bette liegen und scheint vor Begierde zu brennen, die Sappho und *dabei zugleich ein Bischen auch sich selbst* zu spielen', wrote Grillparzer in a letter to Böttiger on 20 Feb. 1818, *Werke*, iii, I, p. 94, ll. 2–5 (italics mine). The first performance of *Sappho* had to be postponed until after the birth in March of Sophie Schröder's first child by Daffinger, which was baptized at St. Stephan's on 9 May 1817, named Moritz after his father, and entered as the son of Theresia Bürger (Sophie Schröder's maiden name). Near this entry appears the intrusive comment: 'angeblich', which (characteristically enough) the person making it gratuitously supplied.

[3] E. Ringseis, *Erinnerungsblätter*, Freiburg i. Br., 1896, p. 66. Sophie Schröder rejected the suggestion made to her on this occasion that Sappho was really too old to be able to command Phaon's devotion!

impression, which v. Weilen's judgement supports, that it was she who from the start provided in her person and circumstances the real source of the most striking motive in Grillparzer's conception of *Sappho*. We may even be justified in stating that this was the immediate source of the work itself, or in other words that at the time when the legend of Sappho and Phaon was mentioned to Grillparzer by Joël, he had promptly associated it with the problem of Sophie Schröder's conduct and resolved to treat it dramatically. If so, it is scarcely accurate to speak of the motive of age-disparity, or that of Sophie Schröder's person and circumstances, as being added by Grillparzer to the material of *Sappho*, as being objectively supplied by him; he did not deliberately introduce the motive or superimpose it: the expression *Grillparzer's Schröder-'Sappho'* might justifiably be coined to characterize his conception and treatment of the piece from the start.

6

If we accept this as the true account of how Grillparzer's plan for *Sappho* came to be conceived, we may discern at the same time that in Grillparzer's over-eagerness to proceed with his *Fiakeridee* lay the source too of the principal artistic defect in the poetic work that grew out of it. If he had given the matter longer consideration he might well have thought it inadvisable to risk alienating sympathy from his heroine by making her appear older than was necessary, in addition to causing her to behave as she does. On the other hand, this may have been an integral part of his original design, a part of the *Aufgabe* which he boldly undertook, because of its bearing upon his personal conviction regarding the artistic temperament and the *malheur d'être poète*: namely, to reveal his artist-heroine's behaviour (like Sophie Schröder's) as by no

means censurable or *ekelhaft*, in spite of her age. But if a
marked disparity of age between Sappho and Phaon was
envisaged from the first, this involved Grillparzer in
difficulties before the end of the work, and caused him to
depart from his original conception, his *Fiakeridee*, not
without damage to its logical accomplishment. This is
the change of plan he seems to have had in mind in his
admission to Müllner. He may not have been conscious
of making it deliberately, he may even have forgotten how
he originally intended to motivate his catastrophe, but
the fact remains that he had to sacrifice adequate motivation of Sappho's end.

Grillparzer's original intention was to show that Sappho
was by her poetic nature a woman of violent passions.
She was a poetess by virtue of this fact, but only so long
as she exercised restraint over her true nature. 'Sie wagt
einen Wunsch an das Leben und ist verloren,'[1] he wrote.
He intended to represent her as a victim of her own
passions. At the time of commencing to write his play
he certainly harboured no lofty belief in the divinity of
Sappho's nature and calling. On the contrary, she is at
first portrayed as being genuinely dissatisfied with her
lot as a poetess, and in this she has much in common with
Grillparzer himself at the time. Contemporary criticism
of his *Ahnfrau*, 'jenes beschrieene, in jeder Hinsicht, zu
früh geborne Wesen,'[2] had provided special cause for his
dissatisfaction with the poet's lot. Sappho is represented,
in 'deserting' her art, as being actuated by considerations
and motives of which Grillparzer at this time distinctly
approved.

There can be no question that at the outset he had no
intention of representing Sappho's desertion of her art

---

[1] An Müllner, loc. cit., p. 99, l. 8.
[2] *Werke*, iii, I (no. 98, An Adolf Müllner, 21 Jan. 1818), p. 88, ll. 18-19.

as her real dramatic guilt. But his conception of her character, conduct, and situation, and of her age in relation to Phaon's, drove him later to represent as preeminently unpardonable her seeking to partake of the common joys of life.

It is because the Sappho of the first plan was so much older than Phaon, and because she behaves as she does in a situation of her own creating, showing such traits as selfishness, spite, anger, jealousy, meanness, cruelty, violence, and cunning, that Grillparzer had seen even then that nothing short of a great compensating emphasis on her merits as a poetess could rescue her for the play. But in the course of the execution of his work he must also have come to see that Sappho was nevertheless alienating herself too much from the sympathy of the audience. The principal reason for this was that she was not youthful enough. To let her commit suicide for reasons that had first suggested themselves to him, not so much because of unrequited love or injured pride, be it said, as because of her very behaviour and in desperation over the *malheur d'être poète*, would not have been sufficient. It had been clear to Grillparzer from the very beginning that after Sappho's 'unclassical' outburst in the middle acts consequent upon the inevitable thwarting of her misdirected desires, she could only become a tragic heroine if she were made to see the error of her ways and atone nobly for the wrong she had done. In the finished work, however, she fails to do so. Grillparzer must have felt that he was unable to contrive this successfully, though without necessarily becoming conscious of the principal cause. What actually happened was that his conception of the wrong she had done insensibly became changed. In the course of writing the work his confidence in his own gifts was restored to him, and he came to look upon Sappho's guilt as consisting not in her conduct after renouncing her art, but in the very fact that she had deserted it. Grillparzer's point of view, or what he refers to as his *Gemüthslage*,[1] had altered. As Petsch puts it:

> Tatsächlich scheint Grillparzer den Konsequenzen seiner ersten Konzeption nachher aus dem Wege gegangen zu sein; aber ich sehe das Neue eben . . . in der Erhebung Sapphos zu einer Höhe, wo von einer eigentlichen Leidenschaftstragödie kaum mehr die Rede sein kann. . . . Hat sich die Heldin kurz vorher, als sie die entflohene Melitta zurückzuholen befahl . . . in einer relativ ruhigeren Stimmung *bewußt* für den Weg der Leidenschaft *entschieden*, so tritt sie uns nun hoheitvoll, zur Entsagung fähig, entgegen, als sei das Ganze bloß eine Verirrung der großen Künstlerin gewesen, die freilich nicht mehr zu der verlassenen Höhe begierdeloser Reinheit wieder aufsteigen kann.[2]

Sappho never really comes to see the error of her ways, and her atonement takes the form almost of condescending forgiveness. She believes that she had formerly wrongfully deserted her art and her gods, in order to partake of the meaner joys of life.

> Ihr habt der Dichterin vergönnt zu nippen
> An dieses Lebens süß umkränzten Kelch,
> Zu nippen nur, zu trinken nicht.

It was to this insight that Grillparzer had now come as a result of the self-confidence and satisfaction with his lot which he had acquired while composing the work. He achieves the feat of making Sappho more appealing to most of his audience and of exonerating her from blame

---

[1] An Müllner, loc. cit., p. 103, l. 16.

[2] Petsch, loc. cit. Here, as in the previous passage quoted from this review, it will be observed that Petsch supports the *Leidenschaftstragödie*-theory. This does not accord with the evidence considered above, and I now no longer associate myself with Petsch in this respect. The implications of his expression *begierdelose Reinheit* are also unacceptable. See next note.

by stressing (partly unconsciously, but of inner conviction) the divinity of her calling, and raising her to more than human heights.

The Sappho of the closing scenes feels that she has betrayed her higher calling in lowering herself to the level of mere human beings, who live to experience and enjoy. This is the only error which she, in her *Dichterstolz*, is capable of recognizing now. Sappho is something higher than life and owes it no explanation. She overlooks her real guilt, namely, that she has behaved as 'ein in der Leidenschaft sich vergessendes Weib', in a manner unworthy of herself as a woman, not merely as a poetess. She, like Grillparzer himself, is now only conscious of having sinned against her art, of having wrongfully succumbed to feelings of dissatisfaction with her lot. She feels incapable of regaining her former Olympian heights. She is a broken woman. Having betrayed her poetic genius, as she believes, she appeals to the gods to summon her to themselves:

> O gebt nicht zu, daß eure Priesterin
> Ein Ziel des Hohnes werde eurer Feinde,
> Ein Spott des Toren, der sich weise dünkt.
> Ihr bracht die Blüten, brechet auch den Stamm!
> Laßt mich vollenden, so wie ich begonnen,
> Erspart mir dieses Ringens blut'ge Qual.[1]

And so she dies, as the legend demands; death, we must feel, is the only escape.

We see now that the 'contrast between art and life' has taken on a very different aspect from that with which the

---

[1] I. Münch's interpretation of Sappho's suicide: 'Sie fühlt, daß sie sich niemals dauernd halten könnte auf der Höhe des reinen Schauens' (loc. cit., p. 33), which is based on these lines (justifiably so?), implies acquiescence in the erroneous conception of 'pure contemplation' as the poet's ideal unchanging state. This is consequently just as subjective and arbitrary as the poet's unsatisfactory motivation for suicide analysed above.

play began. Grillparzer has forgotten his theme of the poet's inherent excessive passions (like Tasso's) and the pitfall they presage. He is also no longer suffering from feelings of *Weltschmerz* or *le malheur d'être poète*: he no longer feels dissatisfied with his lot as a poet, nor longs to partake of the (forbidden) joys of *life*; but is convinced of the exalted nature of his genius and feels now no hardship in renouncing everything in favour of his *art*.

7

Nor was this new attitude unwarrantable in him. He had accomplished a vast stride in his art. The tremendous success of *Sappho* on the stage, though we admit that it was materially contributed to by Sophie Schröder's remarkable performance, was by no means unmerited on the poet's part. Psychologically and poetically (as is confirmed by Börne's and Byron's discriminating praise), structurally and technically, the work is of high quality. With regard to Grillparzer's interesting representation of Phaon's and Melitta's 'awakening' through love, a motive which dates back to *Spartakus* and constantly reappears (notably in *Des Meeres und der Liebe Wellen*), Grillparzer's hitherto unobserved indebtedness to *Romeo and Juliet* is worth noting. The language and metre of *Sappho*, though not as uniformly exalted, smooth-flowing, and polished as that of Goethe's *Iphigenie* and *Tasso*, which Grillparzer apparently sought to emulate, comprise many passages of the highest order of expression. Of the not infrequent 'lapses' into Viennese colloquialisms it may be held, from the dramatic point of view, that these approximations to natural speech (found also in the mature *Libussa*) are praiseworthy, and introduced by design, as by Lessing in *Nathan der Weise*. There are in addition, it is true,

those perhaps somewhat infelicitous figures of speech,
such as Phaon's:

Da meiner Wünsche winterliche Raupen
Als goldne Schmetterlinge mich umspielen. (ll. 493 f.)[1]

and the comparison of Melitta to a snail, so apt is she,
in her *liebevolle Innigkeit*, to withdraw into her shell, and
like the snail again,

Nur zaudernd waget, Fremdes zu berühren,
Doch fest sich saugt, wenn es einmal ergriffen,
Und sterbend das Ergriffene nur verläßt. (ll. 760 ff.)

They remind us of Grillparzer's incongruous allegory of
himself, the poet as the oyster, which secretes its pearls
only after sickness, prolonged suffering, and anguish—in
his 1818 poem entitled 'Abschied von Gastein'. These
metaphors suggest that the young poet carried home from
his imaginative expeditions, at this time, but poor poetical
prey. Like Goethe in Leipzig, who would go out 'hunting
images' (emulating Ewald v. Kleist), Grillparzer seems to
have been equally constrained, lacking objects of beauty or
grandeur for his purposes, to direct his attention to *das
Kleinleben der Natur*; though it is perhaps regrettable that
he thought fit to include the 'dainty proceedings' of cater-
pillars, snails, and oysters from that sphere.

But *Sappho* succeeded; even the critics were impressed;
and this success would appear to have encouraged Grillparzer to continue with his portrayals of women characters.
He was probably in part influenced in this direction,
especially (in the first place) with Sophie Schröder as an

[1] The passage in which Tasso (ll. 3083–91) compares the process of
poetic creation to the silkworm's own, through self-immolation in the
chrysalis stage to metamorphosis and enviable freedom and release, is
related to this one of Grillparzer's (more so than the 'armes Muscheltier'
in 'Abschied von Gastein', cf. *Werke*, i. 10, p. 273 Anm.). Grillparzer's
figure probably derives from this poetic source, but how debased it is in
Grillparzer's formulation by comparison!

ally of his art, to choose a woman, Medea, for the heroine of his next work for the stage. The grim tragedy of that work, 'Wie das Gemüt im eigenen Abgrund endet', provides a still more striking example than *Sappho* of Grillparzer's tendency to draw on his personal experience and observation for his dramatic purposes.

INDEX

LIST OF SUBSCRIBERS

Dr. B. AIKEN-SNEATH, 6 Hans Crescent, London, S.W. 1.

P. ALBERY, Esq., 29 Rosslyn Hill, London, N.W. 3.

J. C. ALLDRIDGE, Esq., 6 Arnside Rd., Birkenhead.

Prof. H. G. ATKINS, King's College, London.

W. G. ATKINS, Esq., Polska 9, Prague XII, Czechoslovakia.

Dr. C. BAILEY, Balliol College, Oxford.

J. B. BAKER, Esq., Nettlebed, Oxford.

Rev. Dr. C. C. BARBER, University of Bristol.

B. BARNES, Esq., 22a Alma Place, Oxford.

Dr. H. G. BARNES, University of Birmingham.

Miss N. BARROWS, Windyridge, Tynell's Wood, Leatherhead.

P. V. M. BENECKE, Esq., Magdalen College, Oxford.

E. K. BENNETT, Esq., Gonville and Caius College, Cambridge.

H. E. BERTHON, Esq., 10 Norham Gardens, Oxford.

Dr. O. D. BICKLEY, St. Hugh's College, Oxford.

K. C. BIRD, Esq., Ryeford Hall, Stonehouse, Glos.

Dr. L. A. BISSON, 83 Woodstock Rd., Oxford.

I. D. BLACK, Esq., Leighton Park School, Reading.

E. G. BLENKINSOP, Esq., 12 Oakfield Grove, Bristol.

Miss E. BLOCHMANN, Lady Margaret Hall, Oxford.

C. E. BOND, Esq., Hurst Cottage, Old Oak Avenue, Chipstead, Surrey.

Dr. J. KNIGHT BOSTOCK, 5 St. Margaret's Rd., Oxford.

Mrs. J. W. BOSTOCK, 5 St. Margaret's Rd., Oxford.

Sir ADRIAN BOULT, 8 Chelsea Embankment, London, S.W. 3.

Dr. J. BOYD, 36 St. Margaret's Rd., Oxford.

Mrs. J. BOYD, 36 St. Margaret's Rd., Oxford.

Miss M. E. BRAUNE, Prince of Wales School, Nairobi, Kenya.

Dr. E. G. W. BRAUNHOLTZ, Goslar, Adams Rd., Cambridge.

Prof. G. E. K. BRAUNHOLTZ, 22 Old Road, Headington, Oxford.

Prof. W. H. BRUFORD, University of Edinburgh.

Miss M. M. BURGESS, Brigg Vicarage, Lincs.

W. C. BURNET, Esq., 15 Brookside, Headington, Oxfrd.

Prof. E. M. BUTLER, University of Manchester.

Miss M. C. CALDWELL, University of Leeds.

A. C. CAMPBELL, Esq., 76 Oxford Terrace, Hyde Park, London, W. 2.

W. H. CARTER, Esq., 13 Buckingham Street, London, W.C. 2.

J. D. CAZES, Esq., Connaught Club, 75 Seymour St., London, W. 2.

Dr. K. CHESNEY, St. Hilda's College, Oxford.

P. W. CHING, Esq., 17 Rawlinson Rd., Oxford.

R. I. CHRISTOPHERSEN, Esq., Woodville, Oaklands Rd., Bromley, Kent.

Miss D. R. CLARKE, Lady Margaret Hall, Oxford.

Dr. A. CLOSS, University of Bristol.

Mrs. A. CLOSS, 30 Cornwallis Crescent, Clifton, Bristol.

Prof. W. E. COLLINSON, University of Liverpool.

Miss A. CRONE, Brockwell, 10 King's Rd., Knock, Belfast.

Dr. C. R. M. F. CRUTTWELL, Principal of Hertford College, Oxford.

Dr. K. CUNNINGHAM, University College, Bangor.

J. C. DAKIN, Esq., Arna, West Nile, Uganda.

Miss. H. DARBISHIRE, Principal of Somerville College, Oxford.

Miss E. DEAN, Stone End, Headington Quarry, Oxford.

Prof. R. M. DAWKINS, Exeter College, Oxford.

Dr. W. H. DAWSON, 23 Latimer Rd., Headington, Oxford.

Mrs. W. H. DAWSON, 23 Latimer Rd., Headington, Oxford.

Dr. W. E. DELP, Royal Holloway College, Englefield Green, Surrey.

Miss H. C. DENEKE, Lady Margaret Hall, Oxford.

Miss M. DENEKE, 19 Norham Gardens, Oxford.

J. D. DENNISTON, Esq., 5 Polstead Rd., Oxford.

Miss U. A. L. DIBB, Bramley Park, Rotherham.

Dr. A. C. DUNSTAN, University of Sheffield.

Dr. O. H. EDWARDS, University College, Cardiff.

H. F. EGGELING, Esq., University of Edinburgh.

Mrs. B. ELLMAN, 29 Weymouth St., London, W. 1.

A. B. EMDEN, Esq., Principal of St. Edmund Hall, Oxford.

Rev. L. P. EMERY, Oscott College, Birmingham.

Prof. W. J. ENTWISTLE, 12 Fyfield Rd., Oxford.

W. G. ETTINGHAUSEN, Esq., The Queen's College, Oxford.

K. A. P. EVANS, Esq., 19 Park Dale, Wolverhampton.

Mrs. E. M. C. EWBANK, 17 Haig Rd., Catterick Camp, Yorks.

Prof. A. EWERT, 214 Woodstock Rd., Oxford.

Miss V. FARNELL, Somerville College, Oxford.

Lt.-Col. A. S. L. FARQUHARSON, University College, Oxford.

Miss H. E. FIEDLER, The Lane House, Norham Rd., Oxford.

Miss J. CORBETT-FISHER, 8 Heathgate, London, N.W. 11.

Prof. C. C. FOLIGNO, 17 Banbury Rd., Oxford.

Miss E. A. FRANCIS, St. Hugh's College, Oxford.

Prof. P. F. FRANKLAND, House of Letterawe, Loch Awe, Argyll.

Prof. J. FRASER, Jesus College, Oxford.

D. GARABEDIAN, Esq., 3 Blackhall Rd., Oxford.

Mrs. A. E. GERRANS, 20 St. John St., Oxford.

Dr. A. GILLIES, University College, Hull.

Dr. G. P. GOOCH, 76 Campden Hill Rd., London, W. 8.

G. GORDON, Esq., President of Magdalen College, Oxford.

Prof. C. E. GOUGH, University of Leeds.

Miss M. M. GREEN, Ludwig Jahnstrasse 6^{II}, Greifswald, Germany.

Dr. J. B. C. GRUNDY, Shrewsbury School.

E. M. GUMMER, Esq., 28 Holywell St., Oxford.

Dr. C. S. GUTKIND, Bedford College, London, N.W. 1.

Dr. K. C. HAYENS, University of St. Andrews.

T. S. THYNE HENDERSON, Esq., The Elms, Hawick, Scotland.

J. R. HIRST, Esq., 16 Rowsley Rd., St. Annes-on-Sea, Lancs.

Miss M. E. M. HODD, 51 Tonge Park Avenue, Tonge Moor, Bolton, Lancs.

R. H. HODGKIN, Esq., Provost of The Queen's College, Oxford.

H. W. HOUSE, Esq., Iffley Turn House, Oxford.

Miss G. CRAIG HOUSTON, Westfield College, London.

Prof. T. H. HUGHES, 204 George St., Glasgow C. 1.

Miss C. G. HUGON, 45 Woodstock Rd., Oxford.

Dr. H. J. HUNT, 24 St. Margaret's Rd., Oxford.

R. M. HYSLOP, Esq., Elthwaite, Morris St., Sheringham, Norfolk.

R. C. JOHNSTON, Esq., Holywell Cottage, St. Cross Rd., Oxford.

Rev. E. SYTHROYD JONES, 76 Bishop Ken Rd., Harrow Weald, Middlesex.

K. C. KING, Esq., 43 Farnaby Rd., Shortlands, Kent.

G. A. KOLKHORST, Esq., Yarnton Manor, nr. Oxford.

Prof. S. KONOVALOV, 4 Oriel St., Oxford.

Miss C. A. M. LAUFS, 4 Clyda Mansions, Gondar Gardens, London, N.W. 6.

Prof. R. W. LEE, Westbury Lodge, Norham Rd., Oxford.

J. G. LEGGE, Esq., 115 Banbury Rd., Oxford.

Mrs. J. G. LEGGE, 115 Banbury Rd., Oxford.

Miss M. D. LEGGE, 115 Banbury Rd., Oxford.

I. LESCHALLAS, Esq., Lynchmere House, Haslemere, Surrey.

Prof. CECIL LEWIS, University of Toronto, Canada.

Mrs. CECIL LEWIS, University of Toronto, Canada.

W. G. LEWIS, Esq., 100 South Hill Park, Hampstead Heath, London.

Prof. M. F. LIDDELL, Trinity College, Dublin.

Prof. R. H. LIGHTFOOT, New College, Oxford.

R. E. LISTER, Esq., King Edward VII School, Sheffield.

C. H. LITTLE, Esq., 72 Heath St. West, Toronto, Canada.

E. A. LITTLEFIELD, Esq., 2 Handel Close, Canons Park, Edgware, Middlesex.

H. L. LITTLER, Esq., University College, Exeter.

E. H. C. LUCKHAM, Esq., Prince of Wales School, Nairobi, Kenya.

Rev. Dr. F. J. LYS, Provost of Worcester College, Oxford.

Dr. R. W. MACAN, Broom Hill House, Boar's Hill, Oxford.

Dr. R. J. McCLEAN, Queen Mary College, London, E. 1.

F. McEACHRAN, Esq., Shrewsbury School.

I. D. MACKENZIE, Esq., 2a Ramsay Garden, Edinburgh.

Sir ARTHUR McWATTERS, 16 St. Giles', Oxford.

J. L. MALLETT, Esq., Headmaster Royal Commercial Travellers' School, Hatch End, Middlesex.

Miss M. L. MARE, St. Ebba's, Shotover Hill, Oxford.

H. M. MARGOLIOUTH, Esq., 14 Bradmore Rd., Oxford.

Dr. R. MARLEYN, University College, Swansea.

P. E. MATHESON, Esq., 3 Brookside, Headington, Oxford.

Mrs. J. E. MATTHEWS, Gothic House, Hunters' Forstal, Herne Bay.

A. H. MEAD, Esq., Elizabeth College, Guernsey, C. I.

Mrs. H. MELCHERS, Rusholme, Rockham Hill, Eden Bridge, Kent.

Dr. D. M. MENNIE, Armstrong College, Newcastle.

W. MILLWARD, Esq., 142 Rosendale Rd., London, S.E. 21.

Miss G. MILVAIN, English Girls' College, Alexandria.

Mrs. M. MONTGOMERY, The Avenue, Woodstock Rd., Oxford.

W. G. MOORE, Esq., St. John's College, Oxford.

K. MORTIMORE, Esq., County School for Boys, Station Rd., Sidcup, Kent.

Mrs. M. MULLER-DARBISHIRE, Verlängerte Liststrasse, Tübingen.

ERNEST NEWMAN, Esq., Polperro, Epsom Lane, Tadworth, Surrey.

Miss J. NICOL, The High School, Stamford, Lincs.

Prof. F. NORMAN, King's College, London.

C. ORD, Esq., 9 All Saints' Rd., Bristol 8.

Miss E. OSWALD, 3 Steele's Rd., London, N.W. 3.

OXFORD UNIVERSITY PRESS.

Miss D. M. PALMER, 195 Harehills Lane, Leeds.

G. PARKER, Esq., The Queen's College, Oxford.

R. PASCAL, Esq., 7 Queen Anne Terrace, Cambridge.

S. H. PATON, Esq., Radley College, Abingdon, Berks.

Miss H. PEACH, 18a Carlingford Rd., Hampstead, London, N.W.3.

Dr. R. PEACOCK, University of Leeds.

Colonel Sir HAROLD PERCIVAL, Christ Church, Oxford.

Miss I. L. PERKIN, 14 Shelley Rd., Bath.

Dr. L. P. DE LA PERRELLE, Royal Naval College, Dartmouth.

Miss A. PICTON, 32 Linnet Lane, Liverpool 17.

Prof. M. K. POPE, University of Manchester.

G. F. A. GORDON POTTS, Esq., 2 Cranleigh School, Cranleigh, Surrey.

Sir E. B. POULTON, Wykeham House, Oxford.

Dr. L. F. POWELL, Taylor Institution, Oxford.

Mrs. R. PRIEBSCH, 23 Heathway Court, West Heath Rd., London, N.W. 3.

Miss K. M. PULLEN, Woodfield, Wylde Green, Sutton Coldfield, Warwick.

Prof. E. PURDIE, Bedford College, Regent's Park, London.

THE PROVOST and FELLOWS, The Queen's College, Oxford.

THE LIBRARY, The Queen's College, Oxford.

J. D. RAINBOW, Esq., Hulme Hall, Victoria Park, Manchester 14.

Miss O. RHYS, Gwynva, Barton Lane, Headington, Oxford.

Dr. M. F. RICHEY, Royal Holloway College, Englefield Green, Surrey.

Miss J. F. RIDDING, 119 Fore St., Hertford, Herts.

C. A. ROBSON, Esq., Christ Church, Oxford.

Miss M. ROSE, The Marl, Rednal Rd., King's Norton, Birmingham.

Dr. W. ROSE, London School of Economics.

Prof. G. RUDLER, 18 Bradmore Rd., Oxford.

Sir MICHAEL SADLER, The Rookery, Old Headington, Oxford.

Mrs. T. SAID-RUETE, 27 Kensington Court, London, W. 8.

H. D. SAMUEL, Esq., Peterborough House, Grove Hill, Harrow.

Prof. F. E. SANDBACH, University of Birmingham.

Prof. O. SCHLAPP, 1 Peel Terrace, Edinburgh 9.

Mrs. B. SCHLESINGER, 15 Templewood Avenue, London, N.W. 3.

Baron BRUNO SCHRÖDER, 145 Leadenhall St., London, E.C. 3.

H. W. B. SCHRÖDER, Esq., Earlywood, Ascot, Berks.

Miss M. G. SKIPWORTH, Lady Margaret Hall, Oxford.

A. J. SMITH, Esq., 20 Blackthorn Close, Bournville, Birmingham.

Prof. H. SMITH, University of Glasgow.

Dr. E. L. STAHL, 9a King Edward St., Oxford.

Miss E. N. STARKIE, Somerville College, Oxford.

J. F. STENNING, Esq., Warden of Wadham College, Oxford.

G. H. STEVENSON, Esq., 10 Chadlington Rd., Oxford.

Dr. S. D. STIRK, University College of the South West, Exeter.

L. R. M. STRACHAN, Esq., University of Birmingham.

M. LE VACK STRUTH, Esq., Exeter College, Oxford.

Mrs. H. S. M. STUART, King's College, London.

Mrs. B. M. STURLEY, 42 Sunningdale Rd., Chelmsford.

B. H. SUMNER, Esq., Balliol College, Oxford.

D. M. SUTHERLAND, Esq., Bodleian Library, Oxford.

J. G. TAHOURDIN, Esq., Sancta Maria, Waxwell Lane, Pinner, Middlesex.

F. A. TAYLOR, Esq., Christ Church, Oxford.

Miss E. M. THOMAS, 82 Mulgrave Rd., Sutton, Surrey.

Prof. F. W. THOMAS, 161 Woodstock Rd., Oxford.

Miss N. M. THORP, St. Hugh's College, Oxford.

Mr. G. F. TIMPSON, Maidenhill House, Stonehouse, Glos.

Mrs. G. F. TIMPSON, Maidenhill House, Stonehouse, Glos.

Flying Officer J. N. TOMES, c/o Lloyd's Bank, Cox's and King's Branch, 6 Pall Mall, London, S.W. 1.

Mrs. M. TREMLETT-SCHWER, Abingdon, Oxford.

GERMAN DEPARTMENTAL LIBRARY, Trinity College, Dublin.

F. H. TROTT, Esq., 20 Addison Crescent, Oxford.

R. V. TYMMS, Esq., University of Manchester.

A. M. URQUHART, Esq., Old Library House, Bournemouth.

Prof. E. VINAVER, University of Manchester.

Prof. E. R. P. VINCENT, 10 Selwyn Gardens, Cambridge.

F. H. VIVIAN, Esq., Wiseman's House, Clifton College, Bristol.

Dr. G. R. VOWLES, Davidson College, Davidson, N.C., U.S.A.

Dr. E. WALKER, 28 St. Margaret's Rd., Oxford.

Rev. Dr. E. M. WALKER, 169*a* Woodstock Rd., Oxford.

Miss E. E. WARDALE, 12 St. Margaret's Rd., Oxford.

Prof. G. WATERHOUSE, University of Belfast.

K. L. WATSON, Esq., 233 Charminster Rd., Bournemouth.

R. WAYE, Esq., Radley College, Abingdon, Berks.

Miss C. E. H. WEBB, 46 Queen's Rd., Hertford, Herts.

Miss G. M. WELFORD, Huyton House, Twitchell Rd., Great
Missenden, Bucks.

Mrs. S. M. WEST, Windyridge, Walmer, Kent.

Miss B. WHITEHEAD, 3 Tavistock Sq., London, W.C. 1.

Miss S. L. WHITELEGGE, 6 Collingham Rd., London, S.W. 5.

J. H. WHITFIELD, Esq., 110 Banbury Rd., Oxford.

Miss M. J. WIGG, Ferry Hinksey, Oxford.

Prof. R. A. WILLIAMS, 35 Millington Rd., Cambridge.

Prof. L. A. WILLOUGHBY, University College, London.

Mrs. J. WRIGHT, 119 Banbury Rd., Oxford.

B. YANDELL, Esq., Clifton College, Bristol.

Dr. D. YATES, University of Aberdeen.

PRINTED IN
GREAT BRITAIN
AT THE
UNIVERSITY PRESS
OXFORD
BY
JOHN JOHNSON
PRINTER
TO THE
UNIVERSITY